DIXIE BETRAYED

DIXIE
BETRAYED

HOW THE SOUTH
REALLY LOST
THE CIVIL WAR

DAVID J. EICHER

LITTLE, BROWN AND COMPANY
NEW YORK   BOSTON

Little, Brown and Company
Time Warner Book Group
1271 Avenue of the Americas, New York, NY 10020
Visit our Web site at www.twbookmark.com

First Edition: March 2006

Library of Congress Cataloging-in-Publication Data

Eicher, David J.
    Dixie betrayed : how the South really lost the Civil War / David J. Eicher. — 1st ed.
        p. cm.
    Includes bibliographical references and index.
    ISBN-10: 0-316-73905-7 (hardcover)
    ISBN-13: 978-0-316-73905-4 (hardcover)
    1. Confederate States of America — Politics and government.   2. Confederate States
of America — Military policy.   3. Davis, Jefferson, 1808–1889 — Military leadership.
4. Davis, Jefferson, 1808–1889.   5. Generals — Confederate States of America.
6. United States — History — Civil War, 1861–1865 — Campaigns.   7. Confederate
States of America — History.   8. Political leadership — Confederate States of America.
I. Title.
E487.E38 2006
973.7'13 — dc22   2005025757

10 9 8 7 6 5 4 3 2 1

Q-MB

Book design by Bernard Klein

Printed in the United States of America

For Chris Eicher, who already knows the meaning of the worst events
in world history, and how they make us appreciate
the best events even more

"It seems to be a law of humanity that generation after generation must rescue its liberties from the insidious grasp of a foe without or within. In our case, we have to seize them from both."

—*Lawrence M. Keitt*

"Revolutions are much easier started than controlled, and the men who begin them, even for the best purposes and objects, seldom end them. . . . The selfish, the ambitious, and the bad will generally take the lead."

—*Alexander H. Stephens*

"I think it important that we should at least seem united & harmonious to the enemy."

—*Clement C. Clay*

CONTENTS

CONTENTS

DIXIE BETRAYED

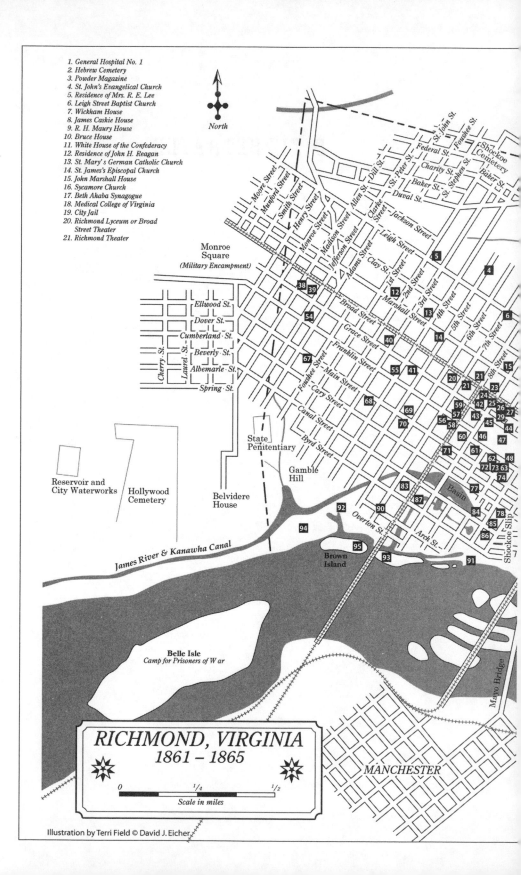

1. General Hospital No. 1
2. Hebrew Cemetery
3. Powder Magazine
4. St. John's Evangelical Church
5. Residence of Mrs. R. E. Lee
6. Leigh Street Baptist Church
7. Wickham House
8. James Caskie House
9. R. H. Maury House
10. Bruce House
11. White House of the Confederacy
12. Residence of John H. Reagan
13. St. Mary's German Catholic Church
14. St. James's Episcopal Church
15. John Marshall House
16. Sycamore Church
17. Beth Ahaba Synagogue
18. Medical College of Virginia
19. City Jail
20. Richmond Lyceum or Broad
    Street Theater
21. Richmond Theater

North

Monroe Square
(Military Encampment)

Reservoir and
City Waterworks

Hollywood
Cemetery

State
Penitentiary

Gamble
Hill

Belvidere
House

James River & Kanawha Canal

Brown
Island

Belle Isle
Camp for Prisoners of War

RICHMOND, VIRGINIA
1861 – 1865

0   1/4   1/2
Scale in miles

MANCHESTER

Illustration by Terri Field © David J. Eicher

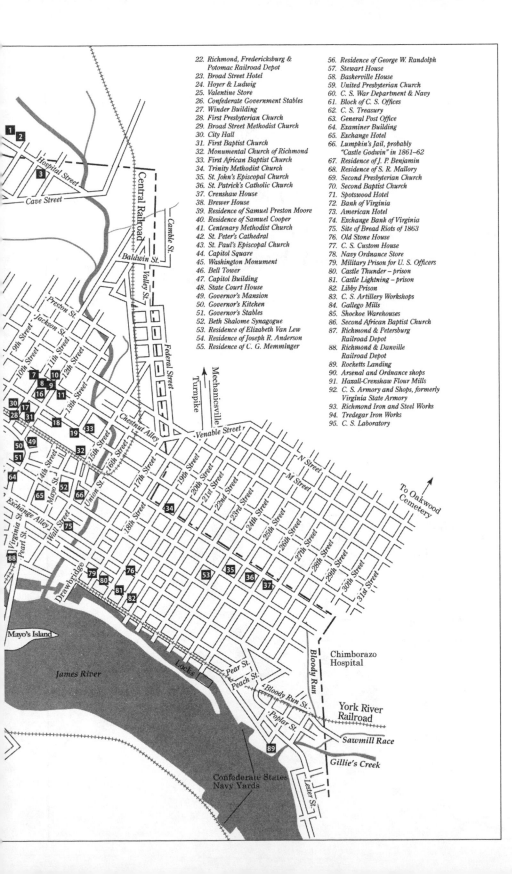

22. Richmond, Fredericksburg & Potomac Railroad Depot
23. Broad Street Hotel
24. Hoyer & Ludwig
25. Valentine Store
26. Confederate Government Stables
27. Winder Building
28. First Presbyterian Church
29. Broad Street Methodist Church
30. City Hall
31. First Baptist Church
32. Monumental Church of Richmond
33. First African Baptist Church
34. Trinity Methodist Church
35. St. John's Episcopal Church
36. St. Patrick's Catholic Church
37. Crenshaw House
38. Brewer House
39. Residence of Samuel Preston Moore
40. Residence of Samuel Cooper
41. Centenary Methodist Church
42. St. Peter's Cathedral
43. St. Paul's Episcopal Church
44. Capitol Square
45. Washington Monument
46. Bell Tower
47. Capitol Building
48. State Court House
49. Governor's Mansion
50. Governor's Kitchen
51. Governor's Stables
52. Beth Shalome Synagogue
53. Residence of Elizabeth Van Lew
54. Residence of Joseph R. Anderson
55. Residence of C. G. Memminger

56. Residence of George W. Randolph
57. Stewart House
58. Baskerville House
59. United Presbyterian Church
60. C. S. War Department & Navy
61. Block of C. S. Offices
62. C. S. Treasury
63. General Post Office
64. Examiner Building
65. Exchange Hotel
66. Lumpkin's Jail, probably "Castle Godwin" in 1861–62
67. Residence of J. P. Benjamin
68. Residence of S. R. Mallory
69. Second Presbyterian Church
70. Second Baptist Church
71. Spotswood Hotel
72. Bank of Virginia
73. American Hotel
74. Exchange Bank of Virginia
75. Site of Bread Riots of 1863
76. Old Stone House
77. C. S. Custom House
78. Navy Ordnance Store
79. Military Prison for U. S. Officers
80. Castle Thunder – prison
81. Castle Lightning – prison
82. Libby Prison
83. C. S. Artillery Workshops
84. Gallego Mills
85. Shockoe Warehouses
86. Second African Baptist Church
87. Richmond & Petersburg Railroad Depot
88. Richmond & Danville Railroad Depot
89. Rocketts Landing
90. Arsenal and Ordnance shops
91. Haxall-Crenshaw Flour Mills
92. C. S. Armory and Shops, formerly Virginia State Armory
93. Richmond Iron and Steel Works
94. Tredegar Iron Works
95. C. S. Laboratory

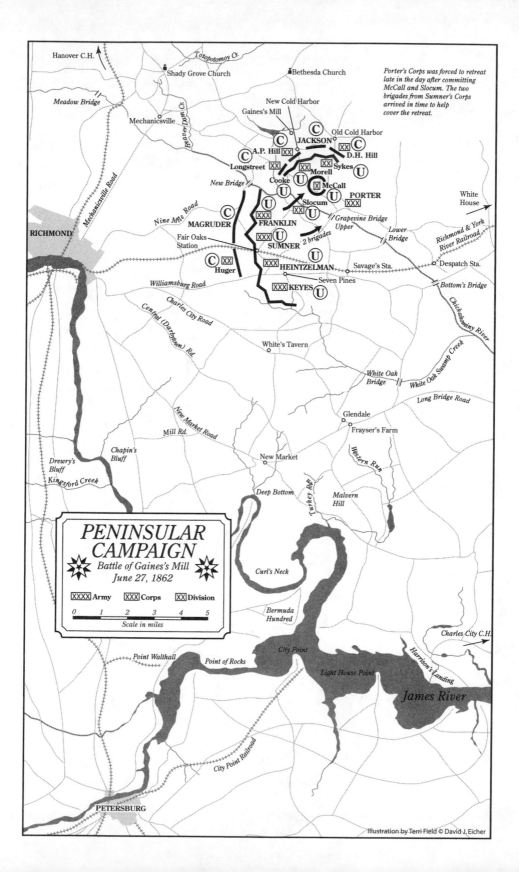

Porter's Corps was forced to retreat
late in the day after committing
McCall and Slocum. The two
brigades from Sumner's Corps
arrived in time to help
cover the retreat.

PENINSULAR
CAMPAIGN
Battle of Gaines's Mill
June 27, 1862

XXXX Army   XXX Corps   XX Division

0   1   2   3   4   5
Scale in miles

Illustration by Terri Field © David J. Eicher

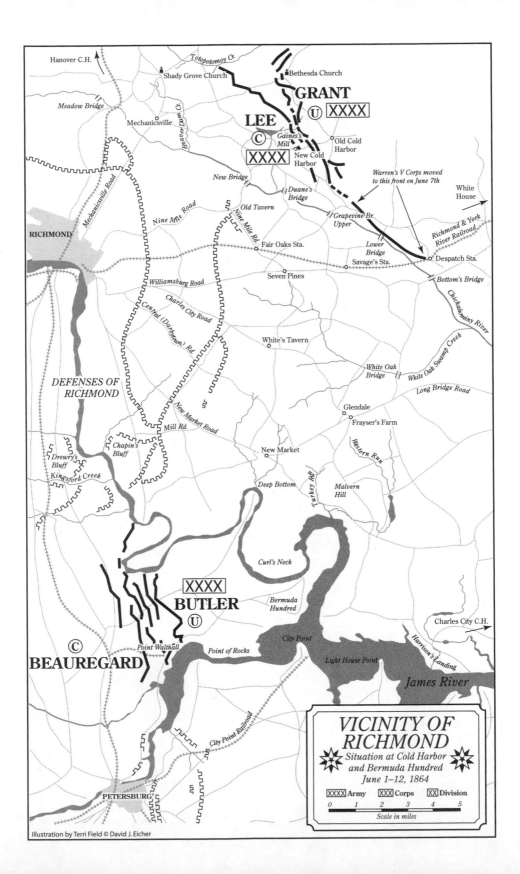

Hanover C.H.

Totopotomoy Cr.

Shady Grove Church

Bethesda Church

GRANT
(U) XXXX

LEE
(C)
XXXX

Meadow Bridge

Mechanicsville

Beaver Dam Cr.

Gaines's Mill

Old Cold Harbor

New Cold Harbor

New Bridge

Duane's Bridge

Warren's V Corps moved to this front on June 7th

White House

Mechanicsville Road

Nine Mile Road

Old Tavern

Nine Mile Rd.

Fair Oaks Sta.

Grapevine Br. Upper

Lower Bridge

Savage's Sta.

Despatch Sta.

Richmond & York River Railroad

RICHMOND

Williamsburg Road

Seven Pines

Bottom's Bridge

Chickahominy River

Charles City Road

Central (Darbytown) Rd.

White's Tavern

White Oak Bridge

White Oak Swamp Creek

Long Bridge Road

DEFENSES OF RICHMOND

New Market Road

Mill Rd.

Glendale

Frayser's Farm

Chapin's Bluff

Drewry's Bluff

Kingsford Creek

New Market

Western Run

Deep Bottom

Turkey Run

Malvern Hill

Curl's Neck

XXXX
BUTLER
(U)

Bermuda Hundred

Charles City C.H.

BEAUREGARD
(C)

Point Walthall

Point of Rocks

City Point

Harrison's Landing

Light House Point

James River

City Point Railroad

PETERSBURG

Illustration by Terri Field © David J. Eicher

VICINITY OF RICHMOND
*Situation at Cold Harbor and Bermuda Hundred
June 1–12, 1864*

XXXX Army   XXX Corps   XX Division

0   1   2   3   4   5
Scale in miles

Chapter

1

PROLOGUE

I T was a typical Virginia spring morning, with a slight breeze cascading and the sweet smell of honeysuckle permeating the humid air. Shafts of bright sunlight shot down through the canopy of forest and illuminated patches of dusty ground. Dense thickets of brush intermingled with the scratchy sounds of life among it; squirrels darted through last fall's leaves; rabbits and raccoons made peace with the forest floor and stayed put, holed up against the commotion of the outdoors. In the distance could be heard faint, shrill tones of music together with the crackle and boom of drums as well as the snapping branches and shuffling leaves as men marched in loose form.

The peace and beauty of the Wilderness, a forested area in Virginia west of Fredericksburg, masked a deepening Southern desperation.

Ulysses Grant and George Meade were bearing down on Richmond, which had narrowly avoided capture two years earlier. Vicksburg had fallen the previous summer, as Robert E. Lee's raid into Pennsylvania failed. Now a Yankee drive deep into Georgia was coming. Federal ships had been tightening control of the coast for months, leaving few seaports open. And the Confederacy's largest city, New Orleans, had long ago fallen to the Union.

Yet there was something powerfully spiritual about this Confederacy: a deep optimism that it would survive, gain independence, and live on as something great. For most Confederates, even the leaders, there was no other way to think. Most of the credit went straight to Providence. Despite some downfalls since the autumn of 1862 — the retreats from Kentucky and Maryland, the losses at Vicksburg and Gettysburg — the Confederacy had whipped the Yankees at Chickamauga in the autumn of 1863. Three years of hard fighting had shaken the rabble out of the ranks of the Confederate armies; now a core of battle-hardened veterans remained, supported by a fringe cast of increasingly older and younger marchers — all true believers in the Cause. Now, if they could beat back Grant, the war might come to a close with a Southern nation intact.

The month of May 1864 was just a few days old.

In the Twenty-first Virginia, making its way into the Wilderness, Sgt. John H. Worsham no sooner heard the word "Forward!" than he found the regiment struck by Yankee fire. Suddenly Worsham and his comrades scrambled and shot back, striking into the Union front, reloaded, and fired madly. The men were armed with a mixture of Springfield and Enfield rifles, Mississippi rifles, and old flintlock smoothbore muskets. In an instant the battle was on, and the crackle of musketry rang out among the line, claps of bullets striking trees behind the Virginians and swishes of minié balls sailing through the air carrying reminders to stay down. As Worsham slowly moved forward, he stopped when he saw a gun protruding from an old tree stump, a Yankee crouched behind it. "Throw down your gun!" Worsham shouted; but before the Union soldier could act, another young boy in Confederate gray shot him dead. Earlier this same boy had been left by the roadside in tears because he seemed too young to keep up with the march.

Pressing on, the Twenty-first Virginia took prisoners and moved toward a pine thicket that shrouded a concentration of the enemy. Now the heavy thud of cannon could be heard in the distance, and all knew a general battle was taking place. Just as Worsham and his comrades settled on the edge of a field and began to fire at more Yankees, both groups of Americans saw an odd sight. The firing dwindled as more and more men watched. One Union soldier and a lone Confederate had slid down into the same gully for protection, into close quarters. After seeing each other and exchanging pleasantries, the two men walked out into an adjacent road and started a "fist and skull fight." All the soldiers within view watched in disbelief. A yell went up across each line, and the Johnny eventually pinned the Yank and brought him back into the Confederate line as a prisoner. This surreal stoppage, in the midst of the start of a great battle, must have given everyone there pause.

====

A T twenty-four, John Worsham was no ordinary Southerner. Born into the middle class of Richmond, the son of a merchant tailor, he grew up in a three-story brick home at the corner of Seventh and Broad streets. Worsham received a good education at Richmond's Shockoe School for Boys and then took his first job at Winston and Powers, Commission Merchants, as a clerk. He was descended from early Virginia settlers, prominent men in Henrico Shire as early as the 1640s. Among the early family associates was Colonial official William Byrd. As with all young Southerners in 1861, Worsham was smitten with patriotic fever. He felt a special connection to the powers that were forging this mighty contest for Southern independence; he could count Joseph Mayo, the mayor of Richmond, among family friends.

Worsham joined a Richmond militia unit known as F Company on April 1, 1861, and twelve weeks later he was mustered into the Twenty-first Virginia Infantry under Col. William Gillam. He went to fight, as did all Confederate boys, with high hopes for absolute success in wresting the new nation away from the tyrannical government of Abraham Lincoln. Worsham and his comrades got their first taste of war in western Virginia. "We are having rather a gay time," he wrote his sister, "marching over mountains with roads as Rocky as can be, and so crooked that we sometimes go over the same place two or three times."[1]

In the spring of 1864, Worsham's hometown was reeling from a recent raid by Union cavalry on the outskirts of the city and by the escape of Federal officers from Libby Prison down on the James River. Another shock to Richmond came when little Joe Davis, the president's son, fell to his death at age five from a second-story piazza at the Confederate White House. Yet life went on. Sallie Putnam, just nineteen and with ultrapatriotic aspirations, spent countless hours as a nurse in the city's hospitals. "So long had the campfires glowed around Richmond," Putnam wrote, "so long had we breathed the sulphorous [*sic*] vapors of battle — so accustomed had our ears been to the dread music of artillery — so signal had been our deliverance from the most elaborate combinations for capture of our city, that more surely than ever before we felt at this time that our Confederate house was built 'upon a rock.' "[2]

Yet, unknown to John Worsham and Sallie Putnam, the Confederacy was far from built on bedrock. The Confederacy was born sick.

━━

O N Thursday, March 7, 1861, Washingtonians awoke to the prettiest day of the season. At the Executive Mansion Abraham Lincoln mounted his horse in the chilly, bright air and readied for a morning journey. Before breakfast, three days after his inauguration (which then occurred in early March rather than January), the new Union president rode a little more than three miles to the Soldiers' Home on the northern outskirts of the city to meet with his cabinet officers, hoping to devise a plan to resupply the Federal garrison in Fort Sumter, South Carolina. The fort, endangered by South Carolina militia and running low on supplies, was not about to be given to the South as a Federal gift. As Lincoln rode north, his horse dislodging clumps of dirt from Fourteenth Street, he did not know that just a couple miles away one of the most influential Southerners in the coming drama also was preparing for a big day.

Inside the U.S. Capitol, its dome unfinished, the new day began, and business resumed as usual. In the two-story rectangular Senate Chamber, its Victorian ambiance complete with mahogany desks, marble columns, statuary busts, and cigar smoke wafting up to the decorated ceiling, senators convened. They had hoped to avoid bloody strife, but it was already too late. A provisional Confederate government had met in Montgomery and elected officers for the new Southern Confederacy. South Carolina had been the first state to secede, signing its ordinance on December 20, 1860. In January Mississippi, Florida, Alabama, Georgia, and Louisiana followed. Kansas had been admitted to the Union as a free state. Texas had left the Union in February. Now Washington politicians recalled with mixed emotions Daniel Webster's celebrated "March Seventh speech," which he had delivered in the old Senate Chamber exactly eleven years before, hoping to ward off conflict. "Instead of speaking of the possibility or utility of secession," said Webster, "instead of dwelling in those caverns of darkness, instead of groping with those ideas so full of all that is horrid and horrible, let us come out into the light of day." The opportunity had come for a "March Seventh answer" to the now-deceased Webster, this time in a new chamber and from a new perspective, one in which a new generation of Americans, in effect, told the old one to go to hell.

Amid a packed and contentious scene, senators crowded inside to hear the debate even as they wondered who might next leave on a southbound train. But as the American nation confronted civil war, the gruff and audacious Texan Louis Trezevant Wigfall had stayed in Washington. Wigfall, age forty-four, was an attorney by training and had been a senator for just one year. He was the kind of Southerner John Quincy Adams had called "pompous, flashy, and shallow."[3] Standing tall, dressed in black, with a thick, wiry beard and black, beady eyes, Wigfall had appointed himself spokesman for the proto-Confederacy. The model of a Southern aristocrat, often on the verge of public drunkenness, always theatrically projecting his voice, he poked, prodded, and bragged at the Yankee politicians. Wigfall was emotional, inflexible, and a hawk, like his hero John C. Calhoun, the radical South Carolina politician who, in the 1830s and 1840s, created what Southerners believed was a constitutional justification for secession. ("Now let the senator from Tennessee put that in his pipe and smoke it," he once shot back at a bewildered Andrew Johnson.) By Wigfall's own admission, "Diplomacy was never my forte."[4]

A South Carolinian by birth and among the most rabid of fire-eating secessionists, Wigfall was one of the supremely influential and vocal Southern politicians of his day. He was a powerful-looking man, according to one English journalist, with a face that "was not one to be forgotten, a straight, broad brow, from which the hair rose up like the vegetation on a riverbank, beetling black eyebrows — a mouth coarse and firm, yet full of power, a square jaw — a thick, argumentative nose . . . these [features] were relieved by eyes of wonderful depth and light, such as I never saw before but in the head of a wild beast."[5] Wigfall had a peculiar blend of power and forceful oratory, even though he was a frequent drunk. His family traced its roots in America back to the 1680s, and he was not about to be told what to do by latecomers, by frontiersmen who were less American.

Wigfall's role as rear guard of the emerging South was a part he had been practicing for all his life. Elected to the U.S. Senate in 1859, he told his fellow senators the following year that Southerners would never accept a "black" Republican as president and let his Northern colleagues know that if Southerners failed to capture Boston, then "before you get into Texas, you may shoot me."[6] Actively spying for the Confederacy on the streets of Washington and emboldened by drinks from various Capitol Hill bars, Wigfall angrily taunted his Northern colleagues with the prospect of Southern independence. He seriously considered kidnapping James Buchanan so Southerner John Breckinridge, the vice president, could succeed him as the chief magistrate. Fellow Texan Sam Houston called Wigfall "a little demented either from hard drink, or from the troubles of a bad conscience."[7]

On March 7 Wigfall proclaimed: "The only question is whether we shall have a decent, peaceable, quiet funeral after the Protestant form, or whether we shall have an Irish wake at the grave? This Union is dead; it has got to be buried. . . . The seven states that have withdrawn from this Union are surely never coming back."[8] The next day he flatly told his colleagues, "We have dissolved the union; mend it if you can; cement it with blood."[9] Wigfall was then expelled from the United States Senate, instantly becoming a celebrity.

A month after his expulsion, prior to the Confederate bombardment of Fort Sumter, Wigfall rowed out to the Federal fort in a small skiff and asked about its surrender. He was considerably drunk. Subsequently branded a hero by the Southern press, Wigfall ingratiated himself with the newly elected provisional president of the Confederate States, Jefferson Davis, while serving as the chief magistrate's aide.

But the relationship between the Texan and the Confederate president would change dramatically, and it would affect how the Confederacy fought the war. Morcover, it was not unique. Key Confederate officials turned on Davis and, indeed, on the Confederacy, when the administration needed them most. The story of the betrayal of the Confederacy is rife with arguments, selfishness, reckless behavior, drunkenness, and the peculiar mind-set of a whole generation of privileged autocrats who had learned, for many years, to put state rights above all else.

Mind you — the Confederacy's internal troubles were not born in a vacuum. The Union had its own complex set of political, military, and social squabbles that unleashed all types of problems for the Lincoln government throughout the war. It would be silly to think that the Confederacy's family arguments were unique or to ascribe the Confederacy's loss of the war entirely to them. But, in the case of the Confederacy, the political and military arguments that echoed throughout Richmond's streets and onto the battlefields made Confederate military success — and independence — far more difficult than it might have been, maybe even impossible. State rights wounded the United States but destroyed the Confederacy.

═══

Davis and the Confederate Congress fought over a wide variety of issues all through the war — from debates over state and federal rights, to suspension of the writ of habeas corpus, to military appointments, to conscripting troops, to emancipation and the arming of slaves to fight, to peace proposals. This was a political nation that could agree on hardly anything. And many of the debates spilled out onto the battlefield through commanders such as Robert E. Lee, Joe Johnston, G. T. Beauregard, John Bell Hood, and others. Grudges, friendships, prewar spats, and stubbornness all played into campaigns of letter writing and personal appearances intended to influence the political spectrum of the South. The story of these relationships begins with the inability to compromise. And it all started with the likes of Louis T. Wigfall.

Wigfall symbolized a huge problem for the Confederacy: his background — and that of many Southerners — would not permit domination by any central government, be it the United States or Jefferson Davis. Many observed this, including William Howard Russell of the *London Times*. One May morning in Montgomery, Russell awakened Wigfall in his hotel room, hoping to discover the secret cause of the Confederate revolution. Groggily, Wigfall ran his hands through his long black hair as he exclaimed to the Brit what seemed perfectly obvious to a Confederate patrician but might need to be explained to a queen. "We are a peculiar people, sir!" Wigfall began. "You don't understand us, and you can't understand us. . . . We have no cities — we don't want them. We have no literature — we don't need any yet. . . . As long as we have our rice, our sugar, our tobacco, and our cotton, we can command wealth to purchase all we want."[10]

Wigfall was a product of his generation in time and space, as were other intellectuals of the Southern cause. They were deeply conservative, privileged, and among the first families of their respective states. They often married each other's cousins, so many became interrelated. They lived among farming or plantation lands. Many were slave owners or had slave owners in their families. They were wealthy, having received large inheritances and having been given significant "pocket monies," even as youths. They were considerable spenders. For the middle period of his life, for example, Wigfall was solvent for only weeks at a time.

The cream of Southern secessionists consisted of socially prominent aristocrats, most of whom were lawyers (like Wigfall) or judges. They drank and smoked cigars and gambled and fought and had affairs. They were well educated, despite spotty behavioral records marked with episodes of arrogance; Wigfall, for one, was described in school as "a nightmare to faculty slumbers" and acquired a reputation for insurgency.[11] These men were dominated by a sense of honor and slight. Over one period of five months, Wigfall was in a fistfight, two duels, three near-duels, and one shooting — leaving one dead and two, himself included, wounded. They felt they could get away with anything. They held slavery as the summum bonum, the height of morality. And they were willing to follow causes to the neglect of both family and fortune — the greatest cause, the one they had been indoctrinated with all their lives, being state rights.

As a result the Confederacy was in trouble right out of the gate. But for a long time, only a relatively small group realized that. Confederate nationalism was doomed. The situation grew worse as resources dwindled and all parties pushed their conflicting agendas, nearly none of which could be granted. Squabbles spread all across the war front. Congress argued with the president. The vice president argued with the president. Governors argued with the president. Generals argued with the president. Military bureau chiefs in Richmond argued with generals and with the president. The press bitterly criticized the president. The Southern government became a mess at all levels, and with a cast of thousands of players, resolution seemed unlikely.

And yet the Confederacy found itself wrapped in a strange paradox. For all its practical troubles, the Southern nation was able to create and sustain a deep passion for the *dream* of a Confederate nation. This passion for an independent South burned so brightly in the hearts and minds of Rebels that it outlived the protonation, in fact, and still has a hold on the descendants of Confederate soldiers — in some cases more strongly than it did on postwar Confederates themselves. The persistent belief that the South should have won the war grew out of this postwar love affair, and many Southern writers continued to fight the war with ink on paper in the decades following Appomattox. The myth building of Lee, Stonewall Jackson, and Jeb Stuart, and the persistent suspicion of federal governments that is part of the human condition, gave birth to and nurtured this dream. The David versus Goliath syndrome, the American fascination with the underdog, the anomaly, captured the fascination of many Southerners.

But more importantly this passion came from the influence of Confederate propagandists who, with noble cause at heart, tried their best to help Jefferson Davis and the young Confederate nation thwart their betrayers. It was a struggle that would turn ugly and play itself out both in the hallways and chambers of the Richmond government and on the battlefields spread across America. It was a struggle in the midst of a national crisis.

2

BIRTH OF A NATION

MONDAY, February 18, 1861, began with a bright, blazing sun rising into a clear, blue sky far above the rooftops and cupolas of Montgomery, Alabama. A vibrant city of 8,843, Alabama's capital was proudly transforming into the center of the whole South. It would be a noble experiment in nation building.

Although its population was modest, Montgomery was accustomed to a flurry of activity from the earliest days on the Alabama frontier. Located in the central part of the state, with Birmingham to the north and Mobile to the south, Montgomery hosted steamboat traffic on the Alabama River and frequent trains on the Montgomery and West Point Railroad. The city's jewel was the neoclassical State House, finished like a great Southern marble cake, with six Corinthian columns and a rust-colored dome that gave it a magnificence above any other buildings in the region.

On the cool morning of the Confederacy's birth, all was bustling within the city. "Montgomery has become a focal point of interest for the whole nation," penned a visiting reporter for the *New York Herald*.[1] It was something of an understatement. From the Capitol Building down to the river, along the city's principal business streets, gas lamps were extinguished one by one as dawn captured the sky above. The residents of fine homes in residential neighborhoods awoke and prepared for the big day, dressing in their best finery to catch a glimpse of the South's new leader.

They were not alone: throngs of visitors clogged the three principal hotels. Others stayed wherever they could, many boarding in private houses, hoping to secure employment in some capacity in this new venture called the Southern Confederacy. Interspersed among the whites in the fancy neighborhoods were African Americans, many acting as house servants. Of the 4,502 African Americans in Montgomery, about 100 were free. They lived in basic cottages that lined the city's outer limits.

The chief revolutionary, president-elect Jefferson Davis, had made an exhausting trip from his Brierfield plantation in Mississippi to attend his inaugural ceremony. Already the Confederate leader felt the pressure of his post; his fatigued frame held a plain, homespun suit, and his voice was so strained by making speeches along his journey that the words he uttered were too soft and flayed for many to hear.

Long before the Confederacy was a glimmer in anyone's eye, Jefferson Finis Davis had a celebrated, successful career as a soldier and politician. Davis's parents, Samuel and Jane, were farmers and innkeepers who had succeeded in Georgia after the American Revolution but soon moved to Christian County, Kentucky, where they cleared a two-hundred-acre farm with the aid of several children and two slaves. By the time Jefferson came along, on June 3, 1808, he was the tenth child, born in a cabin on the farm when his mother was forty-eight. To signify the postscript to their family, Jane and Samuel added the middle name, alerting those who didn't suspect already that Jefferson would be the last Davis child. Eight months later, and fewer than one hundred miles away, another baby would arrive on the Kentucky frontier and be named Abraham Lincoln.

After adding horses and slaves to the clan and in search of better land, Samuel Davis moved the family again in 1810, this time to Louisiana, and a year later, to the southwestern corner of the Mississippi Territory, which would achieve statehood in 1817. There, Jefferson Davis would grow through his adolescent years and become a man, following the course of many youths, rebelling against school despite his bright mind and success. He entered college at Transylvania University, in Lexington, Kentucky, in the heart of the bluegrass region, where he resolidified ties to his native state. His studies went well at Transylvania until June 1824, when he learned his father had died. This shock rattled Davis badly. His melancholy worsened when Jefferson discovered that his father's financial success had reversed itself over his last few years. Jefferson's oldest brother, Joseph, now became a father figure. To further Jefferson's education his older brother secured an appointment for him to the United States Military Academy at West Point through the help of the great political champion of the South, John C. Calhoun. (Calhoun, celebrated U.S. senator from South Carolina, was revered as the author of the most sacred principle of Southern politics: that secession, if desired, could be justified within the bounds of the Constitution.) Jefferson traveled to the Point and commenced his schooling in the autumn of 1824.

Davis performed adequately in his studies at West Point — as well as compiling substantial numbers of demerits — and graduated twenty-third out of thirty-three in the class of July 1, 1828. Commissioned a brevet second lieutenant, he spent seven years in the U.S. Army as an infantry officer. Frontier duty and occasional clashes with Indians marked the period. He was commissioned a first lieutenant of dragoons before resigning, in 1835. That year, he also married Sarah Knox Taylor, daughter of Zachary Taylor, and the couple moved to Mississippi to commence farming. Plantation life on the Davis's eight-hundred-acre estate seemed a reasonable dream, but shortly after their marriage, the newlyweds contracted a fever, and on September 15, 1835, Sarah Taylor Davis died. Ill and depressed, Davis went to Cuba to recover. He eventually returned to Mississippi, to his Brierfield plantation, but stayed in seclusion.

Davis spent the next ten years mostly locked away from the world. When he returned to public life, he turned to politics in Mississippi and the companionship of a very young girl from Natchez, Varina Howell. When they were married in early 1845, Varina was nineteen, Jefferson thirty-six. Independent and volatile, Varina irked her new husband at intervals but eventually transformed herself into an engine of support and encouragement for him. Soon after their marriage Jefferson was elected to Congress as a representative from Mississippi. But Davis's term in Congress was cut short by war clouds looming to the southwest, and he was commissioned colonel of the First Mississippi Rifles, joining his former father-in-law's army in Mexico.

Jefferson Davis's Mexican War career was wholly successful. His regiment, raised in the little town of Vicksburg, was assigned to Maj. Gen. Taylor's army, while much of the army accompanied Maj. Gen. Winfield Scott, general-in-chief of the army, as he marched from Veracruz to Mexico City. As Taylor's force moved against Monterrey, Mexican Gen. Antonio López de Santa Anna attacked Taylor's force, hoping to demolish it and then turn toward Scott. Davis heroically aided the United States' victory, was wounded in the foot, and returned home. In 1847 he was appointed to be a brigadier general in the U.S. Army but was never commissioned as such; instead, Davis was elected U.S. senator from Mississippi.

Throughout the 1850s Jefferson Davis was transformed into the leading proponent of Southern rights in Congress, succeeding John C. Calhoun, who had died in 1850. In that year Davis resigned from the Senate and entered the race for governor of Mississippi, an act designed to help the Democratic Party by keeping his eccentric opponent out of office. Davis joined the race late and faced the irascible, reckless Henry Stuart Foote. Foote had been born a Virginian, in 1804, but settled in Alabama by age nineteen, becoming an attorney and newspaperman. Foote "called 'em as he saw 'em," and soon this shoot-from-the-hip style led to duels with politicians he had called out in the paper. By 1850 Foote was a successful Mississippi politician who, despite his strong advocacy of state rights, fancied himself a staunch Unionist.

Prior to the election the two men already had a checkered relationship. In 1847, on a festive holiday night at Gadsby's bar in Washington, they came to blows after a heated argument over slavery and the territories, a subject that would come to be called "squatter sovereignty." Davis violently disagreed that territories should have the right to decide if they wanted slavery to exist within their boundaries, and the argument turned fiery. Foote said Davis was fueled by "arrogance," and Davis's comment that Foote had uttered "offensive language" is hardly surprising, given the latter's record. Dragging his wounded foot, Davis lunged at Foote and began to "pummel him with repeated blows until others pulled him off."[2]

Davis later wrote that Foote, shocked, had started to leave the room and then turned and emphasized that Davis had struck the first blow, which would mean that in a duel, Foote would choose the weapons. In a complete meltdown Davis shrieked, "Liar!" broke free from those who were holding him, and shook his fist toward Foote. Another senator jumped on Davis and began fighting, and someone shouted that Foote and Davis should be put into a room where they could square off. Foote asked, "Do you have coffee and pistols for two?" Davis replied, "Yes," and Foote hesitated, balking at Davis's military experience. Others in the room finally convinced the two to drop the matter and to write it off as a "Christmas frolic." But the two men would hate each other forever. In the 1851 gubernatorial election, Foote won, further enraging Davis. The two men's paths would cross repeatedly in the coming drama.

Davis rose to his height in 1853, when Franklin Pierce made him U.S. secretary of war, in which role he excelled at army organization and developed a keen sense of military protocol and personalities. In 1857 he again returned to Washington as senator from Mississippi, a position from which he directed a fusillade of Southern spirit at the increasingly Northern-controlled government.

Four years of Yankee-bashing from his post on Capitol Hill had raised Davis to preeminence among Southern politicians. Now, in a new capital city in the making, Davis prepared to take on the leadership of the South. On the morning of his inauguration, Davis left the Exchange Hotel in an open barouche led by six white horses for the journey to the Alabama State House. Bands played for the thousands strewn along Commerce Street, and thunderous cheers, smiles, and screams of joy rang throughout the city, following Alabama politician William L. Yancey's shouted declaration that "the man and the hour have met. . . . Prosperity, honor, and victory await his administration."[3]

"All Montgomery had flocked to Capitol Hill in holiday attire," wrote Thomas Cooper DeLeon, a Southern journalist, of the festive day. "Bells rang and cannon boomed, and the throng — including all members of the government — stood bareheaded as the fair Virginian [Letitia Tyler, granddaughter of John Tyler] threw that flag to the breeze. . . . A shout went up from every throat that told they meant to honor and strive for it; if need be, to die for it."[4]

As the carriage approached the State House, a band struck up the anthem "La Marseillaise," and applause greeted the president-elect. On a platform constructed at the State House, Davis sat beside the vice president–elect, Alexander Hamilton Stephens of Georgia. The band also played a northern minstrel song, "Dixie," which was liked by the crowd and, in time, would become the unofficial song of the Confederacy. Davis and Stephens sat beside Howell Cobb II of Georgia, who had served as president of the Provisional Congress that had commenced its meetings two weeks before.

As Davis looked out over the massive crowd, which perhaps numbered five thousand, he "saw troubles and thorns innumerable."[5] The South in 1861 resembled a set of European-style nation-states, each with its own distinctive flavor and outlook on the world. Unity meant you were friendly with adjoining states, but you had little in the way of official relations with them — governmentally or politically. A shrewd politician, Davis immediately saw trouble in the diversity reflected across the sea of faces spread before him. A strong, unified Confederacy under the control of a central government would be necessary if the war that most saw as inevitable were to come. The unity of this moment, Davis worried, might be short lived.

Waves of cheering cascaded onto the platform as Davis stood up and stretched his tall, lean form and was introduced as savior to the new Southern nation. The Mississippian invoked the spirit of 1776 and referred to "the American idea that governments rest upon the consent of the governed, and that it is the right of the people to alter or abolish governments whenever they become destructive of the ends for which they are established." The crowd erupted into applause. Davis continued, saying that if the Northern states attempted to coerce the Confederacy back into the Union, "the suffering of millions will bear testimony to the folly and wickedness of our aggressors. It is joyous, in the midst of perilous times, to look around upon a people united in heart," Davis shouted, "where one purpose of high resolve animates and actuates the whole — where the sacrifices to be made are not weighed in the balance against honor and right and liberty and equality. Obstacles may retard," he asserted, "they cannot long prevent the progress of a movement sanctified by its justice, and sustained by a virtuous people."[6]

Shouts and applause electrified the air around the State House — Davis had won his audience. Yet Davis was no one's fool. A long, difficult road lay ahead if the Confederacy were to survive and prosper. What he could not yet see, however, were some of the specific obstacles to come, including two who were seated on the platform alongside him.

━━

THE Confederacy's new vice president couldn't have been a worse choice — at least from the president's point of view. Alexander Hamilton Stephens was a tiny, sickly man who had a "ghostly, spectral appearance." Born in 1812, a product of Crawfordville, Georgia, Stephens was called "Little Aleck" by those who knew him, and despite his constant systemic ailments and chronic depression, he had achieved great success. Those who saw Stephens in political meetings often thought he was a visiting teenager, or worse — as one commentator put it, "until he occasionally blinked, he seemed to be stone dead."

He stood five feet seven inches tall and weighed ninety-six pounds and seemed to have aged prematurely. He was ghost white and stooped; at times his weight dropped to a mere eighty pounds. He was a world-class hypochondriac. But his thoughts extended beyond ailments real and imagined. Highly intelligent and gifted as an orator, Stephens had taught school before becoming a prosperous lawyer. He was a quiet intellectual who excelled at nothing more than writing thoughtfully composed letters. Little Aleck maneuvered into politics in 1836 and never looked back. Never married, he was always very close with his half-brother, Linton.

Little Aleck's path to the Confederacy was no less exciting than Davis's had been. Elected to the U.S. House as a Whig in 1843, Stephens became an independent in 1850, upon the party's decline. In 1854 he helped to pass the Kansas-Nebraska Act in the House, one of the key events that propelled America toward war. This act promoted popular sovereignty, the idea that territorial citizens should decide themselves whether their newly formed states should permit slavery.

Exhausted by unsuccessful attempts to promote slavery in the territories and statehood bills, Stephens resigned from Congress in 1859. A political supporter of Stephen A. Douglas in the Democratic Party's race for the 1860 nomination, Little Aleck was a powerful state rightist who, nevertheless, opposed secession; still, he came to Montgomery in 1861, when asked by Georgia's political leaders. Once there he played a leading role in scripting the Confederate Constitution.

To appease politicians in the Deep South (some of whom were anti-secession) and present a united front to the world, Stephens was chosen to be vice president beside Davis in the provisional slate of officers of the new Confederacy. Davis was a more astute politician, and the differences in political savvy emerged quickly. A month after the Montgomery inauguration, Stephens made a speech in Savannah, Georgia, to his friends in the Georgia convention. Given the chance for limelight and the fresh opportunity to summarize the meaning of the new Confederacy, Stephens took full advantage. Having cited the abolitionists' shocking assertions about equality of the races, Stephens proclaimed, "Our new government is founded upon exactly the opposite idea; its foundations are laid, its cornerstone rests upon the great truth, that the negro is not equal to the white man; that slavery — subordination to the superior race — is his natural and normal condition."[7] Davis was understandably upset at Stephens's public remarks — not the remarks, but their public nature. It didn't help that Davis was a simplistic analyst; in his mind, you were either for him or against him. Everything was black or white. Although Davis may have agreed privately, he would not do so publicly — to him, the issue of slavery would be covered under the mantle of state rights versus central government.

For the first weeks of his vice presidency, Little Aleck tried to make the case to the public that the South had attempted to thwart war, that it was Lincoln's government that had brought it about. "No one can more deeply regret the threatening prospect of a general war between the United States and the Confederate States than I do," he said. "Such an unfortunate result, if it should occur, cannot be charged to the seeking or desire of the Confederate States government. On the contrary, I feel assured in saying that every honorable means has been resorted to by the government to avoid it."[8] Privately, Stephens was more candid. "Revolutions are much easier started than controlled," he wrote a friend in late 1860, "and the men who begin them, even for the best purposes and objects, seldom end them. . . . The selfish, the ambitious, and the bad will generally take the lead."[9] Stephens had little idea how prescient he was.

Among the Georgia circle that would congregate around the vice president was one Howell Cobb — a longtime rival of Stephens's. Born on a plantation in Jefferson County in 1815, Cobb rose through the political ranks to become president of the First Confederate Provisional Congress, in Montgomery, where the obese, bearded politician presided over the formation of the South's new government.

Two weeks before Davis's inauguration, delegates from the seven original states that seceded flocked to the new capital to define the Confederacy and how it would work. Trains unloaded parties from South Carolina, Georgia, Florida, Alabama, Mississippi, Louisiana, and Texas as — one by one — the men who would make a new government checked into dusty hotel rooms and into history.

These men were the seedlings of the Confederacy, each selected at secession meetings held in the individual states beginning in December 1860. The forty-three chosen ones represented their home states with the same relative force as representation in the old U.S. Congress, though when it came to voting, each state had only one collective vote. The mission for the Montgomery convention would be to elect a provisional president and vice president, draft a Confederate

Constitution, and write the initial legislation of the New South that would ready it for war with the North.

The Montgomery convention, held in great style within the Alabama State House, assembled in secrecy and with a hell of a task ahead of it. Those gathered were largely attorneys and planters, many of them wealthy enough to own slaves, but by no means all motivated by the peculiar institution. About 60 percent were Democrats and 40 percent were ex-Whigs. The average age of the men was forty-seven. About half were Unionists who had been lukewarm, at best, over secession. Yet the fire-eaters, the rabid secessionists who rattled the door frames with their angry oratory, had no intention of compromising. Alexander Stephens described the men assembled for the convention as politicians of "substance, character, and, most of all, impeccable conservatism."[10] But, as is often the case, one man's "conservative" is another's "radical."

On the first morning of the Congress, Little Aleck awoke at his lodging and entertained breakfast before writing letters, chiefly to his brother Linton. Poised to make history, Stephens walked the half mile to the State House for the opening of the noontime session of the convention. The streets were jammed with visitors from the countryside, all of whom were in town to see the historic opening of the political meeting, and the cloudy, cold skies had opened up to splays of warm sunshine.

Burdened by his heavy coat and a hat awkwardly tipped upon his boyish head, Little Aleck marched past the throngs of curiosity seekers and up the steps of the State House. On entering the building, he walked straight into the rotunda and spied the Senate Chamber where the forty-three representatives would meet (though only thirty-seven were on hand that first day). Stephens walked into the octagonal chamber amid a flurry of others streaming into the building and awaited what would become the birth of the Confederacy.

Patriotic displays covered the white plaster walls inside the chamber. Desks were arranged so as to provide sufficient room for the delegates, and room for many visitors was reserved on the wooden benches in the third-floor balcony. The ladies of Montgomery had assembled an impressive spread of fruits, meats, and bread, all placed outside the chamber's door so that delegates and visitors would not go hungry as they launched a revolution. Presiding over all was George Washington, who peered out of Gilbert Stuart's portrait, hung prominently.

As noon approached, a weird and slightly bemused men's club began to form. Delegates walked from desk to desk introducing themselves, some old acquaintances, but most strangers. After mixed conversations and much anticipation from the gallery above, the gavel struck at 12:30 p.m. to call the session to order. Six judges were present, twelve state legislators, twelve congressmen, seven senators, one governor, and two cabinet secretaries.[11]

Alabama legislator Robert Barnwell served as presiding officer, welcoming delegates from sister states afar. After a blessing from a local reverend, Barnwell asked for a vote on a true presiding officer, a provisional president of the convention. "Howell Cobb of Georgia," he suggested, and asked that the election be accomplished by acclamation. A journalist inside the room noted that Cobb, in making his acceptance speech, appeared like a "fat, pussy, round-faced fellow, who, although he has been Secretary of the Treasury, looks much more like spending money for the comfort of the inner man, than finding out where it comes from."[12]

Getting down to business, the body next elected other officers — a secretary, a doorkeeper, a messenger, and so on — and then Cobb brought down his gavel, with a storm of applause from the floor and from the gallery. The Confederacy had finished its first day of business.

Montgomery's State House would serve as headquarters of the proto-Confederacy for weeks to come, each day witnessing Cobb's opening remarks and the local reverend's prayer. A national correspondent on the scene dubbed the building the "Temple of Mystery and Birthplace of Liberty."[13] Business commenced at 10 a.m., and there was much of it. The work lasted through late afternoon, at which time either a supper break was called or the day was terminated. Some days the delegates returned to the State House to work long into the evening.

Throngs of spectators filled the galleries each day, wild with curiosity or looking for government work. The first major order of business was drafting a Confederate Constitution. This took all of four days. The path to constitutionality might have taken two different avenues: sticking close to the old U.S. Constitution or radically striking out. The delegates chose the former, beginning their revolution conservatively and safely.

With the exception of some differences — significant as they were — the document the Southerners crafted was copied verbatim from the U.S. Constitution. The differences guaranteed state rights and protected slavery. The document explained how each state "acted in its sovereign and independent character" to make a "permanent federal government." There was also hypocrisy: no formula for secession was allowed in the Confederate Constitution.

A provisional constitution in hand, Cobb and friends set about to elect a provisional president and vice president for the nation at large. Jefferson Davis was still on his Mississippi plantation, but in the meantime, Little Aleck Stephens was inaugurated as vice president on February 11, his forty-ninth birthday. Introduced to the delegation, the crowd, and the newspapermen in the chamber, he thanked the assembly briefly before deferring to the as-yet-missing President Davis.

＝

WHEN Stephens and his comrades went home to their Montgomery hotels and boardinghouses, they had plenty to contemplate. Following the spark that ignited the fire, namely South Carolina's secession on December 20, the entire nation had unraveled politically. While the Montgomery convention lumbered on, another meeting would be held in Washington, a so-called Peace Convention. At the request of the Virginia General Assembly, 132 representatives of twenty-one states came together to work out an eleventh-hour peace accord. But few had any hope that it would resolve anything. While President Buchanan remained in office as lame duck for another month, he was not about to do anything during the coming weeks — he would leave the mess for Lincoln.

As for the man from Illinois, a tall, gaunt figure, no one really knew much about him. To Southerners he was certainly that "black

Republican" who would threaten their vital interests and ruin slavery. But Lincoln really hadn't said a lot since his election; what he would do when he arrived in Washington was still unknown.

Although war loomed it certainly didn't seem the only option. Many, including the influential *New York Tribune* editor Horace Greeley, simply wanted to "let the erring sisters go"— to allow the Southern states that had seceded to keep their independence. Why fight to keep them in the Union if they really didn't want to belong? Southerners were experienced as soldiers, skilled outdoorsmen, horsemen, and hunters. Should a war come, certainly a Rebel could lick ten Yankees. Even the Yankees seemed to acknowledge that would probably be the case. Perhaps letting the South go made sense.

Indeed, across Dixie, local militia units assembled, recruited, and drilled for the potential action that might come. Every town seemed interested in raising a company; every county seemed to be full of lawyers, clerks, farmhands, and planters primed and ready to take their respective places in the hierarchy of a fighting South.

Militarily, the center of attention was Fort Sumter, South Carolina, the most powerful and well located of several forts that guarded Charleston Harbor. Tensions at the Federal forts in Charleston had risen to alarming levels by late 1860, and the evening following Christmas 1860, Maj. Robert Anderson and his garrison of Yankees had moved from Fort Moultrie on the shore to the tiny Sumter, well out in the water. Despite his Southern sympathies, President Buchanan staunchly determined that Fort Sumter would not be abandoned to the South Carolina militia.

A few whispers of the trouble to come lay scattered around other locales. On the day Jefferson Davis was inaugurated, Bvt. Maj. Gen. David E. Twiggs, commanding the Military Department of Texas, surrendered military posts to the state militia. Twiggs was a senior general in the U.S. Army whose Georgia birth and proslavery sentiment were no secret. Even though he claimed to have surrendered at San Antonio under heavy pressure from state forces, authorities in Washington would have no part of his explanation and labeled him a treasonist. He would defect from the U.S. Army the day after his surrender, be dismissed by the army on March 1, and subsequently become a Confederate general officer.

━━

Like his Montgomery brethren, Howell Cobb was well educated as a lawyer. He had married a wealthy plantation owner's daughter, Mary Ann Lamar, and settled in Athens, Georgia. Elected to Congress as a Democrat in 1843, Cobb had served as state governor before being re-elected to the House, in 1855. A close associate of all the Washington Democrats, he had been appointed secretary of the treasury by James Buchanan in 1857 before resigning during the secession crisis.

Cobb was a burly man, heavyset, with drooping eyes, a furrowed face, wiry hair that flowed over the back of his head, and a thick, gray beard. He looked and acted somewhat disheveled. Cobb was as furious a state rightist as you could meet, and he had campaigned intensely to sway pro-Union Georgia politicians to secede from the United States. In accepting his presidency of the Montgomery convention, which convened in the State House on February 4, Cobb had declared the separation from the old Union was "perfect, complete, and perpetual."[14] By serving as the leader of the meeting that led to the First Provisional Congress, Howell Cobb had been denied the presidency of the Confederacy itself. Cobb's brother Thomas Reade Rootes Cobb had accompanied him to the meeting and ended up contributing to the draft of the Confederate Constitution.

The spirit of the emerging Confederacy was intense. "I feel utterly unwilling ever again to live under a common government with the free-soil states," a friend wrote Cobb. "Our pride is enlisted to prove to them and to the world that the South is not so poor, weak and destitute of resources as to be unable to hold her own in the great community of nations."[15]

For his part Cobb was willing to paint a shining picture of the new Confederacy to his old chief, President James Buchanan. "So far our movements in establishing the Confederate States upon a firm and lasting basis have been eminently successful," he penned. "Our people are not only content but joyous and happy, and blessed beyond all calculation with prosperity in every department of business. Providence has smiled upon us, and with grateful hearts we go on our way rejoicing. This is not the picture which you had looked for as the result of disunion, and I confess, with all my sanguine feeling, it promises to surpass even my hopes and expectations."[16]

On the day of the inauguration, Cobb wrote, "There is no compromise that the seceded States would accept. There is not a single member of our Congress in favor of reconstruction upon any terms. . . . The idea of going back to the Union is ridiculed."[17]

"We are now in the midst of a revolution," added Stephens. "That may be acted on as a fixed, immovable fact. It is bootless to argue the causes that produced it, or whether it is a good or bad thing in itself. The former will be the task of the historian. The latter is a problem that the future alone can solve. The wise man — the patriot and statesman in either section — will take the fact as it exists, and do the best he can under circumstances as he finds them, for the good, the peace, welfare, and happiness of his own country."[18] The move had been made, and now it was up to the rest of the country to react.

As they sat on the State House platform, Stephens and Cobb listened attentively as Davis's words, forced through his ragged throat, promised the South glory.

———

THE convention, by now called the Provisional Congress of the Confederate States, worked quickly to launch a new nation. It adopted the Stars and Bars, designed by Nichola Marschall of Marion, Alabama, as a national flag. It determined that Federal laws would remain in force until November 1861, unless they conflicted with the Confederate Constitution. It sent commissioners to Britain, France, and other foreign powers to start diplomatic relations, and it dispatched agents to Washington to discuss the status of Federal property in the South. Committees seemed to be forming everywhere — military committees, legal committees, financial committees — nearly every book in Montgomery in danger of being grabbed by Congress for study.

Two major areas of concern confronted Davis, Stephens, and the Congress: money and troops. The most pressing matter was coming up with the dollars to finance both a new nation and a looming war.

Davis did not want to impose taxes immediately, so he drew up plans for exorbitant loans. On the last day of February, the Confederate Congress issued $15 million worth of Treasury bonds, which would be sold for 8 percent interest over twenty years. Not only could buyers grab these government bonds with cash, which was in short supply, but they also could trade military supplies or farm goods for them. Other bond printings and the issuance of Confederate currency would come shortly, too.

Despite Northern fears of a natural Southern affinity for combat, raising the army was a huge challenge. Complicating matters, the Provisional Congress created both the Army of the Confederate States (the regular army) and the Provisional Army of the Confederate States (a volunteer army). The regular army was to be the permanent force, the provisional army the force required during the present war emergency. Officers could hold commissions concurrently in both services. This instantly created an administrative thicket, and few officers and troops ended up serving as "regulars." Some 100,000 men were authorized as provisional soldiers to serve either six-month or one-year enlistments. Few realized at the time how inadequate this seemingly vast number would be.

In getting through the first bits of legislation, Davis learned he would have several vocal opponents in Congress. Chief among them was South Carolinian Robert Barnwell Rhett. A cranky, vitriolic man by the time of the oncoming war, Rhett, sixty, had been a lawyer in Charleston before rising to be a state legislator, attorney general of South Carolina, U.S. representative from South Carolina, and eventually U.S. senator. A bold speaker, incredibly self-assured, he filled the Senate seat vacated by John C. Calhoun, the firebrand of Southern politics, and quickly became a volcanic and unforgiving protector of all things Southern. Rhett offered an odd mixture of pride, obstinacy, and extreme self-righteousness. This made him attractive to many as a symbol of everything Southern, but was a real turnoff for many others.

Rhett — who in 1838 had pretentiously changed his name from Robert Barnwell Smith in order to add distinction — had taken on a dual role in the conflict. In addition to leading the South Carolina radicals, he had bought the *Charleston Mercury,* installing his son and namesake as editor. As the secession crisis approached, Rhett had used the Senate dais to lash out at Northerners who were destroying the Southern lifestyle and used the paper back home to stir up support for leaving the old Union.

Rhett had fiery, ghostly eyes, a prominent nose, and was balding, with wisps of hair on the sides and top of his head. He was clean shaven and had a stark, savage stare that penetrated, leaving the appearance of an evangelical preacher. Rhett had used his amazing powers of rhetoric to play an important role at the South Carolina convention in 1860, earning him the name "father of secession." He argued strongly that slavery could never survive the presidency of Lincoln. But though he urged an independent South, Rhett feared that the new Confederacy would fall victim to its politicians and would never prosper as he imagined it could. He had no idea how right he would turn out to be.

Rhett had traveled to Montgomery as head of the South Carolina delegation. He had recently gone through a difficult personal period, one in which his confidence and ego had received a series of blows. One of these was the death of his granddaughter Ann "Nannie" Rhett from scarlet fever.[19] "Nannies [*sic*] departure has broken one more link which bound me to life," he wrote. "My life appears to me to be as worthless as any body. . . . Let us try to bow with and conform to his will — and at the foot of the cross bury all our rebellion and wrong. Pray for me."[20]

To make matters worse, Rhett's daughter Katherine, Nannie's mother, died shortly afterward. It was perhaps inevitable that his heartbroken anger would search for an immediate target, and as the Montgomery landscape thawed and war became closer, Rhett turned his attention to the new Confederate president. Charged with a bitter spirit and a devout certainty in the absolute correctness of everything he felt, Rhett unloaded on Jefferson Davis in every way he could.

Another caustic member of the Georgia delegation in Congress was Robert Augustus Toombs. His coal black, puffy eyes and robust physical appearance made him a man's man and a magnetic personality for women. He was, physically, the anti-Stephens. He stood six feet tall, weighed more than two hundred pounds, and had long, wavy hair and a bit of a beard. A vehement and overpowering speaker, Toombs was prone to sarcasm and overstatement. He drank, smoked, gambled, and mastered an obscene vocabulary that ranked among the most spectacular and horrifying of his time. From his earliest days he was arrogant, combative, and rebellious toward authority.

Thanks to this combination of traits, Toombs sank to the bottom of his law class at the University of Virginia at age nineteen. But he eventually prospered despite his limitations — and sometimes because of them. Born in 1810 in Wilkes County, Georgia, Toombs was fifty when the war started. He was a large man who lived large. Toombs resided in a Greek Revival mansion in the town of Washington, Georgia — the result of his success as a lawyer whose courtroom speeches often were stunning to both juries and opponents. He had served as a captain in the Georgia volunteers battling Indians in the 1830s and was a veteran of the Georgia House of Representatives, the U.S. House of Representatives, and the U.S. Senate, where he spent most of the 1850s and the days immediately before Georgia's secession.

Toombs was an ardent state rightist, a Southern radical who had been a Whig but converted in the mid-1850s to the Democratic Party. When Lincoln was elected and secession winds blew, Toombs had balked at first, but then his hotheaded rhetoric returned, and he had become an ardent supporter of the revolution. He had been considered by many Southerners a contender for the presidency of the Confederacy and may have succeeded at snatching the nomination, but his excessive drinking sealed his fate. "He was *tight* every day at dinner," wrote Aleck Stephens.

Toombs had strongly disliked losing the presidential bid to Jefferson Davis, and an afterglow of bitterness was left in the fiery Georgian's eyes. As a member of the Provisional Congress, his surly disposition would not be lost on others.

Loyalists to Jefferson Davis made special note of two others in town. William Lowndes Yancey of Alabama, who had introduced Davis when the man met his hour, was thought by many to be the leading fire-eater of his time. A quick-tempered, pasty-faced man with hair that curled behind his ears, a prominent nose, and beady eyes, Yancey had killed his wife's uncle in a fight in 1838. Furiously in support of Southern independence, he was a native Georgian whose life had taken him to Massachusetts under the wing of an abolitionist stepfather. Yancey's relationship with his stepfather was far from close, and the orator savagely attacked abolitionists in every possible public speech.

Yancey's subsequent careers in politics and as a newspaperman led him to prominence. After stints in the Alabama state legislature and the U.S. Congress, he gained notoriety by fighting a duel with Congressman Thomas L. Clingman, a future Confederate general. (The duel ended in a harmless exchange of pistol shots.) He also spoke around the country. He repeatedly asked groups around the South to "fire the Southern heart" against the hated Yankees. Considered too radical to be a delegate to the Montgomery convention — the majority of delegates wanted to project an air of moderation — Yancey instead served as a political envoy for Davis as the weeks passed.

A legitimate member of the Montgomery convention and subsequently of Congress, South Carolina politician Lawrence M. Keitt had been another, with Rhett, in the forefront calling for South Carolina's secession. Keitt was so outspoken about state rights and hating Yankees that he had joined his friend and fellow South Carolinian Preston Brooks in the U.S. Senate when Brooks attacked abolitionist Senator Charles Sumner of Massachusetts with a cane in the U.S. Capitol Building in 1856. A gruff, burly man, with intense eyes, willowy hair, and a thick beard, Keitt may have developed some of his intense hatred for Unionists because his brother had been killed by slaves in Florida. Indeed, Keitt — like Aleck Stephens — remarked plainly about how slavery was indeed the cause of the whole war. "It is the great central point from which we are now proceeding," he flatly said.[21]

Keitt, like Rhett, had made a career out of being a critic of the government, and when he found himself in session in Montgomery under a new government, he could hardly contain himself — it was simply a way of life; his seething antigovernment feelings couldn't screech to a halt, even in Montgomery. They would have to be redirected — if not at Lincoln, then perhaps toward Davis. Rhett and Keitt, after all, each entertained notions of leading the Confederacy, as did many who flocked to Montgomery. That sense of loss coupled with personal unhappiness for Keitt, Rhett, and others was the formula for trouble ahead. Lost dreams change people. And they change revolutions, too.

The stage had been set for disaster.

3

PORTRAIT OF A PRESIDENT

As he sat in his suite at the Exchange Hotel, poring over letters coming in from all over the world, Jefferson Davis's dreams were rapidly coming true. He was now the leader of the newest nation on Earth. He had a large circle of advisers around him. He had a busy Confederate Congress meeting down the street to help him push through legislation that would forge a new government. And he had the will of the South to raise armies against the tyrannical Lincoln administration. What more could the Confederate president want?

When journalist William Howard Russell passed through Montgomery, he sought out Davis and met him, describing his impressions of the Confederate leader in his journal. Russell found Davis a "slight, light figure," presented "erect and straight," but also "anxious," with a "very haggard, careworn, and pain-drawn look, though no trace of anything but the utmost confidence and the greatest decision could be detected in conversation."[1]

Amid the tornado of creating a government, the new president had his comforts. He was both relieved and distracted by the arrival of his family from Mississippi. In March Varina Howell Davis, now the president's wife of sixteen years, arrived at the Exchange Hotel along with their children, the mainstay and focus of Davis's life. The children were Margaret Howell ("Maggie"), age six; Jefferson Davis Jr., age four; and Joseph E. Davis, age two. A fourth child, Samuel E. Davis, had died in 1854, at age two. Two more children would arrive during the war and be christened "babies of the Confederacy."

The Davises all lived in the Exchange Hotel for the next few weeks. Then, in mid-April, they moved to a house two blocks away from their first Montgomery address. Celebrated as the "First White House of the Confederacy," this two-story clapboard, Federal-style structure, the Edmund S. Harrison House, was leased by the Confederate Congress for use as an Executive Mansion. Varina would quickly put her stamp on the place, decorating it and arranging things to be just the way she wanted them, suitable for the household of the leader of a nation.

In the weeks that followed the Confederacy's birth, Davis did his best to incite a national feeling of unity from the people of the South, as well as to justify the South's political stand. In Montgomery in late April, he told the Congress:

> All these carefully worded clauses proved unavailing to prevent the rise and growth in the Northern States of a political school which has persistently claimed that the government thus formed was not a compact *between* States, but was in effect a national government, set up *above* and *over* the States.
>
> An organization created by the States to secure the blessings of liberty and independence against *foreign* aggression has been gradually perverted into a machine for their control in their *domestic* affairs.

After relating how slavery did not work economically in the North, Davis wrote that African slaves had "augmented from 600,000" at the constitutional compact to "upward of 4,000,000." "In moral and social condition they had been elevated from brutal savages into docile, intelligent, and civilized agricultural laborers," he claimed, "and supplied not only with bodily comforts but with careful religious instruction."

"Under the supervision of a superior race," the Confederate leader asserted, "their labor had been so directed as not only to allow a gradual and marked amelioration of their own condition, but to convert hundreds of thousands of square miles of wilderness into cultivated lands covered with a prosperous people."[2] As far as President Davis was concerned, slavery worked well for all parties involved.

===

UNLIKE the purely festive mood of Montgomery, tension plagued the Yankee capital as Illinois attorney Abraham Lincoln stood before the Capitol and was inaugurated. Sharpshooters roamed the rooftops of buildings on Capitol Hill. Nonetheless, Lincoln's inauguration drew throngs. Some twenty-five thousand people came to the nation's capital to see what would happen on this most uncertain of days. Early in the day the early March weather was cool but pleasant; later it turned "bleak and chilly."[3] Such was the national forecast, too: both sections of the country knew they were headed for war, but few knew how fast it might come.

Only the day before Lincoln's inauguration, Bvt. Lt. Gen. Winfield Scott, still general-in-chief of the U.S. Army, had written a note to New York politician William H. Seward, declaring that one of the options available to Lincoln was simply, "Say to the seceded States, Wayward Sisters, depart in peace!"[4] But Lincoln was unlikely to entertain such an idea. He seemed firmly to believe the motto of the United States, *e pluribus unum* —"one out of many"— embodied all that America stood for. As Lincoln rode from the Executive Mansion to the Capitol beside James Buchanan, a military guard stretched throughout the town, boarding and blocking entrance areas, nervously watching windows along the route of travel. It was hardly a confidence builder.[5]

"It is safe to assert that no government proper, ever had a provision in its organic law for its own termination," bellowed Lincoln, when he arose to deliver his inaugural address. After a tedious exploration of the standoff of North versus South, he spoke to the secessionists: "We arc not enemies, but friends. We must not be enemies.

Though passion may have strained, it must not break our bonds of affection. The mystic chords of memory, stretching from every battlefield, and patriot grave, to every living heart and hearthstone, all over this broad land, will yet swell the chorus of the Union, when again touched, as surely they will be, by the better angels of our nature."[6]

But the angels would offer no solutions on that day. Rather, the Yankees faced a growing set of problems, and one in particular that seemed promising to the South was a possible power struggle between Lincoln and Seward. An experienced New York politician who had been chosen by Lincoln as secretary of state, the wily Seward exceeded his authority right away under the guise of helping the lesser Lincoln with valuable advice and counsel. In a memo titled "Some thoughts for the President's consideration," Seward suggested Lincoln alter the platform of opposition to the Confederacy, changing the prime question from the allowance of slavery to one of Union or disunion. He also asked if he could effectively act as a prime minister in approaching the Confederacy and carrying out Lincoln's orders. This might have opened up an avenue of negotiation with the South, but it would also have granted Seward an inordinate amount of power. Lincoln would have no part of it. He, not Seward, would direct the nation, the president informed his startled secretary of state.

As Lincoln and Seward parried, the Virginia State Convention met in Richmond. If Virginia would enter the Confederacy, all knew it would become the largest and most important state in the compact because of its location. In Montgomery, as everywhere else in the South, hopes were high. As they waited for word from Richmond, Varina Davis set about to create a new social Confederacy. She held a levee at the Exchange Hotel and established a regular schedule of receptions that would be attended by the social elite of Montgomery as well as Confederate officials and their wives. Bonding among the new South came easily, and Jefferson Davis himself found time to attend most of the parties. "Playing Mrs. President of this small Confederacy [was] slow work after leaving Washington," Varina's friend and confidant Mary Boykin Chesnut wrote of the First Lady's attitude toward her new role.[7] (Chesnut, wife of South Carolina congressman James Chesnut Jr., was a native Charlestonian who started keeping what would become the most celebrated diary of the Confederacy.)

It was inevitable that discussions at these social gatherings eventually became political. To almost everyone the reason for war seemed to come down to "preserving our way of life." But state rights philosophy often seemed a veneer that covered local conceptions of what "our way of life" actually meant. Money, politics, and control seethed underneath, and with the loss of power in Washington and the potential loss of billions in property (slaves) looming overhead, preserving the way of life meant stirring the collective patriotism of the New South — as well as creating fissures within.

Davis knew his whole political existence and that of his colleagues had been built around state rights as supreme. To have a chance at winning the new war, however, he would need sweeping, central powers — both organizationally and militarily. State rights had allowed sovereign states to secede and determine their own destiny without consultation with other states. But now the Confederate States of America needed to act as one.

Davis felt that in order to have any chance at all, he needed to implement a five-part strategy. First, he would need to build an integrated and well-trained army for the defense of the Confederacy rather than depending on state militias controlled by the governors. The state forces had little uniformity and coordination from state to state, and they depended on local, limited resources in terms of leadership, manpower, money, arms, supplies, subsistence, manufacturing, and transportation, all of which probably could have been better procured and allocated on a national level.

Second, Davis would need to make the most of international politics. A national, Confederate effort would stand a much better chance of obtaining recognition from Britain or France than could the accomplishments of individual states. Davis felt that a comprehensive national plan for the export of cotton, tobacco, rice, and sugar could build credit and trade so as to produce economic stability and recognition.

Third, a national effort would be required to build a navy in order to break the blockade of Southern seaports, open the rivers to commerce, and disrupt Yankee shipping on the high seas.

Fourth, Davis realized that in order to win any war against Lincoln, the South would need to organize massive raids that would threaten Union strongholds such as St. Louis, Cincinnati, Washington, Baltimore, Philadelphia, and Harrisburg. Such offensive moves would cause the Yankees to tire of their "aggressive" warfare, he thought, and yearn for an armistice. It would be far more practical to wage war against the United States from Virginia than from Alabama. But on April 4, a Thursday, the convention rejected — by a vote of eighty-nine to forty-five — a motion to pass an ordinance of secession.

Fifth, Davis desperately needed to believe that the North was only marginally interested in the slavery issue. Although the vast majority of Yankees certainly didn't go to war to end slavery, and many were as racist as the most racist Southerners, Davis risked the question. He hoped that over time most Northerners would decide a war over slaves was not worth the effort.

Whatever the Yankees thought, there was no turning back now. On Saturday, April 6, Lincoln sent a message to South Carolina's governor, Francis Pickens, informing him that the Federal fort in Charleston Harbor, Fort Sumter, would be resupplied with provisions, but no arms. Lincoln also stated that if there was no resistance from the South Carolina militia, the Yankees would not reinforce the fort with more troops or weaponry. It was an aggressive move, but after vigorous debate, the infant Confederate government ordered Brig. Gen. Pierre Gustave Toutant Beauregard to stop any Yankee supply mission, even if it meant firing on the fort. Influenced by the Confederate Congress, Jefferson Davis had appointed Beauregard, the first brigadier general in the Provisional Army of the Confederate States, to supervise the military district around Charleston. One of the most colorful military men of the day, Beauregard was short and slight, bristled with energy, and was expertly trained in a wide variety of subjects. Not only was Beauregard a superb engineer, but he had also been trained in artillery under none other than Robert Anderson, the current commander of Sumter. Beauregard was so liked within the War Department that he had been appointed superintendent of the U.S. Military Academy at West Point in January

1861, an assignment he was relieved of a few days later when his Southern sympathies became starkly clear. With his widespread experience and general popularity — with nearly everyone except Davis — Beauregard was destined to become the first great Southern hero of the conflict.

Beauregard received the news on April 10. By this time the tension among Charlestonians, among Anderson and his men in the fort, and among patriotic Southerners and Northerners had reached a fever pitch. During the first week of April, a large crowd gathered at Charleston's waterfront battery. Anderson and his little garrison sat inside the fort and waited. Surrounding them, scattered about the city and in various forts and batteries in the harbor, were more than six thousand secessionists itching for a fight.[8]

Not all Charlestonians agreed with the Confederate response. James Louis Petigru, a prominent attorney and statesman, said that South Carolina was too small to be a nation and too large for an insane asylum.[9] But the majority of residents felt wronged by the North and saw no other way to react to Lincoln and the rest of the Yankees than to fight. Virginian Roger Atkinson Pryor, a young lawyer, editor, and politician, gave a rousing speech in Charleston on April 10. "I thank you especially that you have annihilated this accursed Union, reeking with corruption and insolent with excess of tyranny," he said. "Thank God! It is blasted with the lightning wrath of an outraged and indignant people."[10]

Advised to surrender by the local South Carolina militia and by representatives of the Confederate government, Anderson would not budge. Instead he drew up a formal reply. "I have the honor to acknowledge the receipt of your communication demanding the evacuation of this fort," he wrote, "and to say, in reply thereto, that it is a demand with which that I regret that my sense of honor, and of my obligations to my Government, prevent my compliance."[11] Informally, Anderson told his potential enemies he was running low on supplies and that he would probably be starved out in a few days if the Southern guns didn't "batter us to pieces." Men inside the fort rolled out powder kegs, worked on the guns, and watched the various positions of Confederate weapons facing them, trying not to expose themselves on the parapets. Night fell over the fort with the stars overhead and the gleam of lights on the horizon in Charleston. Inside the fort Anderson had no oil for lamps, and so the three-story brick fortress stood in near-total darkness.

Early on the morning of April 12 — around 1:30 a.m. — the fort's officers were awakened by a boat bearing a white flag. Four emissaries came: James Chesnut, Stephen D. Lee, Alexander R. Chisholm, and Roger A. Pryor. These aides brought a letter suggesting that if Anderson agreed to evacuate the fort at a stated time without firing on Confederate forces, the transfer of the fort could be accomplished bloodlessly. Anderson stated he would abandon Sumter by noon on April 15 only if his command and flag would not be fired on and unless otherwise instructed by the Lincoln government. By 3:20 a.m. Chesnut and Lee concluded the terms were not acceptable — they wanted the Yankees out of South Carolina immediately — and that the fort would be fired on beginning in one hour. "By authority of Brigadier-General Beauregard, commanding the Provisional Forces of the Confederate States," wrote Chesnut and Lee, "we have the honor to notify you that he will open the fire of his batteries on Fort Sumter in one hour from this time."[12] If they never again met in this world, God grant that they may meet in the next, Anderson replied. The emissaries then withdrew.

Within the fort, sleep was out of the question. "We arose and dressed," wrote Union officer Samuel Wylie Crawford, "and before our arrangements were completed, the firing began."[13] It was almost exactly 4:30 a.m. on April 12 when it started. The great honor of firing the first shot of the war, coveted by officers at Fort Johnson, had been offered to the fiery secessionist Roger Pryor, who had retreated to that point by 4 a.m. Oddly, however, he turned down the offer, later saying, "I could not fire the first gun of the war." The first shot, a ten-inch mortar shell sent as a signal round to activate the other batteries, was fired by the fort's commander, Capt. George S. James. "A flash as of distant lightning in the direction of Mount Pleasant, followed by the dull roar of a mortar, told us that the bombardment had begun," James Chester, a Federal soldier, wrote.[14] In a few minutes' time, the sudden flashes and a surprising number of projectiles, along with the acrid, sulfurous smell of gunpowder and sight of wafting smoke, arced over the fort. After several hours, particularly after dawn, most of the batteries gained an effective range and started spitting shells and balls into the fort with frightening accuracy. In a variety of locations, some Southerners stoked hot-shot furnaces to heat their iron balls into fire starters, hoping to ignite Sumter's wooden barracks. Bricks were smashed, and splinters of wood, brick dust, and mortar chunks cascaded into the air. The soldiers scattered and took cover. "A ball from Cummings's Point lodged in the magazine wall," wrote Union officer Abner Doubleday of the first moments of the war, "and by the sound seemed to bury itself in the masonry about a foot from my head, in very unpleasant proximity to my right ear."[15] What had been one of the most magnificent fortifications in North America was disintegrating into a pile of rubble.

The fire from Southern guns increased in accuracy and frequency after daybreak, when a breeze carried the fumes and sounds of war more effectively into the city. Observers watched the spectacle with amazement as the night turned into day. The youthful Confederacy had struck its first blow.

With such a small amount of ammunition available, Anderson had no reason to react quickly. After breakfasting on a small amount of farina, some of the Federals mounted a response using several cannon, but only a few guns were brought to bear. Doubleday fired the first Yankee cannon of the war. Crawford reported knocking out a gun in the floating battery. But the volume of shells being fired at Sumter was magnificent; it already had ignited a small fire in the wood-framed quarters and knocked away a chimney.

During the afternoon, the Confederate bombardment of Sumter continued without pause, raining shot and shell into and over the fort. Some of Anderson's soldiers were wounded slightly by flying debris; most were unscathed, but the fort's walls were becoming pocked with hits and cracks, and brick dust was accumulating on the parade. Pvt. John Carmody tested the Rebels at Fort Moultrie by sneaking up to the parapet and firing the heavier guns in quick succession at the fort; this only prompted the Confederates into returning a heavy fire onto Sumter. With the approach of nightfall, the firing from Confederate batteries lessened. Amazingly, there had been no deaths on either side.

On the evening of April 12, rain fell on Charleston. Anderson ordered his firing suspended. On the Confederate side, an occasional mortar shell was sent toward Sumter throughout the night. The Federal soldiers finally had the chance to sleep, "well but hungry." Meanwhile, five Federal ships approached, stocked with provisions and the opportunity for escape if necessary. Lincoln's special agent Gustavus Vasa Fox attempted to coordinate the movements of the *Harriet Lane*, the *Pawnee*, the *Baltic*, the *Powhatan*, and the *Pocahontas*. Fox, a former naval lieutenant and woolen goods merchant, was a Massachusetts native who would several months hence become the assistant secretary of the navy. But the movements coordinated by Fox were impeded by heavy seas and a dense fog that formed before dawn.

On the morning of April 13, the storm subsided. Gunfire from Sumter was slowed considerably in order to conserve ammunition. Confederate fire was hot, however, in both senses of the word. By 8 a.m. hot shot from Rebel guns started a fire in Sumter's officers' quarters, and despite the improvised firefighting efforts, the blaze was slowly spreading. Anderson and his officers worried about the possibility of flames or sparks reaching the magazine, which would be catastrophic.

The shot and shell rained in as heavily as ever. Sparks, cinders, and burning pieces of debris launched upward only to rain down on the spreading fire, eventually igniting several shells and kegs of powder, causing a few large explosions. Desperate, Anderson had much of the powder thrown into the harbor.

By now the whole fort was becoming an inferno; the Federal ships were nowhere in sight, and the sally port and heavy entrance gates had been wrecked by shell fire. The flagstaff had been splintered repeatedly. At 1:30 p.m. the flagstaff in Sumter fell. Col. Louis Trezevant Wigfall had returned to his native state and had joined G. T. Beauregard's staff as an aide-de-camp. James Simons, a brigadier general of the South Carolina militia, was determined to find out if this act meant surrender. Before Simons could get an official party off in a nearby rowboat, however, Wigfall demanded that Pvt. Gourdin Young of the Palmetto Guard row him out to the fort. In a bizarre scene aboard a skiff, Wigfall and Young moved north amid the hail of metal. Once Wigfall reached the esplanade, he tied a white kerchief to his sword, got out of the boat, and approached the sally port.

Wigfall found Capt. Jefferson C. Davis (no relation to the Confederate president) and exclaimed that Beauregard had suggested surrender was inevitable. Wigfall then went atop the parapet and waved a white flag, but the firing continued. Anderson approached and said he would capitulate to leave now, rather than on April 15, if the garrison could take its arms and property, honor the United States by saluting its flag, and be transported northward. This was acceptable, said Wigfall. Wigfall had absolutely no authority from Beauregard or anyone else to accept such terms; he did so of his own volition.

The politician returned to Morris Island in the skiff, which flew a white flag, and firing died down from all points. Now, to confuse the issue further, Beauregard's authorized emissaries — Pryor, Lee, and the politician William Porcher Miles — approached the fort. They inquired about Anderson's needs and discussed the situation of the blaze, which was dying down. They asked Anderson about surrender terms, and he replied that terms had already been agreed on with Wigfall. The three Confederates were dumbfounded and explained that Wigfall had no such authority and that he hadn't even seen Beauregard for two days. Confused, the men stood inside the crumbled and burning fort and discussed the surrender. Anderson became upset about the misunderstanding. "Very well, gentlemen, you may return to your batteries," he snapped at his artillerists.[16] But Pryor, Lee, and Miles convinced him to continue a cease-fire until they could talk again with Beauregard, who accepted all the terms except for allowing the Yankees to salute their flag.

After further negotiation, the parties agreed to evacuate and transfer themselves and their supplies on the next morning, Sunday, April 14. The Yankees marched out of the fort "with colors flying and drums beating," Anderson recounted.[17] After thirty-four hours of bombardment, the first engagement of the war was over, and the Confederates had won. The battle had been bloodless. Ironically, however, the pomp and circumstance of the departure ceremony killed two: one of the cannon fired by Anderson's command produced a spark that was blown into a stand of gunpowder. The resulting explosion mortally wounded both Pvt. Daniel Hough and Pvt. Edward Galloway. They were the first to die in America's greatest conflict. Many more were now to come.

Chapter

4

THE WAR DEPARTMENT

ESTABLISHED with the other Confederate agencies in February 1861, the War Department had jurisdiction over all matters pertaining to the Confederate army and to Indian tribes as well. All orders were subject to Jefferson Davis's approval, and because Davis had served as secretary of war for Franklin Pierce and fancied himself the nation's leading military mind, his meddling in the department's affairs soon would become legendary.

Davis's choice for war secretary was a poor one, made to balance political favors handed to various states for representation in the government. Leroy Pope Walker, age forty-four, was an Alabama politician who, as the son of a U.S. senator, grew up with politics in his blood. Balding and with a fluffy gray beard, Walker looked like a small-town lawyer concentrating on petty legal disputes rather than someone who would run a powerful governmental department. A successful attorney, Walker staunchly had defended Southern rights and slavery throughout his career and, in 1860, served as an aide in the Alabama legislature to Senator William L. Yancey. Walker had spoken frequently for Southern candidate John C. Breckinridge in the presidential canvass and served briefly as a brigadier general of the

Alabama militia. When Davis looked to Alabama for cabinet representation, Walker was the third choice. (The two most prominent politicians of the state, Yancey and Clement C. Clay, declined Davis's invitation.) The appointment was a shaky one, as Walker had little military experience, and Davis was determined to start micromanaging the war effort from day one.

In Montgomery the business of the Confederacy was established at the Government Building, a two-story brick edifice standing on Bibb and Commerce streets, within a block of the Exchange Hotel. It was, thus, near where most officials were staying and convenient to those who came downtown to seek office, of which there were many. But the Government Building was not the most attractive of structures. (It appeared as "a great red brick pile" to one observer and "a handsome, first-class warehouse" to another.)[1] Nonetheless, Walker established his office of war to greet the arrivals of hundreds of army officers and would-be officers from all parts of the country. Veterans of the U.S. Army with loyalty to the South — P. G. T. Beauregard, Joseph E. Johnston, and Edmund Kirby Smith included — flocked to see Walker. Indian fighters, including the celebrated officers Earl Van Dorn and Ben McCulloch, also showed up. Soldiers of fortune traveled to Montgomery and offered their services to the Confederacy, including escapees from military adventurer William Walker's Nicaraguan filibustering journey and from the Hungarian revolution of the late 1840s.

Following Fort Sumter's bombardment and surrender by the Yankees, tens of thousands of Southern boys flocked to recruiting stations in scattered towns, anxious for a fight. The men holding these boys' fate represented a mixture of skill and incompetence, some experienced general officers and others glamorized clerks. The War Department's nine bureaus all operated under the direction of Walker, but each bureau chief had considerable authority of his own. The most important of these bureaus was the Adjutant and Inspector General's Department, run by Samuel Cooper. A Yankee who had married a Southern girl, Cooper was a native of Hackensack, New Jersey, and was past his prime at sixty-two when the war started. As adjutant and inspector general of the army, Cooper would be the chief communicator between armies in the field and the Davis administration.

A long-standing veteran of the U.S. Army, Cooper had graduated in the West Point class of 1815 and spent most of his service as an artillerist before becoming a staff officer. He served ably in the Seminole and Mexican wars, after which he was made adjutant general of the U.S. Army, rising to the grade of colonel in the regular army. In 1827 Cooper married Sarah Mason, granddaughter of George Mason of Virginia, a celebrated statesman of the Revolution. This alliance made Cooper a social force in the South and a dedicated Virginian, living on an estate near Alexandria. He became fast friends with Jefferson Davis during the latter's term as secretary of war, an association that would carry over into the Confederacy's struggle for independence, and he joined an intellectual circle that included Robert E. Lee of Arlington House, a significant estate near Cooper's own. Cooper was notable also for his treatises on regulations for the volunteer and militia army troops and for his manual of cavalry tactics. With his earnest yet unremarkable eyes, wavy gray hair, and plain face with its bulbous nose — coupled with a slow, methodical way of thinking — Cooper quickly came to be thought of as a rubber stamp for Davis. One of his subordinates described him as "uniformly courteous and uniformly non-committal . . . self-effacing, something of a mystery."

Cooper had resigned his commission in the U.S. Army on March 7, 1861, just after the inauguration of Abraham Lincoln as president. Cooper might have simply returned to Alexandria to live out his retirement years, but the second aspect of his defection from the North was to go South, offering his services to the fledgling Confederate army. This offer led to Cooper becoming the ranking officer of the entire Confederate army: its senior general. His catapult to the top was, in part, thanks to his relationship with Jefferson Davis. During the days of Cooper as adjutant general and Davis as war secretary, Davis recalled, "my intercourse with him was daily, and I habitually consulted him in reference to the duties I had to perform, as well because of the purity of his character, as of his knowledge of the officers and affairs of the army." Continued Davis,

Though calm in his manner and charitable in his feelings, he was a man of great native force, and [he] had a supreme scorn for all that was mean. To such a man, a life spent in the army could not fail to have had its antagonisms and friendships. . . . The Confederate States had no military organization, and save the patriotic hearts of gallant men, had little on which to rely for the defense of their country. The experience and special knowledge of General Cooper was, under these circumstances, of incalculable value.[2]

Aside from the adjutant general's office, the chief bureau immediately involved with War Secretary Walker was the Bureau of War, also known as the war office, which consisted of clerks and messengers who assisted the secretary. The Bureau, as it would be known, was led by a curious fellow named Albert Taylor Bledsoe. Age fifty-two, a regular army castoff who dabbled in theology, Bledsoe was a friend and Kentucky classmate of both Jefferson Davis and Robert E. Lee's at West Point. After West Point Bledsoe taught mathematics at Miami University in Ohio and then moved to Springfield, Illinois, where he had taken up practicing law next door to another young attorney, Abraham Lincoln. Later Bledsoe taught math at the University of Mississippi and the University of Virginia before emerging into the infant Confederacy, where he was famous for his hatred of all things Northern and his vitriolic diatribes against Thomas Jefferson and democracy.

One clerk in the War Department was John B. Jones, age fifty-one, a Baltimore writer whose *Wild Western Scenes* had sold 100,000 copies in 1841. The father of a large family, he made the journey southward seeking employment in the War Department after publishing the *Southern Monitor* in Philadelphia, a weekly that espoused Southern rights. Jones met President Davis on May 17 in Montgomery and described him as being "overwhelmed with papers." After introducing himself, Jones scrutinized the president during their brief interview. Davis was "tall, nearly six feet; his frame is very slight and seemingly frail; but when he throws back his shoulders he is as straight as an Indian chief. The features of his face are distinctly marked with character," Jones continued, "and no one gazing at his profile would doubt for a moment that he beheld more than an ordinary man."[3]

Two days later Jones visited Secretary Walker, who told the visitor he needed significant help with his correspondence. Walker was "some forty-seven or forty-eight years of age," he penned,

> tall, thin, and a little bent; not by age, but by study and bad health. He was a successful lawyer, and never having been in governmental employment, is fast working himself down. He has not yet learned how to avoid unnecessary labor; being a man of the finest sensibilities, and exacting with the utmost nicety all due deference to the dignity of his official position. . . . The only hope of his continuance in office is unconditional submission to the president, who, being once Secretary of War of the United States, is familiar with all the wheels of the department.

Jones offered to accept a clerkship for relatively scant pay, telling Walker he desired "employment and facilities to preserve interesting facts for publication."[4]

The Confederate Quartermaster-General's Department, charged with providing matériel of war to the troops, got off to a rocky start thanks to its leader, Abraham Charles Myers. Age fifty and a native of Charleston, South Carolina — a descendant of the city's first rabbi — Myers was a particularly poor choice for this position. A West Point graduate, Myers had served as a quartermaster on frontier duty and in the Mexican War, after which he moved to New Orleans and served as a quartermaster there. Resigning his old post at the outset of hostilities, Myers quickly proved unable to cope with the demands of supplying Confederate troops — his miscalculations about supplying uniforms and nonordnance equipment upset numerous officers throughout the army. He fell out of favor with the president almost immediately. Nonetheless, he had many influential friends. He was also the son-in-law of David E. Twiggs, the U.S. brevet major general who had abandoned the Military Department of Texas to Confederate authorities. Myers initially bolstered the nightlife among Confederates, as his wife, Marian, considered herself a social superior to Varina Davis and set out to prove it via parties and receptions.

The Subsistence Department was no better off. Assigned the difficult task of finding food for the swelling army, Lucius Bellinger Northrop, its chief, was "one of the most disliked of all Confederate officials," as a modern historian put it. Fifty years old and a native Charlestonian, Northrop was a West Pointer who went on a campaign against Indians, during which, in 1839, he had accidentally shot himself in the knee. It was an omen of things to come.

Befriending Jefferson Davis early on, Northrop had received a sustained sick leave because of the crippling wound and set up a medical practice in Charleston. Because he was "on sick leave," Northrop kept collecting pay from the army, and many officers deeply resented a situation in which they saw Northrop as collecting two salaries. Nonetheless, Davis did not hesitate to call on his old friend to take on the challenge of serving as commissary general of subsistence. Northrop did not want to accept the post and did so only after Davis's pleading. A writer visiting Montgomery caught a glimpse of Davis and his new commissary general together and published a pen portrait after the war: "With Mr. Davis walks an old gentleman, who bears so striking a family resemblance to him that one would be likely to consider him the wealthy 'Uncle Joe' to whom the nephew owed so much," penned the writer, referring to Jefferson Davis's older brother Joseph, not an uncle.

> He seems an erratic old personage, and jogs along with a limping, lazy stride. What marked features he has — as marked as those of Jeff. [Jefferson] — only more cadaverous. Nature made the two men like enough to be counted kinsmen; art and taste made them prefer similar colors in costume and cut of beard. But there the similarity ends. The old man's coat hangs as loosely as if it were four sizes beyond his measure, and his pants are "shapeless misfits," while his hat — such a shocking bad one.

To make matters worse the Subsistence Department was immediately riddled with corruption, hoarding, and schemes that allowed only poor distribution, the many bad apples more interested in enhancing their own lives than preserving a way of life. Complaints against Northrop's department were voiced right away, and Northrop soon descended into an aura of gloom and despair.[6]

The Confederate Bureau of Ordnance was ably handled by Josiah Gorgas, a forty-two-year-old Pennsylvanian who had graduated West Point and served in the Mexican War as an expert on ammunition. Gorgas was a dark-haired man with a dark beard, prominent nose, and by the time of the Civil War, a receding hairline. He was an independent man who was highly competent yet enjoyed constantly complaining about others. His marriage to an Alabama girl tied him to the South, despite duty at Northern arsenals as the war came. Gorgas began his tenure as a bureau chief with the seizure of about 429 artillery pieces and 154,000 small arms from former U.S. arsenals — a nice start for the fledgling department. It was, in fact, the most significant act in building the storehouse of Confederate weapons.

Gorgas also was acting as chief Confederate engineer, a post that would be taken over by Danville Leadbetter, another native Yankee. Age forty-nine, a Maine man, Leadbetter had graduated high in his West Point class before becoming a career engineering officer. He served on the Pacific frontier and in New York State before transferring to Mobile, Alabama, where he settled in the 1850s. Prior to the outbreak of war, Leadbetter became chief engineer for the state of Alabama, and he remained loyal to his adoptive state when shots were fired at Sumter. His counterpart in the Engineer Bureau, the so-called corps of engineers, was Alfred L. Rives.

Finally, there was the Confederate Medical Department, charged with overseeing the system of hospitals and surgeons assigned to regions and military units. It, too, started on shaky ground, as David C. DeLeon and then Charles H. Smith each acted as bureau chief before Samuel Preston Moore, another Charlestonian, took over as surgeon general. Moore, age forty-seven, was a graduate of the Medical College of South Carolina and a longtime army doctor who agreed to serve as surgeon general only reluctantly.

As Davis was pulling together his War Department, the Provisional Congress of the Confederacy met in Montgomery for the first time. Sessions began on April 29, 1861, just seventeen days after the shelling of Sumter, and lasted for three weeks. Amid all the chaos and furor, Jefferson Davis had a great deal to attempt to balance. There were the politicians who thought they should have received appointments in the Confederate government but didn't. There were old friends who wanted favors and old enemies with scores to settle. There were many who thought Davis would be a fine battlefield commander but would make a lousy executive officer. And there was another problem, bubbling already in the infant Congress, that the president could not have expected: an unpredictable fight between the generals and the politicians.

Every armed conflict carries internal struggles for influence between the military and its civilian commanders, and the Civil War was no different. The first flash point in the Confederacy was Joseph Eggleston Johnston, a veteran of the U.S. Army and an old associate of Jefferson Davis's — yet another of those experienced officers who had come to Montgomery to offer his services to the New South.

Joe Johnston was fifty-four at the time of Sumter, an artillerist and engineer who had graduated high in his West Point class and served ably in the Florida Wars (the 1830s clashes against mostly Seminole Indians) and the Mexican War before rising to staff assignment as quartermaster general of the U.S. Army, in 1860. As such he knew a great deal about the workings of the army and had wide knowledge of many of the officers and politicians involved with it, including Davis.

In April 1861 Johnston and his wife, Lydia, were staying in Richmond, attempting to help Governor John Letcher organize Virginia's state forces for the coming action. Letcher had appointed Robert E. Lee commander of the Virginia forces as a major general; a few days later he commissioned Johnston in the same grade and assigned him to command the forces in and around Richmond itself. Johnston frenetically started drilling, organizing, and supplying the several thousand troops, who had volunteered and marched in from various counties. He also began issuing orders to procure blankets, muskets, uniforms, and tents.

But after just two weeks, the Virginia legislature, not yet part of the Confederacy, determined only one state major general should exist and that it should be Lee. Gravely disappointed, Johnston accepted a brigadier general's commission instead — in the Confederate army, however, not the Virginia militia.

Already disappointed, Johnston and his wife boarded a train for Montgomery, arriving there to meet with Davis, Walker, and Cooper. After much deliberation in the Government Building, the war office sent Johnston to take command of the forces in and around Harpers Ferry, which he did near the end of May. He said good-bye to his wife and boarded a train headed to the front line.[7]

Yet more disappointment was in store for Johnston. During the first term of Congress, in May, Davis determined the Army of the Confederate States of America (the so-called regular army of the Confederacy) should have five full general officers. Davis handled the nomination and made sure they would outrank the many general officers of the state militias, who had been appointed by the governors. He decided the generals should be ranked by seniority, as follows: Samuel Cooper, Albert Sidney Johnston, Robert E. Lee, Joseph E. Johnston, and G. T. Beauregard. Davis evidently based his ranking on year of graduation and class standing at the U.S. Military Academy, which was Cooper (1815), A. S. Johnston (1826), Lee (1829, number 2), J. E. Johnston (1829, number 13), and Beauregard (1838).

But because of his high-ranking assignment as quartermaster general, not to mention his considerable ego, Joe Johnston thought he should be the ranking general of the South. Others argued that the selections should have been made based on their relative rankings at the time of the men's resignations from the U.S. Army. Still others argued that Cooper's and Joe Johnston's staff grades as adjutant general and quartermaster general should have been totally ignored and only their lineal ranks considered. Others argued that special brevet commissions (commissions issued by the president for special reasons) should have been included. Each of these arrangements would have given a different order of ranking among the generals of the Confederacy. (Hindsight would show that Davis's simple method worked pretty well.) Whether Joe Johnston was capable of being the South's leading general is debatable; clearly, Johnston felt he was more than good enough, and Davis felt he wasn't. But the deed was done, and Johnston ranked fourth.

The press had a field day speculating on the different possibilities of what might have been. Johnston, too, would not let it rest. "Cabinet meeting today," Stephen Mallory penned in his diary in mid-September. "The Presdt. shows us a letter from Genl Joe Johnston; a protest against the appt. of Cooper, Lee, and Sydney Johnston over his head in the grade of Genl.— It is an intemperate letter, written evidently under great excitement of feeling. The Presdt's answer is short, and abrupt, & this terminates a lifelong friendship, for a time, at least."[8] In his capacity as president, it was Davis's first lesson in not being able to please all the people all the time.[9]

To be sure, such difficulties with officers were not limited to the Confederacy. The U.S. Army had its own long-standing concerns over command. The term "commander in chief" engendered confusion, for example: by Constitutional specification the president was defined as the supreme military leader, despite the fact that many politicians believed the president to be the nominal head only, dependent on the leadership of a professional soldier during a time of war.

The Union's vague notions of a commander had deep roots. Bvt. Lt. Gen. Winfield Scott, hero of the wars of 1812 and Mexico, was commander in chief of the U.S. Army by custom. He was titled "general-in-chief" to differentiate his role from that of the president. As the ranking officer of the army, Scott was regarded by most as too aged and too infirm to remain in active command. This, despite his engineering of the Union "Anaconda Plan" to infiltrate the South by Mississippi River invasion and weaken its military resolve. As a Virginian Scott was considered by some Yankees as leaning too much toward the South. But in early 1861 no obvious successor to Scott existed. Lincoln needed Scott's expertise as politicians challenged the president's complete lack of military experience, and Scott needed Lincoln's support to thwart any negative comments about his Virginia background. Despite the instability the Scott-Lincoln partnership functioned reasonably well, at least relative to what was happening in the South.

In the midst of the squabbling over rank, the Confederate Congress had business to conduct. The second session of the Provisional Congress, held in Montgomery, lasted from April 29 through May 21. During these early meetings, which continued in the State Capitol, Davis discovered new enemies. Members of the Congress, who considered themselves, not the president, the supreme authority of the Confederacy, now included Robert Rhett, Howell Cobb, Aleck Stephens, Louis T. Wigfall, and Robert Toombs, as well as Virginian Robert M. T. Hunter, Louisianan Edward Sparrow, and South Carolinians James Chesnut, Lawrence M. Keitt, and William Porcher Miles. Although some like Chesnut, Wigfall, and Hunter were Davis friends, others wanted to test the president immediately. On May 11 Congress began that test. Anxious for a location that would serve the war front better logistically, and following Virginia's secession, Congress voted to move the Confederate Congress to Richmond, Virginia. Among the strong supporters of this move were Cobb, Keitt, Miles, Wigfall, and Hunter. President Davis objected, reminding Congress that Montgomery was the seat and that "great embarrassment and probable detriment to the public service must result from a want of co-intelligence between the coordinate branches of the Government incident to such separation."[10] In other words Davis had no intention of moving the executive branch to Richmond following Congress's lead.

Congress again debated the move on May 17, following Davis's objections, and took a vote three days later. After vigorous debate a motion to remove the whole government to Richmond was voted on, and the motion carried by one vote, with the Alabama, Florida, Louisiana, South Carolina, and Virginia delegations voting for the move, and Arkansas, Texas, Mississippi, and Georgia delegations against. Congress had won out, and Davis lost. Preparations for moving the Confederacy's capital began in earnest.

Moving the government was made more complicated by the fact that the government itself was still rather amorphous. Officials needed to be chosen, policies established, defensive preparations made, and all the trappings of society reinvented for the Southerners on the home front. Lacking time to produce a permanent government, the whole experiment was declared a "provisional government" that would explore its workings based on the U.S. Constitution. One discouraged delegate nearly melted at the size of the task that lay ahead:

> With no Treasury at command no machinery of government to raise & collect money, no national existence where credit can be pledged to get money & if it existed no credit upon which to raise it, no commerce to pay duties, no custom house system to give commerce a start, no navy to protect it & no merchant marine with which to carry it on, no army to hold the ports on our seaboard, no postal arrangements for conducting intelligence & all these wants in the face of apparently determined policy on the part of the old government to act quickly in seizing & closing our ports & cutting of our mail facilities I feel really like I was called on to build a great edifice in a short time without any tools or materials to work with.[11]

The Provisional Congress could look at a small but growing list of accomplishments, however. It had produced a provisional constitution that attempted to instill state rights into the document, referring in the preamble to "Sovereign and Independent States." The Constitution allowed states to raise peacetime armies and navies, though it did not allow them to make war on a foreign nation unless invaded first. The word "United" was excised from the document, "The Republic of Washington" rejected as an alternative, and finally, "Confederate" chosen, which according to one delegate, "truly expresses our present condition."[12]

Vice President Stephens, along with Robert Toombs, pushed for the English cabinet form of government, wherein cabinet officers were chosen from within Congress. This was not made mandatory but was possible under the new system, as was simultaneous holding of political and military offices — something the United States Constitution forbade. An export tax initiative suggested that Congress expected to raise significant funds from exporting tobacco and cotton. Congress would determine judicial districts in the New

South, and a Supreme Court would be organized from all the district judges.

The many governmental departments of the Confederacy, although just forming, duplicated the United States system with one exception: the Post Office Department. The U.S. postmaster general was operating under a huge deficit, which Southerners felt was wasteful and, in effect, a subsidy for businesses. So the Confederate Congress ordered their postmaster to turn a profit by March 1, 1863.

The Confederacy also had to plan for expansion, since Congress saw promise among the border states. Such areas, which might support the South or remain behind with the old Union, were critical to the Confederacy's success. Until April the border states had divided loyalties; Lincoln's call for 75,000 men from the North ended this. In response the Confederate Congress had sent commissioners to woo the potential partners. In Missouri the state's pro-Southern governor, Claiborne F. Jackson, called a special session of the legislature, and the state teetered on secession for several months. Secession was brewing in Kentucky, too, and a pro-Southern contingency began meeting in the southern part of the state to start a Confederate government. Arizona Territory considered itself pro-Confederate, and rumblings of secession were heard there. Native Americans scattered across the Plains and American Southwest felt a strong attraction to the Confederacy. Choctaws, Chickasaws, Seminoles, Creeks, and Cherokees held meetings, declared themselves free nations, and appointed commissioners to meet with the Confederacy. On May 3 Lincoln had called for more volunteers, building the Yankee army to nearly 160,000 strong. Virginia, Arkansas, Tennessee, and North Carolina seceded, making eleven Confederate states. The potential for others to join the Confederate cause seemed real.

On the battlefields, events were moving slowly. Soldiers like John Worsham of the Twenty-first Virginia were drilled to within an inch of their lives but wondered if they would see real action. In the late spring of 1861, Worsham's men, equipped with the best uniforms and guns they could obtain, moved slowly into the Shenandoah Valley under the guidance of Brig. Gen. Thomas J. Jackson, an eccentric ex-professor from the Virginia Military Institute in Lexington. The overall commander of this force of several thousand, consisting of Virginia state troops, was Maj. Gen. Robert E. Lee. Near month's end, on May 29, Worsham had his first taste of battle. Near Aquia Creek, Virginia, a Federal gunboat stopped and fired a few shots before voyaging away. It was rather a letdown. But a week later three Yankee gunboats approached the position of the Twenty-first Virginia and, in Worsham's words, "commenced to bombard the earthworks near the wharf."

Worsham reported that "the enemy threw six-, eight-, and ten-inch shots at Captain Walker, who put some of his small three-inch rifled cannon into the works and replied. The firing lasted several hours." During the action, nearly all the Yankee cannonballs whizzed over the heads of Worsham and his comrades. "The family living inside the earthworks had a chicken coop knocked to pieces," Worsham wrote. "The old cock confined in it came out of the ruins, mounted the debris, flapped his wings, and crowed. That was the only casualty on our side."[13]

Action began to sprout elsewhere across the American landscape. Yankee Brig. Gen. Benjamin F. Butler, without authority, moved forces into Baltimore and occupied the city, which had well-known Southern sympathies. Riots erupted in St. Louis, in the center of another area of divided loyalties. Near the end of May, Yankee troops advanced into Virginia, occupying Alexandria and pushing out three small Confederate brigades.

Late in the month the Confederacy pulled up stakes and moved to Richmond.

5

A CURIOUS CABINET

T HE first weeks of summer 1861 produced a terrific swell of war across the South, particularly after Lincoln had called for troops to bring the Confederates back into the Union. As young men rode horses, fitted uniforms, tested weapons, and organized companies all across the South, Davis organized his cabinet. The secretary of state would be Robert Toombs. Christopher G. Memminger of South Carolina would be the secretary of the treasury. The secretary of war was Leroy P. Walker. Floridian Stephen R. Mallory was secretary of the navy. John H. Reagan of Texas was the postmaster general. The office of attorney general was filled by Judah P. Benjamin, an intellectual who many would call the "brains of the Confederacy." (In the U.S. government, the attorney general was not a cabinet-level post; the Confederacy tried to correct this by making it so.)

At the government's formation in Montgomery, no foreign policy for the proto-Confederacy existed; Toombs had to invent it piecemeal as he went along. Before long the Georgian became irritated at being the foreign minister of a nation with no foreign relations. It was Toombs who, when a visitor to Montgomery asked him where the State Department was, famously replied, "in my hat," as he withdrew

some papers from it. As springtime ebbed across the Southern landscape, Toombs increasingly turned his attention to military matters,
becoming bored with the affairs of state.

In addition to everything else, Toombs was a realist. Once summer approached he wrote his friend Stephens with worries over the
coming war:

> The North is acting with wild and reckless vigour . . . They act as tho'
> they believe they will be impotent after the first effort (which I believe is
> true) and seem determined to make that overwhelming and effective. . . .
> [Winfield] Scott has near eighty thousand threatening Virginia and full
> command of the bay, rivers, and inlets. The prospect ahead looks very
> gloomy. It will take courage and energy to avert great disaster and we
> have far too little of the latter for the crisis.[1]

Later he fretted to Stephens over the scant money available to the
Confederacy. "Men will not see that the revolution must rest on the
treasury," he wrote, "without it, *it must fail.*"[2]

The treasury secretary, Christopher Gustavus Memminger, was
an old South Carolina aristocrat. He was a distinguished-looking
fellow, a well-dressed, detail-oriented man, with silvery hair that
waved over his ears, a fit, erect bearing, a prominent nose, and small,
penetrating eyes that exuded a sense of confidence and precision.
Nearing his sixties, Memminger had been born in Nayhingen, Würt-
temberg, in what is now southern Germany, and was brought to the
United States as an orphan at age three. Raised in a Charleston or-
phanage, Memminger eventually was taken into the home of a
trustee, Thomas Bennett, who adopted him. (Bennett later became
governor of the state.) Memminger thereby was grafted into South
Carolina society from complete anonymity. He was a hardworking,
deeply religious young man. Studying law, as many upper-class
young men attempted to do, Memminger was admitted to the bar in
1824. Well known as a leading light in his state by the time war clouds
approached, Memminger served as director of a variety of professional companies in and around Charleston and owned a large plan-

tation house and property in excess of more than $200,000. He also held titles to fifteen slaves.

Memminger had spent a good portion of his youth admiring the Federal Union, but his support for a central government slowly dissipated. By the time of John Brown's raid into Harpers Ferry, Virginia, in 1859 (which scared the daylights out of slave owners as they imagined a mass uprising of ax-wielding former servants), Memminger had solidified himself with the secessionists. As a leading attorney and one of the wealthiest men in Charleston, he was selected to go to the Montgomery convention, where he wasted no time divining thoughts on the proto-Confederacy. Memminger had a treatise printed up, "Plan of a Provisional Government for the Southern Confederacy," and, like Benjamin, stood out as calm and intellectual amid the hyperemotion.

Davis's appointment of Memminger as secretary of the treasury had been a little startling, as the two were not known to each other. The original plan, according to Mary Boykin Chesnut, was that Davis wanted to make the politician Robert W. Barnwell secretary of state and Toombs secretary of the treasury. Barnwell refused, and so the plan was altered, bringing the dark horse Memminger in as a second choice, as recommended by various members of the South Carolina delegation.

The choice to head the Navy Department was also made on political grounds. A significant factor in the selection of Stephen Russell Mallory as secretary of the navy was his residence in Florida, another state Davis wanted to appease by including it in the cabinet. Mallory was about fifty when war commenced; he had been born at Port of Spain, in the British West Indies, in either 1811, 1812, or 1813, depending on which source is to be believed. He was stout, balding, with wavy dark hair trimmed meticulously and brushed with gray, a distinguished-looking, practical politician. His father had been working in the Caribbean as a construction engineer at the time of Stephen's birth, and the family moved around until settling at Key West, Florida, in 1820. During the family moves Mallory had received only snippets of formal education; finally, in his early twenties, he became inspector of customs at Key West and set about improving his education by studying law. Admitted to the Florida bar, Mallory took part in the Seminole War, married, served as a county judge, and spent much of the 1850s as a U.S. senator, elected as a Democrat. As chairman of the Naval Affairs Committee in the Senate, he well understood navy business. He had declined an appointment as U.S. minister to Spain and, despite his initial opposition to secession, resigned from the Senate in 1861 to support his beloved South.

To head the postal department, Davis looked to Texas, appointing John Henninger Reagan, a Tennessee native who had moved to the Lone Star State at age twenty-one. At the time of the firing on Sumter, Reagan was forty-two, a former clerk, bookkeeper, tutor, and plantation overseer. While in his twenties, Reagan had become interested in military affairs and joined the Republic of Texas Army as an Indian fighter. He subsequently was a planter, surveyor, lawyer, judge, and finally, a Texas legislator. Elected a U.S. representative from Texas in 1857, Reagan spent the years leading up to secession in Washington as a staunch Southern supporter, but he opposed radical measures. Hoping that a compromise could be found in the days preceding the Civil War, he had returned to Texas in January 1861.

Reagan had a formidable physical presence, with a hefty frame; jet black hair brushed back over his head and ears; a thick, black beard; and coal black eyes. At the Provisional Congress in Montgomery, Reagan caught the attention of Jefferson Davis when the Texan told him he "would not have voted for you as president." Reagan explained that Davis would have been great as the South's leading general, and this flattery may have laid the groundwork for Reagan's appointment as postmaster general.

The final member of Davis's inner circle wielded enormous influence within the administration. Judah Philip Benjamin, age forty-nine, had been born in St. Croix, British West Indies, a British subject of Sephardic Jewish settlers. He was raised in Charleston and grew to adulthood in New Orleans; at the time these cities were home to two of the largest Jewish communities in the nation. His father was one of the founders of the first Reform Congregation of America, and it's likely Benjamin was confirmed at its temple. At the tender age of fourteen, Benjamin left his deeply Jewish upbringing to attend Yale Law School. He was admitted to the Louisiana bar at the age of twenty-one and married Natalie Martin, the daughter of a wealthy New Orleans planter, which propelled him into the life of a sugar planter and politician. A plump, good-natured man with a perpetual smile, Benjamin had neatly combed, slightly curled hair, a short beard with no mustache, and sad eyes that seemed to signify wisdom in a glance. Elected to the Louisiana legislature, Benjamin was active in state politics in the Whig Party until he exploded onto the national scene with his election as a U.S. senator from Louisiana, in 1853. More than once he had to defend his religion, one time rebuking Senator Benjamin Wade of Ohio with these words: "It is true that I am a Jew, and when my ancestors were receiving their Ten Commandments from the immediate Deity, amidst the thunderings and lightnings of Mount Sinai, the ancestors of my opponent were herding swine in the forests of Great Britain."

Later switching to the Democratic Party, Benjamin was reelected and stayed in the Senate, befriending Jefferson Davis and encountering odd situations and trouble as his influence grew. Benjamin was once so insulted by Davis that he challenged him to a duel, but the future Confederate president apologized, and the situation was diffused. Because of scandalous rumors about Benjamin's wife circulating in Washington, Mrs. Benjamin took the couple's daughter to Paris, and the Benjamins saw each other only about once per year thereafter.

══

ALL these men came together in the great move to Richmond, which was accomplished by the end of May 1861. Before the war Richmond was something of a contradiction. A city of 37,910 built along the James River, it embodied the upper South as well as the cultural and historical richness of old Virginia. Richmond consisted of a blend of old aristocrats, ambitious lawyers and businessmen, farmers and marketers, and plantation aristocracy with their precious slaves. The travelers bustling in and out of the countryside to and from Washington to the north, Petersburg to the south, and Charlottesville and

Lynchburg to the west could be considerable — not to mention the river traffic. To the east lay the Virginia peninsula, with the towns of Hampton, Norfolk, and the old Colonial center of Williamsburg. The mountains of western Virginia spread to the west and north, separating the Virginians from the Yankees in Ohio, though the mountain men were more loyal to the North than Southerners initially imagined, and even most of Richmond initially balked at leaving the Union before Virginia itself adopted its ordinance of secession. Many Richmonders were conservative Whigs who were not particularly keen on seeing the Union dissolve. So the Confederacy would be hosted by a somewhat inhospitable city.

Richmond ranked third in size among Southern cities, after New Orleans and Charleston. About a third of the city's population consisted of slaves. Richmond's mayor, Joseph Mayo, supervised the slaves and free blacks in the city, all of whom had to be careful in their conduct and lived with considerable limitations on their freedoms. For white Richmonders, be they professionals, merchants, farmers, planters, or simply poor, bloodlines were held supreme: if you could trace yourself back to an early Virginia Anglo-Saxon line, you were in good social standing among the city's elite. If not, you simply didn't matter. Many important families with money and accomplishments stuck together in business and social events; they also intermarried, building wealth and networks of social purity and aristocracy. Most labored in the city, which had the greatest concentration of heavy industry in the South and a booming tobacco business fed by vast farms and plantations scattered throughout the Virginia countryside.

Richmond was a gridded city laid along the James River, with its central business and government district built on the northern riverbank, north of what became known as Mayo's Island. Two bridges, Mayo Bridge and the Richmond & Danville Railroad Bridge, spanned the island. A second railroad bridge, that of the Richmond & Petersburg Railroad, stood to the west, halfway to the largest nearby island in the James, Belle Isle. The southern riverbank held the city of Manchester. North of the Petersburg bridge was Brown's Island and the industrial area that was home to the Tredegar Iron Works, the most significant iron factory in the South, chartered in

1837. West of this area sprawled Hollywood Cemetery, the city's extravagant burial ground, founded on a hilly plot in 1848. (James Monroe was entombed here.) Overlooking Hollywood and Brown's Island stood Gamble's Hill, near which the Spotswood Hotel, the city's most famous, was the place to be seen. North of the city lay a geographical rise that came to be known as Shockoe Hill, which contained Shockoe Cemetery as well as many residences. The hill on the southeastern edge of the city supported an extensive military drilling camp and was termed Chimborazo Hill, named after an Ecuadoran mountain. (A Richmonder who had visited Ecuador likened the hill to the South American mountain, and the name stuck.) As the war accelerated, this area was transformed into the largest hospital in the Confederacy. Nearby stood Oakwood Cemetery, another significant burial ground. Southwest along the river was Rocketts Landing, the major docks of the city, and extensive tobacco warehouses, as well as the fledgling Confederate States Navy Yard.

When the Confederacy went to war, Richmonders got organized. The organization focused on one spot: the city's central, monumental building was the Virginia State Capitol, a fantastic, Greek Revival structure with stunning porticoes finished with Ionic columns. The cornerstone was laid in 1785, after the structure had been designed by Thomas Jefferson. By the mid-1800s the surrounding ground, Capitol Square, had become a fashionable city park for all Richmonders. The square stood on high ground overlooking the James River to the south. Inspired by the Roman temple at Nîmes, France, Jefferson had carefully planned the structure, had plaster models of it created in Paris, and had personally overseen the building's detailed construction until the final exterior was finished, in 1797.[3]

A walk of just a few minutes' duration brought Richmonders to several other areas of interest around Capitol Square. Northwest past the green grassy lawns, abundant spring flowers, and tall, handsome trees was the showpiece of the city, a bronze equestrian statue of George Washington, which had been dedicated on Washington's birthday in 1858. Southwest, parallel to Ninth Street, down a terrace of lovely brick steps, was another prominent feature of Capitol

Square, the Richmond Tocsin, or bell tower. Constructed in 1824, this square brick building served both to warn Richmonders of fire and to commemorate glorious or sorrowful events. On April 21, 1861, the Tocsin had sounded, warning of the reported approach of the gunboat USS *Pawnee* on the James. Citizens scrambled along with militia to high ground in the city as well as down to Rocketts Landing on the James. The gunboat never came, however, on what was later recalled as Pawnee Sunday.

The remaining corner of the square, to the northeast, held the Executive Mansion, finished in 1813. This Federal-style house, on the corner of Governor and Capitol streets, served as Governor John Letcher's abode at the start of the war.

Wartime Richmond was, by modern standards, a small city with a downtown district that would today be considered quaint. Most of the government buildings were clustered in the area between Capitol Square and the riverfront to the south. On Main Street, between Tenth and Eleventh streets, on the southern side of the square, was the U.S. Post Office and Customs House, a Tuscan-Italianate edifice constructed in 1858 (and rebuilt and enlarged since). On its move to Richmond, the Confederacy took over this building and used it as the Treasury Department quarters and as an executive office for Jefferson Davis. The Confederate State Department met on the building's second floor, which also hosted cabinet sessions. The Confederate president's office, where much of the business of the war took place, was on the third floor of this building, facing the Capitol. Mechanic's Hall, the site of the Confederate War and Navy departments and the offices of Samuel Cooper and Robert G. H. Kean, chief of the Bureau of War, stood on the corner opposite the Richmond Tocsin. In between the Customs House and Mechanic's Hall stood a block of offices housing the Signal Corps, the Paymaster's Department, the Bureau of Nitre and Mining, and the Quartermaster's Department. The Signal Corps facilitated field and telegraphic communications. The Bureau of Nitre and Mining was charged with mining resources.

Three long blocks northeast of Capitol Square, at Twelfth and Clay streets, stood the John Brockenbrough House, now known as the White House of the Confederacy. This lovely mansion, built in 1818 and lived in by several occupants before the war — including would-be Confederate Secretary of War James A. Seddon — had been purchased in 1861 by the city of Richmond as a residence for the Jefferson Davis family. The beautiful two-story house had a basement that was used as a breakfast room and children's dining room. The first story contained an entrance hall and four large rooms: a dining room, central parlor, drawing room, and library. The second floor included Jefferson Davis's office — where he greeted many Confederate officials and held some memorable meetings — a secretary's office (occupied by Burton Harrison, the president's secretary), a waiting room, the Davises' bedroom, a dressing room, and the large nursery, where all the children slept. A third story, newly added at the time of the war, contained rooms for Harrison, military aides, house servants, and family guests.[4]

Immediately northwest of Capitol Square stood the city's most celebrated house of worship, St. Paul's Episcopal Church. This Greek Revival structure was completed in 1845; the Davis family attended church here, as did the Robert E. Lee family, when in town. On Broad Street, the Monumental Church (Episcopalian) was completed in 1814 as a memorial to seventy-two victims of a theater fire that had occurred on the spot three years earlier. The Old First Baptist Church, another Greek Revival structure at East Broad and Twelfth streets, was built in 1839 and served as a Confederate hospital during the war. To the east, across Shockoe Valley, stood St. John's Church, where Patrick Henry delivered his "Give me liberty or give me death!" speech.

═══

ON July 20, 1861, the ninety-nine members of the Confederate Congress, led by Howell Cobb, met for their first session in Richmond, which would last until the end of August.[5] The military situation was so dominated by organizing, recruiting, and drilling on both sides that little in the way of battles had taken place since Sumter. Minor skirmishes had occurred in Virginia at the towns of Fairfax Court House, Philippi, and Big Bethel, and in the western part of the state the situation was heating up. But so far the war had involved mostly pregame preparation. That was about to change along the banks of a little creek near Manassas dubbed Bull Run. Here, the armies of Gen. Joe Johnston, commanding the Army of the Shenandoah, and Brig. Gen. G. T. Beauregard, leading the Army of the Potomac (the armies adopted geographical names for two of the region's important rivers) met the Yankee army of Brig. Gen. Irvin McDowell, the so-called Army of Northeastern Virginia. The battle of First Manassas (or First Bull Run) commenced on July 21, 1861. Spectators had packed picnic baskets and carried wagonloads of citizens from surrounding villages and from Washington to see the great battle. Some U.S. congressmen were even in attendance — one, Alfred Ely, was captured by the Rebs. When the smoke cleared, most of the Yankee army had bid the battlefield a hasty retreat and skedaddled back to Washington, and the Confederates considered themselves victorious in a day of glory.

Richmond celebrated. At the Confederate Department of State, Robert Hunter reported on Manassas:

> It affords me extreme pleasure to announce to you in my first official communication the glorious victory achieved by our army over the forces of the United States, on Sunday, the 21st instant, at Manassas, in this state. . . . For weeks previous to the battle of Manassas the Northern press teemed with boastful assurances of the vast superiority of the Federal Army over that of the Confederate States. . . . The result has proved how delusive was their confidence in their superiority and in our weakness.[6]

Jefferson Davis himself had ridden out to the field to supervise the effort. "Night has closed upon a hard-fought field," he reported in a message to Congress. "Our forces were victorious. The enemy was routed, and fled precipitately, abandoning a large amount of arms, ammunition, knapsacks, and baggage. The ground was strewn for miles with those killed, and the farmhouses and the ground around were filled with wounded. . . . Too high praise cannot be bestowed, whether for the skill of the principal officers or for the gallantry of all of our troops."[7] In what would turn out to be the single verifiable instance of a "battlefield promotion" in the war, Davis bestowed upon G. T. Beauregard the appointment of full general in the Army of the Confederate States. However, divisive splits already were appearing between Davis and the general.

Beauregard's history with Davis had been good. On Davis's oath as president, Beauregard had immediately sent him a letter of congratulations; in response Davis had made him the first brigadier general in the Confederacy, the ranking brigadier general, and sent him to South Carolina's governor, Francis Pickens. Beauregard had become the first great hero of the Confederacy at Sumter, and as such, he was treated everywhere with the utmost respect and profound awe. Beauregard had become the first commander of the Army of the Potomac (C.S.A.), occupying Centreville, Virginia, after Union forces beat him to Alexandria. At Manassas he and Johnston more or less had combined forces to defeat McDowell, and Davis's battlefield reward sat well with the Little Creole, as he was called due to his short stature.

But Beauregard, bolstered by his ego from successes at Sumter and Manassas, wanted to be an independent army commander, with his own army and no superior to answer to, and Davis wouldn't allow this. Davis pointed out sharply that when Johnston was absent, Beauregard, as number two, would be in command. But Johnston was not about to leave and allow Beauregard to take over.

Although Beauregard did not hold this against Johnston, he was furious with Davis — despite the fact that the Confederate president's refusal of his request made military sense. As for Johnston, he was still furious with Davis over the rank question. As the Confederate armies settled in after Manassas, camping within staring distance of each other, the bad feelings percolated. It was a rocky start for Davis and his two most important field generals.

In the wake of First Manassas, these thistles would be wrapped in a veneer of success and pushed away in the glow of Confederate patriotism. "We arrived here safely on Wednesday evening, and immediately drove out to the Texas camp to see President Davis present a flag that Mama had made for them," wrote Louise Wigfall, daughter of Louis Wigfall, the aide of President Davis and a Confederate senator. "He made a beautiful speech and was vociferously cheered. . . . Oh! how glad I was when I first put my foot on Confederate soil. . . . We went to the President's last night and he was very agreeable as usual, we took tea with him the night we arrived, and I had the honor of a kiss from Jeff, I declare I have almost fallen *in love* with him."[8] In Richmond Howell Cobb, leader of the Congress, penned his wife a letter, suggesting fast independence. "From the tone of the Northern papers I infer that the people there are getting sick of the war and since their disastrous defeat at Manassas they begin to talk of peace," he declared. "Besides their people are not volunteering very freely for the war and their treasury is getting low and their credit lower. From all which it would seem a very natural conclusion that they cannot continue the war much longer."[9]

But a new war actually was brewing, a war of second-guessing between Beauregard and Davis — or perhaps more accurately, between the general and most everyone else. Beauregard began sniping at Lucius Northrop over reportedly inadequate supplies for his army. He pecked at Secretary of War Judah Benjamin for supposedly interfering with his command decisions. And his report to the Confederate Congress on the battle of Manassas caused a bombshell: Davis's political opponents claimed Beauregard's account showed the president prevented the general from pursuing the retreating Yankee army. Davis fumed at Beauregard:

> Yesterday my attention was called to various newspaper publications purporting to have been sent from Manassas, and to be a synopsis of your report of the battle of the 21st of July last, and in which it is represented that you had been over ruled by me in your plan for a battle with the enemy south of the Potomac, for the capture of Baltimore and Washington, and the liberation of Maryland. . . . With much surprise I found that the newspaper statements were sustained by the text of your report. I was surprised because if we did differ in opinion as to the measures and purposes of contemplated campaigns, such fact could have no appropriate place in the report of a battle; further because it seemed to be an attempt to exalt yourself at my expense; and especially because no such plan as that described was submitted to me.[10]

In the autumn of 1861, Davis reflected on his critics in a letter to Johnston. "Though such statements may have been made merely for my injury," penned the president, "they have acquired importance in that they have served to create distrust, to excite disappointment, and must embarrass the Administration in its further efforts to reinforce the armies of the Potomac."[11] Beauregard denied he had said anything designed to damage Davis, but he did suggest that the Confederate leader had blown the chance to capture Washington by rejecting Beauregard's original battle plan and insisting on his own. In fact Davis had arrived on the Manassas battlefield to witness Beauregard directing the battle, and Johnston, who ranked him, playing, in effect, a secondary command role. And while Davis had suggested sober strategy, Beauregard had actually shown himself indecisive at the critical hour. Davis had never been against seizing the momentum and dealing a knockout blow. It had been Beauregard who chose instead to take a defensive stance. The lack of action on his part would haunt everyone in the high command for months to come, as it gradually became clear that the best opportunity for ending the war early would have been immediately following First Manassas.[12] All this was taking place with the knowledge that Beauregard might run against Davis for the permanent presidency of the Confederacy in elections to be held in the spring of 1862. Given Beauregard's immense popularity with Congress and with the people, Davis had plenty of reason to be nervous.

After days and weeks of intense squabbling, the "Report on the Battle of Manassas Affair" took on a life of its own. Davis was furious with Beauregard, flatly stating that the general was attempting to reach loftier heights by attacking his commander in chief. In response Beauregard sent a letter to the *Richmond Whig* attacking the president obliquely and ensuring that their relationship would be fractured forever.

As if to make himself certain of that fact, Beauregard also attacked another front, one close to Davis's heart. Beauregard (aided by Johnston) began making harsh assertions that the Commissary and Quartermaster-General's departments were not properly supporting the armies with food and equipment. While this may have been largely true, the available amounts of food and the logistics of getting it to the right place were difficult questions to work out early in the war. Beauregard didn't give a damn about how difficult the task was — to him, Abraham Myers and Lucius Northrop were clearly failing in their jobs. He was particularly harsh on Northrop regarding the food issue, and Northrop being an old, close friend of Davis's, the president defended him staunchly. Davis angrily wrote Beauregard: "Some excitement has been created by your letter. The Quartermaster and the Commissary Genl. both feel that they have been unjustly arraigned. . . . I think you are unjust to yourself in putting your failure to pursue the enemy to Washington on account of short supplies of subsistence and transportation. . . . Let us . . . give form and substance to the criticisms always easy to those who judge after the event."[13]

None of this boded well for the rebellion. And within the boundaries of the Confederate capital itself, the arguments were just beginning.

Chapter

6

THE MILITARY HIGH COMMAND

In Richmond many hopeful senators and representatives looked at the fight that had arisen over Beauregard's actions at First Manassas in disbelief. Surely this was not the time to fight within the Confederate nation; there were Yankees to kill and, as time marched on, more and more supplies ready for a conquest that might spell Confederate doom. Although Richmonders were flushed with success, Davis knew what lay ahead. He warned that hard battles would follow against a determined enemy, but few believed him until, during a pouring rain, trains rolled into Richmond bearing the Manassas wounded, and men without limbs and soldiers with heads wrapped in bloody bandages were carried off to makeshift hospitals.

"Richmond was then one vast general hospital," wrote Sallie Putnam, the nurse, a native of Madison County, Virginia, who moved to Richmond in 1858 and who kept a celebrated wartime diary. "Our surgeons were kept constantly busy in the rounds of their profession, and we were told, as far as it was in their power . . . they practiced the principles of conservative surgery, although much blame has been attached to the surgeons of both armies for reckless waste and sacrifice of human limbs."[1]

Along with the wounded came Yankee prisoners, to the point where the town was "crowded to the caves."[2] (One of those brought to Richmond was the congressman captured at Manassas, Alfred Ely of New York.) Many houses, schools, and other institutions had been converted into hospitals, and now prisons had to be created. For Yankee officers a warehouse and ship chandlery near the James River, owned by the estate of Luther Libby, was converted and renamed Libby Prison. Common soldiers were held on Belle Isle, an isolated spit of land that housed a tent city for the prisoners. All together some eighteen hundred prisoners were housed in Richmond during the last weeks of 1861.

Not everyone appreciated the growth of Richmond. As Sallie Putnam wrote,

> With the incoming of the Confederate government, Richmond was flooded with pernicious characters. . . . Speculators, gamblers, and bad characters of every grade flocked to the capital, and with a lawlessness which for a time bade defiance to authority, pursued the rounds of their wicked professions, and grew rich upon their dishonest gains. Thieving, garroting, and murdering were the nightly employments of the villains who prowled around the city.[3]

In this arena of strange politics, relations between President Davis and his generals became further strained. The argument between Davis and Beauregard over First Manassas failed to dissipate. Davis was faring no better with Joe Johnston, who also was annoyed with Secretary of War Judah Benjamin. Johnston had added to the Manassas controversy by writing that following the battle the president had been "satisfied with the victory as it was" and that he gave "no instructions" about pursuing the Yankees, later summarized in his memoirs.[4] Davis professed continued anger over the Confederate lack of pursuit. All sides continued to point fingers.

As 1861 dragged on and Johnston's armies stayed encamped at Fairfax Court House and Centreville, Johnston maintained a positive correspondence with the War Department and with President Davis. In mid-September, however, the glue that held the relationship between these old associates came apart. On August 31 Davis finally sent the names of the five full generals of the Army of the Confederate States to the Senate for confirmation, in rank order of Cooper, Albert Sidney Johnston, Robert E. Lee, Joe Johnston, and Beauregard. The news struck Johnston "like a slap in the face," and he immediately sat down to pen a letter to the president. He declared:

> It seeks to tarnish my fair fame as a soldier and a man, earned by more than thirty years of laborious and perilous service. I had but this, the scars of many wounds, all honestly taken in my front and in the front of battle, and my father's Revolutionary sword. It was delivered to me from his venerated hand, without a stain of dishonor. Its blade is still unblemished as when it passed from his hand to mine. I drew it in the war, not for rank or fame, but to defend the sacred soil, the homes and hearths, the women and children, aye, the men of my mother Virginia, my native South.[5]

Sending the letter may have been the worst decision Johnston ever made. Davis was furious, and the relationship never was mended.

Two of the five generals now were very angry with their president. To Davis's credit, he was probably right in both situations. But the tension among the three men would be palpable for years to come.

Such was not the case with Robert Edward Lee, who — after leaving the old Union and taking command of the Virginia state forces in April — had spent the first few months of the war in a succession of assignments. In January 1861 he had turned fifty-four years old, his hair and mustache still black with just a sprinkling of gray, and he had not yet grown a beard. He stood five feet eleven inches in height, and weighed 170 pounds. His father, "Light-Horse Harry" Lee, had been Washington's cavalry commander and governor of the commonwealth before falling from grace, drinking, gambling, and losing his family's money. His son's career as an engineer in the U.S. Army had been stellar, and his service in the Mexican War outstanding. Lee's loyalty to the U.S. Army was intense, but he felt he had no choice but to turn southward when Virginia departed from the Union.

Early in the war Lee had hastily organized a defensive force of militia troops in Richmond, helped to initiate a Confederate naval force, protected Norfolk, and helped to reinforce Manassas, Harpers Ferry, and Fredericksburg. By midsummer about forty thousand Confederate troops were in Virginia's fields. Arms, ammunition, cannon, powder, and other supplies had been furnished for $3.8 million, all in about eight weeks. Six days later, at First Manassas, Lee wrote his wife, Mary, about the battle: "That indeed was a glorious victory and has lightened the pressure on our front amazingly. Do not grieve for the brave dead. Sorrow for those they left behind — friends, relatives, and families."[6]

On July 28 Lee departed for western Virginia to coordinate operations and ensure that commanders were working well together in that mountainous region. It was a bland assignment, and on August 4 he wrote Mary from Huntersville. After mentioning that he had traveled on the same road in 1840, he commented that "if any one had then told me that the next time I traveled that road I would have been on my present errand, I should have supposed him insane."[7]

A few days later, on August 6, the *Memphis Daily Appeal* described the overseer of western Virginia: "His life, since he assumed the chief command of the Virginia forces, has been a model of soldierly patience and energy and watchfulness. Six o'clock in the morning has seen him regularly enter his office, which, with rare exceptions, he has not left, save at meal times, till eleven at night. A man of few words, of unvarying courtesy, but of a singularly cold and distant manner."[8]

This same week at Valley Mountain, young John Worsham recalled seeing the visitor for the first time. "General Robert E. Lee . . . joined us here and pitched his headquarters tent about one or two hundred yards from our company. He soon won the affection of all by his politeness and notice of the soldiers." Articles of food and gifts delivered to Lee were "sent to some sick soldier as soon as the messenger got out of sight." This was consistent behavior for a general already celebrated for showing compassion to his men. Considering the case of a soldier accused of being asleep on guard duty, an offense that could have seen him shot, Lee told the supervising officer, "Captain, you know the arduous duties these men have to do daily.

Suppose the man who was found on his post asleep had been you, or me. What do you think should be done to him?"[9] Suffice it to say this was an uncommon generosity.

In August Lee described his temporary home to Mary. "The mountains are beautiful," he wrote, "fertile to the tops, covered with the richest sward of bluegrass and white clover, and inclosed fields waving with the natural growth of timothy. The habitations are few and the people sparse. This is a magnificent grazing country."[10] A few days later Stonewall Jackson wrote Col. Thomas Bennett, auditor of Virginia: "My hopes for our section of the state [western Virginia] have greatly brightened since General Lee has gone there. Something brilliant may be expected."[11] But difficulties lay ahead. Federal Brig. Gen. William S. Rosecrans had a sizable force in the vicinity of Cheat Mountain, in the hills north of White Sulphur Springs, ready to attack southeastward toward the upper Shenandoah Valley. Rains were relentless, and mud was everywhere. On September 1 Lee wrote Mary, who was now at an estate called Audley, in Clarke County, Virginia: "We have a great deal of sickness among the soldiers, and now those on the sick-list would form an army. The measles is still among them. . . . The constant cold rains, with no shelter but tents . . . with impassable roads, have paralyzed our efforts."[12]

Nonetheless, Lee planned his first battle, an attack on Cheat Mountain beginning on September 11. Lee clashed with the enemy first at Conrad's Mill, and the action proceeded up Cheat Mountain. But the Confederate objectives failed due to confused logistics and terrible weather that made the roads nearly impassable. Newspapers attached a sobriquet to Lee that he most certainly did not appreciate: "Granny Lee," taunting his supposed timidity.

Near the end of September, he wrote Mary from a camp at Sewell's Mountain, near Beckley: "It is raining heavily. The men are all exposed on the mountain, with the enemy opposite to us. We are without tents, and for two nights I have lain buttoned up in my overcoat. To-day my tent came up and I am in it. Yet I fear I shall not sleep for thinking of the poor men."[13]

With cold weather approaching, Lee could barely attempt another offensive movement; stalemate and disappointment were in the air. Lee settled in, got to know his men, whom he lived with closely, and grew a gray beard. Seeing an opportunity, he clashed with Federals again in early October at Sewell's Mountain, where the enemy was now positioned. This also failed due to jealousies between Lee's subordinate commanders, who didn't cooperate or communicate well, and poor logistics; rain-soaked roads were occasionally impassable. "Poor Lee!" editorialized the *Charleston Mercury* on October 16. "Rosecrans has fooled him again . . . are the roads any worse for Lee than Rosecrans? . . . The people are getting mighty sick of this dilly-dally, dirt digging, scientific warfare; so much so that they will demand that the Great Entrencher be brought back and permitted to pay court to the ladies."[14]

Lee did in fact return to Richmond, visiting Mary at Shirley plantation for the first time since leaving her in April. "He came back, carrying the heavy weight of defeat," wrote Jefferson Davis. "And unappreciated by the people whom he served, for they could not know, as I knew, that, if his plans and orders had been carried out, the result would have been victory rather than defeat."[15] Davis fixed blame for the failed campaign on Lee's subordinates because of their omnipresent bickering. In truth a Southern victory in western Virginia may have been irrelevant. Before year's end the region's citizens initiated a movement to break away from Virginia, becoming a separate state loyal to the Union. It was not territory worth fighting over.

On November 1 Jefferson Davis learned that a large Federal naval force was moving southward toward the South Atlantic coast, allegedly to Port Royal Sound, South Carolina. Four days later Lee was given the assignment of commanding the Department of South Carolina, Georgia, and Eastern Florida, a duty that would last until March 5, 1862. He was not happy with the assignment and, due to the public relations damage he had suffered during the western Virginia campaigns, neither were South Carolina authorities. After his arrival, however, opinions changed. South Carolina governor Francis Pickens wrote Jefferson Davis on November 24, saying, "I take this opportunity to say from the interviews I have had with Genl. Lee that I have a very high estimation of his science, patriotism, and enlightened judgment. I am also delighted with his high bred cultivated bearing. If he has a fault it is over caution which results from his scientific mind."[16]

In the words of Jefferson Davis, Lee arrived in Charleston and "his vigorous mind at once comprehended the situation . . . directing fortifications to be constructed on the Stono and the Edisto and the Combahee, he fixed his headquarters at Coosawhatchee, the point most threatened, and directed defenses to be erected opposite Hilton Head."[17] Ten days later Lee and his staff witnessed the great fire in Charleston, when much of the city accidentally burned.

For Robert E. Lee Christmas 1861 would be spent away from his family, this time in Coosawhatchie. He wrote to Mary:

> I cannot let this day of grateful rejoicing pass without some communion with you. As to our old home [Arlington], if not destroyed it will be difficult ever to be recognized. Even if the enemy had wished to preserve it, it would almost have been impossible. With the number of troops encamped around it, the change of officers, the want of fuel, shelter, etc., and all the dire necessities of war, it is vain to think of its being in a habitable condition. I fear, too, the books, furniture, and relics of Mount Vernon will be gone.[18]

On the same day he wrote one of his daughters. "Having distributed such poor Christmas gifts as I had around me," he penned, "I have been looking for something for you. . . . I send you some sweet violets that I gathered for you this morning while covered with dense white frost, whose crystals glittered in the bright sun like diamonds."[19]

====

L EE was not the only general officer who enjoyed the unbridled confidence of the president. Albert Sidney Johnston was perhaps the closest military friend of Jefferson Davis's. No relation to Joe Johnston, this Johnston was a Kentucky-born soldier who, at age fifty-eight, was among the senior military minds adhered to the Confederacy at its outset. A veteran of the Black Hawk War, Sidney Johnston, as he was called, had been caught up in the Texas revolution after migrating there and served as secretary of war for the Republic of Texas. He had gone to West Point with Jefferson Davis and there, at a young age, formed a close friendship with the Mississippian. Sidney Johnston had served as a staff officer in the Mexican War and, thereafter, was consumed with frontier duty as colonel of the Second U.S. Cavalry, serving mostly in Texas. He became renowned in the 1850s for leading an expedition to Utah Territory to quell the so-called Mormon Rebellion, a reported uprising. Sidney Johnston then reverted to frontier post duty, and at the outbreak of war, he had been stationed in California. When the Southern states began to secede, he resigned his army commission and made a long, circuitous journey from California back east. His travels were reported widely in the newspapers, making him something of a Southern hero before the war even started, and his close friendship with Jefferson Davis ensured him an important place in the military hierarchy of the new nation.

Sidney Johnston had been placed in charge of the significant, large area known as Confederate Department Number Two, a tract of land that encompassed much of Alabama, Kentucky, Tennessee, Arkansas, Mississippi, Missouri, and Louisiana. He was, thus, the preeminent western departmental commander of the Confederate armies, and he would be the chief architect of strategy to thwart the Yankees, who — as yet unknown to the Confederates — planned to cut southward along the rivers and deep into Southern territory. Additionally, Sidney Johnston would command the Army of Central Kentucky, organizing and drilling it to prepare for major battles that might erupt in the spring of 1862.

———

For now, the military situation was relatively quiet. August had brought the battle of Wilson's Creek in Missouri, where the Yankees were beaten back after a bloody fight. The following month the Federals had laid siege to the small town of Lexington, Missouri. In the east scattered fighting continued in the mountains of western Virginia, and in the autumn, a sharp fight broke out at Ball's Bluff, along the Potomac near Leesburg, the elegant village named for Robert E. Lee's more famous relatives, where the Declaration of Independence had been hidden during the War of 1812. A massive Federal naval expedition threatened the sea islands near Port Royal, South Carolina, a site of naval actions during the Revolutionary War. As the year waned battles flared at Belmont, Missouri, where a little-known Union commander, Ulysses S. Grant, pushed his force forward, and Alleghany Mountain, Virginia, back in the mountains of the western part of the state.

Meanwhile, the North was having its share of problems with military commands. In November Lincoln replaced Winfield Scott, the old and infirm general-in-chief, with the young and vigorous Maj. Gen. George B. McClellan. This apparent salvation of the Union command structure was a brief illusion. "Little Mac" was energetic and famous for his quick succession of victories in western Virginia and came to Washington with excellent credentials as the ranking major general of the regular army with experience in army organization, training, and military planning. But it didn't take Lincoln long to realize that McClellan was an overcautious tactician, eager to underestimate his readiness and prone to overestimating the strength of the Confederate armies he faced. Moreover, McClellan began to side with the opponents of Lincoln's Republican administration.

Politically, the Union had its hands full late in 1861. Both Missouri and Kentucky seceded in part and were, thus, counted as member states by both the U.S. and C.S. governments. Embarrassingly for the Lincoln government, Confederate diplomats James M. Mason and John Slidell were captured while aboard the British ship HMS *Trent*, which nearly brought England down against the United States until Mason and Slidell were released, and the affair blew over. ("One war at a time!" Lincoln had quipped.)

Politics in the South took the form of elections. Early in the year the Provisional Congress had ordered congressional elections to be held on the first Wednesday of November 1861. Unlike the United States, the Confederacy permitted politicians to hold military office concurrently, and many politicians found the lure of the battlefield irresistible. The men were technically still members of Congress, but they were absent from Richmond and unable to engage in helping run the government. According to one observer, Congress had gotten rid of "nearly all it had of worth and talent."[20]

Transfixed with military affairs, most citizens voted quietly on that Wednesday in November. Some soldiers could cast absentee votes in the field, while the organization of Indian voting was left by the Confederacy to tribal officials. Most candidates were fairly well known and declined to campaign due to the exigency of the military situation, though some candidates unimaginatively advertised in newspapers, calling attention to either their state rights advocacy or vigorous prosecution of the war. Candidates in the field handed over their campaign to be run by friends. Candidate John Goode of Virginia recalled a stump speech by his opponents. "After they all had spoken . . . some friend of mine would arise in the audience and say, 'Gentlemen, you must remember that Mr. Goode is also a candidate. . . . He cannot be here to-day because he is down at the front with the other boys in the army.' "[21] Such proxies were common. The situation was completely different in the Confederate Senate. There, the Constitution required that senators be selected by the state legislatures, not the people, so Senate candidates did no campaigning whatsoever, and a good-ol'-boys network of state politics made the decisions.

For the majority of Southerners, the experience of the Confederacy up to this point was one of relative harmony, of unity in purpose and action. The rifts that occurred politically were mostly hidden behind the seams of the new nation's fabric. But even among such tepid campaigning, some good old-fashioned politics began to shine through. In Alabama Clement C. Clay and John Ralls were accused of land speculation. In North Carolina a debate between two candidates came to a near riot. In Mississippi Henry Chambers forced Col. W. A. Lake into a duel over their contest and shot him dead with his rifle.

Despite such scattered turbulence, the election came off, resulting in a hodgepodge of a now almost meaningless state of various political parties — Unionists, Democrats, Whigs, Secessionists. Now that all were loyal Confederates, the standard political party affiliations lost meaning.

Though few took notice at the time, from state to state within the Confederacy, tiny divisions were beginning to show. The psychology of where various states seemed to stand within the Confederate hierarchy began to play out in the real world. South Carolina's politicians, for example, considered their state the "birthplace of secession" and, therefore, the linchpin of the Confederacy. It should be central to important decisions, the state's citizens felt. This attitude of supremacy began to take effect in the bold actions and the air of superiority among men like William Porcher Miles, James Chesnut, Milledge Bonham, and Lawrence Keitt. The governor, Francis Pickens, also behaved demandingly toward Jefferson Davis, as if Davis owed South Carolina the very reason for his position. Virginia's politicians also began to see themselves as the central focus of the Confederacy; Governor John Letcher, situated right in the beehive of the national Confederate government in Richmond, considered himself uniquely privileged. Those among the Virginia delegations who felt a boost from state influence included Robert M. T. Hunter, James A. Seddon, Thomas S. Bocock, and Roger A. Pryor.

Other states, of course, had less political pull. Texas, for example, began the war as a relatively isolated arena that seemed detached from the "action" out east. Consequently, Texas politicians, and those of other western states, felt left out as the new session of Congress approached. Western politicians who overcame this feeling, like Texas's Louis Wigfall, did so by sheer energy and conniving political tactics, something that not all members of Congress could muster.

Amid this swirl of growing political intrigue, the fifth session of Congress assembled in Richmond on November 8, 1861, with the Senate and House meeting in separate chambers and with separate agendas. There was one special day off, on January 21, 1862, allowing members to attend the Richmond funeral of John Tyler, the former president of the United States who had been a member of the Confederate Congress. Otherwise the session would last until February 17, 1862, and be a relatively quiet gathering as far as legislation was concerned.

The main focus of political thought in Richmond and throughout the South centered on Jefferson Davis and his wartime policy. Although support had been solid when the conflict started, chinks in the armor began to appear through 1861. The war clerk, John B. Jones, reflected this shift in his diary. "No Executive had ever such cordial and unanimous support," he wrote early in the war. But by summertime he reported "murmurs" against the president. Stephen Mallory, secretary of the navy, remarked in August how Congress seemed to be unhappy with Davis and that a "spirit of opposition" was growing. At the same time Confederate senator Lawrence Keitt of South Carolina openly termed Davis "a failure."[22]

The focus was not exclusively on the president. In September Leroy Walker, the ineffectual war secretary from Alabama, had resigned. Judah Benjamin succeeded him, with Thomas Bragg now becoming attorney general, and the legions who didn't like Benjamin were growing. "Benjamin is the supple boot of the President, a Eunuch," wrote Milledge L. Bonham, a brigadier general who would become governor of South Carolina before war's end. Most members of Congress were bothered by this sense that Davis had appointed an administrator and could act as his own de facto war secretary. Not only did they dislike Benjamin's subservience, but those who favored an aggressive war policy found him far too enamored with playing defense.[23]

Political issues were hardly limited to the capital. In the field Toombs, now a brigadier general hoping to win the war by killing Yankees rather than arguing in Richmond, wrote to Aleck Stephens often, sharing his frustration:

> As [to] the assignment of Smith's regiment, [Judah P.] Benjamin wrote me the President instructed him to suggest to me to call Genl. [Joseph E.] Johnston's attention to it; that he was commander of both corps of the army. I replied to Benj[amin] that I had good reasons to know that fact, "and in common with the army, not without reasons to lament it." I never knew as incompetent [an] executive officer. As he has been to West Point, tho', I suppose he necessarily knows everything about it. We are doing nothing here, and will do nothing. The army is dying. . . . Set this down in your book, and set down opposite to it its epitaph, "*died of West Point.*"[24]

The following week Toombs turned his ire more directly toward the president. "Davis is here," he confided to Stephens. "His generals are fooling [him] about the strength of our force in order to shield their inactivity. [Davis] talks of activity on the Potomac but I fear he does not feel it strong enough to move this inert mass."[25] Toombs was hardly alone in his vilification. "Pres. Davis was up the other day and reviewed about 12,000 troops at Fairfax Court House," wrote Thomas Thomas, colonel of the Fifteenth Georgia Infantry. "There was not a single cheer, even when some one in the crowd among the staff called out for three cheers there was not a single response, everything was as cold as funeral meats."[26]

Members of Congress fancied themselves better managers of the army than their president, whether or not that may have been the case. Since First Manassas, it seemed, nothing at all had been accomplished by the Southern armies. The repeated skirmishing in western Virginia had led nowhere. Federal troops had landed along the southeastern coast, capturing positions at Cape Hatteras, North Carolina, and Port Royal Sound, South Carolina. What had the Confederate armies accomplished? The gloom over Davis's management of the army spread during the inactive autumn. "All governments are humbugs and the Confederate government is not an exception," Thomas told Stephens in October. He went on:

> Its President this day is the prince of humbugs and yet his nomination for the first permanent presidency meets with universal acceptance, and yet I do know that he possesses not a single qualification for the place save integrity. . . . Imbecility, ignorance, and awkwardness mark every feature of his management of this army. He torments us, makes us sick and kills us by appointing worthless place-hunters to transact business for us on which depends our health, efficiency, and even our lives. . . . He would make a good ordinary [judge of probate] of a county in Georgia and his capacity is not above that; but he is king, and here where we are fighting to maintain the last vestige of republicanism on earth we bow down to him with more than eastern devotion.[27]

Late in the year the clash between Beauregard and the president's inner circle heated up again, disrupting the harmony between Richmond and the field officers. In November Beauregard had argued repeatedly and over a multitude of subjects with Secretary of War

Benjamin. Davis had written Beauregard, trying to soothe him, but Beauregard replied that his "motives must not be called into question" and that if his "errors are pointed out, it must be done in a proper tone and style." Davis had responded that he did not feel "competent to instruct Mr. Benjamin in the matter of style."[28]

As the armies stood inactive, the weather turned cold, and the Congress reconvened in Richmond, patience for military victories seemed to be running thin. They would come, but much more slowly than the people on the home front and the soldiers would have liked. Davis, meanwhile, was saddled with a vast job, and the cards were stacked against him. The naysayers were growing in numbers, and their complaints growing in volume. No one embodied the antiadministration rhetoric better than Robert Rhett. "Jefferson Davis is not only a dishonest man, but a liar," he wrote at year's end. "What is to become of us, under this man for six years?"[29]

7

STATE RIGHTISMS

WITH the turn of the new year, hope sprang: Confederate commanders drew up plans for springtime battles; politicians planned their returns to the House and Senate chambers in Richmond's Capitol, thinking of how best to whip the Yankees as well as how to put the best spin for their constituents on what was happening.

For his part Jefferson Davis planned on taking greater charge. The Confederacy remained mostly under his control, despite the arguing and politicking that was growing slowly like an infection in Richmond. But just when Davis thought he had enough to worry about, another deleterious effect appeared. A theme had emerged in this winter of discontent: who would wield the real power of the Confederacy — the executives or the legislators? Davis began to wonder if the states would remain loyal to his leadership. This was particularly scary because, after all, the states were held to be supremely powerful by nearly all the politicians of the Confederacy.

The new fears were bound up most completely in the form of Joseph E. Brown, the governor of Georgia. Joe Brown, who often wore stark black suits, was balding, with tufts of white hair on the sides. He sported a long, white-and-gray beard and looked every inch like a preacher. To Davis he symbolized everything that could spin the Richmond government out of control. Infused with supreme confidence from his South Carolina roots, Brown applied that fanatical sanctimoniousness to his adopted state. Georgia was itself in a politically influential position at this time because it had to be held in solid, loyal form — militarily, it was the gateway to the Deep South. If Georgia fell, Union troops could destroy the Confederacy from within by marching and fighting through its heart. To Davis, Brown's loyalty to Richmond was crucial.

A native South Carolinian, Brown was forty years old as the second calendar year of the war began. He had studied at Yale Law School before winning election to the Georgia State Senate, where his family had moved. A leading Democrat, he was elected governor in 1857. At the outset of war, Brown enthusiastically called for volunteers and vowed to support Confederate military operations. But he would not budge on one issue: he wanted to maintain control of the Georgia troops — how they were supplied, who commanded them, and where and when they fought. This sent chills through the War Department. A conflict with state governors attempting to call the shots on the battlefield simply wouldn't work. A sniping campaign commenced between members of the Georgia State House and the authorities in Richmond.

Brown supported the Confederate war effort during the first months of the conflict, and he was a masterful state politician, keeping the spirits of both his civilians and troops high. He acted ceaselessly to procure clothing and blankets for the Georgia troops, pulling strings everywhere he could to obtain cotton for basic goods and salt to preserve the troops' food. But Brown felt the mounting wrath of Davis and the Richmond War Department, as well as another factor that was starting to turn public sentiment at home: inflation. Like most state politicians of the time, Brown could not bring himself to see affairs through a lens larger than the local view. He, therefore, dragged his heels on issues of Confederate unity, and the president could see that a time would come when Brown would have a head-on collision with the Confederate States of America.

The other Confederate governors were a mixed bag. In North Carolina Henry Clark, the product of a plantation upbringing, was no model of ambition and had failed to inspire the people of his state. A Yankee blockade made it impossible to get supplies to the Tar Heel troops, so the state had to scramble to supply many of its own men. Federal troops had landed and secured positions along North Carolina's coast, so Clark initiated a draft of one-third of the state's militia to help defend adjoining areas along the coast. This created ill feeling in the now less-defended inner, central counties, which began to question North Carolinians' loyalty to the Confederate effort. Scattered protests against the Confederacy sprang up in the weeks following secession; by 1862 Unionism in the state was real, though only among a small number of the citizens. More so than in other Confederate states, however, a resentment by many over class distinctions — the war had to be fought for the rich and by the poor — and a general distrust of the state and national governments began to erode the feeling of support for the Confederacy. In Richmond this began to put Clark and other North Carolina politicians in a somewhat precarious position.

In Virginia Governor John Letcher was the middle-class product of comfortable Lexington, in the Shenandoah Valley. A moderate conservative, Letcher worked frantically to mobilize Virginia in the early months of the war. The philosophical opposite of Brown, Letcher realized that compromising state principles and closing ranks behind Jefferson Davis would be necessary if the South were to have a chance of winning its independence. He continued to be demanding, though, expecting privileged treatment for Virginia and her interests, which he generally got.

Another pro-Davis man, Francis Lubbock, was a South Carolinian who had become a Texas rancher and governor. A Democrat and strong supporter of secession, Lubbock was a strong militarist who delighted in discussing strategy and tactics; in fact he would not be able to keep himself away from the battlefield as the war drew on. Texas's isolated nature meant that it held limited political sway in Richmond.

In Florida Governor John Milton was a secession Democrat who had amassed a personal fortune as a planter and slave owner. He was limited in ability by the scant resources the state had to bring to bear in the war. Pleased with Richmond's plans to defend the approaches to Apalachicola, the harbor at Fernandina, Jacksonville, and other towns along the coast, Milton would be disappointed early in 1862, when Davis failed to follow through with them. As Federal forces began to threaten Kentucky and Tennessee, Richmond ordered Florida's forces and resources northward and, thus, began disillusionment in the Sunshine State.

In Louisiana Governor Thomas Moore was a native Tar Heel who had become one of Louisiana's largest sugar planters before the war. He was a fanatical secessionist who seized Yankee property even before his state left the Union. Louisiana's political leaders offered trouble for Richmond authorities over the national government's ability to build defensive works to protect the state, but the state supported the Davis administration on most matters. Governor John J. Pettus of Mississippi was a frontier lawyer and cotton planter who, politically, was another rabid secessionist. Support for the war in Mississippi started strong, but strain on the home front quickly became apparent. Pettus felt the Davis administration did not adequately provide for the state's defense and, in early 1862, wanted to secure the state with its own troops under his control. South Carolina's governor, Francis Pickens, who had been involved in the Fort Sumter drama, was the grandson of a Revolutionary War general. Pickens found himself publicly criticized for his inability to act independently since he was bound by a five-member state Executive Council that limited his powers.

Arkansas governor Henry Rector was a Kentucky native who had led a revolt within Arkansas's Democratic Party, subsequently ordering the seizure of the U.S. Arsenal at Little Rock before the state seceded. Rector began his relationship with Jefferson Davis in a series of clashes, partly because the state's military board, which he chaired, wanted Arkansas troops employed only within their home state — mirroring Joe Brown's position in Georgia. In Alabama Governor John G. Shorter was a Georgian who migrated to Alabama before becoming a lawyer, planter, and slave owner. A Davis supporter, Shorter told the folks in his state in December 1861 that they would face "unaccustomed burdens" in the future. He had no idea what an understatement that would turn out to be.

The governorships of Kentucky, Tennessee, and Missouri were more muddled. Late in 1861, following pro-Confederate meetings in Russellville, Kentucky was admitted as a Confederate state under the governorship of George Johnson. However, the government's jurisdiction extended only as far as Confederate troops in the state advanced, so it withdrew from the state in early 1862. The pro-Southern prewar governor, Beriah Magoffin, continued to act as the state's government leader as recognized by the Lincoln administration, although many Northern politicians didn't trust him. Tennessee had seceded and set up a pro-Richmond government under Isham G. Harris, but eastern Tennessee citizens refused to follow its authority. So Tennessee began as a divided state, and the divisions would only deepen as time moved on. Missouri, another area with deeply split loyalties, left the Union after a rump session had met at Neosho, late in 1861. The state's prewar governor, Claiborne F. Jackson, was a rabid secessionist. After raiding the U.S. Arsenal at St. Louis, Jackson's militia troops thwarted Union efforts to maintain control of the state. As with Kentucky and Tennessee, two governments arose in the state, and Hamilton R. Gamble led the one recognized by the Yankees.

───

STATE governors who might not comply with Jefferson Davis's wishes were just another growing worry for the Confederate president. Comfortable in the Confederate White House, on January 1, 1862, Davis and his family opened their abode to anyone who wanted to come and see it. For four hours on this New Year's Day, the president welcomed all who stopped by, greeting them with cheer and high spirits for the Confederacy. (His wife, Varina, stayed in her room, too ill to join the fray.) A continuous string of visitors was treated to the music of the Armory Band and a "very large bowl of apple brandy toddy."[1]

At the war's outset Davis and Stephens had been inaugurated as president and vice president of the provisional government of the Confederate States. Now February 22 would mark their inauguration as president and vice president of the permanent government. The symbolism was intentional: the birthday of George Washington would provide the Southern nation with a touchstone of credibility that recalled the earliest days of the Republic. To strengthen the philosophical bond, Davis was set to deliver his inaugural address at the base of the great equestrian statue of Washington that stood adjacent to Richmond's Capitol. It was a neat public-relations package, one that seemed fluently constructed, and with the new president commanding armies that stretched from the Atlantic coast to west of the Mississippi River, the Confederacy seemed in good shape.

In Richmond February can be mild, but this year, the sky was gray, the temperatures cold, and the streets wet with rain. This dampened the mood for the city's inaugural festivities, but Davis was determined to press on with his speech. Numerous umbrellas dotted the hillside around the Capitol, and despite mud that approached being "ankle-deep," a throng of visitors pushed forward to hear the president, amid a band that belted out "Dixie," just as at the Montgomery inauguration.

The Senate and House assembled at 7:30 a.m. and then moved to the House of Delegates. Davis and Stephens were conducted there at 11:45 a.m. At 12:30 p.m. the procession moved from the House of Delegates to the Washington statue.[2] Prayer was followed by the inaugural address. As Davis rose he seemed oblivious to the rain that fell on him, and a guest nearby stuck an umbrella up to cover him. With, according to one observer, "a fine manner and with a loud voice," the president told his fellow countrymen that "on this birthday of the man most identified with the establishment of American independence, and beneath the monument erected to commemorate his heroic virtues and those of his compatriots, we have assembled to usher into existence the Permanent Government of the Confederate States."

Justifying the war, he flatly said, "The tyranny of an unbridled majority, the most odious and least responsible form of despotism, has denied us both the right and the remedy. Therefore we are in arms to renew such sacrifices as our fathers made to the holy cause of constitutional liberty." Davis pointed to the "lights and shadows" of the first year of the war and commented that difficult times lay ahead. But he had no doubt that Southerners would prevail in the "great strife" they suffered through.

Following his remarks, which were met by loud cheers and sustained applause, the oath of office for Davis and Stephens was administered by Judge J. D. Halyburton, and the result announced by the Confederate Senate. The band commenced playing "La Marseillaise," and Davis, this time along with Varina, hosted a reception at the White House that evening. All around town was a sense that Richmond was back on its feet with a permanent president. The country could move forward; the confidence with which the president spoke gave all hope for a speedy end to the war.

It didn't take long for the president and Congress to begin to have sharp differences about their permanent government. State rights reared its philosophical head right away. The president, jealously attempting to hold onto his national power, vetoed a bill that would have allowed the state of Texas to assign a regiment to frontier duty after it had joined the Provisional Army of the Confederate States. Davis would have none of that; he wanted to preserve his authority over how and where troops would be assigned.[3] Rationality departed the chambers. Robert Toombs and Robert Barnwell Rhett, along with eight others in the House, strongly protested a bill that would furnish Davis with one million dollars to connect the Richmond & Danville Railroad with the North Carolina Railroad in downtown Richmond in order to expedite the transportation of military supplies. Casting an immense spotlight on state rights over national ones, Toombs and Rhett were willing to forgo what was clearly best for supplying battlefronts because they wanted Virginia to make such decisions — not the national government.

There were other problems, too. A week after the session opened, for example, Davis wrote Congress complaining of the short-term (one year or less) enlistment of soldiers and their frequent absences home, both practices Congress approved of and the War Department fought tooth and nail against. "The policy of enlistment for short terms, against which I have steadily contended from the commencement of the war, has, in my judgment, contributed in no immaterial degree to the recent reverses which we have suffered," Davis said. "Now that it has become probable that the war will be continued through a series of years, our high-spirited and gallant soldiers, while generally reenlisting, are, from the fact of having entered into the service for a short term, compelled in many instances to go home to make the necessary arrangements for their families during their prolonged absence."[4] The "recent reverses" Davis spoke of to Congress referred to the loss of Forts Henry and Donelson in early and mid-February at the hand of the then little-known Yankee general Ulysses S. Grant. Grant had attacked the perimeter line of Kentucky defenses held by Davis's trusted friend and admired general Albert Sidney Johnston, and Johnston's failure to hold his line and to supervise the defense of the forts on the Tennessee and Cumberland rivers, which now opened up a potential deep penetration southward by Grant, became a hot topic in Congress. In the House of Representatives, meddlesome politician Henry S. Foote of Tennessee argued that the cause of the disasters in Kentucky, Tennessee, and North Carolina should be investigated. Not only had Johnston, touted as the South's greatest general, completely failed in his duty, but a succession of commanders on-site, John B. Floyd and Gideon J. Pillow, had escaped and left the Confederate troops to surrender under a junior general officer, Simon B. Buckner. The whole affair smacked of total incompetence and wholesale evasion of responsibility for what happened. The matter was discussed and then tabled. A week later Foote again argued about the cause of the disasters at Fort Henry, Fort Donelson, and Nashville. The inquiry was again tabled, but it wouldn't go away forever.

In March the House finally passed a resolution to determine what prevented Johnston, who was at Bowling Green, from relieving Fort Donelson during its investment by Grant. Congress also overwhelmingly passed a bill demanding an explanation from the executive branch[5] and debated holding a vote of no confidence in Johnston, a discussion that was inconclusive.[6]

Davis hoped to cheer up a shocked Congress. "The hope is still entertained that our reported losses at Fort Donelson have been greatly exaggerated," he wrote, "in as much as I am not only unwilling, but unable to believe that a large army of our people have surrendered without a desperate effort to cut their way through the investing forces, whatever have been their numbers, and to endeavor to make a junction with other divisions of the army."[7] But it was clear to everyone in Richmond that disaster had struck. The surrender at Fort Donelson sent about 11,500 Confederate soldiers to Yankee prisons. Moreover, Nashville — also under Johnston's jurisdiction — fell into Federal hands at month's end. "The terrible disaster at Fort Donelson is a terrific shock upon weak nerves — and somewhat trying to strong ones," wrote Howell Cobb, former president of the Provisional Congress.[8] Moreover, Roanoke Island, North Carolina, fell to Union forces, and the South lost 2,500 soldiers to prisons.

It didn't take long for the finger pointing to begin. Judah Benjamin tried to help Davis and Johnston escape the blame. "The bearer Capt. Wickliffe, aid of Genl. A. S. Johnston, can give you some interesting details of the escape of Genls. Floyd and Pillow from Fort Donelson," he wrote Davis. "He says we had 17,000 men there, and the enemy only 30,000, and that all the army could easily have been saved."[9] Replied the president, "The reports of Brig. Genls. Floyd and Pillow of the defense and fall of Fort Donelson are unsatisfactory. . . . You will order Genl. A. S. Johnston to relieve both of these officers from command."[10] This did not sit particularly well with senators and representatives. The anger and sense of frustration with Johnston in Congress simmered on.

Nevertheless, Davis, ever true to his close friends, seemed to shake any sense of holding Johnston responsible. "You have done wonderfully well," he wrote his old friend late in March, "and I now breathe easier in the assurance that you will be able to make a junction of your two armies. If you can meet the division of the enemy moving from the Tenn. before it can make a junction with that advancing from Nashville, the future will be brighter. If this can not be done, our only hope is that the people of the South West will rally en masse with their private arms."[11]

Meanwhile, the distrust between Congress and the friends of Davis grew. With no one in the administration apparently holding anyone accountable for the Fort Donelson disaster, Congress discussed a vote of no confidence against Secretary of War Benjamin. They tabled the debate after much talk, and Davis responded by appointing Benjamin secretary of state, replacing Robert M. T. Hunter. In this way Davis could move his close friend and intellectual aide out of the direct fire of Congress when it came to military affairs. In his place Davis chose Virginia loyalist George Wythe Randolph, who became secretary of war on March 18.

Randolph was a gentleman from Charlottesville who happened to be a grandson of Thomas Jefferson's. He had a diverse background as a naval officer, an attorney, and a militia captain and was an influential member of Richmond's City Council. Randolph had spent the first months of the war in the field as a major and subsequently as a colonel of Virginia troops, conducting himself well in the Army of the Peninsula. He had just become a brigadier general a month before his appointment as war secretary, and Randolph's credentials seemed impeccable: his family pedigree was exceptional; his experience as an administrator and lawyer was solid; his education and military experience were unassailable; and he had the confidence of the president. However, within days of inhabiting the War Department building, receiving frequent communication from Davis, it became clear to Randolph that the president really wanted to run the war. Instead of being a leader in his own right, Randolph quickly found himself a Davis functionary and a relative nonentity.

The Navy Department — what there was of it — was not shaping up well, either. In the Senate South Carolinian James L. Orr led a fight to block the confirmation of Secretary Stephen Mallory; a significant group of politicians in Richmond lacked confidence in Mallory's ability and was not particularly sympathetic to the enormity of the job before him. On March 18 the Senate debated Mallory's confirmation, tabled the issue, and then returned to it and voted to confirm the Floridian, thirteen to six. Davis had dodged another political bullet — but it was clear further shots would be fired.[12]

Still contentious were Davis's executive authority versus that of the Provisional Congress and the provisional government's authority versus the new, permanent government. For example, the House passed a bill allowing generals who had been confirmed during the provisional session to continue in their grade throughout the entire war. Debates about the status of general officers ensued. In the House the Judiciary Committee tried to determine whether army officers also could hold seats in Congress. The South Carolina fire-eater Roger Pryor introduced the first of many attempts to create an enlarged general staff for the army. The Congress also argued over the confirmation of Davis's friend Lucius B. Northrop as commissary general of subsistence, the officer charged with providing food to the armies. Congress then resolved that its members could not concurrently hold commissions in the army or navy, thereby mixing legislative and executive functions. This regulation was not always obeyed, however. Members believed this did not apply to the militia. The issue was debated from time to time without a clear regulation.[13] Two weeks after Pryor's proposed legislation, the Senate followed suit by introducing a bill to expand the general staff. This time the bill came from the chair of the Military Affairs Committee, Edward Sparrow.

To the administration all this was Congress sticking its nose into the business of the War Department — plain and simple.[14] And it kept going. In March Congress, alarmed over what appeared to be a lack of leadership among military officers in the field and the War Department, called for and debated the merits of assigning a general-in-chief for the entire Confederate army. This was the last thing Jefferson Davis wanted, of course, given his desire to manage every military campaign and all aspects of the war office. In the House of Representatives, Pryor raised the issue, and subsequently, Foote jumped in with an even more radical approach: Foote moved that a commander in chief should *replace* the secretary of war, whose office would be discontinued. Jefferson Davis was not amused.

Two days after Foote's motion, on March 3, the issue again came up in the House. William Porcher Miles, chairman of the Committee on Military Affairs, said he was frustrated that various important topics were brought up only to be subjected to "long, rambling, and desultory debate." Hines Holt of Georgia declared that if Miles pressed for the topic to be discussed, he would respond by moving for a postponement. Nothing but stalemate resulted. Later on the same day, noting that the subject of replacing the secretary had risen in secret session — in a subcommittee behind closed doors — South Carolinian Milledge L. Bonham cautioned against discussing the matter publicly. Pryor, who had brought up the bill, claimed he did not wish it to go into secret session, and Foote testily cut in to say that the subject should be resolved in the open. He was overruled, and the point went into secret session.[15]

On March 10 the general-in-chief debate heated up when the House bill was discussed in the Senate. Davis now clearly felt that the issue couldn't be avoided, and four days later, he reacted angrily. With the bill passed in the House and pending in the Senate, the House received a startling veto message from the president. Davis announced that he feared the legislation would create a quasimilitary dictator. He refused to have an officer who could "take the field at his own discretion and command any army or armies he may choose, not only without the direction but even against the will of the President, who could not consistently with this act prevent such conduct of the general otherwise than by abolishing his office."[16]

But the House of Representatives seemed willing to fight. A representative at this moment wrote that "Congress is raising a perfect storm" over the issue and would have rid the government of President Davis if only any of them had faith in the abilities of Vice President Stephens.[17] On March 20 the House attempted to override Davis's veto, and a vote was taken in open session. In the end, however, not wishing to seem against prosecution of the war, of sixty-nine representatives, only Joseph P. Heiskell of Tennessee voted to override.

The backing off of the House resulted in one change: for the rest of the war, Davis would assign a general officer to act as a sort of executive assistant. This would be a highly capable military mind — at least in Davis's view — and also someone who politically would not threaten him. His choice was none other than Robert E. Lee, who lately had been supervising field operations down in the Department of South Carolina, Georgia, and East Florida, while stationed in the swampy outpost town of Coosawhatchie, South Carolina. Certainly, Davis felt, another general could take over there, and Lee was told to make his way north to Richmond, becoming chief adviser to the president.

In Washington, meanwhile, adjustments on the fly were being made fairly effectively. In the Lincoln cabinet the least competent and most troublesome member had been Simon Cameron, a corrupt Pennsylvania politician, as secretary of war. The appointment had been made as a concession to Pennsylvania Republicans. Not only did Cameron possess no particular qualifications for the office, but he clashed with the president and other cabinet members over the building of the army, its training, and army logistics. For example, Cameron believed that volunteer and militia officers should rank along with the regular army — that their relative ranks should depend only on the seniority of their commission. Long-prevailing regulations allowed all regulars to outrank volunteers, who in turn outranked all militia officers of the same grade, regardless of their commission dates. Cameron's desires favored the political generals, while the regulations favored those with experience, training, and competence. After much debate the traditional viewpoint prevailed, which influenced the command structure at the very top. Cameron was finally appointed minister to Russia (a move most called, with a smile, exile to Siberia), which removed him from the political scene, allowing Lincoln to appoint the Ohio politician Edwin M. Stanton to take over the War Department. When situations became too tense or unworkable, Lincoln found a way to resolve them, unlike his Confederate counterpart.

———

DURING war, in any time or place where constitutional principles apply, civil liberties and fundamental rights of citizens always spark considerable controversy regarding the government's ability to control despotism. With the feud over the commanding generalship simmering down, Congress and President Davis formed a tense alliance over another sensitive topic — suspension of the writ of habeas corpus. In a statedom steeped in personal liberties and individual rights, no issue so fueled the fire of controversy.

Early 1862 was a troublesome time for Confederates, both on the battlefield and on the home front, and everyone seemed to understand the dire consequences if the Yankees won the war. In late February Congress passed a bill suspending the writ of habeas corpus. This allowed the president to suspend civil rights and declare martial law in cities, towns, and areas in danger of assault by the Yankees. Extensive discussions and arguments flared within Congress, the administration, and the press and with governors over the wisdom and right of suspension. Among other things the bill would allow the government to hold suspects in confinement for long periods without bringing them to trial.[18] Davis's old friend Louis T. Wigfall of Texas spoke eloquently in the Senate and argued that such a law rarely would be needed, that individual rights of Southerners would be held as sacred as possible, and that Jefferson Davis could be trusted.

Davis didn't wait long to act. On February 27 he issued a proclamation suspending the writ in Norfolk and Portsmouth and "the surrounding country to the distance of ten miles from said cities, and all civil jurisdiction and the privilege of the writ of *habeas corpus* are hereby declared to be suspended within the limits aforesaid."[19] Two days later the president extended his suspension to include Richmond itself, to a distance of ten miles out. He assigned Brig. Gen. John H. Winder to carry out the proclamation; liquor was prohibited immediately. On the same day Winder assigned Capt. Archibald C. Godwin as provost marshal of the city. He also ordered all persons with arms to deliver them to the Ordnance Department. Winder assembled a gang of provost marshal "plug-uglies" who marched around town, keeping order and intimidating citizens, many of whom were alarmed by "seeing the glimmer of bayonets in the streets." All of a sudden Richmonders began to take a sterner look at the national government to which they played host.[20]

Seeing the effects of martial law on the streets of Richmond, the very places where they walked and talked and went to church, the members of Congress began to rethink their position. Certainly in a climate of such strict control, even Davis, who justly felt suspension of the writ necessary to keep chaos from sinking in, had to wonder about how his own people saw him. This was especially true in an age when he was now regularly receiving threats. One letter read, "You rebel traitor here is the beauty of America one of the greatest treasures that ever wavest over your sinful head. How I want you to look at this motto and think of me for I say death to cesession [*sic*] and death to all traitors to their country and these are my sentiments exactly." This little ditty was scrawled on patriotic letter sheet with the imprinted motto Death to traitors! and an American flag.[21] It had not, to state what was becoming obvious to Davis, been sent from the North.

━━

WHEREAS Davis often wanted to restrict power, reserving it for himself, in other ways he was happy to give it away. For the judicial branch the president favored formulating a Confederate Supreme Court. The House of Representatives discussed the matter in mid-March. In fact the Confederate Constitution had provided for a Supreme Court, but without sufficient detail on how it would be put together. On March 11 Senator Thomas J. Semmes of Louisiana introduced a Supreme Court bill, which proposed a chief justice and three associate justices. The sessions would commence in January and August, and the chief would make seven thousand dollars per year, the associates six thousand. The bill was ordered to be printed and placed on the calendar. In the House William Porcher Miles brought out the legislation about a month later. The subject was then infected with a disease that pervaded much of the new Southern law: debatitis. Day after day after day, representatives and senators discussed how a Supreme Court might work. Before long it was clear that the whole topic may as well have been buried in the subbasement of the Capitol Building. The bill was going nowhere.[22]

As the Supreme Court legislation stagnated, another hot topic reared its head. Among his other worries President Davis was daily growing more and more concerned that the South could lose its army to attrition. Twelve-month volunteers, who had enlisted for a period that originally seemed to be longer than any war could last, might well not reenlist, the president reasoned. And yet there was no method in place to conscript soldiers to fight out the rest of the war. On March 28 President Davis delivered a message to the Senate, telling his countrymen, "There is also embarrassment from conflict between state and Confederate legislation . . . on conscription." He pleaded with Congress for a conscription act, which would help raise a large, standing army for defense. The next day debate erupted. Davis wrote that a general conscription law was needed to provide for uniformly organizing, arming, and disciplining the militia to execute the laws of the Confederate States. Williamson S. Oldham of Texas bluntly shouted that Congress "does not have the power to force citizens into the Army of the Confederate States." Fellow Texan Louis Wigfall disagreed, saying he "is and always will be a state rights man, but the right to make war was transferred by the States to the central government."[23]

As the debate continued, Wigfall's temperature rose. "Cease this child's play!" he screamed. "The enemy are in some portions of almost every State in the Confederacy; they are upon the borders of Texas; Virginia is enveloped by them. We need a large army. How are you going to get it? . . . No man has any individual rights, which come in conflict with the welfare of the country." In response Oldham said, "It was the object and theory of our government to secure and preserve the liberties of the people. If they are to be destroyed, I don't care a fig whether it is effected by the General or State government."[24] The topic was referred to the Committee on Military Affairs, where it would live another day — and longer. But by April 16 Congress passed the First Conscription Act, which drafted for military service all white males between the ages of eighteen and thirty-five for a period of three years, unless the war came to an end. For the time being Davis had bested his opponents.

━━

Somehow life in Richmond carried on. At the White House Varina Davis gave birth to another son, William Howell, on December 16. The Davises were both exhausted and feeling rather ill, independent of the demands of the Confederacy. The president confided in his closest associates his worries about the state of the country. "Recent disasters have depressed the weak," the president declared to Joe Johnston, away in the field, "and are depriving us of the aid of the wavering. Traitors show the tendencies heretofore concealed, and the selfish grow clamorous for local, and personal, interests."[25]

And the spring brought little comfort. Virginia governor John Letcher might have declared conscription "the most alarming stride towards consolidation that has ever occurred" but would not fight Davis because the alternative would be ruin. Brown, however, believed the draft was a measure aimed at destroying the states. Addressing Davis, the Georgia governor wrote:

If the State Regiments are broken up, and the conscripts belonging to them forced into other organizations against their consent, it will have a very discouraging effect. . . . This Act, not only disorganizes the military system of all the States, but consolidates almost the entire military system of the State in the Confederate Executive, with the appointment of the officers of the militia, and enables him at his pleasure, to cripple or destroy the civil government of each State, by arresting, and carrying into the Confederate Service, the officers charged by the State Constitution.[26]

Davis, predictably, was incensed. He wrote:

I have received your letter of the 22nd inst. informing me of your transfer of the Georgia State troops to General Lawton commanding Confederate forces at Savannah, suggesting that there be as little interference as possible on the part of the Confederate authorities with the present organization of those troops. . . . Interference with the present organization of companies, squadrons, battalions, or regiments tendered by Governors of States, is specially disclaimed.[27]

So began a bitter clash, a wicked one — and the Union had no intention of waiting until the Southern leaders stopped fighting among themselves.

Chapter

8

──

RICHMOND, THE CAPITAL

T HE conscription bill that President Davis pushed through Congress alarmed the city as much as the military setbacks had. So had the suspension of the writ of habeas corpus and the authorization of martial law within the city. Soldiers on leave from their regiments filled the city's streets, dining halls, and private houses. Crime was picking up; rioting erupted occasionally as gangs of drunken soldiers and civilians spoke too loosely. John Winder's military agents made the situation only worse — Richmond felt like a police state, complete with the hypocrisy that seems requisite of tyranny. For example, in no time at all, recorded one historian, Winder's agents were "forging prescriptions for brandy, drinking the brandy and then arresting unfortunate apothecaries who had sold it to them."[1] No one was immune: "Every Virginian," wrote a clerk in the war office, "and other loyal citizens of the South — members of Congress and all — must now, before obtaining Gen. Winder's permission to leave the city for their homes, bow down before the *aliens* in the Provost Marshal's office, and subscribe to an oath of allegiance, while a file of bayonets are pointed at his back!"[2]

Sallie Putnam, the Richmond diarist, recorded the frustration with the growing scarcity of food in the city. "General Winder, the Provost Marshal of the city," she wrote, "in order to remedy the evil, laid a tariff of prices on all articles of domestic produce, but did not legislate upon groceries, liquors, and articles imported from abroad. The consequence was, the markets were so ill supplied that they had almost as well been closed."[3] Meats became increasingly scarce, and fish took over as the main dinnertime item — but only if one got to the fish market "before the break of day," Putnam recorded. Buyers were fortunate to land a pair of rockfish or shad for dinner, and the situation eased only slightly as springtime brought a slightly larger number of vegetables in from the country. The prices for beef, butter, eggs, vegetables, poultry — and especially imported items such as brandy, sugar, and tea — were astronomical. Butter sold for one dollar per pound (this equates to twenty dollars per pound in 2006).

Despite such challenges the administration of the war had to carry on. Not surprisingly, this included some shuffling. A loyal Virginian, Robert Garlick Hill Kean, was appointed chief of the Bureau of War, replacing Albert Bledsoe, who had been made an assistant secretary of war. Kean won the job not only by his sterling record as an attorney and soldier but also as a nephew of the new secretary of war, George Wythe Randolph. Over the coming months Kean would keep a close watch on his uncle's affairs within the war office. At the same time Isaac M. St. John took command of the newly created Bureau of Nitre and Mining, which would undertake the tasks of procuring and manufacturing saltpeter to produce gunpowder, as well as mining iron, copper, lead, coal, and zinc.

But military bureaucracy was not an immediate worry of Richmonders in the early spring of 1862. The Yankees were bearing down on the Confederate capital, and actions were flaring on many battlegrounds on land and even on the water. The war was splashing across the frontiers of disunion.

In the east came a peculiar show of innovative naval technology. The Confederate ship *Virginia* was the retrofitted "screw steamer" *Merrimack*, scuttled by Union forces when they abandoned the Norfolk

Navy Yard, in April 1861. Confederate naval engineers had turned the hull into a new type of warship with heavily armored, canted sides. The 263-foot-long ship was protected by 4-inch iron laid over 22-inch oak beams. Nothing like it existed before. The ship's armament consisted of six 9-inch Dahlgren guns, naval cannon, and four rifled 6-inch and 7-inch guns. Clad by iron and buoyed by the knowledge of technical advantage, Capt. Franklin Buchanan's crew of 350 steamed into Hampton Roads, Virginia, on March 8 to destroy all the Federal ships they could find.

At about 2 p.m., the *Virginia* rammed the USS *Cumberland* and fired mercilessly on the USS *Congress*. The former sank at 3:30 p.m., and the latter surrendered and was run aground. By 10 p.m. a peculiar vessel arrived, the USS *Monitor*. The invention of John Ericsson, a Swedish-American mechanical engineer, the ship appeared like a flat skiff spanning 172 feet with a single turret extending only 9 feet above the waterline that contained two 11-inch Dahlgren guns. By 9 a.m. the *Monitor*, commanded by Lt. John L. Worden, moved astride the *Virginia* and opened fire. "The contrast was that of a pygmy to a giant," wrote Gershom J. Van Brunt, commander of the nearby USS *Minnesota*, on March 10. "Gun after gun was fired by the *Monitor*, which was returned with whole broadsides by the rebels, with no more effect, apparently, than so many pebble-stones thrown by a child."[4] The Confederate warship withdrew from Hampton Roads, and it would not play a further role in the war, being scuttled two months later. The *Monitor* itself foundered off Cape Hatteras on December 31, 1862. A new era in naval war had, nonetheless, emerged; the era of wooden ships was gone.

In the western theater Ulysses S. Grant's success had shoved Albert Sidney Johnston southward along a line from Memphis to Corinth, Mississippi, to Huntsville, Alabama. Gradually Johnston was reinforced by Maj. Gens. Braxton Bragg, who had been in Mobile, and Leonidas Polk, who had been at Columbus, Kentucky, concentrating about forty thousand men under his command. Grant's thirty-five thousand men were encamped south of the Tennessee River, at Pittsburg Landing near Shiloh Church, by early April. Maj. Gen.

Don Carlos Buell's Army of the Ohio, consisting of fifty thousand, lay well to the northeast at Columbia.

On the night of April 5, Johnston, now also supported by Gen. G. T. Beauregard, advanced northward toward Grant's encampment. Grant did not suspect an attack from the south, but a massive assault came. Between 6 and 7:30 a.m. on April 6, a battle line stretching from southwest to northeast exploded. "Fill your canteens, boys. Some of you will be in hell before night and you'll need water!" advised Isaac C. Pugh, colonel of the Forty-first Illinois Infantry.[5] The battle of Shiloh, the costliest thus far in the war, had begun.

The enormity of the battle seemed evident to soldiers in the ranks from its earliest hours. Leander Stillwell, a private in the Sixty-first Illinois Infantry, wrote:

> Suddenly, away off on the right, in direction of Shiloh Church, came a dull, heavy "Pum," then another, and still another. Every man sprung to his feet as if struck by an electric shock, and we looked inquiringly into one another's faces. . . . Those heavy booms then came thicker and faster, and just a few seconds after we heard that first dull, ominous growl off to the southwest, came a low, sullen, continuous roar. There was no mistaking that sound. That was not a squad of pickets emptying their guns on being relieved from duty; it was the continuous roll of thousands of muskets, and told us that a battle was on.[6]

Johnston hoped to push Grant's army in between two creeks, cutting it off from reinforcement via the Tennessee River, and initially, it looked as if he would succeed. All along the Union battle line, regiments were falling back in the face of the Confederate attack. A Union division under Brig. Gen. Benjamin M. Prentiss stubbornly held fast along a sunken farm lane in an area that became known as the Hornets' Nest due to the intensity of the fighting. Twelve separate Confederate assaults, supported by heavy cannonading, failed to dislodge Prentiss and Brig. Gen. William H. L. Wallace from their positions. But their perseverance seemed the exception rather than the rule, and the Confederate commanders — knowing well the power of momentum in addition to recalling the criticisms that had followed earlier engagements — rushed forward. As the action flared Johnston personally led an attack in which he was wounded behind the knee. The Confederate commander, blood gushing from his leg, slumped off his horse and died near the base of a tree. Now command devolved on Beauregard.

The death of Johnston momentarily stunned parts of the Confederate line, but they pushed forward and successfully pinned Grant's force back against the Tennessee River. Meanwhile, Prentiss had surrendered the Hornets' Nest, and wounded soldiers crawled to drink from a small pond nearby. The little body of water became known as Bloody Pond after it was stained from the soldiers' wounds. As darkness fell on April 6, the Federal army's position seemed tenuous. A rainstorm moved in and depressed the Yankees further.

By daybreak, however, the tide turned. Although tardy Brig. Gen. Lew Wallace finally had arrived to support Grant, more important, Buell's army began to cross the river and reinforce Grant. Refreshed with three new divisions, Grant attacked and, by late morning, had forced Beauregard's troops back in disarray. By early afternoon Beauregard had his whole army retreating southward toward Corinth. The rapidity of the shift surprised some soldiers, including the young Confederate and future explorer Henry M. Stanley, who wrote,

> I became so absorbed with some blue figures in front of me, that I did not pay sufficient heed to my companion greys. . . . Seeing my blues in about the same proportion, I assumed that the greys were keeping their position, and never once thought of retreat. . . . I rose from my hollow; but, to my speechless amazement, I found myself a solitary grey, in a line of blue skirmishers! My companions had retreated! The next I heard was, "Down with the gun, Secesh, or I'll drill a hole through you! Drop it, quick!"[7]

As Beauregard retreated southward into Mississippi, he left behind some 3,477 men dead on the fields and another 20,264 wounded or missing. The scale of the bloodshed shocked the nation. Shocked, too, were the Confederate leaders.

They did have some cause for relief, though. In the Shenandoah Valley — the rich, fertile region so critical to supplying the war in Virginia — Stonewall Jackson, now a major general, was busy making trouble for a succession of Union commanders. Jackson was a Virginian, a close ally of Robert E. Lee's, and an eccentric former professor at the Virginia Military Institute. He was given the nickname "Stonewall" after standing stoutly (or in the way) at the first battle of Manassas. Jackson was a man on a mission, charged with a fervent religious doctrine that overshadowed all else. "The religious element seems strongly developed in him," wrote observer Garnet Wolseley, "and though his conversation is perfectly free from all puritanical cant, it is evident that he is a person who never loses sight of the fact that there is an omnipresent Deity ever presiding over the minutest occurrences in life, as well as over the most important." Jackson indeed took his calling seriously. "You appear much concerned at my attacking on Sunday," he wrote his wife on April 11. "I was greatly concerned, too; but I felt it my duty to do it, in consideration of the ruinous effects that might result from postponing the battle until morning. . . . I hope and pray to our Heavenly Father that I may never again be circumstanced as on that day."[8]

Jackson's brilliance as a tactician became clear during the Valley campaign, when he moved against Union Maj. Gen. James Shields at Kernstown. Despite significant casualties, Jackson was able to divert three Yankee armies from reinforcing a troop buildup on the Virginia peninsula, designed to threaten Richmond.

Meanwhile, military events of differing character transpired far to the south. Near Savannah, Georgia, Fort Pulaski — one of the great brick masonry forts of the coastal southeast — on Cockspur Island fell to Union forces on April 10–11. Union Capt. Quincy A. Gillmore had placed batteries of heavy rifled cannon on Tybee Island, one to two miles from the facade of Fort Pulaski (which had been constructed in part under the supervision of a young Robert E. Lee). The fort's fall signaled the demise of brick masonry forts as an effective defense against the new technology of the rifled cannon. In northern Georgia, at the same time, a band of Yankee spies launched a raid to disrupt the important railroad supply line between Atlanta and Chattanooga. Led by civilian James J. Andrews, twenty-two volunteers traveled to Big Shanty, where on April 12 they captured an engine, the General, and hastily moved northward, destroying track and telegraph wires along the way. The raiders nearly made it to safety in Union-occupied Chattanooga as they were pursued vigorously by the Texas. "With no car left, no fuel, the last scrap having been thrown into the engine or upon the burning car, and with no obstruction to drop on the track, our situation was indeed desperate," wrote William Pittenger, one of the raiders. "A few minutes only remained until our steed of iron which had so well served us would be powerless."[9] Indeed, the raiders were caught, and Andrews along with seven of his men were executed in Atlanta, their bodies sent to the Union lines at Chattanooga, where they were buried. Six of the raiders imprisoned for the longest time were the first men to receive the Medal of Honor.

Far to the west the Confederacy was not faring as well. With a population of nearly 170,000, New Orleans was by far the largest city in the Confederacy. It was also a vital port for supplying the Mississippi River operations and the Deep South. Some ninety miles south of the city, on the river, stood Forts Jackson and St. Philip. These positions and their five hundred men, along with several ships, attempted to block the Federal fleet commanded by Capt. David G. Farragut, who commanded twenty-four wooden vessels and nineteen mortar boats. Instead, Farragut pummeled the defenders at Jackson and St. Philip before capturing New Orleans itself; the citizens were now under Federal occupation. "These people have complimented us highly," wrote Southern diarist Julia LeGrand on April 25. "To quell a small 'rebellion,' they have made preparations enough to conquer a world." A well-known Northerner viewed the problem from a slightly different perspective. "We woo the South 'as the Lion wooes his bride,'" wrote Nathaniel Hawthorne, in Concord, Massachusetts, the following summer. "It is a rough courtship, but perhaps love and a quiet household may come a bit at last."[10]

All these springtime actions, significant as they were, paled in sheer size relative to the great eastern campaign about to unfold on Virginia's peninsula. Lincoln and most of his advisers favored a movement on land back toward Richmond, as had been attempted the previous summer. Maj. Gen. George B. McClellan had succeeded the aging Winfield Scott as general-in-chief, in late 1861. Instead of using Lincoln's plan, he preferred to transport his troops by ship to the eastern tip of the peninsula and approach Richmond from the southeast. After considerable argument and consternation, McClellan got his way.

By April 2 McClellan had arrived at Fort Monroe, near Norfolk, the point of debarkation, where fifty thousand Federal troops were massed for the Peninsular campaign. Confederate Maj. Gen. John B. Magruder represented the first line of defense, thirteen thousand troops. The main Confederate army between McClellan and Richmond, which consisted of forty-three thousand men, was that of Gen. Joseph E. Johnston. Bluffed by Magruder's movements, McClellan laid siege to Yorktown rather than attacking it. For a month McClellan was inactive, preparing for a heavy bombardment of the Confederate defenses. But on May 3 Johnston withdrew toward Richmond, and the Federal army struck at his rear guard, opening the battle of Williamsburg. McClellan abandoned his positions and followed, attacking along a new battle line that stretched around the town that had been Virginia's Colonial capital. Despite his army's lackluster performance in this engagement, McClellan celebrated the battle in a letter to his wife written on May 6. "As soon as I came upon the field the men cheered like fiends," he wrote, "and I saw at once that I could save the day. I immediately reinforced Hancock and arranged to support Hooker, advanced the whole line across the woods, filled up the gaps, and got everything in hand for whatever might occur. The result was that the enemy saw that he was gone if he remained in his position, and scampered during the night."[11]

Johnston's force of 60,000 now moved north and east of the city to defend Richmond. McClellan's army, which consisted of 105,000, established a base at the White House on the Pamunkey and threatened the James River with gunboats that moved as far north as Drewry's

Bluff, a mere seven miles from Richmond. The booming of cannon plainly heard, life for the 38,000 citizens of the capital city soured. "Oh, the extortioners!" wrote John B. Jones on May 23. "Meats of all kinds are selling at fifty cents per pound; butter, seventy-five cents; coffee, a dollar and half; tea, ten dollars; boots, thirty dollars per pair; shoes, eighteen dollars; ladies' shoes, fifteen dollars; shirts, six dollars each."[12]

By May 31 the armies clashed along the Richmond and York River Railroad line in the battle of Seven Pines. A muddy confrontation complicated by poor weather, the engagement presented an opportunity for Confederate success that slipped away. And the army's commander, General Johnston, was carried from the field. As Davis wrote Varina,

> General J. E. Johnston is severely wounded. The poor fellow bore his suffering most heroically. When he was about to be put into the ambulance to be removed from the field, I dismounted to speak to him; he opened his eyes, smiled and gave me his hand, said he did not know how seriously he was hurt, but feared a fragment of shell had injured his spine. . . . I saw him yesterday evening, his breathing was labored but he was free from fever and seemed unshaken in his nervous system.[13]

Johnston would be recuperating for a long time to come. This would prove to be providential for the Army of Northern Virginia. The replacement for Johnston was Gen. Robert E. Lee.

"General Lee had up to this time accomplished nothing to warrant the belief in his future greatness as a commander," wrote Col. Evander M. Law. He continued:

> The general tone, however, was one of confidence, which was invariably strengthened by a sight of the man himself. Calm, dignified, and commanding in his bearing, a countenance strikingly benevolent and self-possessed, a clear, honest eye that could look friend or enemy in the face, clean-shaven, except a closely-trimmed mustache which gave a touch of firmness to the well-shaped mouth; simply and neatly dressed

in his uniform of rank, felt hat, and top boots reaching to his knee; sitting [on] his horse as if his home was in the saddle.[14]

Whatever the case, Lee's nominal accomplishments on the battlefield were not the point — that he and Davis had established a clear, trusting bond was.

As the Yankees moved closer to Richmond, a major council of war was held at the White House. President Davis hosted this get-together all day on April 14 in an effort to decide whether to hold the line at Yorktown. The group included Davis, Robert E. Lee, Joe Johnston, Secretary of War George Randolph, and senior generals James Longstreet and Gustavus W. Smith. Held in the state dining room of the Davis residence, the war council offers a good snapshot of how Confederate military decisions were made at the highest level. At the time Johnston's Army of Northern Virginia was just moving from its lines along the Rappahannock River to the peninsula; meanwhile, McClellan's Yankees were disembarking and moving up the peninsula toward Williamsburg. Magruder's Confederates had established defensive positions along the Warwick River from Yorktown to Mulberry Island, while McClellan's soldiers were marching northward into their position. The question the council faced was should Johnston's entire army move down to occupy the Warwick River line or move into some other closer to the Confederate capital?

Davis began by asking Johnston to summarize his situation. The general claimed that McClellan, no doubt, could move around the Warwick line and force his way closer to Richmond, so Magruder's line might as well be abandoned. Johnston then handed the president a paper, written by Smith, which he said he had been given just before the council began. Davis read Gustavus Smith's memorandum aloud, which confirmed Johnston's notion that the Warwick line was indefensible; it should be abandoned, as well as Norfolk. Instead, Smith contended, reinforcing a line close in to Richmond should be the course, and if McClellan laid siege to the capital, the Confederates should march on Washington and Baltimore immediately.

Johnston told the president he wanted to draw McClellan inland, to concentrate his forces at Richmond and fight the Yankees there. Longstreet believed McClellan would not strike quickly and that Washington, therefore, could be attacked. But Davis criticized Longstreet for underrating McClellan. Meanwhile, Secretary Randolph argued against abandoning the Norfolk Navy Yard, and Lee insisted that defensive positions could be found along the peninsula.

Johnston and Smith continued to argue, much of the day, that the Warwick line simply could not be held. Hence, Davis sat and listened, Longstreet sat and listened, and the Johnston-Smith and Lee-Randolph sides hammered it out. The whole group pored over maps spread all about. After eight hours of this, a break ensued at 6 p.m. The meeting resumed at 7 p.m. and dragged on until 1 a.m. the next day, with all parties stuffed into the cozy dining room. Then, suddenly, the president announced that Johnston's army would return to the lower peninsula to unite with Magruder and that they would, in fact, hold the Warwick line and that Yorktown and Norfolk would be held for as long as could be. It was a striking confirmation of two things: the inability of the Confederate leadership to reach consensus and the president's confidence in Lee over any other. That confidence would continue throughout the war.[15]

To help the president make the most of his military men, in April four aides-de-camp, authorized by Congress, were assigned to him. They were Davis's old friend James Chesnut of South Carolina; William Montague Browne of Georgia; Joseph Christmas Ives, a Confederate captain; and William Preston Johnston, a lieutenant colonel. The last of the four was the son of Albert Sidney Johnston.

The elder Johnston's death at Shiloh had struck his close friend Davis like a hammer blow. The president called the loss "the greatest our country could suffer from" and wept considerably in private. He told Preston Johnston some time later, "My dear Boy, I cannot think calmly of your Father. I cannot speak or write of him without immotion."[16] Subsequently, Preston Johnston not only acted as an aide to the president, but he moved into the Confederate White House and was essentially a surrogate son. This coincided with the Davis family's escape to Raleigh, North Carolina, to flee the enemy, which was now at the doorstep of Richmond. "I have a fine room in the third story," Preston Johnston wrote his wife, Rosa, "with a fine view & everything comfortable. The President lives simply, but delightfully. The hours are rather late to suit me." A week later he wrote his wife again: "From ten or eleven until five are the usual office hours then going to bed at midnight I have to wait an hour or two to breakfast."[17] Before long Davis would return to Richmond, leaving his family behind but taking Preston.

With bleak military prospects Davis, nonetheless, attempted to put on a brave face to Congress and to the rest of the world. In the wake of Shiloh, he reported to Congress:

> I am able to announce to you, with entire confidence, that it has pleased Almighty God to crown the Confederate arms with a glorious and decisive victory over our invaders. . . . The last lingering hope has disappeared, and it is but too true that General Albert Sidney Johnston is no more. . . . My long and close friendship with this departed chieftain and patriot forbids me to trust myself in giving vent to the feelings which this sad intelligence has evoked.[18]

Johnston's death continued to elicit strong feelings among Confederate officers. "The tears of the South now freshen the grave," wrote the South Carolina politician and officer Lawrence M. Keitt, "and the gratitude of the South now embalms the memory of Sydney Johnston. . . . I believe that we shall win."[19]

Nevertheless, political fighting still raged over some of Johnston's past responsibilities. In the House Henry Foote and colleagues delivered a report on the fall of Forts Henry and Donelson, with many members blaming the loss on Johnston. Foote and Horatio Bruce of Kentucky drew up additional reports, which laid blame for the fiasco squarely on the dead general and vindicated Floyd and Pillow, who had been censured by the president and relieved of command.

Other controversies burst forth into Congress. Severe tension over the conscription law had failed to dissipate, especially with the more cantankerous of the governors. "The constitutional question discussed by you in relation to the conscription law had been duly weighed before I recommended to Congress the passage of such a law," Davis angrily wrote Joe Brown of Georgia, who implied the president was trying to put one over on good Confederates on the home front. "It was fully debated in both Houses; and your letter not only has been submitted to my cabinet, but written opinion has been required from the Attorney General."[20]

In April Congress resolved that the president should appoint a military chief of railroads; this constituted the first of many attempts to improve transportation and eliminate communication problems. Davis resisted, however, feeling that it was not Congress's place to order him to do such things.[21] Nor had the details regarding a Confederate Supreme Court been settled, with House member William Porcher Miles peskily continuing to raise the subject. Miles was also dealing with an impending financial crisis. "Our Department is entirely out of funds and we have pressing requisitions on us," wrote Josiah Gorgas, chief of ordnance, in a letter to him.[22] Too little money and too much debate was a dangerous combination. Indeed, it seemed like free debate was preferable to expensive resolution. Familiar arguments over nominations of officers continued. Davis wanted (and justly held) the only responsibility for appointing officers, while various state governors disputed that power, feeling they should have the authority. "It is the province of the executive to nominate and of the Senate to confirm or reject," Davis scolded Senators William Yancey and Clement Clay of Alabama. "Recommendations are willingly received and respectfully considered by me, but I will not argue as to their propriety and do not recognize the fairness of the within statement of my course and assumption as to what it should be."[23] Davis further questioned Congress's acts to distribute naval prize monies and the pay of deceased soldiers. Davis blocked payment of the monies to the wives of sailors held as prisoners and to the widows or heirs of dead soldiers and sailors. He saw both of these as invasions of Congress into unconstitutional ground.[24] Others must have seen such measures as, at the least, good politics.

Not that Davis had no sense of political priorities: he was constantly dealing with politicians second-guessing his military plans for reasons that had little to do with winning the war. Occasionally this was acknowledged by the petitioners. "That Charleston should be defended 'to the last extremity,' seems to me, in a *political* point of view, if not a military, a matter of grave importance," William Porcher Miles wrote to the president about his home city from the House Chamber in the Capitol.[25] But such confessions were rare. So, too, Davis had to deal with the near-continuous arguments between commanders about what was happening in the field. Francis Pickens, for example, complained to Robert E. Lee about the field commanders at Charleston. "Ripley dislikes Pemberton, Pemberton dislikes Ripley, and everything is dysfunctional. It strikes me that it is all important that some able and independent officer should be sent to inspect the forts by your authority."[26] Lee replied, telling Pickens that Porcher Miles wanted Roswell S. Ripley kept in position. Eventually, when the situation degraded further, Ripley was reassigned — but only after a great deal of ink and sweat and tears had been expended on this one question among hundreds. Talk may have been cheap, but inaction was costly.

In Virginia the fighting politicians on the peninsula also had their own evolving ideas about the president and military strategy. "We were kept in the trenches, often times a foot deep in water, for eighteen days, without any necessity or object that I could [learn, except] the stupidity and cowardice of our officers," Bob Toombs wrote his friend Aleck Stephens, who was still sick and bedridden back in Georgia. He continued:

> McClellan was there with his whole army, a good deal less I think than ours, and we could have whipped [them] as easily there as anywhere else. But as usual we burnt up everything and fled, were attacked in the retreat, and left in the hands of the enemy some ten or twelve hundred of our killed, wounded, and sick, and that *after a decided victory.* This is called generalship!! . . . Davis's incapacity is lamentable, and the very thought of the basement of Congress in the impressment act makes me sick. I feel but little like fighting for a people base enough to submit to such despotism from such contemptible sources.[27]

Toward the end of May, the president rode out to inspect the Confederate lines around Richmond. Davis wrote to Varina:

> Riding on the bluff which overlooks the Meadow Bridge, I asked Colonel Anderson, posted there in observation, whether he had seen anything of the enemy in his front. There, by the use of a powerful glass, were distinctly visible two cavalry videttes at the further end of the bridge, and a squad of infantry lower down the river, who had covered themselves with a screen of green boughs. . . . I then rode down to the bank of the river, followed by a cavalcade of sight-seers, who I suppose had been attracted by the expectation of a battle. The little squad of infantry, about fifteen in number, as we approached, fled over the bridge, and were lost to sight.[28]

The walls seemed to be closing in. "I packed some valuable books and the sword I wore for many years," Davis reported to Varina at month's end, "together with the pistols used at Monterrey and Buena Vista, and my old dressing case; these articles will have a value to the boys after time and to you now."[29] But the Confederacy was far from done. Indeed, it was about to roar.

THE RISE OF LEE AND BRAGG

THE summer of 1862 saw the Confederacy in a precarious position. Alarm was palpable on the streets of Richmond, as McClellan's Yankees were spread widely around the city's outskirts, threatening the capital and the very livelihood of the South. "McClellan has been quiet for several days," war clerk John B. Jones wrote his wife in June. "If we do not attack him and beat him soon, Richmond must be evacuated. He is digging his way to it, and may soon have his siege guns in reach of the city."[1] With Confederate military campaigns on multiple fronts in full swing, long, sweltering, dangerous days were now being experienced by a huge number of troops. The tally of deaths was growing, and the examples of men running away from the army to visit home, even with the intention of returning, was alarming Southern commanders.

With Joe Johnston wounded and Lee taking over the Army of Northern Virginia, no one was exactly sure how the Confederate forces would fare. Lee, after all, had been notable in western Virginia early in the war as "Granny Lee," too timid to attack the Yankees in force and preoccupied with digging entrenchments, earning him the additional sobriquet "King of Spades." President Davis, though, was hopeful regarding his military adviser.

But the president and Varina were worried, too, as sickness had struck their own family. From Raleigh Varina wrote of the travails of wartime loneliness and longed to be with her husband in Richmond. Preston Johnston sent her frequent news of the president, in addition to Davis's own letters. With Richmond in jeopardy, Sidney Johnston dead, and having heard about Joe Johnston's wounding, she wrote her husband, "Why are our best friends killed?" The Davises' young son William was intermittently sick with boils and cholera, and most of the medications tried for him did no good. "My heart sunk within me at the news of the suffering of my angel baby," wrote the president. "Your telegram of 12th gives assurance of the subsidence of disease. But the look of pain and exhaustion, the gentle complaint, 'I am tired' which has for so many years oppressed me, seems to have been revived."[2]

Around Richmond McClellan moved most of his force south of the Chickahominy River and, characteristically, waited. The weather was poor, and several weeks passed before any significant action came. Then, on June 25, the armies began a series of battles that collectively came to be called the Seven Days. On June 25 occurred the battle of Oak Grove. A more significant action, the battle of Mechanicsville, was fought along Beaver Dam Creek the following day. Lee's sound plan to force the Yankees from their trenches by flanking movements went awry when Stonewall Jackson arrived late for his attack and Brig. Gen. A. P. Hill attacked without orders. The following day Lee and his subordinates attempted to regroup. Robert Stiles, a young soldier in the Richmond Howitzers, was present when Lee met Jackson. He wrote:

> The two generals greeted each other warmly, but wasted no time upon the greeting. They stood facing each other, some thirty feet from where I lay, Lee's left side and back toward me, Jackson's right and front. Jackson began talking in a jerky, impetuous way, meanwhile drawing a diagram on the ground with the toe of his right boot. He traced two sides of a triangle with promptness and decision; then starting at the end of the sec-

ond line began to draw a third projected toward the first. This third line he traced slowly and with hesitation, alternately looking up at Lee's face and down at his diagram, meanwhile talking earnestly; and when at last the third line crossed the first and the triangle was complete, he raised his foot and stamped it down with emphasis, saying "We've got him."[3]

The generals believed they knew how to defeat the Yankees by striking them before they could establish a solid defensive line. The bloody battle fought on June 27 was termed Gaines's Mill. Lee planned to envelop Union Brig. Gen. Fitz John Porter's right, but again, Jackson was slow. Nevertheless, a massed Confederate assault late in the afternoon turned the battle into a Confederate victory. So close to the zone of war, Davis could not keep away. On June 26 he commenced a tour of the battlefields, and he actually slept a number of days out under the stars with the troops. At Oak Grove Davis approached so close to the front lines that Lee had to ask him to leave, which he eventually did. Shortly thereafter Davis toured the troops and their encampments along the Chickahominy River and encouraged the men to fight on stubbornly. He was shaken by the terrible wounding of a friend, Brig. Gen. Richard Griffith, whom he saw carried away on a litter to die. Elsewhere the president came under fire and — again after Lee's prodding — he left a house that was later struck by artillery shells.

On June 28, as McClellan began a retreat to the James River, the more minor battle of Garnett's and Golding's Farms took place. Jackson struck the Federal army from the north at the White Oak Swamp on June 30. And finally, on July 1, Lee's army attempted a frontal attack at Malvern Hill to crush the retreating Federals, but his men were hammered by well-placed Union cannon that fired with devastating effect — sometimes even to Union soldiers. As Thomas L. Livermore, a New Hampshire soldier, described it,

> Shells flew all around us, and the wonder was that more were not hurt. I turned my head to the left and saw the battery and the gunners, springing to their work amid the smoke. I saw one pull the string, saw the flash of the piece, heard the roar, and the whiz of the shell, heard it

burst, heard the humming of the fragments, and wondered if I was to be hit, and quicker than a flash something stung my leg on the calf, and I limped out of the ranks, a wounded man.[4]

Despite the success at Malvern Hill, it was by now clear that McClellan's Peninsular campaign was a strategic failure. By July 3 he had withdrawn the Army of the Potomac to Harrison's Landing and awaited a northward movement. It was over.

Other wheels were turning, however. In mid-July, Lee dispatched Jackson northward to Gordonsville to threaten the advance of Maj. Gen. John Pope, whose Army of Virginia occupied the Shenandoah Valley. This established the basis for the Second Manassas campaign, also called Second Bull Run.

Jackson hit Union Maj. Gen. Nathaniel P. Banks at Cedar Mountain on August 9 in an affair significantly mismanaged on both sides. Subsequently, both armies moved northward, and by late August, Jackson interposed himself between Pope's army and Washington. "His sun-burned cap was lifted from his brow, and he was gazing toward the west, where the splendid August sun was about to kiss the distant crest of the Blue Ridge, which stretched far away, bathed in azure and gold," wrote Jackson's staff officer Robert L. Dabney of his celebrated commander. "And his blue eye, beaming with martial pride, returned the rays of the evening with almost equal brightness. . . . His face beaming with delight, [he] said, 'Who could not conquer, with such troops as these?'"[5] The opposing Federal commander heard no such praise from his fellow soldiers. Pope's competence had been brought into question a number of times, and a common feeling of distrust had developed. "I don't care for John Pope one pinch of owl dung," Union Brig. Gen. Samuel D. Sturgis wrote on August 23.[6] He was far from alone in his sentiments.

Pope's seventy-five thousand faced about fifty-five thousand men commanded by Lee as the armies converged on the old battleground of Manassas. By August 27 Jackson had concentrated his forces at Manassas Junction, capturing a vast array of Union supply trains. Confederate Maj. Gen. James Longstreet approached from the west. Two days later Federal troops occupied the old battleground at

Henry House Hill, as well as the towns of Centreville and Haymar-
ket and lay scattered southward toward Brentsville. Deciding the
moment had come, Pope attacked Jackson from both east and west.
The Federal attacks westward were poorly coordinated, piecemeal
affairs. Vicious fighting erupted at Groveton and along an unfinished
railroad that passed by the base of Jackson's position at Stony Ridge.
"I can see him now," wrote Edward McCrady of the Confederate
Brig. Gen. Maxcy Gregg at Groveton, "as with his drawn sword, that
old Revolutionary scimitar we all knew so well, he walked up and
down the line, and hear him as he appealed to us to stand by him and
die there. 'Let us die here, my men, let us die here.' And I do not
think that I exaggerate when I say that our little band responded to
his appeal, and were ready to die, at bay, there if necessary."[7]

On August 30, the battle's second day, a massive attack by Longstreet on the southern end of the Union line transformed the battle
into a great Confederate victory. Jackson struck at Pope's northern
flank, and the Federal army fell back. Pope withdrew toward Centreville, but a rear-guard action ensued on September 1 at Chantilly.
There, the Confederate divisions of Maj. Gen. Dick Ewell (who had
lost his leg at Groveton on August 28) and Maj. Gen. A. P. Hill
struck Federal forces commanded by Maj. Gen. Philip Kearny and
Brig. Gen. Isaac I. Stevens. The Confederates were turned back, but
both Union commanders were killed. Charles F. Walcott, a captain
in the Twenty-first Massachusetts Infantry, described Kearny's
death:

> The General, entirely alone, apparently in uncontrollable rage at our
> disregard of his peremptory orders to advance, forced his horse through
> the deep, sticky mud of the cornfield past the left of the regiment, pass-
> ing within a few feet of where I was standing. I watched him moving in
> the murky twilight through the corn, and, when less than twenty yards
> away, saw his horse suddenly rear and turn, and half-a-dozen muskets
> flash around him: so died the intrepid soldier, Gen. Philip Kearny![8]

In the east Robert E. Lee was beginning his ascent to greatness
and fame by beating back the Yankees from Richmond. In the west

Gen. Braxton Bragg was rising to great notoriety by outflanking Union forces in Tennessee. Significantly alarmed about Charleston, Davis sent Bragg to investigate the situation and then a week later dispatched his old friend Samuel Cooper there also to find out what was going on.[9]

The problem of Charleston's defense festered. The city was nominally under the supervision of Maj. Gen. John C. Pemberton. According to Francis Pickens, Pemberton was "confused and uncertain about everything."[10] Against nearly everyone else, Davis vigorously defended Pemberton. Late in August Pickens complained again about Pemberton. "[Pemberton] had no idea of defending the city [following orders to do so]," wrote Pickens, who implored Davis to remove him. The president stood by his old friend, however.[11]

Along the Mississippi River, combined action resumed on August 5 with an attack on Baton Rouge by Confederate infantry. Yankees had occupied the city on May 12, before commencing operations toward Vicksburg. After their failure in Vicksburg, the Union troops had retreated to Baton Rouge by July 26. During this period some changes took place among the Confederate commanders. After being commissioned a full general in April, Bragg, who held President Davis's favor, was assigned to replace P. G. T. Beauregard as commander of the Army of Mississippi, assuming charge on August 15. "The great changes of command and commanders here has well nigh overburdened me," Bragg wrote his wife on July 22, "but I hope yet to mark the enemy before I break down."[12]

For his part Beauregard was once again furious. "If the country be satisfied to have me laid on the shelf by a man who is either demented or a traitor to his high trust — well, let it be so," he confided to his friend and staff officer Thomas Jordan. Beauregard went on:

> I require rest & will endeavor meanwhile by study and reflection to fit myself better for the darkest hours of our trial, which, I foresee, are yet to come. . . . My consolation is, that the difference between "that individual" and myself is — that, if he were to die to day, the whole country would rejoice at it, whereas, I believe, if the same thing were to happen to me, they would regret it.[13]

The fate of Vicksburg was a terrific worry back in Richmond. The fortified bastion on the Mississippi River meant control of the lower part of the waterway. If lost to the Yankees, the result would be disastrous. Yet with so much action in the east, there seemed to be little Davis could do to bolster his support for the garrison there. Corinth, Mississippi, where Beauregard had retreated following the battle of Shiloh, was under a slow, tedious advance by Union Maj. Gen. Henry W. Halleck.[14] "If Miss. troops lying in camp when not retreating under Beauregard, were at home," mused Davis, "they would probably keep a section of the river free for our use and closed against Yankee transports."[15] Writing the state's governor Davis confessed, "My efforts to provide for the military wants of your section have been sadly frustrated."[16]

Davis continued to urge governors to provide soldiers and allow his government to assign them for duty and made vague promises about helping the states resist attacks by Federal troops. "With respect to conscripts, the law of Congress does not allow new Regts. to be formed from their number," the president wrote Governor Thomas Moore of Louisiana. "I trust that the new Commandg. Genl., with your assistance, and the co-operation of the patriotic citizens of Louisiana will be able to keep the enemy in check . . . until we shall be able to drive the invader altogether from the soil."[17] But such words were of little comfort to recipient or sender.

A more explosive situation was brewing in Arkansas, where Governor Henry Rector wanted to pull his state away from the Confederacy altogether. "Arkansas lost, abandoned, subjugated, is not Arkansas as she entered the confederate government," Rector declared in a proclamation. "Nor will she remain a confederate State, desolated as a wilderness." Rector threatened to build "a new ark and launch it on new waters, seeking a haven somewhere, of equality, safety, and rest."[18] Responding to Rector's proclamation, Francis Lubbock of Texas wrote the president, reassuring him as best he could that support would come from the Deep South. "This is no time for bickerings, heart-burnings, and divisions among a people struggling for existence as a free Government," wrote Lubbock.[19] True, but false, too.

Davis, worried over the independence of governors and what they might try, continued his run-ins on paper with the most cantankerous of them all, Joe Brown of Georgia. Brown wrote his friend Aleck Stephens, still in Georgia:

> I deeply regret that the President, whom I have regarded as a lead State Rights man, should have given in his adhesion to the doctrines of unlimited congressional powers. I am satisfied however that my position is the position of the old State Rights leaders from the days of 1798 till the present time, and I am willing to stand or fall by these doctrines. I entered into this revolution to contribute my humble mite to sustain the rights of the states and prevent the consolidation of the Government, and I am still a rebel till this object is accomplished, no matter who may be in power.[20]

As Stephens lay in bed, away from his post in Richmond, he not only reflected on letters from his partners in opposition to Davis, but he also had time to write out a list of his "negroes, with their values." He listed thirty-one names, starting with "Harry" and ending with "Melissa, a child," and placed their collective value at $12,950. (A year later he calculated their total value at $32,150. For some, at least for a time, the war seemed to be profitable.) While the Confederate vice president was not willing to help his government in Richmond, he was able to tally his estate.[21] It was an unencouraging sign.

Even the friendliest of Deep South governors had their apparent demands, or at least concerns, to share with the president. "The isolated condition of the States West of the Miss. River, since the fall of New Orleans, and the virtual possession of that River by the enemy rendered it proper that the several executives of those States should confer together freely and fully as to their wants and necessities, and the best means for their protection and defense," Lubbock and his colleagues from Arkansas, Missouri, and Louisiana informed Davis. "We should have a Commanding General, having territorial jurisdiction over all the States West of the Mississippi River. . . . We must have money for the support of the Army. . . . We must have arms, and also ammunition . . . [and] the General sent should be eminently gifted with administrative ability."[22]

At Chattanooga Maj. Gen. Edmund Kirby Smith was preparing an invasion of Kentucky that hoped to retake much of the territory captured and occupied by Federal troops. The Confederate plan called for Bragg to concentrate at the rail center of Chattanooga while Kirby Smith would move against the Union forces controlling the Cumberland Gap to open a thoroughfare into central Kentucky. The two Confederate armies would then unite to destroy the army of Union Maj. Gen. Don Carlos Buell, which had been moving toward Chattanooga, and push him from Tennessee. Because of its complexity, it was an audacious plan strategically, but one that might work if the timing were handled perfectly and if preliminary events favored the South.

Smaller-scale operations were a part of the Confederate effort. Col. John Hunt Morgan was assigned the task of trapping Union Brig. Gen. George W. Morgan, who was presently at Cumberland Gap. Beginning a forced march from Sparta, Tennessee, John Morgan's raiders attempted to cut the Louisville & Nashville Railroad and attack Gallatin on August 12, northeast of Nashville. There, they skirmished with a Union garrison and destroyed an eight-hundred-foot-long railroad bridge over the Cumberland River as well as a railroad tunnel between Gallatin and Bowling Green. The commander of the Federal force, Col. William P. Boone, had left camp to visit his wife, who was lying ill in a hotel in town. On leaving the hotel Boone was surrounded and captured. John Morgan's men infiltrated the town so quietly that most of the pickets and guards were asleep and surprised as well. The result was, in the words of Union Capt. Walworth Jenkins, "a shameful and complete surprise within two hours after Colonel Boone had left his guards 'on the alert and doing their duty,' and the surrender of the whole camp, on guard, and at the tunnel and bridges without a shot being fired for the defense of their position, the reputation of their State, or the honor of their country."[23]

T HESE actions in the western theater, especially in the critically important border state of Kentucky, were fought against the politically volatile backdrop of coming emancipation. On July 17 President Lincoln had signed the Second Confiscation Act, after considerable

131

debate in Congress. The act stated that slaves held by those in rebellion against the government of the United States would be set free after coming into regions of Federal control or occupation. Vigorously supported by radical Republicans, and seen as not going far enough by many abolitionists, the act was highly controversial in the North. It called for the confiscation of slaves as property, suggested that other types of property also could be seized, and allowed the government both to employ freed slaves in various tasks as well as to establish a provision for colonization somewhere outside the United States (an idea that had been batted around in Congress as a solution to the slave dilemma for several decades). Although Lincoln was not satisfied with all parts of the act, and many elements were never enforced (as is the case with many complex laws), he had signed it. It signaled another step toward transforming the character of the war, and it upset nearly everyone in one way or another.

"We think you are strangely and disastrously remiss in the discharge of your official and imperative duty with regard to the emancipating provisions of the new Confiscation Act," implored the powerful, radical, eccentric editor Horace Greeley in an open letter to Lincoln. The letter, titled "The Prayer of Twenty Millions," was published in the *New York Tribune* on August 20. "We think you are unduly influenced by the councils," continued Greeley, "the representations, the menaces of certain fossil politicians hailing from the Border Slave States. . . . The Rebels from the first have been eager to confiscate, imprison, scourge, and kill; we have fought wolves with the devices of sheep."[24] In response to this public stab at his policy, Lincoln sent a reply to the editor and his paper two days later. "My paramount object in this struggle *is* to save the Union," Lincoln wrote, "and is *not* either to save or to destroy slavery. If I could save the Union without freeing *any* slave, I would do it; and if I could save it by freeing *all* the slaves, I would do it; and if I could do it by freeing some and leaving others alone, I would also do that. . . . I intend no modification of my oft-expressed *personal* wish that all men, everywhere, could be free."[25] Greeley printed the text of Lincoln's letter on August 25.

While Lincoln was stepping into considerably more controversial waters as chief executive, Secretary of State William H. Seward wrote off concerns about the violent war spilling over into politics. "Assassination is not an American practice or habit," he told John Bigelow, the U.S. consul in Paris, on July 15, "and one so vicious and so desperate cannot be engrafted into our political system."[26]

═══

Meanwhile, the Lincoln administration continued to experiment with command structure, as it had throughout the first part of the war. Having given up on the timid George McClellan in March, Lincoln next appointed a "War Board" to run the army consisting of his bureau chiefs, along with Secretary of War Edwin Stanton. When this arrangement proved too cumbersome, with too many cooks in the kitchen, Lincoln found a western general whom he lacked faith in on the battlefield but who might serve as an excellent glorified clerk — Henry Halleck. In July he brought Halleck to Washington and reinstated a conventional general in chief role for him.

In the South there were no such neat solutions. Yankee armies still held close to the Confederate capital, and Navy Secretary Stephen R. Mallory confided to his diary, "I feel that if my life would gain this victory [before Richmond] it should be instantly offered; nay, I would seize and glory in, the chance of sacrificing it for so great a result." He also began to sour on the prospects for the Confederacy. "England . . . may be here fitted by the annihilation of our cotton producing power," he wrote. "Her efforts to raise this staple in India, Egypt & Africa indicate her determination to look elsewhere than to us for it." Mallory also reflected on his lack of confidence in Jefferson Davis. "The Presdt. does not consult his cabinet either as to plans or arrangements of campaigns, or the appointments of military men to office."[27]

While Mallory lacked confidence in Davis, others lacked confidence in Mallory. Blaming him for the inaction of Confederate forces on the water and the failure to raise any kind of naval force that could respectably take on the Yankees, Congress took action. It appointed a Joint Select Committee in the House to investigate the Navy Department and Mallory. The second session of the First Regular Congress of the Confederacy was just getting under way, called to open on August 18. It would be the most contentious yet.

Chapter

10

———

AN UNEASY BROTHERHOOD

As autumn 1862 approached, the whole country watched and waited with eager anticipation. Richmonders felt a degree of calm they had not known in some time. The Union invasion of the previous spring had melted away, and now Lee was on the attack. A sense of security flowed back into the city as politicians gathered once again to join another session of Congress on Capitol Hill.

The session commenced on August 18, with the chambers on the first and second floors of the Capitol Building again packed with light, debate, cigar smoke, and numerous politicians. From day one the issue of state rights versus a strong national government had plagued the fledgling Confederacy, but never more squarely than during this period.

On the first day of sessions, Jefferson Davis delivered a jubilant message to Congress reminding them of the administration's success the previous spring. "The vast army which threatened the capitol of the Confederacy has been defeated," Davis reported, as if they hadn't heard. "Rapine and wanton destruction of private property, war upon non-combatants, murder of captives, bloody threats to avenge the death of an invading soldiery by the slaughter of unarmed civilians, orders of banishment against peaceful farmers engaged in the cultivation of the soil, are some of the means used by our ruthless invaders to enforce the submission of a free people to foreign sway."[1] At the same time, the president reminded Congress of his standing relative to the states — at least as he saw it. "You can best devise the means for establishing that entire cooperation of the State and central governments which is essential to the well-being of both at all times, but which is now indispensable to their very existence."[2] The president desperately wanted Congress to take responsibility for getting the states to cooperate.

One of the issues the national government and states of the Confederacy were still clashing over was military appointments. Davis wanted, among other things, the power to eliminate from the service officers he saw as incompetent. He wrote:

> In the election and appointment of officers for the Provisional Army, it was to be anticipated that mistakes would be made, and incompetent officers of all grades introduced into the service. In the absence of experience, and with no reliable guide for selection, executive appointments as well as elections, have been sometimes unfortunate. The good of the service, the interests of the country, require that some means be devised for withdrawing the commissions of officers who are incompetent for the duties required of their position, and I trust you will find means of relieving the Army of such officers by some mode more prompt and less wounding to their sensibility than the judgment of a court martial.[3]

Boards of inquiry and boards of retirement were suggested. In early September arguments erupted in the Senate over whether generals should be nominated based on their previous rank (seniority) or by merit demonstrated on the battlefield. Many similar questions arose. Should brigadier generals be appointed with regard to state representation proportional to their numbers of troops?[4] Further, President Davis asked for a clarification on the matter of renominations. Should the president have the exclusive right to nominate generals?[5] In the Senate on September 27, a dustup flared over the perception that the president had appointed too many generals from Virginia, relative to other states. Senators from virtually all the other states felt this was the case and were envious of the supposed unfair elevation of Virginia. The Senate resolved to regulate the appointment and nomination of brigadier generals in the future and decided that nominations should be made with reference to the numbers of troops in service from that state, giving preference to the state having the least number of brigadier generals in proportion to their troops. The Military Affairs Committee then hit their fellow senators with a dose of reality, reporting the president had the exclusive right of nomination but the Senate had the exclusive right of confirmation, and therefore, it may not also control or regulate appointments or nominations. Predictably, debate continued.[6]

In the Senate James Phelan of Mississippi asked, "Can Congress demand military service of a State Officer?" He believed that by constitutional power, "Congress has the right to go into the States and take the militia as individuals. . . . We trust that Congress will not abuse these powers, as we trust the States, who have the power to raise armies, if in their opinion they think themselves in danger of invasion, will not raise those armies and plunge the Confederacy into war."[7]

A few days later Thomas Semmes of Louisiana asked, "If the Confederate government can take state officers, what is stopping them from conscripting governors and legislators as well as justices of the peace?" Williamson Oldham of Texas said that if Semmes were right, then "every person, male and female, could be forced into the Confederate army." His fellow Texan Louis Wigfall said that if Congress had the right to call out the militia, as it does, then "'it also has the right to define who the militia are. . . . And I do not believe that Congress will ever be guilty of declaring that a woman shall be a militia *man*."[8] Had there not been a war on, it might all have been comical.

——

O N August 18 the president sent a message to the Senate asking for a more comprehensive conscription act that would cover men of ages thirty-five to forty-five. The same day the Senate received the president's message, South Carolina congressman William Porcher Miles, chairman of the Military Affairs Committee, offered a bill extending conscription to white males between eighteen and forty-five. He also offered a bill suggesting that all black soldiers taken in arms against the Confederacy — and all white officers leading them — should be hanged at capture or turned over to the state in which they are captured to be dealt with as the states saw fit.[9]

Porcher Miles was an unusual character, a one-time teacher of mathematics at the College of Charleston who was born in rural South Carolina on Independence Day in 1822. In a brief autobiography Miles noted, "I believe I am the *eighth generation* born upon the soil of Carolina which may account for my intense Southern sentiments."[10] Following a stint as a hospital worker during the yellow fever epidemic of 1855, Miles ran for mayor of Charleston and won. He then ran for Congress and won a seat in the House in Washington, serving until 1860, when he resigned along with the other South Carolina politicians. He had served as a member of Beauregard's delegation to arrange for the surrender of Fort Sumter as the war broke out, and now he was emerging as a powerful politician. A solid-looking man with a neat hairstyle, sincere eyes, and a beard and mustache that fitted neatly above his trim suits, he also had served as chairman of the committee that approved the Confederate flag and wielded great influence as head of the Military Affairs Committee.

Over the summer of 1862, Porcher Miles's standing, and sway, would grow week by week. At times he supported the administration, but overall, his strident state rights stance pushed against it. He had allies. Four days after the House first confronted conscription, the cantankerous Henry S. Foote of Tennessee, Davis's old nemesis, took the floor. He warned against extending the act and argued over the impression that the First Conscription Act had passed by a large margin; in fact many in Congress had voted for it with regret, and the president said that he signed it into law with reluctance. Foote called the law unconstitutional. "If agents of the Confederate Government had the right to go into any State and take therefrom the men belonging to that State," screeched Foote, "how was States Rights and State sovereignty to be maintained?" Ethelbert Barksdale of Mississippi said that he thought Mississippians would support conscription. In a huff Foote countered that he knew the people of Mississippi, read the newspapers, and — by God — they "were states rights people." Otho Singleton of Mississippi said he "saw nothing new" in Foote's speech and that "it was a useless waste of time" to discuss the act. "Mississippi would rally to a man" over conscription, said Singleton. The question was carried over into secret session.[11]

The next day the debate exploded once again. Nearly immediately Foote began arguing with Augustus Kenan of Georgia, who staunchly defended Joe Brown's raising of troops in Georgia. Caleb Herbert of Texas then declared that if it became necessary to violate the Constitution to win the war, he would favor "raising the 'lone star' flag that had twice been raised before." Porcher Miles asked if conscription were not extended, then how would the Confederacy fill up the army's ranks, "many of which are reduced to mere skeletons"? Burgess Gaither of North Carolina said the present laws, if correctly executed, would fill up the regiments. This was absurd, but the argument was not based on logistics but political logic. Nearly every step taken by a representative was taken with the thought of their own state foremost in mind — and most states by now were feeling an increasing separation from the Richmond government.[12]

If some in Congress did not support supplying the army with more white troops, then they could contemplate forcing slaves to serve the army in support roles. On August 26 in the House, Thomas Foster of Alabama offered a resolution to call up all male slaves between ages twenty and thirty to be used as teamsters, cooks, and nurses in hospitals or laborers and mechanics in railroads, workshops, furnaces, foundries, and factories of the Confederate States. Congress would secure the owners of the property "a just and reasonable compensation for the labor of said negroes," said Foster. The measure was adopted.[13]

The day after the resolution was adopted, the Senate took up the conscription debate. Some senators were particularly worried about the administration empowering enrolling officers to seize conscripts. Louis T. Wigfall claimed that because of the passage of the conscription bill, every white male in the land was, ipso facto, a soldier, "and when now found traveling about, the assumption was fair that he was a deserter." Still, if a provost marshal did catch someone who was shirking duty, Wigfall stated, "it would do them no harm to be subjected to a little drill, and if they should happen to kill one of the enemies of their country, so much the better." The amendment passed.[14]

Conscription continued to arouse emotion throughout the autumn. On September 1 in the House, Porcher Miles reported on a bill that would allow the president to increase the size of the army by calling for those between thirty-five and forty-five years old to serve for three years.[15] Two days later in the Senate, William Yancey of Alabama attempted to circumvent the president by offering his own version of a conscription act that would have allowed new military companies to form with troops that had not yet been mustered into service — something the president opposed.[16]

On September 3 the debate reignited in the House. Samuel Miller of Virginia believed that "some thought conscription doubtful constitutionally, and many viewed it as a breach of good faith towards the soldiers who had contracted to serve for a certain period." But he now thought the majority of the country supported it. John Crockett of Kentucky originally argued that conscription was unconstitutional and that he could not vote for the bill. But now he could. Fear of the Yankees taking over Kentucky won him over. Still, he was "opposed to leaving the exercise of a power on which the fate of the country might depend, to the sole discretion of the President."[17] Milledge Bonham of South Carolina stated that the governors should call quotas for troops and organize them in certain states rather than giving that power to the president. He criticized the president and secretary of war for not acting sooner and disagreed with them that there was no immediate need for troops. "Our armies are victorious everywhere, and we have time to fill up our forces in the constitutional mode," he fantastically suggested.

Finally, on September 17, 1862 — the day a battle raged far away along a little Maryland creek called the Antietam and a month after the conscription debate had begun — the House passed a new conscription bill. Miles led the vote for it; Bonham and Foote fought against it. The bill passed forty-nine to thirty-nine.[18] On September 27 the

Second Conscription Act was passed in the Senate by a vote of fifty-four to twenty-nine, requiring service of all able men ages eighteen to forty-five. Implementation was delayed until July 15, 1863. The first such Union army conscription would also take place in the summer of 1863, sparking brief riots in New York by those who opposed such compulsory service. On both sides of the war, citizens at home would begin to feel that their governments were infringing on their free will and personal liberties.

=

CONSCRIPTION was not the only tiger this contentious Congress had by the tail during the summer and autumn of 1862. Continuing its investigation of the navy secretary, the House resolved on August 27 that it "lacked confidence" in Stephen Mallory. After some discussion a motion to table the resolution was passed forty-seven to forty-one; nevertheless, Foote then introduced a resolution to form a committee to investigate the affairs of the Navy Department. For some members of Congress, their own feelings about Mallory mattered little; they smelled blood in the water and adored the opportunity to attack Davis, albeit via his navy secretary. After further debate the House adjourned, but not before Hines Holt of Georgia and George Jones of Tennessee said that if members did not stop condemning government officials and set about doing the work of government, then history would remember the Confederate Congress as "the most inefficient branch of Government existing in this revolution."[19]

Congress also had it out for Gen. Braxton Bragg, who, like Mallory, was a close friend of the president's. "You have the misfortune of being regarded as my personal friend," Davis wrote Bragg, "and are pursued therefore with malignant censure by men regardless of truth and whose want of principle to guide their conduct renders them incapable of conceiving that you are trusted because of your known fitness for command, and not because of friendly regard. Revolutions develop the high qualities of the good and the great, but they cannot change the nature of the vicious and the selfish."[20]

Bragg incurred the ire of the entire Georgia cabal by invoking martial law over Atlanta. "I have viewed this proceeding as I have others of our military authorities of late with painful apprehensiveness for the future," Governor Joe Brown wrote Aleck Stephens, still ailing at Liberty Hall. "It seems military men are assuming the whole powers of the government to themselves and setting at defiance constitutions, laws, state rights, state sovereignty, and every other principle of civil liberty, and that our people engrossed in the struggle with the enemy are disposed to submit to these bold usurpations tending to military despotism without murmur, much less resistance."[21]

Then came another storm over Bragg, this time in the Senate. The contentious, egotistical South Carolinian James Orr inquired whether General Bragg had had any citizens "executed . . . without trial, the number thus executed, and the crimes or offences imputed to them."[22] Senators angrily requested clarification from Jefferson Davis. Orr claimed he had heard "from officers in the army of this tyrant" that executions of three citizens had taken place. Others objected to what they saw as hearsay and slander. "The names assassin and General Bragg should never be linked together, and driven into the public ear," said James Phelan of Mississippi. "There is a common law in the army," said Louis Wigfall, "by which a Lieutenant even may shoot down a soldier, when, during battle, he is deserting or creating disorder." Robert M. T. Hunter said that Bragg should be present if he were to be brought into an inquiry, though he believed the Senate actually lacked the power to insist on the removal of a general officer. "Citizens may be shot down in this city and the Senate take no notice of the circumstances," added Wigfall.[23]

The next day the arguments raged on. Orr continued to ask for a resolution seeking information from Jefferson Davis over Bragg's alleged executions. In one case, Orr said, the soldier had been ordered not to shoot his gun and had fired at a chicken, instead hitting a black man. The soldier was summarily executed. The execution occurred not because of shooting the man, however, but because the army was in retreat and silence was mandated. He had violated an order to not make noise. "The guns of the sixteen men ordered to perform the execution," said Orr, "made more noise than the one gun fired at the chicken."[24]

Bragg was a target largely because his campaign in Kentucky was failing. On October 8 he had fought the Yankees at Perryville but had since fallen back and was retreating from the state. By late October Bragg's army had arrived at Cumberland Gap, planning to move back toward Knoxville and Chattanooga. A week later Bragg met with the president, hoping to mend his standing, as recorded by Preston Johnston. "I think Bragg in Ky. a signal failure," he penned on October 27. "He is here, & in conference with the President."[25]

Not only could Congress interfere with decisions about military commanders they did not like, Davis found, but they could interfere to attempt to help officers Davis *didn't* like. On September 13 a large number of congressmen signed and sent a letter to the president asking him to restore G. T. Beauregard to command of the Army of the West, taking him out of Charleston. They reflected great confidence in Beauregard and urged the president to move him into command out west, especially in the wake of Henry, Donelson, and Shiloh. The document was carried to Davis by Edward Sparrow and Thomas Semmes and signed by them and many others, including Miles, Bonham, Wigfall, and Foote. It was one more thing for the wartime president to deal with.[26]

AND then there was the unresolved matter of habeas corpus. The fight to preserve individual rights against the tyrannical Davis administration, as some extremists saw it, soldiered on. On August 26 in the House, Ethelbert Barksdale of Mississippi introduced a law to limit the president's ability to declare martial law to twenty days, unless continuation was allowed by Congress. In the discussion that followed, Muscoe Garnett of Virginia angrily alluded to arbitrary proclamations like those of Provost Marshal Gen. John Winder in Richmond, which attempted to silence the press, fix prices for goods and services, and commit other abuses. The bill was referred to the Judiciary Committee.[27]

In mid-September the Senate Judiciary Committee declared the president's use of martial law had effects "far beyond a mere suspension of the writ of habeas corpus." It reaffirmed that only Congress should have the authority to suspend the writ of habeas corpus and asked for new legislation to limit the president's authority. At the same time in the House, Virginian Charles Russell offered a resolution to authorize suspension of the writ of habeas corpus in certain cases. Foote strongly opposed it. "I will never again consent to a suspension of the writ of Habeas Corpus unless the enemy is within sight of the city," he said, "and then only so long as circumstances might render absolutely necessary."[28]

A few days later Thomas Semmes of Louisiana reported that the Judiciary Committee had formulated a bill enabling the president to declare suspension in towns or cities in danger of rebellion, in the neighborhoods of armies, or in areas of potential attack. Such arrests would be confined to those to maintain discipline of the army or for crimes against the Confederate States.[29]

Early in October the debate flared again in the House. Foote argued to limit the powers of the president so Davis could not threaten the Constitution. The next day Foote's amendment was defeated, forty-five to fourteen — an easy fail, and yet the minority in support constituted almost a quarter of the House, and they would not let the issue die.[30]

As habeas corpus bubbled, so did issues relating to the general staff. Davis saw most of this as interference in matters that should be purely in the domain of the executive branch, and for the most part, he was right. Nonetheless, on September 23 Orr introduced a bill asking for the quartermaster general to have the "rank, pay, and allowance" of a brigadier general. This was an attempt to have his friend Abraham Myers, the quartermaster general, promoted. "The experience of seventy years under the old government shows the necessity of giving to the quartermaster general a higher rank than colonel," Orr declared. Davis, however, disliked Myers, whose wife had cracked that Varina Davis was "an old squaw," and would not stand for his promotion. John Clark of Missouri suggested extending the bill to cover the commissary general, chief engineer, and chief of ordnance as well. The bill went to committee and was sent to the House.[31]

The next day in the House, Miles reported on the bill and recommended it should be approved. Barksdale supported the extension to include the commissary, ordnance, and engineering chiefs. Miles opposed the amendment. Barksdale argued that the four offices were equally important. Foote objected to any amendment. The bill passed without amendment, and Davis responded with a veto once the Senate sent up its version.[32]

A week later the House introduced a bill to make the surgeon general a brigadier general. Again Davis struck with a veto. On the same day he returned a bill regarding the building of warships, claiming it afforded insufficient discretion for the secretary of war. Davis also returned an act to provide relief for the Confederate States Bible Society, concluding that Congress did not have the authority to use government funds for repaying civilians whose property may have been damaged or destroyed through acts of war.[33] What chemistry there was between Davis and Congress seemed to have broken down completely. The chemistry between senators wasn't so positive, either. Nothing, it would seem, was destined to get done anytime soon.

On the day of the battle of Antietam, September 17, House members passed a resolution requesting that the Judiciary Committee organize a Supreme Court. A week passed, and then the Senate got involved. Benjamin Hill of Georgia, chair of the Judiciary Committee, proposed taking up the Supreme Court bill. Edward Sparrow opposed the motion, feeling any such court would be too powerful over the states. Louis Wigfall was strongly in favor of organizing the court. "There should be some tribunal to decide questions between the States and the Confederate States," he said. After further debate the topic was postponed. The next day the debate flared again but was then postponed. As with many topics, nothing would be resolved at present because of the divisive split between viewpoints. And Union generals had no plan to pause until the Confederacy was ready with its paperwork.[34]

On September 12 Davis asked the advice of the Senate on military reappointments, reminding senators that the sixth article of the Constitution had something to say about the appointments that had already been made: "All the officers appointed by the [Provisional Government] shall remain in office until their successors are appointed and qualified, or the offices are abolished." On September 23 the Senate debated renominations and how they should be made.

This was a sensitive issue because it allowed a weeding out of undesirable officers whose commissions were carried over from the Provisional Congress, and many of these officers had powerful advocates in Congress. Little was resolved despite the intensity of debate.

The same issues dragged on through autumn. On October 10 Davis requested an extra Executive Session of the Senate to process a backlog of pending nominations. These were simply referred to the Judiciary Committee. On the same day a bill allowing the president to make recess appointments, subject to later confirmation, passed in the Senate but failed in the House.[35]

Also in October a long debate erupted in the Senate over the confirmation of Joseph R. Davis as a brigadier general. Aside from being the president's nephew, Davis had a serviceable record in the army, having entered as a Mississippi captain. By the summer of 1861, the younger Davis was commissioned colonel and joined his uncle's staff; this apparent nepotism upset many congressmen. After considerable argument the Senate confirmed Joseph Davis as a brigadier general by a vote of thirteen to six. The Senate also argued over the confirmations of others of Davis's friends, including John Pemberton, who would become famous as the defender of Vicksburg, and Henry Heth, who would end up as a trusted lieutenant of Robert E. Lee's. The confirmation of Pemberton as a lieutenant general was shot down thirteen to five, with Sparrow and Wigfall voting for and Robert M. T. Hunter against the motion. The confirmation of Heth as major general also failed, Hunter, Sparrow, and Wigfall all voting for disapproval. On October 13, 1862, however, Pemberton's confirmation was reconsidered and approved, with Wigfall still holding out. Such was how they spent their days.

With troop shortages a big factor in the minds of everyone during this summer and autumn of battle, a new, almost unspoken subject arose in the arena of Confederate politics. Along Antietam Creek, west of Frederick, Maryland, the bloodiest single day of the war had occurred on September 17. Lee's Army of Northern Virginia clashed with McClellan's Army of the Potomac, sending 4,808 men to their graves, with another 21,000 wounded or missing. The Union infantry struck southward into Lee's Rebels early in the morning, thrusting forward in savage attacks, and heavy artillery and infantry battles raged along a huge line of battle all day. In the end the Confederates, endangered and forced back, were reinforced late in the afternoon and counterattacked handsomely. But at nightfall they abandoned the field and retreated southward, ending what was effectively a gigantic raid onto Northern soil. The battle, a strategic victory for the Yankees, had enabled President Lincoln to issue the preliminary Emancipation Proclamation. Shocked Confederate politicians were outraged at the freeing of slaves who, in their point of view, were theirs and living in their nation. On October 1 the Confederate House issued a response to Lincoln: "Resolved that after the first day of January 1863, no officer of the Lincolnite army or navy ought to be captured alive, and if so captured should be immediately hung." The resolution was sent to committee, and the next day a final resolution was drafted. It included the inflammatory clause, "All slaves taken in arms against the Confederate States shall be delivered to the authority of the State in which they were taken, to be punished or otherwise dealt with according to the law of such State or States." The final response continued, "Every white person who shall act as a commissioned or non-commissioned officer, commanding negroes or mulattoes in arms against the Confederate States, or who shall arm, organize, or prepare negroes or mulattoes for military service against the Confederate States, or who shall voluntarily aid negroes or mulattoes in any military enterprise, attack, or conflict, in such service, shall, if captured, be put to death by hanging."

In the Senate Semmes declared the Emancipation Proclamation was "leveled against the citizens of the Confederate States, and as such is a gross violation of the usages of civilized warfare, an outrage upon private property and an invitation to a servile war, and therefore should be held up to the execration of mankind and counteracted by such severe retaliatory measures as, in the judgment of the president, may be best calculated to secure its withdrawal or arrest its execution." John Clark of Missouri thought the proclamation so shocking that he felt "every person found in arms against the Confederate Government and its institutions, on our soil, should be put to death." Likewise, Gustavus Henry of Tennessee believed the time had come to "declare a war of extermination upon every foe that puts his foot upon our soil, no matter what the bloodshed it may cause."[36]

O N the battlefield the bloody war certainly did continue. The awful struggles of the Antietam campaign in Maryland, which soon would be shown in battlefield photographs in exhibitions in American cities, would shock the American nation with up-close evidence of death and woe. The scale of the carnage seemingly knew no bounds.

In Mississippi, at Corinth, Confederates under Earl Van Dorn and Sterling Price battled fiercely with Yankees commanded by Maj. Gen. William S. Rosecrans, leaving a body-strewn town with the Yankee army pursuing the retreating Southerners. As the year wound down, a bloody fight took place in the far west at Prairie Grove, Arkansas, as a genuine brawl shaped up at Fredericksburg, Virginia, between Robert E. Lee's Army of Northern Virginia and the Yankee army commanded by Maj. Gen. Ambrose Burnside. After hellish fighting in which the Northerners attacked across the Rappahannock River and uphill through the town of Fredericksburg, the battle accomplished little but more death.

The bloody horrors of the battlefield touched everyone on a personal level. Casualties meant losses of sons and fathers and brothers in thousands of families, and if your own family didn't lose someone, you certainly knew a family who did. Even Howell Cobb, who had served as the Confederacy's provisional president, had to write his wife a heartfelt letter on the day of Antietam. "My telegraph from Richmond will have informed you of the death of your brother [Col. John B. Lamar]," he penned, "who fell in the hottest of the fight, struggling to rally our broken columns. He lived until the next day and suffered no great pain. . . . I need hardly, my dear wife, say how my own heart has bled and how it flows with sympathy for you in this trying hour."[37]

And death had not finished with the Cobb family. The talented soldier and attorney Thomas R. R. Cobb, who had helped his brother in the early days of the Provisional Congress, fell mortally wounded at Fredericksburg as a colonel, never having been confirmed as a brigadier general (as he often is reported to have been). Having written a tender letter informing his wife of the death, Cobb now received one from a fellow officer. "In performing the sad office of having sent to you today a dispatch of Major Lamar Cobb [Howell Cobb's son] informing you of the death of your noble and gallant brother, I cannot refrain from expressing to you my heartfelt sympathy in this terrible bereavement. His death has cast a gloom over this city."[38]

Amid the wreckage one thing was clear: now it was Lee's army, and the soldiers adored their commander, whose beard and gray hair made him look grandfatherly and wise. Gone were the barbs about Lee's timidity in western Virginia; he was now seen as a magnificent leader — by his boss, most of all. "Too much praise cannot be bestowed upon the skill and daring of the commanding General who conceived, or the valor and hardihood of the troops who executed, the brilliant movement," wrote Davis following the Second Bull Run campaign.[39] For his part Lee now had to command the battlefield but also play politics. In touch with Congress as well as with the president, Lee lobbied for help for his army, the preeminent force of the South. "I have not yet heard from you with regard to the new Texas regiments which you promised to endeavour to raise for this army," he inquired of Louis Wigfall shortly after Antietam. "I need them much. I rely on those we have in all tight places and fear I have to call upon them too often. . . . With a few more such regiments . . . I could feel much more confident of the results of the campaign."[40]

⸺

THROUGHOUT all the military actions, Jefferson Davis persisted with his micromanagement, using his War Department chieftain like an executive secretary. By November 1862 the toll was too much for George Wythe Randolph, who suddenly resigned his post. Randolph had been frustrated not only by Davis's henpecking, but also because he fundamentally disagreed with the president on grand strategy. Davis's primary strategy was an offensive-defensive one, in which he could maximize the effect of interior supply lines and lines of movement and use inferior Southern resources against Northern strength.

In this way Southern armies would employ men and matériel conservatively, retreating in the face of superior forces. They would choose the great moments for boldness on their own, as Lee had with the Antietam campaign. Chief among the disagreements between Randolph and Davis was where the strategy would best be employed. The secretary repeatedly emphasized the western theater, whereas Davis focused mostly on the east. In the west Pemberton and Bragg were not succeeding against Grant and Rosecrans, and this frustrated Randolph almost beyond measure. When Davis belittled Randolph's ideas about rectifying the situation during October and the first days of November, the secretary bailed.[41]

Davis seemed shocked. "As you have thus without notice and in terms excluding inquiry retired from the post of a constitutional advisor to the Executive of the Confederacy," he wrote, "nothing remains but to give you this formal notice of the acceptance of your resignation."[42] Others seemed shocked, too. "Usually when a cabinet member resigns," wrote Navy Secretary Stephen Mallory, "he remains in possession of the post until the installation of his successor; but Genl. Randolph walked out of it on Saturday, leaving much business that he might have concluded on that day, unattended to. . . . The fact is that the Presdt's familiarity with army matters induces his desire to mingle in them all & to control them & this desire is augmented by the fear that details may be wrongly managed without his constant supervision."[43]

For his new war secretary, Jefferson Davis turned to another Virginian, James A. Seddon, an attorney and former U.S. representative who had served in the Confederate Congress. Seddon, Davis knew, would be content to be subservient. He suffered from neuralgia, was an Episcopalian, and a staunch follower of John C. Calhoun. In 1845 he had married Sallie Bruce, a daughter in a very wealthy family, who bought for them the mansion on the corner of Clay and Twelfth streets, which later became the Confederate White House. Seddon was a staunch defender of state rights but also could remember very clearly for whom he worked. He established residence at the Spotswood Hotel to be near the government offices, while his family lived at an estate known as Sabot Hill, about twenty miles up the James River.

Seddon's office was in Mechanic's Hall, on the southwestern corner of Capitol Square. Assistant Secretary of War John A. Campbell and Clerk John B. Jones worked alongside him in the two-room war office. Seddon concentrated on recruiting men and gathering supplies, while the president handled most of the strategy and personnel details. By this time it was becoming clear to Richmond's politicians that Seddon, Judah Benjamin, Lee, and Bragg were the president's closest friends — which meant they were good candidates as potential enemies.[44]

Some had doubts about the new secretary. "I see that Mr. Randolph has resigned," wrote Albert Bledsoe, who had recently left his post as assistant secretary of war. "I have taken up my pen to suggest, for your consideration, Genl. Polk as his successor. . . . Seddon would be a failure. A man of fine parts, a most estimable character, an accomplished gentleman, and as fine a patriot as ever lived; but his *physique* is too feeble. The labors of the office would kill him in a month."[45]

After one month in office, Seddon was still breathing, but hard; he faced considerable challenges spread across the whole landscape. One missive, from Louis Wigfall, underscores the nature of what Seddon faced. "I have just received a letter from Genl. Johnston which contains gloomy forebodings as to our future in the west," Wigfall advised. "Pemberton he says has fallen back before a superior force & he [Johnston] is ordered to reinforce him with troops from Bragg's command. Consider the positions of these armies. As Pemberton falls back he will be each day one march further from Bragg. Grant is between them with, I suppose, a superior force to either. If he falls upon either before their junction may he not destroy him & then turn upon the other?"[46]

Such difficult challenges on the battlefield sparked a strange twist in Congress from one of its most unusual members, Henry Foote. Why not simply send peace commissioners to Washington to see if they would call off the whole war? Foote suggested negotiating a "just and honourable" peace. "I have but little confidence, I confess, sir," said Foote, "in the wisdom and sagacity, the statesmanship, or the true manliness of spirit, of Mr. Lincoln and his deluded cabinet counselors," said Foote. But he still felt the effort worthwhile:

Jefferson Davis faced a nearly impossible task as leader of the Confederacy: forging a group of political separatists into a unified team, which ultimately miserably failed. *National Archives and Records Administration*

The president's wife, Varina Howell Davis, led the Richmond wartime social scene even as some aristocratic women scorned her and criticized her pedigree. *The Museum of the Confederacy*

Richmond's central, monumental building was the Virginia State Capitol, a fantastic Greek Revival structure with stunning porticoes finished with Ionic columns. The cornerstone was laid in 1785, after the structure had been designed by Thomas Jefferson. The Confederate Senate met in a second-floor committee room adjacent to the governor's room, above the House of Delegates Chamber; the House met in what is now termed the Old Senate Chamber, on the first floor. *Library of Congress*

The Bruce-Lancaster home near Twelfth and Clay streets hosted Vice President Alexander Stephens when he frequented Richmond in 1861 and 1862. The camera's viewpoint in this 1865 image is from a position near the White House; the sentry box housing the president's guard stands between the two houses. *Library of Congress*

Gruff, audacious Louis T. Wigfall started the war as a Jefferson Davis confidant and transformed into the president's most vocal critic in the Senate. *Library of Congress*

The Confederacy's vice president, Alexander H. Stephens, was a sickly, frail man who never weighed more than ninety pounds and, according to one newspaperman, "looked like a freak." Although charged with presiding over the Confederate Senate, Stephens spent most of the war at home in Georgia, bedridden. *Library of Congress*

Dedicated on Washington's birthday in 1858, the monumental equestrian statue of George Washington gracing Capitol Hill served as a rallying point for Confederates during the war. Others claimed the statue issued a warning, as the general pointed his arm toward the state penitentiary. *Library of Congress*

Three long blocks northeast of Capitol Square, at Twelfth and Clay streets, stands the John Brockenbrough House, now known as the White House of the Confederacy. This lovely mansion, built in 1818 and lived in by several occupants before the war — including would-be Confederate Secretary of War James A. Seddon — was purchased in 1861 by the city of Richmond as a residence for the Jefferson Davis family. *Library of Congress*

As chairman of the Military Affairs Committee, South Carolina Congressman William Porcher Miles was the most powerful man in the House of Representatives. He disagreed with Davis over a variety of issues, including the need for a Supreme Court and the suspension of the writ of habeas corpus. *The Museum of the Confederacy*

A Virginian who thought like President Davis on most issues, Robert M. T. Hunter was a slow, methodical planner who became Confederate secretary of state and later a senator in Richmond. He staunchly supported state rights and disagreed violently with Davis over the matter of freeing and arming slaves. *Library of Congress*

Henry Stuart Foote was one of the most explosive characters in the Civil War South. In 1847 he fought with and nearly dueled Jefferson Davis at a Washington tavern. In Richmond as a Confederate congressman, he claimed to be a "voice of the people" as he constantly attacked the administration. His troublemaking career in the House came to an end when he sneaked away from Richmond on a self-appointed peace mission behind the Yankee lines. *Library of Congress*

South Carolina's celebrated "father of secession," Robert Barnwell Rhett was the consummate Southern "fire-eater." A former U. S. senator and owner of the influential *Charleston Mercury*, Rhett was spurned in Montgomery in trying to seize leadership of the Confederacy. He attacked Davis with a passion before leaving Richmond to criticize the administration in angry editorials in the *Mercury*, terming Davis "criminally incompetent." *Library of Congress*

A large man who lived large, Robert A. Toombs was a Georgia politician who was considered too radical for the Confederate presidency. His hard drinking in Montgomery during the genesis of the Confederacy sealed his fate: Davis named him secretary of state for a nation that had no foreign relations. He tired of this and turned to a generalship in the field before returning to Georgia and creating a full-time job of criticizing Davis and his administration. *Library of Congress*

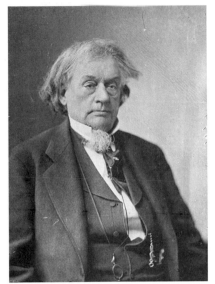

This panoramic view of central Richmond includes part of the "burnt district," the territory of the evacuation fire, and was made by Alexander Gardner on April 6, 1865. The Capitol is visible on the horizon; the Spotswood Hotel stands in front of it. This view was made from Gamble's Hill. *Cook Collection, Valentine Museum*

The Stars and Stripes again flies from the staff atop the Capitol in this Richmond image taken across the James River in April 1865. The burnt district lies between the Capitol and the river; the Customs House, where Jefferson Davis had his office, stands right of the Capitol. *Library of Congress*

Alexander Gardner's image of the burnt district on April 6 includes picturesque destruction from the evacuation fire. The size of the inferno was staggering. *Library of Congress*

A view of the city from the Gamble's Hill area reveals the skeletons of buildings that stood throughout the war only to fall at war's end. Visible on the horizon are the Capitol and Customs House, as well as church steeples. *Library of Congress*

Richmond's City Hall (right) stands on Broad Street as a magnificent Greek Revival structure, built in 1815. The Broad Street Methodist Church is at left. In the foreground of this 1865 image are Union occupation troops resting amid stacked rifles. *Library of Congress*

City Hall housed all the functions of the city government during wartime Richmond. The city grew by several factors as soldiers and office seekers swelled in from the countryside, creating impossible problems that would frustrate the population throughout the struggle. *Library of Congress*

The "brains of the Confederacy" and "Jeff Davis's right hand," Judah P. Benjamin was born in the British West Indies, the child of Sephardic Jewish settlers. A close friend of Jefferson Davis's, he served as attorney general and then secretary of war in the Confederacy. He quarreled with P. G. T. Beauregard and Stonewall Jackson and was chastised regularly by the Confederate Congress. Benjamin resigned under intense pressure but was then named secretary of state. He was the most influential Jewish politician in American history. *National Archives and Records Administration*

Stephen R. Mallory, born in Trinidad, was a Floridian chosen for political balance to be Jefferson Davis's secretary of the navy. He began with a navy consisting of twelve small ships. Bitterly attacked by members of Congress for inefficiency and lack of aggressiveness, he weathered the assaults and lasted throughout the entire war. *National Archives and Records Administration*

Aristocratic Richmonder Joseph C. Mayo served as the city's mayor during the war. He faced the task of placating civilians in a rapidly growing city that was often short of supplies and under a government that seemingly didn't care. In April 1863 a "bread riot" erupted in the city, with more than one thousand assembling and protesting the lack of available food, ransacking stores, and screaming in anger. Mayo appealed to the crowd as Jefferson Davis passed out a few coins to try to suppress the rioters, who eventually dispersed. *Cook Collection, Valentine Museum*

Alabama lawyer Leroy P. Walker was chosen as the Confederacy's first secretary of war for balance of representation across the South after the state's two most prominent politicians turned down the office. Jefferson Davis made all the decisions and treated Walker mostly as a figurehead; after seven months Walker no longer could bear the arrangement, and he resigned to take up a short-lived military command. He then returned to practicing law in Alabama. *Library of Congress*

A grandson of Thomas Jefferson, George Wythe Randolph drafted Virginia's conscription law and, in 1862, became Jefferson Davis's secretary of war. He constantly advised Davis to attend to battles in the west, with only partial success. Frustrated with Davis's reluctance to follow his advice, Randolph resigned in late 1862 and two years later left for Europe to ride out the rest of the war. *Library of Congress*

Another Virginian, James A. Seddon, held the longest tenure as Confederate secretary of war, from late 1862 to early 1865. Inexperienced as an administrator and lacking military knowledge, he nevertheless served very capably and weathered criticism from nearly all quarters, save for his good relationship with the president. After the war he "considered his life to be a complete failure." *National Archives and Records Administration*

The U.S. Post Office and Customs House, a Tuscan-Italianate edifice constructed in 1858, stands on Richmond's Main Street, between Tenth and Eleventh streets. The Confederacy took over this building and used it as the Treasury Department building and as an executive office for Jefferson Davis. The Confederate State Department met on the building's second floor, which also hosted cabinet sessions. The Confederate president's office, where much of the business of the war took place, existed on the third floor of this building, facing the Capitol. *Library of Congress*

The Spotswood Hotel, newly built when the war commenced, was Richmond's place to see and be seen. Jefferson Davis and his family lived here until a home could be found, as did cabinet members and many congressmen and senators. After the Confederate victory of First Manassas, Jefferson Davis made a stirring speech from a window of the hotel. *Library of Congress*

The consummate Virginian, Robert E. Lee opposed secession until his own state left the Union. He began the war inauspiciously, serving as a general in western Virginia and in South Carolina and then as adviser to the president in Richmond before Joseph E. Johnston's wounding thrust him into command of the Army of Northern Virginia. Lee's performance in the field was legendary; distrustful of diluting his own power, Davis resisted naming Lee general-in-chief until near war's end, when it was too late to make any difference. *Cook Collection, Valentine Museum*

The Lee Home at 707 East Franklin Street in Richmond housed Mary Custis Lee and various family members from early 1864 to the end of the war. Lee arrived at the house after Appomattox and stayed until September 1865, when the family moved to Lexington. This image is from 1865. *Library of Congress*

Braxton Bragg, one of six full generals in the Confederacy, survived scathing attacks on his generalship due to his friendship with Jefferson Davis. A North Carolinian, he fought at Shiloh, invaded Kentucky, and clashed with Yankees at Stones River and Chickamauga and Chattanooga. Following harsh criticism, he was summoned to Richmond to serve as Davis's military adviser during the last year of the war. Davis's loyalty to his friends sometimes caused severe damage, as was the case with Bragg. *Library of Congress*

Like Bragg, Joseph E. Johnston suffers from a record stained with frequent criticism. This Virginia general, another close friend of Lee's, commanded the Confederate Army of Northern Virginia before being wounded at Seven Pines. However, in the first weeks of war, he had already become outraged at Jefferson Davis for ranking him lower than he believed just. He had a testy relationship with the administration throughout his whole career — from First Manassas to his surrender to Sherman at Durham Station, North Carolina. *National Archives and Records Administration*

The senior general officer of the Confederacy, Samuel Cooper served as adjutant general and inspector general and was characterized by War Department insiders as a "glorified clerk." He never wore a uniform, seemed dull and was distracted by trivial matters, and lived in a cramped rooming house in Richmond, his family often away. He was a paperwork general whom two famous Richmond diarists both thought simply "incompetent," but Davis could trust him, and so he stayed throughout the whole war. *Library of Congress*

The first great hero of the war, P. G. T. Beauregard drove the Yankees from Fort Sumter and helped to retain the field at First Manassas. Relations between Beauregard and Davis soured because the general wanted an independent command, and Beauregard was subordinate to others. He fought all over the western theater and was never happy with his treatment by the president. *National Archives and Records Administration*

A Kentuckian who relocated to Texas, John Bell Hood was known as an aggressive fighter from the early days of the war. He was also a close friend of Senator Louis T. Wigfall, who looked after him. Hood rose through the command ranks and accompanied his Texas Brigade as it screamed the rebel yell into attacks. He lost the use of his left arm at Gettysburg and lost his right leg at Chickamauga. After leading a foolhardy campaign in Tennessee late in the war, he was forgotten by Davis. *Library of Congress*

Son of a brigadier general of the War of 1812, Marylander John H. Winder was a harsh man who drew a difficult assignment as provost marshal of Richmond. As such, Winder tried to keep law and order in a town that tripled in size over the course of the war. He was hated by Richmonders for trying to restrict too much and finally was sent to Andersonville Prison in Georgia to clean it up, but couldn't. He died in 1865, before Federal authorities could capture him, thus saving a trial and hanging by the Yankees for mistreating Union prisoners. *Library of Congress*

At times Kentuckian John C. Breckinridge was the only politician in the South who seemed to keep his head. A former U.S. vice president under James Buchanan, Breckinridge became a general and fought at Shiloh, Vicksburg, Chickamauga, and Chattanooga. Moving east, he checked the Yankees at Cold Harbor before returning to Richmond as the Confederacy collapsed, in February 1865. As the last Confederate secretary of war, Breckinridge judged the situation hopeless, so tired from the struggle he termed himself "an extinct volcano." *National Archives and Records Administration*

A North Carolina professor of mathematics, D. H. Hill was a bitter, combative, and aggressive general officer. He fought in one of the first land battles of the war at Big Bethel and went on to the Virginia peninsula, Antietam, and Chickamauga. He criticized his superiors and got entangled in a grave dispute with Braxton Bragg over a petition requesting removal of Bragg from army command. Davis supported his friend Bragg, and Hill's career was ruined. He spent the rest of the war trying to clear his name. *Library of Congress*

Robert E. Lee's senior corps commander and most trusted lieutenant was Georgia-born James Longstreet. This corps commander led his troops well throughout the war, though he has been blamed by hard-core Virginians for the loss at Gettysburg and everything else that ailed the Confederate cause. *Library of Congress*

Thomas J. Jackson, known as "Stonewall" ever since First Manassas, was the South's great hero general of the first half of the war. A Virginian and friend of Robert E. Lee's, Stonewall set a spirit of aggressiveness the South felt it needed for victory. His mortal wounding at Chancellorsville and subsequent death stunned the South and coincided with a strategic backslide that saw Union victories at Gettysburg and Vicksburg. *National Archives and Records Administration*

As a young Virginia cavalry officer, James E. B. (Jeb) Stuart epitomized the hope of Confederate civilians. He served gallantly and rose to major general over the course of First Manassas, the Peninsular campaign, Chancellorsville, and Gettysburg. At Yellow Tavern outside Richmond in May 1864, however, Stuart was mortally wounded, and he died the next day in Richmond. *Library of Congress*

Hollywood Cemetery, begun in 1847, stands west of the city on high ground overlooking the James River. It served as the principal burying ground for Confederate soldiers returned to Richmond, including Jeb Stuart, in early 1864. Stuart's first gravestone stands starkly in an 1865 image. *Library of Congress*

The Tredegar Iron Works, the most significant iron factory in the South, was chartered in 1837. The factory operated throughout the war, supplying much of the armament of the Confederacy, under Brig. Gen. Joseph R. Anderson, the firm's president. The canal bridge in this April 1865 image leads to Brown's Island, site of Confederate ordnance experiments. *Library of Congress*

Located on the James River along the eastern quarter of the city, Rocketts Landing served as the city's wharf and docks. This view, taken in April 1865, shows the Confederate Navy Yard on the opposite shore and Union naval vessels anchored downstream. Lincoln docked here on his journey into the fallen city. *Library of Congress*

In 1862 Confederate officials commandeered a variety of warehouses to serve as prisons, housing the swell of Yankees captured during the Peninsular campaign. The most famous was Libby Prison, which contained Union officers. A notable escape occurred here in 1864, before the warehouse was torn down brick by brick and — in 1892 — rebuilt at the Chicago World's Fair. *Cook Collection, Valentine Museum*

Rubble in the burnt district in Richmond, photographed in April 1865, testifies to the wanton destruction within the capital as the end of the war came. *Library of Congress*

In sheer magnanimity, we are bound to offer terms of peace to the enemy. With us alone can a proposition of peace originate, without the deepest dishonour. . . . Mr. Speaker, I know well that I shall be denounced in certain quarters for my present conduct. I shall probably be charged with excessive moderation, and perchance even of pusillanimity. I shall not be at all surprised if all who are specially interested in the continuance of the war shall resort even to ridicule and denunciation.

John Wilcox of Texas asked if the Confederacy didn't already have great commissioners in Robert E. Lee and Stonewall Jackson. Hines Holt of Georgia offered a modified resolution, similar to Foote's. The president, on hearing of all this, must have simply shaken his head.[47]

As if his worries weren't enough, Jefferson Davis spent the final weeks of 1862 with a growing level of noise from a collection of Southern governors who felt he should do more for each of them — much more. Often he could do little other than simply thinking on paper. "I have not been unmindful of the condition of the Eastern portion of your State and can make allowance for the anxiety felt by those who reside there," the president wrote newly elected governor Zebulon B. Vance of North Carolina.[48] Davis's thoughts about Joe Brown, who carped at him, were no more specific. "Nothing could be more unfortunate," wrote the president, "not only for the success of the cause in which we are engaged, but also for the future reputation of the great State of Georgia than any other conflict between the authorities of that State and the Confederate Government."[49]

He was mildly reassuring to Governor John Shorter of Alabama that the Richmond government sympathized with the potential loss of Mobile to the Yankees. "I entirely concur with you as to the immense importance of Mobile and the adjacent country," Davis penned, "and the unfortunate results that would follow its fall. I have felt long and deeply the hazard of its condition and an anxious desire to secure it, but have vainly looked for an adequate force which could be spared from other localities."[50] Shorter was outraged, feeling left alone by the Richmond government. Governor John Milton of Florida also received vague assurances of support. "Your letter of the 10th ult., calling my attention to the dangers now threatening the State of Florida," wrote Davis, "and asking for additional forces and munitions of war, was submitted to the perusal of the Secretary of War and Genl. Lee. . . . General Lee reports he cannot send the Florida regiments home; and we have no other reinforcements that could be spared without injustice to other sections equally important and equally threatened." Could the national government of the Confederacy do much of anything for Confederate States that existed away from the central war zone of the east? It seemed to many the answer was a clear no.[51]

Yet the governors still pleaded for help from Richmond, which in turn, actually needed all the help it could get from the states. "Can you not spare us a few thousand arms for this State?" wrote Francis Lubbock of Texas, increasingly seeming an island in the far west. "If we could get back the old rifles & shot guns that have been cast off by our men, & which we trust have been laid aside for more improved ones, we would feel better able to defend our state."[52] This, when the Confederate army begged for manpower.

Near the end of 1862, Davis begged the governors to help the Confederacy as a whole. He wrote asking them for special cooperation with enrolling conscripts, restoring to the army all officers absent without leave or who had recovered from disability, and sending to the Confederacy all supplies not absolutely essential to home state use. He also begged the governors to enact legislation that "will enable the Governors to command slave labor to the extent which may be required in the prosecution of works conducive to the public defence."[53]

The war was a desperate struggle, and the resources of the Confederacy were stretched badly. Yet those who should have known better seemed to have blind faith in the Cause and self-interest. They still felt that victory was inevitable. "Lee has an army which I believe is invincible," wrote the politician-turned-soldier Lawrence Keitt.[54] Indeed.

JOCKEYING FOR POSITION

WITH the New Year the topic on everyone's mind — in the South and the North — was exactly what Abraham Lincoln's Emancipation Proclamation would mean to the country and to the world. "The Emancipation proclamation upsets the peaceful and contented condition of the slaves in the Confederacy," wrote Davis. "[The black soldiers of the North] are encouraged to assassinate their masters. . . . All commissioned officers of such assassins, hereafter captured by our forces, will be turned over to State authorities to be dealt with as criminals inciting servile insurrection."[1]

By now the toll of tens of thousands of deaths had saddened, shocked, and grieved every family in the land either directly or by acquaintance. Soldiers in the army and sailors in the navy felt a sad, sinking feeling that they might not return to see another New Year's Day at home. There was good reason for such dread. As 1863 opened, with Congress convening again in Richmond, the sounds of battle spread thickly across the fields and in the woods of Tennessee. Farther east the principal army of the Union, the Army of the Potomac, was entrenched in the hills around Fredericksburg, Virginia, and Robert E. Lee's Confederates could pause to rest for a short time —

but only a short time. Other threats from the Union army and navy existed. Along the Mississippi River the stronghold of Vicksburg was endangered, and Union forces slowly occupied more of the Atlantic coastline. Amid these conflicts many in the South began to consider geography in a new way: east versus west. Which area was more important? Which should garner the preeminent resources? Which should the Richmond government bolster most quickly?

But despite the challenges the Rebels had plenty of reason to hope. The Confederacy's military necessities were still far different from those of the Yankees. Rebel armies were fighting essentially a defensive strategy, hoping that Union citizens would grow weary of war and that Britain or France would recognize the burgeoning Southern nation. As long as the Federals had to attack southward, sustaining heavy losses, and as long as the daring chances taken by commanders such as Lee and Jackson paid off, the Confederacy could look forward to increasing odds for a peace movement and an armistice. The chances looked good during the first few weeks of 1863, and during the coming months, they would look even better. In both theaters, east and west, short-term military successes seemed to favor the Confederacy. The South had the momentum and the spirit. Lee's Army of Northern Virginia had been turned back from Northern soil the previous autumn, but it had scored a stunning victory over the disorganized and apparently dazed Federal army at Fredericksburg just two weeks before New Year's Day 1863. Braxton Bragg's inconclusive campaign in Tennessee had, nevertheless, upset the Federal army under Rosecrans, and Bragg had the notion to telegraph President Davis from the battlefield at Stones River that God had "granted us a victory." In the far west John Pemberton seemed to be holding off a succession of attacks aimed at capturing Vicksburg, the Confederate stronghold on the Mississippi.

For the armies in the field, the first weeks of cold winter in 1863 were quiet. As the Confederacy anticipated a spring thaw and a new series of victories, the aims of the war were slowly changing in Washington. The issuance of Lincoln's Emancipation Proclamation on New Year's Day transformed the struggle in the minds of many Yankees into a holy war for freedom. No longer was it simply a fight for the continuance of the Federal government, but now was for a nobler, higher cause.

Yet in the ranks the conflict remained earthbound, a soup of mud and blood. "In every direction around men were digging graves and burying the dead," wrote David Hunter Strother, a western Virginian colonel in the Federal army, following the battle of Antietam. He continued:

> Many [dead soldiers] were black as Negroes, heads and faces hideously swelled, covered with dust until they looked like clods. Killed during the charge and flight, their attitudes were wild and frightful. One hung upon a fence killed as he was climbing it. One lay with hands wildly clasped as if in prayer. From among these loathsome earth-soiled vestiges of humanity, the soldiers were still picking out some that had life left and carrying them in on stretchers to our surgeons. All the time some picket firing was going on from the wood on the Hagerstown turnpike near the white church.[2]

Such terrible losses hung heavily over both sides. In Washington Lincoln had removed Maj. Gen. Ambrose E. Burnside from command of the Army of the Potomac following the disaster at Fredericksburg and a pointless, muddy march, but he had no ideal replacement in mind. In desperation Lincoln turned to Maj. Gen. Joseph Hooker, a brash, forty-eight-year-old, hard-drinking egotist. Lincoln wrote Hooker, "I have heard, in such a way as to believe it, of your recently saying that both the Army and the Government needed a Dictator. Of course it was not for this, but in spite of it, that I have given you the command. . . . Beware of rashness, but with energy and sleepless vigilance go forward and give us victories."[3] The great eastern Union army had a new chief.

Between January 10 and 11, Yankees under Maj. Gen. John A. McClernand and Acting Rear Adm. David Dixon Porter attacked the Confederate stronghold, Fort Hindman, at Arkansas Post, Arkansas. There, on the Arkansas River, some thirty-two thousand men together with three ironclads and six gunboats assaulted the fort, which was garrisoned by three brigades commanded by Brig. Gen.

Thomas J. Churchill and Col. John W. Dunnington. The action demonstrated the value of river gunboats in shelling a position, as Porter's naval forces contributed substantially to the fort's capitulation following a murderous bombardment. The result was a surrender of more than five thousand Confederates, a major loss to the South.

In the east little of note occurred until March 17, when a cavalry battle erupted at Kelly's Ford, Virginia. Three weeks before the battle, Confederate Brig. Gen. Fitzhugh Lee's cavalry had stunned a series of Federal outposts, capturing 150 prisoners. Lee left a note for a Federal division commander, his old friend Brig. Gen. William Woods Averell, asking him to "return the favor and bring some coffee." Averell arrived at Kelly's Ford on the Rappahannock before sunrise, and the battle was joined at about noon. Both mounted and dismounted, the troopers fought all afternoon, the Yankees repulsing Lee's attacks. The battle ended inconclusively except that Union cavalry had withstood their legendary opponents with great skill.

During recent battles in the last several months of fighting and maneuvering, several Confederate leaders had begun to stand out. They were not the army's top leaders, but they were important young generals who were making their presence felt strongly. Following his heroic actions in the Shenandoah Valley campaign of 1862, at the battle of Second Manassas, at Antietam, and at Fredericksburg, Stonewall Jackson had become the most celebrated of the bunch. On the cusp of his thirty-ninth birthday, Jackson was now a lieutenant general and commanded the second army corps of the Army of Northern Virginia. He engendered a great fighting spirit in the South that would grow as the weeks rolled on.

Jackson's brother-in-law, Daniel Harvey Hill, was a cantankerous South Carolina native who had been a professor of mathematics and commandant of the Military College of Charlotte in North Carolina before the war. Two years senior to Jackson, D. H. Hill began the war as a colonel of North Carolina troops before being commissioned a brigadier general and moving around to a voluminous number of assignments in part because of his argumentative persona. Now a major general and veteran of leading troops at Antietam, Hill had quit the army on January 1 in a huff but was quickly talked into withdrawing his resignation. Hill would continue to bounce around the army over the coming weeks, serving as something of a barometer of the relationships between army officers and the War Department and the importance given to various theaters of the war. Plagued by poor relations with the War Department, he drew their least glamorous assignments.

And then there was John Bell Hood. The Kentucky native, just thirty-two years old, had served on the Texas frontier before commanding Texas infantry for the Confederacy. Wounded on the peninsula at Gaines's Mill, Hood subsequently led troops at Second Manassas, Antietam, and Fredericksburg and was commissioned a major general late in 1862. Young, yet appearing beyond his years due to sunken eyes and a full beard, Hood had a growing reputation as a hard and reckless fighter who left everything on the field. His adventures also would prove to serve as a measurement of Congress's involvement with military matters.

═══

Congress had reconvened in Richmond on January 12, 1863, with this third session of the First Congress scheduled to remain in convention until May 1. Many of the old areas of dispute and argument would again rear their heads, with other, new areas of concern added to them. One of the fresher topics was the possibility of foreign intervention — something that Davis had dreamed about since the shots were fired at Sumter. If only England or France would come to the aid of the South, he believed, the war might draw to a speedy close with Southern independence intact. And without foreign monetary support, it seemed the Confederacy would go broke sooner rather than later. "The increasing public debt, the great augmentation in the volume of the currency, with its necessary concomitant of extravagant prices for all articles of consumption" was devastating, said the president.[4] On January 17 Davis furnished the Congress with lengthy arguments for recognition of the Confederacy by Britain, France, Italy, and Russia to increase foreign trade and to help break the blockade.

But the new issues could not displace the old. The question of the Supreme Court had been postponed — again — back in September

1862, and senators now came out with heated vigor to resolve the issue. But the heat did not transform into light. Making no headway, senators argued heatedly over the salaries justices should receive and then adjourned.

Two days later the subject arose again. A much revised bill now included a controversial section proposing that a Confederate Supreme Court could review State Supreme Court decisions, allowing for state courts to employ precedents from United States court decisions. The matter was again tabled.[5]

It wouldn't remain tabled for long. On February 2 Wigfall declared that it was "the greatest misfortune that ever befell the country that a man of [John Marshall's] imperial genius and unspotted virtue should have been so long connected with the old Supreme Court." Other senators opposed the court for declaring constitutional the United States Bank, an act that strengthened Federal authority. If the Supreme Court bill should pass, several agreed, "the fatal stab would be given to our new Government."[6]

On and on it went. On February 5 James Phelan of Mississippi shouted that if Clement Clay's amendment repealing the ability to establish a Supreme Court were adopted, then "the same questions which dissolved the United States would be renewed under this Government."[7] On March 17 Alabaman William Yancey warned his fellow senators that power of the Supreme Court over state courts "would subvert and destroy the power of the States." Two days later the Supreme Court bill passed by a fourteen to eight margin and was sent to the House for consideration.[8] However, the bill was revised, and by March 28 another bill was introduced. No action was taken, and the whole affair dropped back into the arena of indefinite delays.

Meanwhile, an even greater shocker rose to the floor of the Senate. On February 5 the Senate heard a proposed amendment to the Confederate Constitution that would allow an aggrieved state to secede from the Confederacy. "It shall do so in peace," read the proposal, "but shall be entitled to its *pro rata* share of property and be liable for its *pro rata* share of public debt to be determined by negotiation." The idea was referred to the Judicial Committee. Two days later senators failed to recommend the amendment, and the whole thing was dropped as a dangerous idea.[9]

══

A SIDE from arguments about the Confederacy itself, the new session of Congress also entertained much disagreement over the army and its internal policies. From Davis's point of view, the Senate was becoming increasingly meddlesome about who should be commissioned in a particular grade or given a particular assignment in the field. No one was more so than Edward Sparrow, the Louisiana senator who chaired the Committee on Military Affairs. And yet Davis needed the Senate's approval for commissions, so he often acquiesced to their demands.[10]

As was always the case, many officers in the field felt they were not getting due recognition for services performed, and they often complained in letters to the president or to Congress. Even important politicians who had left Richmond to fight in the field complained heartily: "For five months I have been acting Brigadier," wrote South Carolinian Lawrence Keitt to Davis's nemesis, Louis Wigfall, "and want the commission of one. Genls. Beauregard, Ripley, Jordan, and Gist have recommended me. I now have under me all the guns on Sullivan's Island."[11] Even with Wigfall's support Keitt never would be commissioned a general.

Most senators felt Davis was not providing sufficient information in order to help other politicians work to commission their favorite officers into the army. They were right. From Davis's point of view, the senators were interfering far beyond their legal rights to confirm appointments by the president, so dragging his heels on providing specific information was wholly justified. On January 30 Sparrow requested that Davis submit a list of all regimental, brigade, and division commanders with commissions in the provisional army both under provisional and permanent governments. Six weeks passed without a response from the White House. By mid-March Sparrow resolved that it "is inexpedient for the Senate to confirm any more generals until a response is obtained from the President on the numbers of regiments, brigades, and divisions in the army." On March 19, 1863, Davis finally furnished a list of brigadier and major generals, but the tension would continue for months.

Army commanders in the field, meanwhile, asked for more and more slaves to use as common laborers for the army. "I trust some arrangement will be made at a very early date to secure a proper number of negro laborers, who should be promptly relieved at the expiration of the period for which they have been sent," Beauregard wrote South Carolina governor Milledge Bonham. "As it is, those negroes who come to work for 30 days, have been necessarily detained from 60 & 90 days, because none were sent to take their places in the works. . . . I have been subjected to the daily strenuous applications of owners to have their slaves released from the detail."[12]

Inevitably politicians and generals alike worried about both the possibility of Northern African Americans fighting in the field and the lack of troops in the South, some imagining that freeing and arming slaves might be necessary. But few mentioned such a radical idea publicly — at least yet. More so, the white Southern politicians were worried about their own inconveniences and those of their constituents.[13]

Black Americans were not the only group being oppressed — although they obviously had the worst situation. In the House on January 14, the matter of enlisting Marylanders who resided in the Confederacy, and particularly those of Jewish heritage, arose. George Vest of Missouri suggested that displaced Marylanders living in the Confederacy should be compelled to serve in the military. He yelled out that Richmond held plenty of "roughs," "shoulder-hitters," and "blood tubs" who stood on the street corners in fine clothes, always ready to break out in the strain of "Maryland, My Maryland" but unwilling to strike a blow for the Confederacy. This drew considerable laughter. Henry Foote turned the question of "foreigners" within the Confederacy to Jews, who he said had "deluged" the Confederacy and controlled "nine-tenths of the trade in each city." If the present trend continued, Foote announced, "the end of the war would probably find nearly all the property of the Confederacy in the hands of Jewish shylocks."[14]

The most prominent shots fired across the bow of the Confederate White House, however, were saved for matters of military operations — chiefly those felt to be failures. Congress seemed hell-bent on destroying the reputation of Braxton Bragg, whom they squarely blamed for the outcome of the battle of Stones River, also known as Murfreesboro, fought December 31, 1862, through January 2, 1863, in Tennessee. Despite Bragg's and Davis's declarations of glory associated with the fight, the Confederate retreat from the field engendered great debate and anger on the House and Senate floors.

At the end of February, in the House, discussion arose a day after Bragg had been given a vote of thanks by Congress, a prestigious recognition, for the Murfreesboro campaign. Henry Foote rose to clarify some newspaper reporting of the events. He did not "commend General Bragg's skill in commanding armies," as the papers reported. Foote had "never regarded him as capable of commanding a large army in the field." He had only voted for the resolution because of the recommendation of Joe Johnston, he explained, out of respect for the latter.[15] Three Kentucky congressmen — Robert Breckinridge, James Chrisman, and Willis Machen — said they would now change their votes against Bragg if possible.

With Bragg's reputation falling, Johnston felt his growing, and he tried to direct his good friend to set things straight for him in Richmond. "I am told that the president & secretary of war think that they have given me the highest military position in the Confederacy," Johnston wrote Wigfall, "that I have full military power in all this western country. . . . If they do so regard it ought not our highest military officer to occupy it? It seems so to me. That principle would bring Lee here. I might then, with great propriety, be replaced in my old command." He then complained about how far apart the troops of Pemberton and Bragg were and how impractical it would be to coordinate their efforts together. "Now you, who are a military man, can understand this case, which Mr. Seddon apparently can not. I want you to convince him. . . . If the government cannot be convinced of the correctness of my views, it seems to me that the assignment of Lee to this command, & of me to my old army, would be a good & pleasant solution."[16] It was all further evidence of the undercurrent of ego that ran through the Confederate effort.

In early February discussions arose in the House over the fall of New Orleans the previous year and exactly who should be held responsible. The answer came through loud and clear: "The main offenders who were responsible for the catastrophe at New Orleans were the former Secy. of War and the present Secy. of the Navy." Although representatives named Randolph and Mallory, their attack was a very thinly veiled one at the president, who had stood by the two cabinet members as their friend.[17]

Davis himself had it out for certain officers. One of them was Bob Toombs, the Georgia politician and friend of Little Aleck Stephens and the Georgia clan of anti-Davis agitators. Frustrated, Toombs finally reached a boiling point. "I have resigned my commission as Brigadier General in the Provisional Army of the Confederate States," he wrote in a proclamation to his soldiers. "This separation from you is deeply painful to me. . . . It is only necessary now for me to say, that, under existing circumstances, in my judgment, I could no longer hold my commission under President Davis with advantage to my country."[18] Toombs went home to Georgia to take up criticizing Davis as a full-time enterprise.

Given the close scrutiny from the public and from the press, Davis had to tend house. One day he sent Abraham Myers, the much-criticized quartermaster general, an article from the *Richmond Examiner* lambasting officers for supposedly selling excess army fabric to stores at a profit when enlisted men were short of proper clothing. "The enclosed slip cut from a morning paper is sent to you for your attention," wrote the president. "If the abuse described exists it should be promptly corrected and the offenders held to a due responsibility."[19] But such interventions did virtually nothing to pacify his critics.

While Davis was busy trying to mend fences, others spent their time second-guessing strategic and tactical decisions sent from Richmond to the battlefront. "If we had [an engineer] corps now, with pontoons," wrote John Bell Hood to his mentor, Wigfall, "I believe we could destroy the Yankee army in our front."[20] Wigfall also heard more from Joe Johnston, who softly criticized the strategy under way in the west. Johnston wrote:

> It is unfortunate that [Edmund] Kirby Smith was not sent across the Mississippi in September. In that event, both Grant & Rosecrans would probably have been beaten. . . . At present we can't do otherwise than stand on the defensive on the Missi. The whole of its valley is said to be impassable for large wagon trains, while the enemy, on the river, can avoid without difficulty, any movement of ours. . . . I don't think the government appreciates the value of our position in Middle Tennessee. If we lose it East Tennessee can not be held. It is not considered in Richmond either, that Rosecranz' N. Western troops are worth double their number of Yankees. . . . Troops of ours from Va. ought to reinforce Bragg. Tell Mr. Seddon so.[21]

—

FOR most Confederate civilians on the home front, the war seemed to be making matters far worse, not better. Sons and husbands were being killed by the scores, fear and disorganization dominated everywhere, the economy virtually had collapsed, and food was getting scarce. So serious a problem was this as 1863 opened that the Georgia legislature enacted laws prohibiting the growing of cotton in the state and requiring the growth of food crops to supply the Confederate army. Why supply the army and not the home front? President Davis pressed the matter hard with the governors. "The possibility of a short supply of provisions presents the greatest danger to a successful prosecution of the war," he wrote Joe Brown of Georgia.[22]

Brown was so disgusted with Davis and the national government in Richmond he considered melting away from public life altogether. "I do not intend to be a candidate for election to another term in the Executive office," he wrote Aleck Stephens. "But I feel a deep interest in seeing someone elected who, while he does his whole duty to the Confederacy, will contend for and sustain to the extent of his ability the rights and sovereignty of the state. . . . In looking over the field for such a man my mind rests upon your brother [Linton] as my first choice."[23] Two weeks later, informed that Linton Stephens might not be a viable candidate, Brown suggested that Bob Toombs should run. The politics of Georgia would continue in flux for weeks to come. Davis, meanwhile, wanted to see if some of the war debt could be transferred to state governments, which Aleck Stephens violently opposed. "You are right in opposing the assumption of Confederate debt to the States," his friend Toombs wrote. "I would not endorse a dime of it. It is puerile and disastrous. . . . As to Geo[rgia], I suppose Joe Brown will run again."[24] In the end Toombs was right: Brown would run again.

In the House of Representatives, a lengthy discussion about state rights occurred centered on North Carolina's loyalty. Because of pro-Union sentiment scattered around the state, Southerners sometimes questioned whether North Carolina favored a restoration of the Union. Burgess Gaither and William Lander, representatives from North Carolina, reassured the House that the state would remain loyal to the Confederacy.[25]

North Carolina was not the only state wavering. "I take the liberty of informing you of the condition of affairs in this State," wrote Col. Guy Bryan, an aide of Lt. Gen. Theophilus H. Holmes's, to President Davis, from Waco, Texas. "There is a growing feeling of discontent among the people at what is regarded as 'the unwarranted exercise of powers by the military authorities, and the unwise and illegal interference of the same with the rights of the citizen and civil authorities.' "[26]

Arkansas also offered a bubbling controversy. On March 30, 1863, Davis wrote the senators and representatives from Arkansas, telling them he had already or would look after their requests about the Trans-Mississippi being cut off and most of their state being occupied by the Yankees. Davis reported he had placed Kirby Smith in command of the Trans-Mississippi, as they had wished; that Thomas C. Hindman had been withdrawn from command of the army in Arkansas, as they had wished; that arms and ammunition should be sent at every possible opportunity; and that Lt. Gen. Theophilus H. Holmes should be continued in service in that theater. "It is not in my opinion wise or proper to encourage the idea of retaining in each State its own troops for its own defence," Davis added, "and thus giving strength to the fatal error of supposing that this great war can be waged by the Confederate States *severally* and *unitedly,* with the least hope of success. Our safety — our very existence — depends on the complete blending of the military strength of all the States into one united body, to be used anywhere and everywhere as the exigencies of the contest may require for the good of the whole."[27] That the statement sounded like a straight call for a national — even "federal"— government was an irony lost on few.

While Davis was hoping that all politicians, local and national, would join to form one grand effort for war, some politicians began to walk in another direction. On March 11, 1863, in the House, Charles Conrad of Louisiana introduced a resolution for the restoration of peace. The states of the Confederacy and the Union, he said, "must ever be intimately connected by identity of race, of language and of religion, and by the unalterable laws of geographical affinity and of mutual demand and supply."[28] The resolution was referred to the Committee on Foreign Affairs. It was the second time any such peace offering came to the floor of Richmond's government and the first time it seemed to be taken seriously — at least by some. It would not be the last.

Chapter

12

POLITICS SPINNING OUT OF CONTROL

WHILE a major war transformed the nation, spreading death to countless battlefields and gloom over the civilians of Richmond, everyday life in the Confederate capital continued. The ladies of Richmond would settle for nothing less.

Many women in the Confederate capital not only operated their households, looked after the events on the military side, and paid careful attention to the politics of what was happening in the halls of Congress but also carried on full social schedules during the war. This was particularly true of the high social circles of Richmond, where soul mates of top Confederate officials mingled with an exclusive set of friends and wondered among their politically connected friends where the war would take them.

The ladies of Richmond had matured and stiffened by now, having passed through a first, intoxicating summer of life among the elite during a period when no one knew what the war would bring. They next settled into a routine, accepting the hardships and uncertainty of war. During the second autumn and winter of the conflict, the ladies seemed to come to peace with themselves, their roles solidifying as mates of the esteemed and privileged, hostesses to a growing variety of social events, nurses to the sick and wounded, and cheerleaders to a republic. "In various offices under the government," Sallie Putnam wrote, "and particularly in those of the Treasury Department," the services of females were found useful. "Employment was given and support secured to hundreds of intelligent and deserving women of the South, who, by the existence of the war, or other misfortunes, had been so reduced in the means of living as to be compelled to earn a support."[1]

A relatively small number of women, probably several hundred, took a far more creative and aggressive approach to warfare. They impersonated men and enlisted as soldiers, fighting in the Civil War. One of these ladies, Loreta Janeta Vasquez, a Cuban who was just twenty-five, aspired to be a "second Joan of Arc" after her husband died in Confederate service. She raised and equipped a cavalry company, the "Arkansas Grays," and, dressed as a man, called herself "Lieutenant Buford," leading the company into battle. After fighting at First Manassas, Vasquez traveled to fight in Kentucky and Tennessee and was wounded twice.

Late in 1862 Vasquez came to Richmond to find out what she could do to help further the Confederate cause. She recalled,

> Richmond was a very different place from what it was on my first visit to it [in 1861], as I soon found out to my cost. Martial law was in force in its most rigorous aspect, and General Winder, the chief of the secret service bureau, and his emissaries, were objects of terror to everybody, rich and poor. . . . It is not surprising, therefore, that almost immediately upon my arrival in Richmond I fell under the surveillance of Winder as a suspicious character, and was called upon to give an account of myself.

Imprisoned, Vasquez confessed her soldierly activities and was urged not to repeat such unladylike functions and released on an assignment to carry dispatches to Maj. Gen. Earl Van Dorn.[2]

The Confederacy's girls also had varied and amazing experiences in Richmond. The daughter of Senator Louis Wigfall, Louise, was a schoolchild in Richmond during the last part of 1862. In spending time with her parents (and undoubtedly hearing a great deal about the machinations of Congress), Louise counted Gen. and Mrs. Joe Johnston as housemates, as Johnston was still recovering from his wound received at Seven Pines the previous spring. Shortages of fuel and goods were enough to put their mark on the little girl: "Mama says as soap is $1.25 a cake you must economize!" she wrote her brother Halsey in the army.[3]

The center of the social galaxy of the Confederacy was the White House, and its chief star, from a social standpoint, was Varina Davis. In the Davis White House, receptions occurred weekly or every other week, with most of them taking place during the winter months. Some were so-called levees, which invited the public. The most important of these was the New Year's event, which took place from noon to 3 p.m. on the first day of January. After paying respects to the first family of the Confederacy, callers then would move on to other houses, in a sort of crawl around the city. At the White House a band serenaded visitors, who entered the house on the Clay Street side. The first to greet — and announce — the guests were the president's aides, including Joseph R. Davis, the president's nephew, and later William M. Browne and Joseph C. Ives, who acted as secretaries for the president. After being received and saying hello to the president and Varina, visitors moved through the parlor and then back out through the entrance hall. Most presidential receptions, however, accommodated a more select set of guests and were held on Tuesday nights from 8 to 10 p.m.

Accounts of the frequency of other White House receptions vary, but it's clear the Davises held many events. Mary Chesnut assisted Varina Davis with a levee as early as March 1861, when the government was still in Montgomery. On moving to Richmond the Davis family was caught up in a social scene that revolved around activities at the Spotswood Hotel. Richmond socialite Mary Tucker Magill recalled a Christmas reception at the White House late in the war as "a wide hall brightly lighted," in which she waited with "the masses of people" and various officers as she listened to "the voice of our master of ceremonies murdering our names most atrociously." After moving into the house, Magill recalled "a gentleman in the uniform of a Colonel ask our names and [took] us into the presence and the acquaintance of the President." The crowd was filled with military and civilian celebrities.[4]

Thomas Cooper DeLeon, who wrote a book filled with his observations about the social life of wartime Richmond, claimed "bimonthly levees" were held at the White House at which Davis and Varina received guests openly, but they seemed "a Washington custom and smacked too much of the 'old concern' to become very popular." (DeLeon's writings suggest the big levees were rare during the middle period of the war but reawakened in 1864, when a sense of togetherness in the cause fired a new social life into the city.) "Evenings" and "drawing rooms" hosted regularly by Varina would bring together "a staff that numbered some of the most noted men and brilliant women both of the stranger and resident society [and] assured all her varied guests a warm welcome and a pleasant visit." After finishing his business for the day, the president would join the group for an hour's relaxation before rejoining his business at candlelight deep into the night.[5]

Informal get-togethers were fairly common as well, and the Davises sometimes hosted meals in the White House, but after a time the president decided that government should come first, and according to Varina, "We ceased to entertain, except at formal receptions or informal dinners and breakfasts given to as many as Mr. Davis's health permitted us to invite." Late in the war, as social events were on the upswing, Varina hosted a great many of these breakfasts and luncheons. Mary Chesnut recorded the fare included "gumbo, ducks, and olives, supreme de voaille, chickens in jelly, oysters, lettuce salad, chocolate jelly cake, claret soup, champagne, etc., etc."[6] While Jefferson Davis's workaholic nature and frequent bouts of illness held in check the social life of the White House, events did carry on without him. Davis also sometimes held breakfasts with cabinet members.

═══

At the end of April, the opposing eastern armies approached each other west of Fredericksburg along the Rappahannock and the Rapidan. "Fighting Joe" Hooker marched the "finest army on the planet," as he called it, the Federal Army of the Potomac, westward away from Falmouth, hoping to hit Gen. Robert E. Lee's army from the side and rear. Lee split his force, leaving part of it facing the Federal troops positioned along the Rappahannock River at Fredericksburg and marching the other westward to face Hooker's main force, near the crossroads of Chancellorsville.

On April 29 Federal troops crossed the Rappahannock. At first the situation looked poor for Lee's Southerners, who were in danger of being crushed by the pincer movement. Lee's army of sixty thousand, much undersupplied, faced both Hooker's seventy-five thousand and Sedgwick's slowly advancing forty thousand. One-third of the enormous Union army would assault Lee's flank and rear; another third, under Maj. Gen. John Sedgwick, would repeat Burnside's maneuver of attacking across the river at Fredericksburg and plowing westward. The final third of the Federal army lay in reserve.

Rather than a Confederate disaster, however, Chancellorsville would be Lee's masterpiece. The bold commander gambled by splitting his army and relying on Stonewall Jackson's corps in a crucial role. Jackson's men smashed directly into the Union army on May 1, unleashing a tremendous firefight. That evening Lee and Jackson held a war council, and the following day Jackson led his troops on a fourteen-mile flank march around the Federal right. Late in the afternoon Jackson's men struck, crushing Hooker's lines. "The events of the few hours of this afternoon and evening are imprinted on my memory in a grand picture," wrote Capt. Thomas L. Livermore of the Eighteenth New Hampshire Infantry. "I can now, and probably always shall be able to again bring before my eyes the dusty plain bounded by long lines of men on all sides; the smoke of musketry and batteries, whose thunders still reverberate in my ears."[7] On the other side jubilation and confidence were the order of the day. Johann August Heinrich Heros von Borcke, a staff officer of Maj. Gen. Jeb Stuart's, noted, "A more magnificent spectacle can hardly be imagined than that which greeted me when I reached the crest of the plateau, and beheld on this side the long lines of our swiftly advancing troops stretching as far as the eye could reach, their red flags fluttering in the breeze, and their arms glittering in the morning sun; and farther on, dense and huddled masses of the Federals flying in utter rout toward the United States Ford."[8]

But the emerging victory would come at a great cost to the Confederacy. While reconnoitering his troops and riding into a patch of woods alongside the Orange Turnpike, Jackson was fired on accidentally by his own men. As described by Jackson's chaplain, James Power Smith, "Under this volley, when not two rods from the troops, the general received three balls at the same instant. One penetrated the palm of his right hand and was cut out that night from the back of his hand. A second passed around the wrist of the left arm and out through the left hand. A third ball passed through the left arm halfway from shoulder to elbow. The large bone of the upper arm was splintered to the elbow-joint, and the wound bled freely."[9] Jackson was carried off the field, his left arm amputated, and plans made to transport him by ambulance to a railroad station and on to Richmond.

While Lee directed the battle and worried over Jackson, Hooker was having a disastrous day on the field. Not only had he ignored the admonitions of his corps commanders regarding Confederate troop movements, convincing himself that Jackson's men were retreating, but the next day, leaning on a column at the Chancellorsville Tavern, which he employed as a headquarters, Hooker was knocked to the ground when the column was hit by a shell. "General Hooker was lying down I think in a soldier's tent by himself," wrote Maj. Gen. Darius N. Couch following the incident. "Raising himself a little as I entered, he said: 'Couch, I turn the command of the army over to you.' . . . This was three-quarters of an hour after his hurt. He seemed rather dull, but possessed of his mental faculties."[10]

The Confederate victory was complete. Although Sedgwick had fought his way westward from Fredericksburg and a sharp clash erupted about Salem Church, Hooker's force was demoralized, and he was discredited completely. With the Union army on the retreat, Lee could celebrate a terrific triumph.

Eight days after his wounding at Chancellorsville, Jackson died at Guinea's Station, Virginia, his last words reputedly being, "No, no, let us cross over the river, and rest under the shade of the trees." The South had lost its most celebrated general of the hour. Much later, the Federal general Oliver O. Howard wrote, "Stonewall Jackson was victorious. Even his enemies praise him; but, providentially for us, it was the last battle that he waged against the American Union. For, in bold planning, in energy of execution, which he had the power to diffuse, in indefatigable activity and moral ascendancy, Jackson stood head and shoulders above his confrères, and after his death General Lee could not replace him."[11]

And of course there were other casualties. Back in Richmond many women had become nurses and administered to the sick and wounded. One such nurse, Kate Mason Rowland, served at Winder Hospital just outside the city. In early May casualties streamed in from the Chancellorsville battlefield. Rowland wrote:

> The sick and wounded are pouring in. We all went out to the wards with lanterns, tin buckets of water and sponges and wet the wounds, we carried a supply of lint and bandages, but with only two surgeons it was a long while before all could be attended to. Sounds of misery greeted our ears as we entered, some groaning, others crying like children, and some too weak and suffering to do anything but turn a grateful look upon us as we squeezed the cold water from the sponge over their stiffened and bandaged limbs.[12]

Meanwhile, in the western theater, the Confederate military situation appeared alarming. Along the Mississippi River the Rebel bastion at Vicksburg was the target of Federal military operations that moved north from New Orleans and south from Tennessee. The campaign for Vicksburg originated in the autumn of 1862, when Union Maj. Gen. Ulysses S. Grant struck south along the railroads following the battle of Corinth. The approach didn't work, and Grant discovered that attempting to maintain long and imperiled supply lines over this route was too problematic.

In April 1863 the stubborn Federal commander opened a second campaign to control the Mississippi. This time Grant marched his troops south of Vicksburg, crossed the Mississippi River, and prepared to attack eastward. It was one of the most daring military maneuvers attempted to that time, as Grant relied on long, tenuous lines of communication and planned to fight "behind enemy lines" without sources of fresh supplies. Union Brig. Gen. Benjamin H.

Grierson led a diversionary raid from La Grange, Tennessee, to Baton Rouge, Louisiana, confusing the Confederate response to the impending assaults. "Much of the country through which we passed was almost entirely destitute of forage and provisions," wrote Grierson. "It was but seldom that we obtained over one meal per day. Many of the inhabitants must undoubtedly suffer for want of the necessities of life, which have reached most fabulous prices."[13]

Confederate forces consisted of the garrison at Vicksburg under Lt. Gen. John Pemberton, a Northern-born officer who, nonetheless, enjoyed the good graces of Jefferson Davis; and an army near Jackson commanded by Joe Johnston, back in commission but not in his old post. During the first two and a half weeks in May, Grant's men accomplished amazing feats: marching eastward following a battle at Port Gibson, they fought and won four battles, separating the two Confederate forces, casting off Johnston into a northward retreat, capturing the city of Jackson, and turning to attack Vicksburg from the east. It was a stunning beginning to what became a siege of Vicksburg itself.

The fierce determination of the Federal campaign was reflected in a letter Maj. Gen. William Tecumseh Sherman wrote toward the end of the siege. "Vicksburg contains many of my old pupils and friends," wrote Sherman. "Should it fall into our hands I will treat them with kindness, but they have sowed the wind and must reap the whirlwind."[14]

In the city itself Pemberton and his strong defensive lines held off the Yankee juggernaut. Life in the city for the soldiers and the civilians was slowly becoming unbearable, however. Food was scarce and matériel was dwindling rapidly, and the Rebel army's ability to fight off attacks was diminishing. The psychological effect on the Southerners was disastrous. In March a civilian who happened to be a Northerner caught in the city wrote this diary entry: "The slow shelling of Vicksburg goes on all the time, and we have grown indifferent. It does not at present interrupt or interfere with daily avocations, but I suspect they are only getting the range of different points; and when they have them all complete, showers of shot will rain on us all at once." Soldiers and townsfolk lived in cellars, caverns, or earthen caves carved out of the landscape, approximating crude bombproof shelters. The same diarist later penned, "The cellar is so damp and musty the bedding has to be carried out and laid in the sun every day, with the forecast that it may be demolished at any moment. The confinement is dreadful. To sit and listen as if waiting for death in a horrible manner would drive me insane."[15]

The suffering continued through May and June as the siege dragged on with infrequent attacks but scattered, intense fighting along the lines north, east, and south of the city. One of the most notable attempts to break the lines occurred on May 25, three days after the siege began. Engineers working under the supervision of Union capt. Andrew Hickenlooper, chief engineer of the Seventeenth Army Corps, had constructed a mine under the Third Louisiana Infantry Redan, the principal fort protecting the Old Jackson Road approach into town. On May 25 Hickenlooper exploded twenty-two hundred pounds of black powder set along the mine, as a prelude to a massive attack.

Later Hickenlooper recalled the scene:

> At the appointed moment it appeared as though the whole fort and connecting outworks commenced an upward movement, gradually breaking into fragments and growing less bulky in appearance, until it looked like an immense fountain of finely pulverized earth, mingled with flashes of fire and clouds of smoke, through which could occasionally be caught a glimpse of some dark objects — men, gun-carriages, shelters, etc.[16]

But still this attempt to break through the lines, and another attempt six days later, failed. The siege at Vicksburg ground on, not one Yankee certain of the competency of the Federal commander Grant. Nor did the Confederates' faith rest in the abilities of Pemberton.

B ACK in Richmond many in the government worried greatly over the fate of Vicksburg, but the people of the South were more distracted and heartbroken over the death of Stonewall Jackson. Charlotte Wigfall, wife of Louis Wigfall, relayed the country's lament over the fallen leader. "We are all saddened to the heart to-night by hearing [of] the death of our hero Jackson," she wrote. "It will cause mourning all over our land and each person seems to feel as if he had lost a relative. I feel more disheartened about the war now than I have ever felt before. It seems to me it is to be interminable, and what a wretched life of anxiety it is to look forward to!"[17]

"We had great excitement here on account of Gen. Jackson's death, and a long procession passed by Mama's house," wrote the youngest Wigfall daughter, Fannie, just ten years old. She continued:

> And just before it passed 3 thousand Yankees arrived [prisoners of war], and I had to walk by them nearly the whole way from the capitol square to Mama's house, and then as I was on the wrong side of the pavement I had to pass right through them. Directly after the hearse went his horse came with his coat pantaloons boots, and spurs, and the flag all draped in black crepe, and Gens. Longstreet, Elzey, and Pickett, and President Davis, and all of General Winder's staff.[18]

The Confederate president attempted to boost hopes for victory that spring. Davis told the Confederacy:

> At no previous period of the war have our forces been so numerous, so well organized, and so thoroughly disciplined, armed, and equipped as at present. Disaster has been the result of their [Union forces'] every effort to turn or to storm Vicksburg and Port Hudson, as well as of every attack on our batteries on the Red River, the Tallahatchie, and other navigable streams. Within a few weeks the falling waters and the increasing heat of summer will complete their discomfiture and compel their baffled and defeated forces to the abandonment of expeditions on which was based their chief hope of subjugation.[19]

Privately, however, the president knew how fragile the war standing was on several fronts. Joe Johnston, having returned to the field, reported from Tennessee. "Should all, or a large part of [Grant's] troops, come into middle Tennessee," he wrote the president, "this army would be forced to leave it. We can not attack now with probability of success & should strong reinforcements arrive, we could not hold our ground against the Federal army."[20]

Davis also received alarming news from governors, none more so than from Zebulon Vance of North Carolina. "I receive information from our Generals in the field that desertion is alarmingly on the increase in the army," Vance wrote, and went on,

> I do not believe that one case in a hundred is caused by disloyalty — have no apprehensions whatever on this score. Homesickness, fatigue, hard fare, &c., have of course much to do with it. The promise of the law of Conscription, that they *should* have furloughs, which has never been redeemed, is one *principal* cause beyond a doubt. . . . Another great cause — in fact almost the only one assigned by the last class of conscripts, is that they were refused permission to enter the regiments of their choice with their neighbors and relations. Large numbers actually threaten to desert before they leave camp and generally make good their threats.[21]

Davis replied that he did not believe calling out the militia to force the return of Confederate troops to the field, as Vance suggested, was the answer.

Generals in the field went right on with meddling in Richmond politics, as they had for months. "There is a fair prospect of forward movement," wrote James Longstreet, Lee's senior corps commander, to his old friend Louis Wigfall. The letter was headed: "None of these matters are mentioned to anyone but Genl. Lee and yourself." "That being the case," Longstreet continued, "we can spare nothing from this Army to re-enforce in the West. If we could cross the Potomac with one hundred & fifty thousand men I think we could demand of Lincoln to declare his purpose. If it is a Christian purpose enough of blood has been shed to satisfy any principles. If he intends extermination we should know it at once and play a little at that game whilst we can."[22]

Wigfall also heard from his old friend Beauregard. "Knowing your zeal, energy, and enlarged views on all military matters," wrote the Little Creole, from Charleston, "I send you herewith the copy of a hastily written letter to my friend Genl. J. E. Johnston, proposing to him the plan of a campaign in his Department, which I feel confident, if it met with the cordial support of the War Department, would soon give us back Tennessee, Kentucky, and Louisiana, relieve the States of Mississippi and Arkansas of the presence of every Yankee in them — and probably give us Missouri also."[23] Beauregard's enthusiasm for Johnston's ideas may have been overzealous, but it would give Wigfall more ammunition to interfere with Davis and the War Department as the war dragged on.

Davis, for his part, became frustrated not only with officers who seemed to be fighting the War Department, but also with his old favorites. The foggy communication between Davis and the field generals, not always transformed into clarity by Samuel Cooper, the adjutant general of the army, gave rise to Davis venting to his most trusted field officer. "It is embarrassing to be called on for orders," he wrote Robert E. Lee, "and when they are given to be met with opinions previously invited but withheld."[24]

For its part the Confederate Congress continued on with arguments over a great array of topics big and small. They debated the merits of a Confederate motto at length, the House desiring an improvement on *e pluribus unum* ("one from many"), which several members thought should be "translated" as "The eagle's flight is out of sight." The proposed motto, to be placed on the official seal, was *Deo duce vincemus* ("With God as our leader, we will conquer"). After much discussion, however, the motto was changed to *Deo vindice* ("Under the protection of God") and placed below the equestrian statue of George Washington on the official seal of the Confederacy.[25]

In the House Henry Foote proposed moving the seat of government away from Richmond. "Richmond is no place for the capital of the Confederacy," he shouted. Foote complained of "a lack of supplies" and "a spirit of extortion manifested here which I hope to never encounter elsewhere." Charles Conrad of Louisiana said that moving the government would appear to the Yankees like "Congress was taking steps for the evacuation of Richmond" and that "nothing [would be] more dangerous than a transfer of the seat of government during war."[26]

Many of the squabbles seemed petty. Davis wrote the Senate regarding an act to authorize newspapers to be mailed to soldiers free of postage. Davis objected to the bill, claiming it would be "unconstitutional" for the post office's charges to become a burden on the Treasury. Nevertheless, Davis believed that the official mail of the government being sent for free was a different matter. This infuriated some senators, who saw the verdict as an attack on the little people, while privileges were held fast for wealthy officials.[27]

In the Senate arguments erupted over the requirements for the chief of ordnance, and — once again the issue of rank — whether he should be a brigadier general in the provisional army. Several senators believed that all bureau chiefs should be made brigadier generals. But the problem, according to Albert Brown of Mississippi, was that "many [incumbent bureau chiefs] never led a squadron in the field, and knew no more of battle than a spinster. . . . By what justice should high military rank be conferred upon them?"[28] The bill was postponed indefinitely.

Still webbed in personal disputes, Davis did his best to untangle. "In the last [letter] you inform me that you had learned after writing the first [letter] that I entertained personal enmity towards you," the president wrote Senator William Yancey of Alabama, who frequently referred to Davis as "a military dictator." "Will you have the goodness to inform me how you acquired that information? Not having made any declaration to that effect, I think I have a right to inquire. It is true that for some time past the impression has been made upon me that you were in opposition to my Administration."[29] That was a major understatement, and the rift only would widen between the Alabaman and the president.

When Davis and his war secretary, Seddon, attempted to solve problems, as with asking Howell Cobb to replace the beleaguered quartermaster general, Abraham Myers, they often did not meet with success. "I beg to assure you that the offer you have tendered to me to take the head of the Q.M. General's Department is received in the spirit in which it was offered," Cobb replied to Seddon. "So far from regarding it as an unpleasant light, I receive it as an expression of confidence both on yours and the President's part — to which I do not feel entitled. . . . I cannot accept it because I feel certain that I am not qualified for the place."[30]

During the spring of 1863, a lot seemed to be on the verge of being out of control for the Confederacy. Not all were surprised. "I do not know that events have taken a different turn from what I had contemplated in the beginning," penned Assistant Secretary of War John A. Campbell, "& which I labored with all my energy to avert for the country."[31] And yet perhaps one, grand campaign could turn it all around.

13

CAN'T WE ALL GET ALONG?

THERE had been one preeminent battlefield hero in the minds of many Southerners. With Stonewall Jackson dead, where would the Confederacy turn?

Robert Edward Lee now had the supreme confidence of his men and of the Southern nation, and he believed his Army of Northern Virginia could do nearly anything he asked. He needed much from them, no doubt: the Confederacy was feeling the crunch of a war that had lasted two years, killing many of its young men, exhausting many of its resources, and destroying much of Lee's beloved Virginia. As the summer of 1863 approached, Lee sought a plan that would strike fear into the Northern populace, accelerate Northern cries for peace, carry the burdens of the war away from Virginia, and perhaps gain foreign recognition for the Richmond government. It was a bold gamble, but such risks had worked in a tactical sense before, during the Peninsular campaign and at Chancellorsville. Lee needed to begin with a grand strategic victory, and Pennsylvania would be the target.

Meanwhile, the Army of the Potomac was in disarray. Haunted by the failures at Fredericksburg and Chancellorsville, the soldiers utterly lacked confidence in Joe Hooker. Lincoln had no choice but to change commanding generals once again, this time opting for the bookish and occasionally quick-tempered Maj. Gen. George Gordon Meade, reputedly only after the senior corps commander, Maj. Gen. John F. Reynolds, declined the assignment.

On June 9, as the armies began moving northward, a great cavalry battle erupted at Brandy Station, near Culpeper, Virginia. It would be the largest cavalry battle ever fought in North America, and the Yankees under Brig. Gen. Alfred Pleasonton held their own against the fabled Maj. Gen. Jeb Stuart's troops. As the Confederates moved northward toward Pennsylvania, screened by the Blue Ridge Mountains, Hooker and then Meade groggily pursued. The Confederate movement was really a giant raid; Lee had no intention of attempting to occupy Pennsylvania. But while penetrating he could strike toward Harrisburg, York, or even Philadelphia, terrorizing the North's sense of security and perhaps winning a pitched battle on Yankee soil.

By the last hours of June, the Confederate corps under Lt. Gen. A. P. Hill, and particularly the division under Maj. Gen. Henry Heth, was moving slowly eastward toward Gettysburg, Pennsylvania, having been ordered to scout for supplies. Also in the vicinity, where there was a major convergence of roads, was a brigade of Federal cavalry under Brig. Gen. John Buford. When the two forces first clashed, early in the morning of July 1, neither side anticipated a battle at that position or at that time, but piecemeal attacks and counterattacks escalated as Confederate reinforcements moved in from the west and, eventually, under Lt. Gen. Richard S. Ewell, from the north.

Buford's cavalry stubbornly resisted the Confederate infantry for a short time before Reynolds's First Corps arrived and deployed west of town. Shortly thereafter, Reynolds was killed. "He had taken his troops into a heavy growth of timber on the slope of a hill-side, and, under their regimental and brigade commanders, the men did their work well promptly," wrote Joseph Rosengarten, a major in the Union army. "Returning to join the expected divisions, he was struck by a Minié ball, fired by a sharpshooter hidden in the branches of a tree almost overhead, and killed at once; his horse bore him to the little clump of trees, where a cairn of stones and a rude mark on the bark, now almost overgrown, still tells the fatal spot."[1]

Pushed back through the town by superior Confederate forces, the Federals made a stand on Cemetery Hill, where Maj. Gen. Winfield Scott Hancock, dispatched by Meade to command the field, assembled the men in order. By the end of the first day, Union corps were still marching toward the field, and Meade himself had not yet arrived. Hancock had analyzed the situation with foresight, however, and formed the basis for a fishhook-shaped battle line that would hold the high ground east and south of the town — Culp's Hill, Cemetery Ridge, and the Round Tops, hills on the southern terminus of the Federal line of battle. Lee, desperately attempting to control a fight that had spiraled away too quickly, deployed Ewell to the north, assigning him the task of taking Cemetery Hill, with A. P. Hill and his most experienced corps commander, Lt. Gen. James Longstreet, forming a line of battle along a ridge running southward from the town's Lutheran Theological Seminary into the countryside.

Early in the morning of July 2, major portions of the battle lines exploded, and intense fighting in various regions flared all through the day, multiple attacks and counterattacks capturing and recapturing the same parcels of ground. The fight for Culp's Hill required several bloody Confederate assaults, the position having been attained by the Federals after dark. Cemetery Hill, with the town's small plot, Evergreen Cemetery, erupted into a scene of terror. Gunshot victims were strewn around the grounds, as well as those who had been grotesquely wounded by artillery shells. A sign beside the small cemetery gatehouse warned that anyone using firearms on the premises would be prosecuted.

To the south huge attacks moved on spare words such as those of Hancock, who at one point snapped: "Do you see those colors? Take them!" Nothing more needed saying. Soon dead men and horses from both sides littered regions of the battleground.

It was now clear that one of the largest battles yet was well under way, and many soldiers felt the war would turn on this conflict. Maj. Gen. Gouverneur K. Warren, Meade's chief engineer, realized that Little Round Top was the key position. Artillery posted on this hill could command the field. (Big Round Top, also known as Round Top, was too heavily wooded to serve usefully.) A scramble ensued, and elements of the Union Fifth Corps posted themselves along the ridge of Little Round Top, a craggy, rocky hill.

The attack would come from Maj. Gen. John Bell Hood's division of Longstreet's corps. Hood's soldiers faced a long assault over a relatively open stretch, a slight elevation to the boulder field of the Devil's Den, and then an uphill march through the draw between Round Top and Little Round Top. During the maneuver Hood himself would be wounded and lose the use of his left arm. "With this wound terminated my participation in this great battle," Hood later wrote. "As I was borne off on a litter to the rear, I could but experience deep distress of mind and heart at the thought of the inevitable fate of my brave fellow-soldiers . . . and I shall ever believe that had I been permitted to turn Round Top mountain, we would not only have gained their position, but have been able to finally rout the enemy."[2]

The small regiment posted on the extreme left of Little Round Top on the warm afternoon was the Twentieth Maine Infantry, commanded by Col. Joshua L. Chamberlain, a former professor at Bowdoin College. As the repeated attacks struck along the lines from the woods, Chamberlain's Twentieth Maine was running desperately low on ammunition. It was a moment of crisis for the Union cause at Gettysburg. "A critical moment has arrived, and we can remain as we are no longer," wrote Theodore Gerrish, a private in the Twentieth Maine. "We must advance or retreat. It must not be the latter, but how can it be the former? Colonel Chamberlain understands how it can be done. The order is given 'Fix bayonets!' and the steel shanks of the bayonets rattle upon the rifle barrels. 'Charge bayonets, charge!' "[3]

Although Gerrish's account is embellished (he was not present at the battle, and no such order was dispatched), the passage helped immortalize the legendary fight of the Twentieth Maine on Little Round Top, which sent Col. William Oates's Alabamans downhill in a scramble. Other actions along the crest of Little Round Top held the position for the Federal army, and the many other concurrent fights slowly wound down into the silent campfires of the night.

The second day at Gettysburg may have decided the outcome of the battle, but the next day, July 3, would offer its greatest spectacle. Dissatisfied with the prospect of pulling away without a decisive victory, Lee ordered a desperate charge toward the one area that had not been struck forcefully the previous day — the Union center, held by none other than Hancock's Second Corps. In hindsight it was a foolish move, and some commanders — most notably Longstreet — chafed at the idea on the spot. But the Confederate commander believed the Federal guns were running low on ammunition, and he reasoned that if he could split the Union center, he could drive a wedge through the army and rout the Yankees yet. The frontal attack came on the afternoon of July 3 and consisted of divisions under Maj. Gen. George E. Pickett and Brig. Gens. James J. Pettigrew and Isaac R. Trimble. All together more than twelve thousand men would march more than a mile across the plain toward a copse of trees and an angle in the stone wall, beyond which Union blue coated the landscape, rifles and ordnance ready.

The relative silence at noontime on July 3 didn't last long. "The cannonade in the center soon began, and presented one of the most magnificent battle-scenes witnessed during the war," wrote Evander M. Law, the Confederate brigadier general who inherited Hood's division. "Looking up the valley toward Gettysburg, the hills on either side were capped with crowns of flame and smoke, as 300 guns, about equally divided between the two ridges, vomited their iron hail upon each other."[4]

The artillery barrage, designed to prepare the Union center for the assault, carried on in full force as the assembled Southerners readied to move out of the woods. In Longstreet's words, "Pickett said, 'General, shall I advance?' The effort to speak the order failed, and I could only indicate it by an affirmative bow."[5] Pickett scurried to the assembled troops, blaring, "Up, men, and to your posts! Don't forget today that you are from old Virginia."

The attack proceeded, the Union soldiers momentarily stunned at the vision of such a long line of gray moving toward them. The Federal artillery belched long-range shell, shot, and finally short-range canister, and waves of bluecoats poured lines of fire into the approaching Rebels. It was a desperate moment of the war. As Edmund Rice, lieutenant colonel of the Nineteenth Massachusetts Infantry, recalled, "Voices were lost in the uproar; so I turned partly toward them, raised my sword to attract their attention, and motioned to advance. They surged forward, and just then, as I was stepping backward with my face toward the men, urging them on, I felt a sharp blow as a shot struck me, then another; I whirled round, my sword torn from my hand by a bullet or shell splinter. My visor saved my face, but the shock stunned me." Rice won the Medal of Honor for his action that afternoon. Another Federal officer, Col. Frank Haskell, remembered the chaos: "The line springs — the crest of the solid ground with a great roar, heaves forward its maddened load, men, arms, smoke, fire, a fighting mass. It rolls to the wall — flash meets flash, the wall is crossed — a moment ensues of thrusts, yells, blows, shots, and indistinguishable conflict, followed by a shout universal that makes the welkin ring again, and the last and bloodiest fight of the great battle of Gettysburg is ended and won."[6]

Gettysburg indeed had ended. Lee's spectacular attack was a failure, most of those who marched toward the Union line dead, wounded, or captured. The following day Lee marched his army southward, back toward Virginia, Meade's battered force too depleted of energy, ammunition, and supplies to pursue with any meaning. To make matters worse, however, on the same day the siege at Vicksburg came to a close, Pemberton and his remaining Confederates surrendered to Grant. The double victory marked a major turning point of the war and the beginning of the end for the Confederate nation.

At Vicksburg the celebration of the weary Union troops was vigorous, the terms offered by Grant typically magnanimous. "As soon as our troops took possession of the city, guards were established along the whole line of parapet, from the river above to the river below," wrote Grant. "The prisoners were allowed to occupy their old camps behind the intrenchments. No restraint was put upon them, except by their own commanders."[7]

In Washington, although he was disturbed by Meade's lethargic pursuit of Lee, Lincoln finally had a major event to celebrate. He had found not only a victory at Vicksburg but also a reliable and forceful commander.

As the major war news was unfolding at Gettysburg and Vicksburg, the summer of 1863 also brought action along the Atlantic coast and at the gateway into the Deep South. In Charleston, South Carolina, a hotbed of rebellion, the Federal navy and army made slow progress by a series of movements on land and water. A naval attack in April by Rear Adm. Samuel F. Du Pont failed, but by July the Federal army initiated another set of engagements designed to disable the forts protecting Charleston Harbor. The troops would assault James Island and Morris Island, capture Fort Wagner and Battery Gregg, and place guns to concentrate fire on Fort Sumter.

Leading the attack through a thin strip of sand on Fort Wagner was Col. Robert Gould Shaw's Fifty-fourth Massachusetts Infantry, a national regiment of African American soldiers, one of the first deployed in combat. The attack on Wagner became a test of whether black American troops could fight effectively. An account of the attack of July 18 published in the *New York Tribune* records the outcome: "In the midst of this terrible shower of shot and shell they pushed their way, reached the Fort, portions of the Fifty-fourth Massachusetts, the Sixth Connecticut, and the Forty-eighth New York dashed through the ditches, gained the parapet, and engaged in a hand-to-hand fight with the enemy, and for nearly half an hour held their ground, and did not fall back until nearly every commissioned officer was shot down."[8] The attack failed, but the gallant efforts of Shaw's regiment strongly supported the emerging role of black Americans in the crucial first summer of emancipation.

<hr/>

$\mathbf{B}$ACK in Richmond political squabbles continued at a frenzied pace despite the fact that the third session of Congress had ended on May 1 and the fourth session would not begin until December. With battles east and west raging, every politician on hiatus and officers in the capital city or in the field speculated on where the whole war was headed. Greatly upset at the loss of Vicksburg, Jefferson Davis asked Joe Johnston how he possibly could have allowed it to happen, having been in the area (though not the commanding general holding the city). "Painfully anxious as to the result," Davis wrote, "I have remained without information from you as to any plans proposed or attempted to raise the siege. Equally uninformed as to your plans in relation to Port Hudson, I have to request such information in relation thereto as the Government has a right to expect from one of its commanding Generals in the field."[9] Davis was further irritated with Johnston over the latter's seemingly cavalier grasp of authority to do what he wished. "After a full examination of all the correspondence between you and myself and the War Office, including the despatches referred to in your telegrams of the 20th inst., I am still at a loss to account for your strange error in stating to the Secretary of War that your right to withdraw reinforcements from Bragg's Army had been restricted by the Executive, or that your command over the Army of Tennessee had been withdrawn."[10] For weeks Davis and Johnston continued to bicker over the responsibility and authority of the Mississippi theater and who was responsible for the loss of Vicksburg.

Former South Carolina governor Francis Pickens, still fuming over the loss of Vicksburg and John Pemberton's alleged incompetence while stationed at Charleston, could not resist playing "I told you so" to his confidant in Richmond, Louis Wigfall. "You know I wrote you three months ago, that we would lose Vicksburg & the S. West from the incompetency of Pemberton," Pickens wrote, "and now the facts . . . have no room to doubt in any man's head, and if Pemberton is put in responsible command again, I assure you it will be a great public calamity. It will produce deep seated disaffection, & endanger any army. I know him well."[11] This provided still more authority to rail against Davis, who was Pemberton's friend.

On August 1 Davis wrote again to Johnston, sending a newspaper clipping critical of Davis and pointing out that it clearly had been written by "someone having access to your correspondence." Moreover, a staff member of Johnston's had been found showing similar material around Richmond. "A copy of a letter written by one of your staff has been exhibited in this city which contains passages so identical with the published communication as to leave little room for doubt as to its origin," Davis fumed. He asked Johnston to "take the proper action."[12]

Johnston looked to his old friend Louis Wigfall for help, writing him a heartfelt letter in August. "I write [because] my wife, who apprehends that the whole power of the government is preparing to overwhelm me, insists on it," Johnston admitted. He then gave Wigfall a lengthy treatise on how he could not possibly have conducted the operations in Mississippi any better.[13]

Soon thereafter Davis wrote again to Johnston. He now knew that Johnston's medical director, John M. Johnson, had allowed a newspaper editor to copy some of Johnston's private correspondence. Davis found the medical director's explanation "not satisfactory" and wrote to Johnston that "I feel that it would be unjust to you to have on your staff an officer, who copies your official correspondence without your knowledge, and sends it to another who permits its publication."[14]

Davis also continued his fight with the powerful Alabama senator William Yancey. "I have now received your letter of 11th inst.," the president wrote, "in which you not only omit entirely any answer to my inquiry, but make the very grave charge that in my official action I have been 'influenced by feelings of personal hostility' to yourself, and not satisfied with reporting that this charge is based on information received by you, you add that you 'believe it.' Repelling this charge as utterly untrue, I again claim the right of inquiring on what information it is based."[15] It was nearly a carbon copy emotionally of what he had written Yancey months before, and as then, it had virtually no effect. The controversy would smolder for months to come.

The governors also continued to pelt Davis with requests for help, which he most often felt he could not comply with. For example, cantankerous Joe Brown pressed Davis for more troops to help guard Georgia's railroads. "I regret, however, that the pressing exigencies of the service at other points actually invaded or immediately menaced by the enemy will not permit that a regiment of cavalry should be detached from the armies in the field for the service which you suggest," the president told him.[16]

Davis's good friend Francis Lubbock, governor of Texas, continued to push the Confederate leader for more of practically everything for the Lone Star State. "I am satisfied your Excellency does not underrate the importance of Texas to the Confederacy," Lubbock wrote. "We need but arms; with an adequate supply, we will battle manfully, and, I trust, with success. The Confederate Government it is reported, have on hand a large quantity of arms."[17] Davis, however, could not help.

From South Carolina, Governor Milledge Bonham implored the people of his state to loan more slaves to the state government. "An immediate necessity exists for three thousand laborers," the governor requested, "for a period not exceeding one month. . . . Let every citizen, without a moment's delay, send every hand he can spare. . . . A discreet [*sic*] overseer to every fifty hands should be sent. The hands should bring spades and shovels. . . . The Executive ventures to say the negroes will be properly cared for."[18] The call was answered by some, but ignored by many. On August 27 Bonham issued a declaration increasing the required furnished labor for the construction of coastal defenses in and around Charleston. Slave owners now were ordered to send "all they can share."[19] While he was appealing to his own people, Bonham also sent unsatisfied missives to congressmen in Richmond.

Davis was putting out fires across the Confederacy. For example, he felt he had no chance but to turn to Governor Zebulon Vance for support in the case of William Woods Holden, a newspaper editor and would-be politician who was openly attacking the Davis administration in the newspapers, mostly the *Raleigh Standard*. "This is not the first intimation I have received that Holden is engaged in the treasonable purpose of exciting the people of North Carolina to resistance against their Government," penned Davis, "and cooperation with the enemy." Davis asked the governor's help in stopping these editorials, which "mislead a portion of our own people." However, Davis would find that Vance could be only so supportive toward the Richmond government, as he had his own suspicions about the primary Confederate leaders.[20]

The increasingly pessimistic mood was shared by many Confederate leaders. Their losses were "a terrible revulsion," wrote Senator Clement Clay of Alabama to Louis Wigfall. "The fall of Vicksburg & Port Hudson, the loss of all of Middle Tenn. & North Ala. & the expulsion of Lee from the enemy's territory!! Superadded to all this comes my own little griefs, with selfishness . . . my home & parents & most of my kindred in the hands of the enemy."[21] In Georgia Bob Toombs became so panicked over the Confederacy's lack of funds that he began a letter-writing campaign to the newspapers, starting with one to the editor of the *Augusta Constitutionalist:*

> The Confederate Government have committed two radical errors in the management of our finances which produced our present calamitous condition by the operation of laws of currency as fixed, certain, and immutable as the laws which govern the planetary system. . . . The first great error was in attempting to carry on a great and expensive war solely on credit — without taxation. . . . [The second great error] was the use of the public credit almost exclusively in the form of currency. The natural result of this policy was plain, inevitable, overwhelming.[22]

Privately, Toombs wrote the vice president, Aleck Stephens, despondent. "We are gloomy and in great trouble," he reported, "North, South, East and West the clouds look dark and threatening. . . . We must fight this thing out, and I shall try to be with the militia of Georgia in the prospective defense of our homes. . . . We shall have to call out the 'melish.' "[23]

The governor of Georgia himself was even more alarmed than usual. "There seems to have settled upon the minds of our people a sort of feeling of despondency," Joe Brown wrote Stephens, "which is stimulated by the constant croaking of a class of speculators who have made money and are preparing to curry favor with Lincoln if he should overrun the country, with the hope of saving their property. These men put the worst face upon every mishap to our arms, and while they are guilty of no act of positive disloyalty they do all in their power to discourage our people."[24]

Stephens, meanwhile, had a plan of action that seemed to come out of nowhere. Fed up with the war, and angered over the lack of prisoner exchanges, the Confederate vice president hatched a plan to proceed north and talk with the Yankee authorities. Stephens would begin by reestablishing the exchange of prisoners, which had broken down following Lincoln's issuance of the Emancipation Proclamation and the Confederate government's threats to execute African American troops and their white officers. What Stephens really wanted, however, was to offer peace to the Yankees. Writing Davis, he said, "I am not without hopes that *indirectly* I could now turn attention to a general adjustment upon such basis as might ultimately be acceptable to both parties and stop the further effusion of blood in a contest so irrational, unchristian, and so inconsistent with all recognized American principles."[25]

Davis accepted the Stephens plan just as the battle began to rage at Gettysburg. "Having accepted your patriotic offer to proceed as a military commissioner under flag of truce to Washington," Davis wrote, "you will receive herewith your letter of authority to the Commander in Chief of the Army and Navy of the United States. . . . War is full enough of unavoidable horrors under all its aspects to justify and even to demand of any Christian rulers who may be unhappily engaged in carrying it on to seek to restrict its calamities and to divest it of all unnecessary severities."[26] Davis further wrote two identical letters to Abraham Lincoln, one addressed to the "commander in chief" and the other to "the president," which described the attempt at reconciling a prisoner exchange, and sent Stephens to Washington with them. Incessant rains caused the vice president to travel by steamer. Stephens left Newport News on July 4, and after waiting two days in Washington, the Lincoln government refused to consider the Stephens proposal. The official response from the U.S. government was, "The request is inadmissible. The customary agents and channels are adequate for all needful military communications and conference between the United States forces and the insurgents."[27] Stephens was furious that his influence had amounted to nothing, and he returned to Georgia more embittered than ever. There, Stephens's old friend Joe Brown tried to console the vice president. "I fully agree with you that our matters are being badly managed," he noted, "and do not know what may be the result if we do not have a change of policy. I am advised by the commissary at Atlanta, Maj. Cummings, privately that the supply of meat is now very short and that we cannot subsist the army through the fall unless we get the cattle out of Florida and lower Ga. faster than we are now doing. I have called the attention of the President to this."[28]

Many other formerly influential politicians felt helpless at what appeared to be an aimless policy that stung badly in the wake of the double defeats at Gettysburg and Vicksburg. Lamenting his apparent loss of influence, Robert M. T. Hunter, the president pro tempore of the Senate, wrote Wigfall: "I suppose the point upon which you wish to confer with me is connected with the conduct of the war and if so as *you know* I am entirely without influence in such matters."[29]

The military situation seemed to be coming to a head: either Confederate armies would need to rebound from the recent disasters quickly or they would be in dire straits. "Our people have not generally realised the magnitude of the struggle in which we are engaged," Davis lamented to Senator Robert Johnson of Arkansas. "Had Missouri and Tennessee furnished the number of troops which you say they could not supply, if in our possession, our banners would be flying on the upper Missi. And the Ohio."[30]

Bob Toombs had other culprits in mind, as did many in the political world of Richmond. He complained,

> The real control of our affairs is narrowing down constantly into the hands of Davis and the old army, and when it gets entirely there it will collapse. They have neither the ability nor the honesty to manage the revolution. Many of our ablest and most reliable col[onel]s who brought troops into the field have been killed by the blunders and jealousies of the old army, and the morale of the army is now pretty much gone. We never had a desertion until we had conscription, for the very good reason that there were thousands outside who wanted to take the places of those inside. . . . Conscription and conscription alone destroyed all that feeling.[31]

"I am raising a regiment," Toombs confided to his fellow Georgian Howell Cobb, "it is only a body guard to protect me when we have all to flee to the mountains. Davis will soon bring us to that point."[32]

Davis, meanwhile, looked to the states to stand up against the Yankee army just as they looked to him for protection. "The enemy is reported in large force threatening our army in East Tenn.," he wrote Aleck Stephens. "That is the gate of Northern Georgia. We have sent all disposable reinforcements, but require an addition to our army there. . . . If you concur as to the propriety of sending [the militia] up to co-operate with Bragg or Buckner you will oblige me by conferring with Governor Brown on the subject."[33]

Politicians, generals, civilians — all felt that what was needed was a strong commanding general who could run the show. And by this time there was only one candidate, Robert E. Lee. A general-in-chief would stand up to the Yankees, solve the problems that seemed to rise out of a lack of coordination here, there, and everywhere. On this virtually everyone agreed. Everyone except Jefferson Davis.

Chapter

14

—

SOILED REPUTATIONS

As the summer of 1863 waned, the situation was fluid throughout the South. Maj. Gen. William S. Rosecrans and his Yankees were pushing into Alabama with their eyes on Chattanooga. Bragg, already under heavy criticism, would need to block him. Knoxville and eastern Tennessee were under duress. Actions in Texas, Louisiana, and Arkansas threatened to place even more Confederate territory under Federal occupation. While Gettysburg and Vicksburg had fallen, it was becoming clear that the war would go on for a long time. The Confederacy was still in business.

The hot and deadly summer transformed into a cooler autumn, and the western armies positioned for a great clash in the vicinity of Chattanooga. The importance of railroads in the Tennessee city and the geographical nature of the region made Chattanooga crucial to the South. In June the Army of the Cumberland under Rosecrans moved south against Gen. Braxton Bragg's Army of Tennessee. The same armies had grappled in the bloody slugfest at Stones River that proved strategically inconclusive at the outset of the year. Bragg fortified the city and entrenched but was forced to move south in September after Rosecrans's army crossed the Tennessee River and entered Chattanooga.

Bragg massed his forces at Lafayette, Georgia, and engaged portions of it with small, isolated Federal elements. He then marched his men to a position along Chickamauga Creek, a small riverway named in Cherokee dialect for the smallpox outbreak that had occurred along its banks. Chickamauga translated to "river of death."

By September 18 Bragg tried to force Rosecrans's hand by placing himself between the Yankees and Chattanooga. The movement precipitated a major battle that would result in an enormous Confederate victory.

On September 19 the battle erupted at Jay's Mill and spread south. The fields, cabins, and woods in the area witnessed repeated, rolling attacks that washed over the same ground, resulting mostly in temporary gains. The next day the battle was renewed, and again Bragg stabbed toward Chattanooga, inciting engagements along the entire north-south battle line. The struggle excelled with unspectacular results until timing struck just right: Union Brig. Gen. Thomas J. Wood was ordered to move his division to support another area, creating a quarter-mile-wide gap in the Federal line. Nearly at this moment Lt. Gen. James Longstreet sent six divisions forward, plowing through and sending the Yankees back in startled confusion. It was one of the greatest frontal attacks of the war.

"Now the enemy are in plain view along the road covering our entire front," James R. Carnahan, a captain in the Eighty-sixth Indiana Infantry, wrote of the attack. "You can see them, as with cap visors drawn well down over their eyes, the gun at the charge, with short, shrill shouts they come, and we see the colors of Longstreet's corps, flushed with victory, confronting us." On the Confederate side Capt. William Miller Owen, a staff officer of Brig. Gen. William Preston's, recorded his impressions: "The men rush over the hastily-constructed breastworks of logs and rails of the foe, with the old time familiar rebel yell, and, wheeling then to the right, the column sweeps the enemy before it, and pushes along the Chattanooga road towards Missionary Ridge in pursuit. It is glorious!"[1]

Pushed to a series of hills northwest of the center of the field, the last Union remnants held fast to a region called Horseshoe Ridge, which included Snodgrass Hill and a small cabinlike house owned by George Washington Snodgrass. Only Maj. Gen. George H. Thomas and the remainder of the Federal army held the ground here, earning Thomas the sobriquet "Rock of Chickamauga." Thomas's resistance prevented a rout and allowed Rosecrans and the bulk of the Union army to scurry back to Chattanooga.

The battle was a Union disaster — a spectacular, albeit brief, Confederate return to domination. Chickamauga caused panic in Washington, and Lincoln sparked an enormous movement to reinforce Rosecrans's stunned and mauled army. The new star of the Federal effort, Grant, would arrive to supervise personally the rebuilding of the army, now penned in Chattanooga and depleted of food and supplies.

The reinforcements sent to the Federals in Chattanooga included troops of Maj. Gens. Joseph Hooker and William Tecumseh Sherman, and by October Grant was in town taking charge. Starving and surrounded, the Yankees opened a tenuous "cracker line" of supplies from Bridgeport, Alabama, across a peninsula of land called Moccasin Point alongside the Tennessee River, and into the city. Bragg's victorious Confederates held the high ground: Lookout Mountain to the south and Missionary Ridge to the east. The river bordered the town on the west and north. Along the Confederate lines, picket duty was tense. Joseph B. Polley, a soldier in Hood's Texas Brigade, wrote: "All too soon the dreaded and fateful hour arrived; all too soon the whisper order 'Forward' was passed from man to man down the long line, and, like spectral forms in the ghastly moonlight, the Confederate pickets moved slowly out into the open field in their front, every moment expecting to see the flash of a gun and hear or feel its messenger of death."[2]

Bragg's army was not well supplied and lacked confidence in its commanding general, despite the victory at Chickamauga. Thomas attacked and captured Orchard Knob, a hill midway between the river and Missionary Ridge, on November 23. The following day Hooker's men assaulted and captured Lookout Mountain, partly aided by a blinding fog that gave the action the name "battle above the clouds," but mostly aided by the retreat of most of the Confederate troops. On November 25 Bragg concentrated his army along Missionary Ridge. As the bulk of the Federal army fanned into several attack points along the ridge, casualties mounted.

Just as the Union attack seemed desperately stalled, one of the spectacular events of the war occurred. Maj. Gen. Thomas's men, ordered to proceed from Orchard Knob to the base of Missionary Ridge and capture the rifle pits, proceeded after a pause up the mountain. Waves of blue coated the mountain and slowly captured the Confederate guns high atop its crest. "This, I confess, staggered me," wrote Maj. James A. Connolly. "'Charge' is shouted wildly from hundreds of throats, and with a yell such as that valley never heard before, the three divisions rushed forward. Our men, stirred by some memories, shouted 'Chickamauga!' as they scaled the works at the summit."[3] The Federal high command, watching from Orchard Knob, was stunned.

Bragg had no choice but to retreat into Georgia. Immediately, Federal troops occupied Chattanooga and controlled its railroads and communications. The movement opened up the possibility for Sherman's invasion of Georgia, the Atlanta campaign, and the March to the Sea that would follow. "The disaster admits of no palliation, and is justly disparaging to me as a commander," Bragg wrote in a letter to Jefferson Davis. "I trust, however, you may find on full investigation that the fault is not entirely mine."[4]

As the armies clashed at Chattanooga, other events occurred in eastern Tennessee, at Knoxville, where Rebel Lt. Gen. James Longstreet had been sent following Chickamauga, partly because of his animosity toward Bragg. Eastern Tennessee with its pro-Union sentiment had long been a problem for the Confederacy, and Longstreet wished to attack Maj. Gen. Ambrose E. Burnside's Yankees, who were operating in the region. Small actions erupted before Burnside retreated into Knoxville, pursued by Longstreet. Longstreet attacked Fort Sanders on November 29, but a deep, icy ditch prevented Confederate success. "For fully twenty minutes the men stood around the ditch unable to get at their adversaries but unwilling to retreat," wrote Col.

Edward Porter Alexander, Longstreet's acting chief of artillery. Capt. Orlando M. Poe, Burnside's chief engineer, recalled, "Meanwhile those who remained in the ditch found themselves under a deadly flank fire of musketry and canister, supplemented by shells thrown as hand-grenades from inside the fort, without the slightest possibility of returning a blow."[5] The Confederate attack failed, and Longstreet was ordered back to support the Army of Northern Virginia.

Before the year ended the United States president solidified the sense of purpose brought into the war the previous New Year's Day. For his trip to Gettysburg to dedicate the new National Cemetery, Lincoln struggled to express the meaning of all the death, the suffering, the smoke and battle. On November 19, speaking for little more than two minutes after the two-hour discourse by Massachusetts orator Edward Everett, Lincoln concluded, "It is rather for us to be here dedicated to the great task remaining before us — that from these honored dead we take increased devotion to that cause for which they gave the last full measure of devotion — that we here highly resolve that these dead shall not have died in vain — that this nation, under God, shall have a new birth of freedom — and that government of the people, by the people, for the people shall not perish from the Earth."[6]

———

THROUGHOUT the struggles on the battlefield, Confederate Richmond held its head high, hoping for turnarounds that would signal progress against the Yankees. And yet a sort of hopelessness had set in among some politicians in Richmond and army officers in the field. To some it hardly mattered what happened anymore. If you were a crony of the administration, you got a free pass despite the troubles that might surround you. Otherwise, it would be an uphill struggle for recognition and influence. It seemed that a new theme was emerging in Richmond: playing favorites. If your name was Bragg, Lee, or Cooper, you were above reproach. Sometimes the bonds seemed to come from the unlikeliest directions. "I know not what to think of Davis since he professed to be Yancey's friend!" penned Clement Clay of Alabama. "By the way he quite persuaded Y. that he was his friend. He left D. his telescope (wh. was [George] Washington's) by his will. Yet his wife is very bitter against D. and even blames him for her husband's death!"[7] For the most part, however, the favorites were predictable and immutable.

For his part Davis enjoyed looking to Johnston as chief scapegoat. Bragg, meanwhile, remained an almost indestructible friend of Jefferson Davis's. But confidence in Bragg was draining from almost everyone else at nearly lightning speed. In the wake of Chickamauga, Bragg blamed several subordinate officers for supposed incompetent behavior on the battlefield, most notably D. H. Hill and Leonidas Polk, both of whom were relieved of command by Bragg. Bragg's army felt their commander had overreacted, and a spirit of disunity and insubordination followed. Trying to assuage the troops, Davis addressed them: "He who sows the seeds of discontent and distrust prepares for the harvest of slaughter and defeat. To zeal you have added gallantry; to gallantry, energy; to energy, fortitude. Crown these with harmony, due subordination, and cheerful support of lawful authority, that the measure of your duty may be full."[8] Such words were cold comfort.

On October 15 several important officers of the army wrote a memorandum in support of Hill's actions at Chickamauga, testifying that he had the confidence of the army now. Moreover, Maj. Gen. John C. Breckinridge, the former vice president of the United States, wrote Hill: "I was present on the night of the 19th Sept. at an interview between Lt. Gen. Polk and Lt. Col. Anderson of your staff and think I heard all that passed between them. I do not recollect that Lt. Gen. Polk ordered you to attack at daylight."[9]

Polk, meanwhile, had the good fortune, like Bragg, of being the president's close friend. "After an examination into the causes and circumstances attending your being relieved from command with the army commanded by General Bragg," Davis wrote Polk, "I have arrived at the conclusion that there is nothing attending them to justify a Court Martial, or a Court of Inquiry, and I therefore dismiss the application."[10]

The Hill matter lingered for weeks, however. On November 13 Hill wrote Samuel Cooper asking that a court of inquiry be ordered to investigate Hill's conduct at Chickamauga. He wanted to remove the feeling of any "delinquency, mismanagement, or misconduct on the field" he may have committed.[11]

Three days later Hill addressed President Davis directly about the Chickamauga incident. He also complained that respected officers such as Longstreet, Simon B. Buckner, and Benjamin F. Cheatham also lacked confidence in Bragg but had not been relieved.[12]

But Davis wanted the matter simply to fade away. On November 20 Cooper wrote Hill formally telling him that a court of inquiry was not justified. "You have been simply relieved from duty at the request of your Commanding General," Cooper declared bluntly.[13]

While Hill was struggling with his reputation, Grant was making his way east. Brought to Chattanooga in the wake of the fiasco at Chickamauga, Grant was now ready to take on a major, shaping role in the war. Not all in the Confederacy were convinced this little man was a threat. More worried about Rosecrans. Lawrence Keitt of South Carolina wrote, "Rosecrantz [*sic*] is superseded by Grant — good for us, for Rosecrantz is far the ablest man."[14]

The new focus of the Confederate leadership was the loss at Chattanooga. "The disaster at Chattanooga gives much uneasiness here," lamented Joe Brown to his friend Aleck Stephens. "I fear it will be followed by other Federal victories which will cost us Upper Georgia for a time and expose our people there to extreme suffering. I wish we had a more able man at the head of our forces in that Department."[15]

For his part Jefferson Davis continued to worry over the command structure of the army. Davis hated the fact that various offices were appointed as political favors and not with regard to the best men. "My observations convince me that I have not overestimated, but rather underrated the importance of organizing the several staff corps as 'general staff corps of the army,'" he worried to Secretary of War Seddon in late October.[16]

As had been the case since the beginning of the war, chaos trumped coordination. The situation in North Carolina seemed to be getting out of control. An Alabama brigade on duty in the state supposedly had committed some outrages against the population, such as stealing, creating a feeling of minor anarchy at local levels.

"This thing is becoming unsupportable," Governor Zeb Vance reported to Jefferson Davis, "for sixty hours I have been traveling up and down, almost without sleep or rest, making speeches alternately to citizens and soldiers — engaged in the humiliating task of trying to defend the laws and peace of the State against our own bayonets!"[17]

Vance later informed the War Department about the arrival of his brother, Gen. Robert B. Vance, into the state. "Gen. R. B. Vance has arrived [in western North Carolina] and has not a single man with which to defend this country!" he exclaimed. Seddon endorsed the verso of the letter: "Any would cheerfully furnish the forces, if it could spare them." The situation was so perilous in parts of the state that Vance could not get any flour for locals to make the troops bread, and Abraham Myers in Richmond had to send him four barrels by special train. To restore order in the state, the Confederacy suggested detaching the Sixty-third North Carolina Infantry from Lee's army, but Lee refused, and Seddon finally had to write, limply, "If another good regt. from N.C. could be sent to take its place, there would be no objection."[18]

In South Carolina getting enough slaves released by their masters to help the Confederacy dig ditches and build fortifications continued to be a problem. Governor Milledge Bonham vented his frustration to anyone who would listen, including G. T. Beauregard. "They do not complain that they have to send their slaves," he wrote, "but they do complain that when impressments are resorted to, the slaves of those who have neither paid the money or sent the negroes are not impressed and carried to the coast . . . [and] that the negroes are not returned at the end of the month, as required by the Act of the Assembly."[19]

Bob Toombs, frustrated with the whole Davis government, contemplated running for political office once again. "I shall leave here Wednesday morning for Milledgeville [Georgia] with the purpose, if I can be elected, to run for the Senate," he told Aleck Stephens.

> Mr. Davis's present policy will overthrow the revolution in six months if the enemy only [gives] him time enough to stand still and do nothing. I shall do what I can to avert so dire a calamity. Of course in adopting

the proposed course towards Davis I am fully aware of the nature of the contest. We shall both fight under the same flag. *Vae victis,* — with this difference: I shall avow it and he will quote scripture, say "God bids us to do good for evil" and thus "clothe [his] naked villainy in old odd ends stole forth from holy writ and seem a saint when he plays the devil."[20]

⸻

WHILE all hell was breaking loose elsewhere, Congress reconvened in Richmond on December 7 for the fourth session of the First Congress. This would last until February 17, 1864. Previous campaigns, particularly those of Chattanooga and Vicksburg, continued to cast long shadows on the proceedings. In his opening message to Congress, President Davis chose to focus on the difficulty of securing international relations, now increasingly unlikely but viewed as the most credible route by which the Confederacy might establish its independence. "I regret to inform you that there has been no improvement in the state of our relations with foreign countries since my message in January last," Davis wrote. "On the contrary, there has been a still greater divergence in the conduct of European nations from that practical impartiality which alone deserves the name of neutrality, and their action in some cases has assumed a character positively unfriendly." He then moved on to other serious challenges:

> The state of the public finances is such as to demand your earliest and most earnest attention. . . . An organization of the general staff of the Army would be highly conducive to the efficiency of that most important branch of the service. . . . Having begun the war in direct violation of their Constitution, which forbade the attempt to coerce a State, they have been hardened by crime until they no longer attempt to veil their purpose to destroy the institutions and subvert the sovereignty and independence of these States. We now know that the only reliable hope for peace is in the vigor of our resistance.[21]

The congressmen, however, were focused on other things. In the Senate, for example, various legislators inquired about whether Davis really meant, as he had apparently been quoted, that "the disasterous [*sic*] defeat before Chattanooga [was caused by] . . . the want of valour on the part of our army." An outraged Senate as a whole took issue with the president and anyone else who charged the army with want of valor. A countercharge was made that the president was responsible, for he had not replaced Bragg, who had previously been shown to be incompetent. Some senators demanded that Bragg be replaced by Joe Johnston. The same arguments were applied also to Pemberton in connection with the Vicksburg campaign.[22]

In the House on the same day, Bragg came up as a prominent subject. Henry Foote inquired about raising a committee to investigate the country's "late disastrous defeat before Chattanooga." Foote was incensed by Davis's comments. "A more valiant body of men the world never saw," he exclaimed. He yelled violently, charging "Jefferson Davis with the responsibility of the defeat. . . . The President has persisted at keeping Bragg in office against the protest of both the army and the people." He accused Davis of treating Pemberton, "his bosom friend," the same way. "I charge the President with gross misconduct in retaining his favourites in office," he barked. If continued, he suggested, it "will prove fatal to our course."[23]

Three weeks later in the House, a discussion arose about the letter sent by officers of the Army of Tennessee which had been signed by twelve generals. The generals requested keeping the men in the ranks, without reorganization, for the duration of the war. They also wanted to extend conscription to an age range of fifteen to sixty and to prohibit leaves and furloughs. Incensed, Foote addressed the House. He defended the rights of the common soldiers by insisting they be able to choose their own officers and reacted most violently to the notion of expanded conscription. "If you extend the conscript law in the manner now recommended, the President, as the commander-in-chief, would have more power given to him than any monarch now living," he bellowed. Davis, said Foote, would not be likely to wield such power "either wisely or with a due regard to the rights of the States or the people. . . . When this country is called on to select a dictator, Jefferson Davis will not be, and ought not be . . . chosen, but . . . General Lee."[24]

Congress also fought bitterly — once again — over the issues of the general staff. It was as if they were a team arguing about uniform colors as their opponents rounded the bases unmolested. On the session's opening day in the Senate, the body received a message from President Davis recommending abolition of the gradation in rank for staff officers who served in different levels of command — Davis wanted to systematize everything. Rather than taking this seriously, however, the Senate and House attacked one of Davis's pet staff officers, Commissary of Subsistence Lucius Northrop. The allegation arose that Yankee prisoners were not getting enough to eat, which was true. "It is the fault of the Commissary-General, Mr. Northrop," barked Foote, "and his way of doing business. This man has been a curse to the country. He is a pepper doctor from South Carolina. . . . He should be dragged from his position."[25]

Also in the Senate, Edward Sparrow, chair of the powerful Military Affairs Committee, resolved to determine whether Quartermaster General Abraham Myers was discharging his duties correctly. Secretary of War James Seddon wrote the Senate reporting that Alexander Lawton had been serving as quartermaster general since August 7, 1863. The secretary's reply to a query directed at the president infuriated members of Congress. "I do not understand it," Wigfall said of the letter. "I do not understand why the President has been shuffled to the bottom and the Secretary turned up. General Myers is still the quartermaster general," he said, "and that General Lawton had been assigned to the duties does not effect [sic] the case. . . . The Senate has been cheated by his assignment." Essentially ignoring Davis's assignment of Lawton to the post, on December 23, seventy-six members of Congress sent a letter to the president recommending that "Abraham C. Myers, Quartermaster General, be appointed a brigadier general."[26] This infuriated Davis.

The old issue of a Confederate Supreme Court came up again, about which no progress had been made since the first time it was mentioned on the House floor. Rufus Garland of Arkansas nevertheless wanted to push ahead. "It is dangerous to society to be without the properly established tribunals of justice," he proclaimed. "While the pending war is in progress we have no use for a supreme appellate tribunal," said Foote. "No, sir, the establishment of the court would have inevitable effect of bringing the sovereign States in our system in dire conflict with the central government." Moreover, Foote asserted, he would never assent to a Supreme Court as long as "Judah P. Benjamin shall continue to pollute the ears of majesty with his insidious counsels," further evidence of Foote's anti-Semitism.[27]

And in the midst of this arguing, indications of the wheels coming off surfaced in North Carolina. Confederates there were becoming increasingly discontented, and support for the war in the Tar Heel State seemed to be waning. On December 30 Davis received a letter from Governor Vance referring to the unrest in his state. "After a careful consideration of all the sources of discontent in North Carolina," the governor wrote, "I have concluded that it will be perhaps impossible to remove it, except by making some effort at negotiation with the enemy."[28] On receiving this barrage, Jefferson Davis must have felt a sting as deep as a shot through the side at Chattanooga or Vicksburg. And, like the wounds that brought down Stonewall Jackson, the pain was all the greater knowing the assailant was supposed to be a friend. The sparks that were supposed to ignite a great Southern torch were drifting apart in the wind, extinguished in the wet and cold of the December midnight.

Chapter

15

THE PRESIDENT VERSUS
THE CONGRESS

T HE nature of the war would transform considerably during the year 1864. No longer would the Confederacy feel such confidence in its ability to outlast the conviction of the North or to win support from foreign powers. Never again would the eastern Confederate army bring the war onto Northern soil, apart from small-scale raids. Now the issues of diminishing supplies and an increasingly harder life for citizens on the home front would begin to plague the decisions being made by Confederate commanders. And the decisive Union victory at Chattanooga would allow a Yankee penetration deep into the South that would endanger the Confederacy's ability to continue waging war.

During the final weeks of 1863, the eastern armies under Lee and Meade had engaged in a fruitless exercise known as the Mine Run campaign. Lee's army, somewhat scattered, constructed quarters south of the Rapidan River, west of Fredericksburg, Virginia, to serve as winter lodging. Meade's plan of attack was poorly executed, and by the opening days of December, both armies sat inactive, resigned to the harsh weather. In part due to Lincoln's ongoing frustration with the eastern commanders, and largely due to Grant's successive victories in the West, Lincoln had appointed Grant general-in-chief of all armies in the field. Grant was also commissioned lieutenant general in the regular army, the first use of that grade since George Washington. Now Grant would direct all military operations, save for those of the navy. Warned to stay away from Washington by his good friend William T. Sherman, Grant established his headquarters in the field, where politicians couldn't meddle with him. As a result he would accompany Meade and the Army of the Potomac.

This assignment of Grant's would prove to be the solution Lincoln had been looking for all along to the problems of command. The arrangement eased friction that had existed between Secretary of War Stanton and Grant, both of whom now had direct access to Lincoln. Lincoln had allowed the assignment of two chiefs of staff, one in Washington (Halleck) to continue on as the chief military paper pusher, and the other, Brig. Gen. John A. Rawlins, in the field, to serve as Grant's personal attaché to military departments and field forces. Both Halleck and Rawlins now performed at their full potential, filtering communications, summarizing the consequential and blocking the trivial, interpreting military and political jargon, and effectively interacting with Lincoln and Grant. Thus, Lincoln was freed to concentrate on policy matters, while Grant considered matters of strategy. It was a smooth, efficient system in the making, hit on by pure experimentation. The Confederates, by contrast, would never discover such efficiency.

=

THE calendar may have turned, but familiar subjects continued to upset congressmen and members of the administration. The touchy business of who could appoint officers to act in the field still, after months of war, presented problems. On January 9 the Senate, led by Edward Sparrow, discussed Davis's custom of antedating his nominations, which the Senate felt was an abuse of power. Davis had had enough. On January 15 he sent the Congress an angry explanation of his powers and why he should be enabled to order military commissions as he chose. Responding to the Senate's Military Affairs Committee Report Number 15, which disapproved of the president's action and challenged his authority, he wrote,

I confess my surprise at finding myself apparently charged with a violation of the Constitution . . . the only difficulty . . . is that . . . the date [of] rank is anterior to the last session of Congress. The Committee are of the opinion that the Constitution contemplates that all officers appointed in the recess of Congress shall only hold under such appointments to the close of the next session of Congress . . . and that they should be renominated, if it is intended to retain them in their office. . . .

The Senate cannot but agree with me that the plain inference from these passages is that the Constitution has been violated by my having appointed these offices during the recess and retained them in office without nominating them to the Senate at its next session. It has thus become incumbent on me . . . to repel any inference that might hereafter be drawn from my silence on the subject, by stating that not only had no appointments of these officers been made prior to the nominations on which the Senate has just acted, but in fact of the necessity for the appointments reached the Executive only since the commencement of your present session, by communication received last month from the Trans-Mississippi Department.

Upon the point suggested in the close of the resolution, that the Executive is without the right to make a nomination to a military grade, coupled with a rank from a date prior to a former session of the Senate, it is not deemed proper to anticipate any future disagreement with the Senate by presenting the reasons for the opposite conclusion as being the only one consistent with the laws for the regulation of the Army, as well as with long-settled usage and the necessity of the service.

Davis went on almost endlessly, the words gushing with volume but not force,

When the occasion shall arise I cannot doubt that the Senate will, notwithstanding this resolution, refuse to abandon its own constitutional power to act on nominations at its pleasure, according to the mer-

its of each case and the good of the service. I am confirmed in this conclusion by observing that the resolution passed without a call for the yeas
and nays, and therefore with probably less than the usual consideration,
as well as by the further reflection that as Executive nominations which
meet the disapproval of the Senate on any ground are always subject to
rejection without assignment of reasons, experience will show that no
advantage can arise from the Senate's curtailing its own discretion in future cases by binding its own judgment in advance.[1]

Most senators were dumbstruck by Davis's angry, long legalese.
Wigfall ordered that Davis's reply be tabled, and the situation smol-
dered without resolution.

On January 21 the Senate resolved that Abraham Myers was
legally recognized as the quartermaster general of the army, not
Alexander Lawton, whom the president had appointed the previous
August.[2] A showdown over the Myers-Lawton controversy now began. On January 27 Davis decided to go back to square one. "I submit to the Senate herewith," he wrote, "the Nomination of A. R.
Lawton, of Georgia, to be Quartermaster General, with rank of
Brigadier General to take rank from the 13th day of April 1861, and
deem it proper to communicate the reasons which induce this
course." In an effort to appoint the most competent person, Davis
reported that

> the office of Quartermaster General was offered to General Lawton,
> who was adverse to accepting it if it involved a nomination and new ap-
> pointment, for the reason that it withdrew him from service in the field,
> interfered with his chances for promotion, and that, as he was then the
> oldest [sic; senior] brigadier in the service, he would, by acceptance of a
> new commission, be deprived of his relative rank as compared with other
> brigadiers. There were two other officers recommended to me . . . and
> they were both Major Generals and could not therefore be expected to
> accept a lower grade in the staff than that which they held in the line.

Davis then continued with his explanation of the Lawton case,
and just as with his response to the antedating report, his argument

lacked all conclusion. On and on he went, for pages, with technical detail and legal qualification.

The name of the officer then performing the duties of Quartermaster General was also presented to me [But Davis did not approve of the promotion or retention of the incumbent, Myers]. . . . On examination of the law above referred to, its language, although not free from doubt, was held, after consultation and advice, to justify the conclusion that the intention of Congress would be fulfilled by assigning to the performance of the duties of Quartermaster General an officer already confirmed as Brigadier General in the Provisional Army, without again submitting his nomination to the Senate. The grounds for this conclusion were that the eighth section of the Act of 6th March, 1861, organizing the Regular Army, expressly authorized the Executive to assign Brigadier Generals to any duties he might specially direct, and when the five Brigadier Generals were raised to the rank of General in the Act of 16th May, 1861, the president was again empowered to assign them to such command and "duties" as he might specially direct. As it had therefore been permitted by Congress that any one of the Generals of the Regular Army might be assigned to staff or any other duty at Executive discretion, it seemed a fair inference that when by the law of last session provision was made that the rank, pay, and allowances of Quartermaster General should be those of a Brigadier General in the Provisional Army the will of the Legislature was as well fulfilled by assigning to the duties of that office one who was already a Brigadier General of the Provisional Army as by nominating a new officer.

Incensed, Davis continued his barrage:

This view of the question was fortified by the fact that the law last referred to did not create an office, but only provided that during the war the officer discharging the duties of Quartermaster General should have the rank of Brigadier General, and by the further fact that the original act of 26th February, 1861, for the establishment and organization of the general staff, contained a provision, still in force, that officers of the

Quartermaster General and other staff departments might by order of the President be assigned to the command of troops, according to their rank in the Army, thus indicating that positions in the Quartermaster's and other staff departments were not distinct offices, but were posts of duty to which officers of the Army were appointed, and from which they might be withdrawn and assigned to other duties at Executive discretion. This provision of our law that did not exist in the former service of the United States, in which when an officer of the Army entered the Quartermaster's Department he surrendered his commission in the line and his right to command troops.

"I am advised, however," Davis continued, "that such is not the construction given to the law by many Senators" — an understatement to say the least.[3] The Senate was not about to take up Davis on his nomination offer. The House, for its part, worked on its own general staff bill. The controversy would smolder for months, leaving Lawton in place. The president seemed to have won the technical debate but lost potential supporters in Congress by doing so. He was not the only loser: regarding the staff bill, Joe Johnston wrote Wigfall from the field, full of fury. "My objection to the bill is that it will take so many of the best officers from their proper places with the troops," said Johnston, "for others in which they have not been tried. . . . The officer who had distinguished himself in the command of a brigade might utterly fail as a staff officer."[4] Another major area seemed to have been resolved to the satisfaction of nearly no one in the Confederacy.

━━

MEANWHILE, soldiers on both sides survived as best they could through the long winter and wondered about the campaigns to come. Religion filled the lives of an increasing number of soldiers in 1864, as the war dragged on. "The church was very neat and filled with soldiers, but one woman in the audience," wrote Jenkin Jones of the Sixth Wisconsin Artillery, at church in Huntsville, Alabama, on January 17. "Chaplain of 18th Wisconsin officiated, of the Calvinistic school, and but ill agreed with my views, but it seemed good to be once

211

more listening to an earnest speaker and hear the old-fashioned tunes swell in the bass voices that filled the room. Returned to camp, if not better a more thoughtful man."

In the Army of Northern Virginia, however, earthly concerns made for a tone that was becoming increasingly grim. "Short rations are having a bad effect upon the men, both morally and physically," wrote Lee to Seddon on January 22. "Desertions to the enemy are becoming more frequent, and the men cannot continue healthy and vigorous if confined to this spare diet for any length of time. Unless there is a change, I fear the army cannot be kept together."[5]

With the Rapidan River separating the opposing eastern armies, little action occurred. A number of relatively small engagements took place in the western theater, however. In Mississippi Sherman launched an expedition to destroy railroads and military resources in the central portion of the state, in somewhat of a dress rehearsal for his March to the Sea later the same year. On February 3 he moved from Vicksburg with twenty-five thousand men and faced scattered forces under four Confederate commanders. After five skirmishes Sherman's army wrecked the facilities at Meridian before withdrawing to Vicksburg.

As Sherman was busily ruining the military value of Meridian, the largest battle of the war fought in Florida occurred. At Olustee, west of Jacksonville, the clash was a relatively small engagement, but nonetheless it ended as a spectacular Confederate victory, with heavy losses. On the same day to the north, fighting in northern Georgia accelerated. Since the Union occupation of Chattanooga, Joe Johnston had positioned forces around Dalton, Georgia. A reconnaissance on February 22 by Union major general John M. Palmer checked the enemy's positions and produced clashes at Tunnel Hill, Rocky Face Ridge, and Varnell's Station. Johnston's defensive tactics constituted an approach that would be debated heavily in the weeks to come.

The recapture of Arkansas and Louisiana continued to trouble the Lincoln administration. Lincoln also worried over the French governance of Mexico and desired a strong show of Federal force in Texas. He, therefore, acquiesced to Henry Halleck's request to launch an operation that became known as the Red River campaign. This befuddled series of maneuvers, led by Maj. Gen. Nathaniel P. Banks, was coordinated with Sherman and Maj. Gen. Frederick Steele. It was a combined operation, with naval gunboats providing support. The campaign lasted until May 18, produced a large series of small skirmishes and a few battles, and entrapped the gunboats near Alexandria due to low water. Only Lt. Col. Joseph Bailey's engineering genius saved the fleet. Wrote Porter from his flagship *Black Hawk* to Navy Secretary Gideon Welles on May 16: "I have the honor to inform you that the vessels lately caught by low water above the falls at Alexandria, have been released from their unpleasant position. . . . Lieut.-Colonel Bailey, Acting Engineer of the 19th Army Corps, proposed a plan of building a series of dams across the rocks at the falls, and raising the water high enough to let the vessels pass over."[6] The campaign ended with virtually nothing accomplished but causing a great deal of disarray on both sides.

═══

WHAT is wanting in Richmond is '*brains*,'" Howell Cobb wrote to his Georgia friend Aleck Stephens, vice president of the Confederacy. "I did not find the temper and disposition of Congress as bad as I expected, but there is a lamentable want of brains and good sound common sense."[7] Lawrence Keitt, writing his wife, echoed Cobb's fears:

> I hear that Toombs is on the stump in Geo., and is arraigning Davis in a terrible manner. I have always feared the divisions, which I saw would spring up among us. You cannot have liaison — connexion — unity — among a planting community. Too many Revolutions have shipwrecked upon internal division. This Revolution proves that canonized imbecility is but a straw before the wrath of masses — it seems to be a law of humanity that generation after generation must rescue its liberties from the insidious grasp of a foe without or within. In our case, we have to seize them from both foes — we have a worthless government, and are reduced to the humiliation of acknowledging it, because we cannot, with safety, shake it.[8]

Some congressmen tired of the constant bickering and grew fearful of the potential advance of Grant's army toward Richmond. Wrote Wigfall in April,

> If Lincoln has, as the Northern papers say, at last found out, that he cannot . . . wound the armies of the United States longer with safety to either his country or himself & Grant is not a greater fool than he is usually taken to be, Lee will have no child's play this spring & the sooner Congress adjourns & we get South the better. Richmond is an entrenched camp without depots & subsistence & if Lee is ever driven with the lines around the city & it is thoroughly invested, the surrender of his Army will be only a question of time.[9]

Those were strong words from the fire-eating Texan.

If the conventional war was appearing increasingly unlikely for the Confederate authorities to win, then they would introduce and experiment with other options. "I have not been unmindful of the necessity for prompt action in the matter to which you refer," Jefferson Davis wrote Robert M. T. Hunter, on April 14, 1864, "and have made attempts to engage for the service in Canada several gentlemen deemed competent; but they have declined for various reasons. The subject is too delicate to permit entering into details until I have the pleasure of seeing you. I confine myself to saying that two persons specially qualified are now on their way here from the South. . . . One of them, the General Agent, is well known to you."[10] Davis was referring to hiring spies who would conduct secret operations on behalf of the Confederacy, one of which would be a raid on St. Albans, Vermont. Other actions also were planned, such as blowing up ships on the Great Lakes. These quasiterrorist acts reflect the onrushing sense of despair that Davis and other Southern politicians were beginning to feel this spring.

Two weeks later, Clement Clay began a mission. "I am on my way to Canada, for the purpose of arming the country as I best can," he wrote to his friend Wigfall. "You know how as well as I do. It is a very responsible, difficult, and delicate duty, for which I am not suited by my talents, tastes or habits. . . . I cannot enjoy secret service. I expect to suffer daily annoyances from the hounds who will be set to watch & pursue me."[11]

While future terror plans were being drafted in Canada, another radical act, this one by the Yankees, was unfolding. In February Union cavalrymen hatched and carried out a raid on the outskirts of the Confederate capital that sent a chill through the spines of Richmonders. Civil War prisons held thousands of Southern and Northern soldiers in their brutal grip throughout the war. The most notorious prisons in the South were part of a group in Richmond that included Libby Prison (for Yankee officers) and Belle Isle (for enlisted men). During the late winter thaw of 1864, a dashing young Union cavalry brigadier general named H. Judson Kilpatrick had hatched a plan to raid Richmond, free Northern prisoners, and generally wreak havoc on the city. This was prompted by intelligence reports of horrible overcrowding in the prisons, inadequate food, and a supposed garrison force in Richmond of only 3,000. The Union high command approved of the plan, and Kilpatrick, Col. Ulric Dahlgren, and 3,584 troopers set out on the raid on February 28. Dahlgren was of particular value to the Yankee general. He was just twenty-one years old and the son of the highly respected Union rear admiral John A. B. Dahlgren, a close friend of President Lincoln's. Young Dahlgren had a reputation for hard fighting — he had lost a leg at Hagerstown, Maryland, the previous summer.

On the twenty-ninth the raiders reached Spotsylvania Court House, where Dahlgren took a detachment of five hundred to attack Richmond from the south. Kilpatrick — with enemy forces behind him — would enter the city from the north. The only nuisance was a cold rain that transformed into sleet by the following night. Meanwhile, Confederate Brig. Gen. George Washington Custis Lee — Robert E. Lee's eldest son — shifted his local defense forces to block an attack he predicted would come from the west.

Strangely, Kilpatrick — who was known for reckless bravery — halted at the outer defenses of Richmond on March 1, even though only a small opposing force met him there. By nightfall Confederate cavalry had caught up with Kilpatrick and attacked him in camp. Kilpatrick retreated, aborted the plan, and left Dahlgren in the lurch.

At Goochland, twenty miles northwest of the city, Dahlgren split his force and then recombined it, finally reaching a point two and a half miles south of the city on the evening of March 1. After dark General Lee's forces fought a sharp skirmish with Dahlgren. One day later, during Dahlgren's retreat, Confederates ambushed his men, capturing ninety-two and killing Dahlgren.

Then came the controversy. A thirteen-year-old boy named William Littlepage found on Dahlgren's body papers that disclosed a plan to release fifteen thousand prisoners, who would act as a guard until fresh Federal troops arrived. The papers also contained information about burning the city and killing Jefferson Davis and his cabinet.

The papers, at the time alleged by some to be either Confederate forgeries or at least not written in Dahlgren's hand, sparked intense debate in the South. (In modern times the papers have been conclusively judged authentic.) The responses ranged from Confederate Col. Josiah Gorgas's proposed plan to execute all Yankee prisoners to Robert E. Lee's more rational and restrained response of sending a letter of inquiry to the Federals. Kilpatrick issued a statement to George G. Meade, his commanding general, that he knew nothing. Therefore, officially, the responsibility for the idea had died with Dahlgren. But in a time of war and heated passions, such plots undoubtedly were contemplated more than once in both Washington and Richmond.

To coordinate Southern military affairs and prevent such attacks, many Confederate politicians had long wanted a general-in-chief. Jefferson Davis was always reluctant to dilute his nearly absolute power, but in February he came as close as he could get by appointing a special adviser to the president on military affairs — the same role, in essence, that Lee had played before taking command of the Army of Northern Virginia. He now gave that lofty post to none other than Braxton Bragg, his good friend in whom many others, including most congressmen, had almost no faith. Nevertheless, on February 24, 1864, Bragg was "charged with the conduct of military operations in the armies of the Confederacy." About the same time Congress toyed with two volatile ideas that infuriated Davis. First, the Senate introduced a bill to limit the terms of the president's cabinet members. The matter was debated to no conclusion, but the discussion sent Davis into convulsions of anger over the assumed power of Congress over the executive branch. Further, Virginian Thomas S. Bocock, Speaker of the House, introduced a vote of no confidence in the administration. This, too, was debated with no significant conclusion.

There was some cooperation. Congress passed the Third Conscription Act on February 17, which made white men aged seventeen to fifty eligible for service. Now nearly every man would have to report. But while relations between Davis and Congress would work out regarding conscription — most congressmen at this point felt no alternative was left — stormy times lay ahead on the issue of habeas corpus. Davis felt he was losing control. In February, in a mood bordering on paranoia, he had written to Congress of "discontent, disaffection, and disloyalty . . . treasonable design . . . plots to release prisoners . . . conspirators . . . spies . . . deserters . . . Having thus presented some of the threatening evils that exist, it remains to suggest a remedy. And in my judgment, that is only to be found in the suspension of the privilege of the Writ of Habeus [*sic*] Corpus."[12]

Other powerful forces continued to work against suspending the writ, however, including Davis's own vice president. From his bed in Georgia, Stephens wrote:

> I am now comparatively comfortable — free from violent pain and able to sit up. I have great interest in what's doing in Congress and shall go on just as soon as I feel able. The thing I would say to your great apprehension is beginning to be felt amongst the public here that Congress will pass an act suspending the writ of Habeas Corpus and putting the country under martial law. Such an act would in my judgment be exceedingly [unconstitutional], and I trust if it should pass it will never achieve the executive approval.[13]

Davis continued to work for congressional support on the issue in whatever way he could. He declared,

While brigade after brigade of our brave soldiers who have endured the trials of the camp and battlefield are testifying their spirit and patriotism by voluntary reenlistment for the war, discontent, disaffection, and disloyalty are manifested among those who, through the sacrifices of others, have enjoyed quiet and safety at home. . . . On one occasion, when a party of officers were laying a torpedo in the James River, persons on shore were detected communicating with the enemy, and were known to pilot them to a convenient point for observing the nature of the service in which the party were engaged. They were arrested and were discharged on habeas corpus, because, although there was moral certainty of their guilt, it could not be proved by competent testimony. . . . In my judgment [a remedy] is to be found only in the suspension of the privilege of the writ of habeas corpus. It is a sharp remedy, but a necessary one. It is a remedy plainly contemplated by the Constitution.[14]

The assumption was clearly that a true patriot would go along with the administration's position.

Too many others disagreed, however, and the issue remained at a standstill. Lawrence Keitt flatly stated,

The act reproaching the Habeas Corpus, I believed, when I read it, to be unconstitutional. For the past year, Congress has been acting under the idea of "Independence now — Liberty hereafter" — If the two are not reconcilable now, they will not be reconciled in the future. Our whole system of government has been gradually passing into a new phase — common abroad — but not known to us in the past — all powers are fast trending to the Executive control. . . . I confess the shameful wish on the part of the Confederate government to overlook, and slight even, the States, bodes not well for the future.[15]

While nothing happened with habeas corpus, another, even more explosive issue was arising. A significant discussion had erupted on the floor of the House on February 1 regarding the use of African American troops in the Confederate army, which to some implied the possibility of a form of emancipation. Joe Johnston wrote to his friend Wigfall, from a position north of Atlanta,

I propose to substitute slaves for all soldiers employed out of the ranks on detached service, extra duties, as cooks, engineer labourers, pioneers, or on any kind of work. Such details for this little army amount to more than 10,000 men. Negroes would serve for such purposes better than soldiers. The impressment of negroes has been practiced ever since the war commenced, but we have never been able to keep the impressed negroes with an army near the enemy. They desert & their owners, if they do not investigate, do not prevent it. If you can devise & pass a law to enable us to hold slaves or other negroes with armies, this one can, in a few weeks, be increased by the number given above.[16]

Congress agreed on the following terms regarding free African Americans used as soldiers: not using free blacks while using poor whites as soldiers is discriminatory; black soldiers should be used for menial tasks only since those who could read and write might desert to the enemy; blacks make good laborers but poor soldiers; "free negroes . . . are inimical to our cause"; up to twenty thousand African Americans, aged between eighteen and fifty, should be employed for labor on fortifications, government workshops, hospitals, mess tents, etc.; the pay of slaves should go to their masters; and should too few slaves volunteer or be furnished by their masters, they should be impressed.

In the House Porcher Miles brought up the act, which would increase the army by adding slaves and free blacks to labor in it. All black males between eighteen and fifty would be required to serve. Erasmus Gardenhire of Tennessee asked that if the bill passed, "would it not recognize Lincoln's right to conscribe our negroes?" Porcher Miles said, "We have a right to do what we please with our slaves, and Lincoln has no control over them." Henry Foote said that a difficulty might exist relative to prisoner exchange. "Suppose some of them are taken prisoner," he asked. "What would be done with them?" Miles reported the committee had not considered that.[17]

A few days later in the Senate, a bill was introduced to place free blacks in the military; it was then referred to committee. By order of the Senate leadership, the committee was discharged from considering the bill on February 5, 1864. Meanwhile, in the House, Miles again reported that he believed the act to employ slaves and free blacks would increase the army by forty thousand men. John Baldwin of Virginia wanted to exempt any free blacks engaged in food production, particularly in the Shenandoah Valley. Ethelbert Barksdale of Mississippi objected, saying that free blacks "are a blot upon our escutcheon, and pernicious to our slave population. . . . [Baldwin] says to the free negro, you shall not bear the burdens of this war — while [the white citizen] must take his place in the army."[18] After further argument and slight massaging of the language, the bill was passed. Whether African American soldiers would serve in the Confederacy, however — whether they would be armed and whether slaves would be emancipated in compensation — was a thorny topic to be held for another day. Like so many policy and military decisions the South needed to make, it was deferred.

——

A s always President Davis found another source of pain and interference, as he saw it, at least. North Carolina seemed to be coming apart at the seams. Wrote Governor Zeb Vance,

> The final plunge which I have been dreading and avoiding, that is to separate me from a large number of my political friends, is about to be made. It is now a fixed policy of W. Holden and others to call a convention in May to take N.C. back to the United States, and the agitation has already begun. Resolutions advocating this course were prepared here a few days ago in the *Standard* office and sent to Johnson County to be presented at a public meeting next week. If I should go down before the current I shall perish . . . at bay, destroying many a foe.[19]

Anti-Richmond sentiment had been growing in the Tar Heel State, fueled by state rights philosophy and a feeling that the war had worsened lives rather than improved them.

In response the president warned Vance and his allies against seeking a peace movement away from the military victory of the Confederacy. "Peace [without liberty and independence] is now impossible," wrote Davis. "This struggle must continue until the enemy is beaten out of his vain confidence in our subjugation. Then and not till then will it be possible to treat of peace."[20] Vance sought the counsel of his fellow governor Joe Brown in Georgia as well. "While there is no considerable discontent at the action of the Confederate authority in this state," Brown responded, "and a sincere desire for peace, there is not a great deal of disloyalty, and no despotism manifested to take any course by separate state action to correct the errors or abuses by the Confederate government, at so critical a period in our struggle." Brown agreed with Vance that the government had done too little to build up Northern groups who were "hostile to the Lincoln policy."[21]

Davis and Vance then entered into an argumentative correspondence, with Vance asserting that Davis excluded anti-secessionists from the important offices of the government and from army promotions. Vance suggested that "the great body of our people have been *suspected* by their Government, perhaps because of the reluctance with which they gave up the old Union." Vance also complained about conscription, which had been "ruthless," "unrelenting," and only "exceeded in the severity of its execution by the impressment of property frequently entrusted to men unprincipled, dishonest, and filled to overflowing with all the petty meanness of small minds, dressed in a little brief authority." In response Davis wrote Vance: "I warned you of the error of warming *traitors* into active life by ill-timed deference or timid concession, instead of meeting their insidious attempts to deceive the people, by tearing the mask from the faces of the conspirators."[22] With that, the governor of North Carolina and the leader of the Confederacy let their relationship cool to an icy near-nonexistence.

Brown, meanwhile, was experiencing increasing paranoia. "I would be obliged if you would mark all your letters private across the seal of the envelope," he wrote his friend Aleck Stephens, "as I often have to leave my mails to be opened by secretaries and prefer that your letters should always be handed to me unopened."[23] Brown didn't want even his own staff to see the thoughts he harbored toward Davis.

Little Aleck wasted no time in informing his friend that authorities in Richmond were growing tired of his lack of cooperation and wanted to find a way to get rid of him and install a pro-administration governor in the state. "I thank you for your suggestions and for advising me of the prospect of a war to be waged against me at Richmond," the governor wrote Aleck Stephens. "I regret that such may be the intention of those in authority. If it must come I shall try to be prepared to meet it."[24]

Davis, aware that North Carolina and Georgia were now attempting to block his policies, if not splinter the Confederacy, heard whispers of hope in the Northern states from his political friends. "There exists in the North West and North a secret political organization," penned J. W. Tucker, a Mississippi newspaper editor, "having a Lodge in St. Louis, with one thousand members." The principles of the group included: preservation of state rights, opposition to Republicanism, recognition of the Southern Confederacy, the formation of a "North West Republic," and making open war against the "perverted government" of the United States.[25] But hoping for assistance from distant cousins when his brothers-in-arms were increasingly against him seemed like foolish behavior on Davis's part. And the rhetoric of his fellow Confederates was more and more barbed and sharpened. Wrote Bob Toombs, "I am greatly delighted at the vote on Linton's resolutions concerning the suspension of *habeas corpus*. . . . I shall certainly give Mr. Davis an early opportunity to make me a victim by advising resistance, resistance to the death, to his law."[26]

While this splintering of the South has been ignored or downplayed by many Southern historians, subversive, secret societies in the North have received quite a lot of press. Called "dark lanterns" in the 1850s, underground political groups gained momentum as the war grew unpopular among some citizens when casualties mounted after 1863. Such antiadministration groups as the Knights of the Golden Circle, the Order of American Knights, and the Sons of Liberty attempted to thwart the goals of the Lincoln administration and bring about a swift peace movement. The most vocal inciter of this type was the radical Ohio politician Clement Vallandigham, whom Lincoln exiled to the South to quell his rabble-rousing speeches. But the influence of secret societies in the North has been overblown. In the end, as historian Frank Klement has meticulously documented, these societies never amounted to much more than paper-based organizations with vague goals and "little ability to carry them out."

A far more skilled orator, the old "father of secession," Robert Barnwell Rhett, commented on the Davis administration and its military policies in a letter to Louis Wigfall:

> During the war, I cannot advise you to propose in Congress an alteration of the Constitution in any particular; for it is impossible in the condition of the country, to get a hearing, or in the second place to get any efficient cooperation. The greater part of the People are in the army, where a rigid despotism prevails; and men used to it, cannot feel, in the face of the dangers and excitement which surrounds them the insolence of Constitutional provisions to protect liberty, or to correct inadequacies in the Constitution. . . . We will win our liberties and independence, I believe; but it will be in spite of the most terrible incompetency . . . in our Executive, which has ever afflicted a noble people.[27]

The venom went both ways. "I learn that Genl. [Howell] Cobb is getting crazy in the state of fury," Brown wrote Aleck Stephens. "A friend from Atlanta writes me that he denounced me on the R.R. car between Macon and that place the other day as a *traitor*, a *Tory;* said I ought to be hung and would be soon; that he had never been to a hanging but would go some distance to see it done, etc. . . . He did all he could to serve his master [Davis]."[28] A true Confederate this was not.

16

MILITARY HIGHS AND LOWS

I N the east the armies were positioning themselves for what might be the decisive campaign of the war. The Federal command now understood fully that geography was not the issue — destruction of the enemy armies and their ability to wage war was. Particular cities were subtext. "Lee's army will be your objective point," wrote Grant at Culpeper Court House on April 9 to George Meade. "Wherever Lee goes, there you will go also."[1]

By the first days of May, with the onset of warm weather, Grant's 119,000 men were spread north of the Rapidan from Culpeper Court House to Manassas Junction in Virginia. Lee's 64,000 lay south of the river from Gordonsville to near the Wilderness, the forested area west of Fredericksburg, with Stuart's cavalry south of Fredericksburg. Without risking staggering casualties, Lee's position could not be attacked frontally. Instead, Grant would need to turn Lee's right, interposing his army between Lee's army and Richmond, to preserve his own line of communications and force Lee to retreat southward. The stage was set for what would become the Wilderness, or Overland, campaign. So on May 3 Grant ordered the army corps under Maj. Gens. Winfield Scott Hancock, John Sedgwick, and Gouverneur

Warren south to Germanna Ford and Ely's Ford on the river, where they would cross and move into the Wilderness.

Just after midnight on May 4, Hancock's Second Army Corps and Warren's Fifth Army Corps crossed the fords and moved into the Wilderness, unsupported by artillery or cavalry. Grant hoped to move the men through the brushy, heavily wooded region quickly, but by early afternoon Warren had halted at Wilderness Tavern, three miles west of Chancellorsville, and Hancock near Chancellorsville itself. Meanwhile, Confederates under Lt. Gen. Richard S. Ewell were approaching Warren, and those under Lt. Gen. A. P. Hill were nearing Hancock. Longstreet was approaching, too, but farther behind. "You will already have learned that the army of Gen Meade is in motion, and is crossing the Rapidan on our right, whether with the intention of attacking, or moving towards Fredericksburg, I am not able to say," Lee reported to Jefferson Davis on May 4. "But it is apparent that the long threatened effort to take Richmond has begun, and that the enemy has collected all his available force to accomplish it."[2]

On the morning of May 5, Ewell clashed with Warren, opening the battle of the Wilderness. Sedgwick arrived from the north, supporting Warren with three additional divisions, and Hancock approached from Todd's Tavern, three miles south of Wilderness Tavern. The Yankees, spread along a northwest-southeast line across the Orange-Fredericksburg Turnpike, faced the five divisions of Ewell and Hill. Poor visibility and difficulty of holding formations meant attackers normally were heard well before they could fire on the defenders. It was far from ideal for the Northerners: Confederate troops seemed better adapted to the woods, and Federal troops were relying on poor maps. Moreover, Confederate attacks in such conditions were especially unnerving to the Yankees, due to the fearsome rebel yell. "The Federal, or 'Yankee,' yell, compared with that of the Confederate, lacked in vocal breadth, pitch, and resonance," explained Harvie Dew of the Ninth Virginia Cavalry. Dew continued, "This was unquestionably attributable to the fact that the soldiery of the North was drawn and recruited chiefly from large cities and towns, from factory districts, and from the more densely settled portions of the country. In an instant every voice with one accord vigorously shouted that 'Rebel yell,' which was so often heard on the field of battle. 'Woh-who-ey!, who-ey!, who-ey! Woh-oh-ey! who-ey! etc.' "[3]

The Confederates worked their psychological advantages well, and because of various hesitations on the Federals' part, held their lines in strong fashion until darkness fell. Each army planned an attack for the next morning. At 5 a.m. on May 6, much of the Federal line lunged forward on the offensive, with Ewell defending well on the north, and Hill, to the south, breaking in confusion. As the Confederate right was crumbling, Longstreet arrived and reinforced the position. On the northernmost end of the line, Confederate Brig. Gen. John B. Gordon launched an attack that succeeded until halted by darkness. On May 7 the armies reinforced their lines and mostly stayed inactive, with fires consuming parts of the Wilderness brush that separated them — fires that burned some wounded to death. Already the casualties were heavy, amounting to possibly as many as thirty thousand total, and neither side had gained a meaningful outcome. But rather than retreat, Grant chose to turn Lee's left and race toward Richmond, necessitating the Confederate commander to block him at the junction of roads near Spotsylvania Court House.

On the Confederate side A. P. Hill was sick, and Longstreet, the senior corps commander, had been seriously wounded, accidentally, by his own men on the Brock Road on May 6. On May 8, as elements of both armies vied for position near Spotsylvania, Warren's infantry clashed with Confederate units of Longstreet's corps, now commanded by Maj. Gen. Richard H. Anderson. A Federal attack late in the afternoon was too poorly coordinated to achieve a significant result.

By May 9 the Confederate corps of Anderson, Ewell, and Maj. Gen. Jubal Early (replacing Hill, temporarily) formed a semicircle near Spotsylvania Court House, with the Federals approaching from the northwest (Hancock, Warren, and Sedgwick) and the northeast (Maj. Gen. Ambrose Burnside). On this day, as aides worried over his exposure to Confederate fire, Sedgwick was killed, hit below the left eye by a minié bullet. (Among his last words were, "They couldn't hit an elephant at this distance.") The following day, the

Confederate line tightened, and part of Ewell's position formed a Mule Shoe salient, a semicircular bulge, around two local houses. Grant had the opportunity to turn Lee's left but remained determined that Hancock should assault from the front. At 4 p.m. on May 10, Hancock, Warren, and Maj. Gen. Horatio Wright (having replaced Sedgwick) struck vigorously into Anderson's corps. The resulting casualties were monstrous. "Ambulances and army wagons with two tiers of flooring, loaded with wounded and drawn by four and six mule teams, pass along the plank, or rather, corduroy road to Fredericksburg," wrote Augustus Brown of the Fourth New York Heavy Artillery. "Many of the wounds are full of maggots. I saw one man with an arm off at the shoulder, with maggots half an inch long crawling in the sloughing flesh, and several poor fellows were holding stumps of legs and arms straight up in the air so as to ease the pain the road and the heartless drivers subjected them to."[4]

The following day, May 11, was quiet, masking a grim determination on Grant's part to engineer the end of the war. "I propose to fight it out on this line, if it takes all summer," he wrote Henry Halleck on this day. All knew the heavy fighting — in what was becoming a micro-siege at Spotsylvania — would continue. "I shall come out of this fight a live major general or a dead brigadier," wrote Brig. Gen. Abner Monroe Perrin, who commanded a brigade in A. P. Hill's corps.[5] He was killed the next day. On May 12 a vicious frontal attack by Hancock plunged into the Mule Shoe. Attacks and counterattacks continued until dusk. The fighting was stubborn, and Lee slowly began to develop a new line, this time positioned south of the Mule Shoe.

During all this, Union cavalry under Maj. Gen. Philip H. Sheridan had been raiding Richmond, drawing J. E. B. Stuart away from Lee's army. The approach to Richmond culminated in the battle of Yellow Tavern, where Stuart was mortally wounded on May 11, dying the next day. After destroying supplies and railroad, Sheridan returned to Grant's army on May 24. After continued fighting around Spotsylvania Court House, Grant sent Hancock to Guinea's Station, ten miles east of Spotsylvania, and interposed Federal forces between Lee's army and Richmond. A rush to a potential next line of defenses ensued for Lee, who withdrew to a position along the North Anna River. After a fight on May 23, both armies again raced southward, Lee's army arriving astride the old battlefields of the Peninsular campaign of 1862 by May 28. Elements of Grant's army arrived east of Atlee's Station and Cold Harbor by May 30 and June 1.

At Cold Harbor Lee's army of about 59,000 faced Grant's force of about 108,000. Between Richmond and Petersburg, Maj. Gen. Benjamin F. Butler's Army of the James, consisting of 14,600 men, faced Confederate general G. T. Beauregard's 9,000 soldiers. Planning to take the offensive, Lee sent Anderson to strike Sheridan at Old Cold Harbor, with disastrous effect: once opposed, the Confederates scattered in retreat.

The next day both armies moved toward Cold Harbor. In the early morning of June 3, Grant ordered a frontal attack designed to push Lee to the Chickahominy, but more than seven thousand Yankee soldiers were cut down in less than one hour. "The dead and dying lay in front of the Confederate lines in triangles, of which the apexes were the bravest men who came nearest to the breastworks under the withering, deadly fire," wrote Charles Venable, a staff officer of Lee's, of the attack. The armies stubbornly fought from the trenches for the next nine days, with the cost in suffering and casualties fearfully high. "We are now at Cold Harbor, where we have been since June 1," wrote Federal colonel Emory Upton on June 5. "On that day we had a murderous engagement. I say murderous, because we were recklessly ordered to assault the enemy's intrenchments, knowing neither their strength nor position. Our loss was very heavy, and to no purpose. Our men are brave, but cannot accomplish impossibilities." Despite the savagery of the fighting and the newspaper reports of monstrous casualties, young men were still anxious to support both armies with their sweat and blood. Richard Corbin, a young Southerner in Paris, ran the blockade to join his beloved army. "*Veni, Vici,* and as Julius Caesar remarked, we have gone in and won," he wrote on June 5 from Wilmington. "Thank Heaven I am at last on Confederate soil, having most successfully passed through that awful ordeal . . . the blockade."[6]

On June 12 Grant initiated a movement that would set up the final act of the war. His plan was to shift his base of operations south of the James River, capture Petersburg, and threaten the last railroad supply line connecting Richmond with the outside world. To do this he established a second line at Cold Harbor and withdrew under the cover of darkness, sending Maj. Gen. William F. Smith's Eighteenth Corps to Bermuda Hundred, on the James River twenty miles south of Richmond, where it arrived on June 15. The remaining corps also sped southward, and when Lee heard about the Yankee movements, he relocated Anderson and A. P. Hill south toward Malvern Hill to block an approach toward Richmond.

Having fooled Lee entirely, Grant ordered Smith to attack and capture Petersburg at daybreak on June 15, but he approached cautiously and reconnoitered the city's defenses so extensively that an attack was not launched until 7 p.m. He captured two redans, small gun emplacements, with ease, and by the fall of darkness nothing prevented him from marching straight into Petersburg. Unduly concerned about possible growing Confederate strength in the area, Smith stayed put, and the opportunity was lost.

On June 16 heavy reinforcements arrived, along with Grant, who ordered an assault at 6 p.m. A light attack on the following day and a heavier one on June 18 both failed against the strengthening Confederate defenses. "I shall never forget the hurricane of shot and shell which struck us as we emerged from the belt of trees," wrote Augustus Brown of the battle on June 18. "The sound of the whizzing bullets and exploding shells, blending in awful volume, seemed like the terrific hissing of some gigantic furnace. Men, torn and bleeding, fell headlong from the ranks as the murderous hail swept through the line."[7] The Petersburg operations were transforming into a siege. Indeed, sporadic fighting around a deepening network of trenches — punctuated by infrequent major attacks — would characterize the remainder of the war on the Petersburg front.

WHILE these many developments were transforming the war's character in Virginia, Union Maj. Gen. William T. Sherman was transforming the war another way in Georgia. In May Sherman, who commanded the Military Division of the Mississippi, moved his three armies southward toward the Army of Tennessee, commanded by Gen. Joseph E. Johnston. He was not alone: Sherman brought the Army of the Tennessee (24,000 men commanded by Maj. Gen. James B. McPherson), the Army of the Cumberland (61,000 under Maj. Gen. George H. Thomas), and the Army of the Ohio (13,500 under Maj. Gen. John M. Schofield) against some 50,000 of Johnston's defenders. The plan was for Sherman to crush Johnston's army, move against the rail center of Atlanta, and destroy the heart of Georgia's capacity to support wartime operations.

The armies clashed at Rocky Face Ridge, north of Dalton, between May 5 and 7. On May 13 Johnston fell back to Resaca, south of Dalton, hoping to lure Sherman into a foolish attack. Elements of the armies skirmished at this position for three days before Johnston again pulled back, allowing Sherman to capture the manufacturing town of Rome. After additional minor engagements, Johnston retreated to the heavily defended position of Allatoona Pass. Between May 25 and 27 the armies clashed, and Sherman continued turning movements that forced Johnston southward toward Atlanta. Thereafter, Union soldiers established a supply depot at Big Shanty — the position from which James Andrews's raid had departed two years before — and by late June Johnston constructed a heavy defensive line along Kennesaw Mountain, northwest of Marietta. There, on June 27, a savage frontal assault from Sherman resulted in bloody casualties, particularly for the Union attackers, who amassed three thousand killed, wounded, and missing.

The armies of Sherman and Johnston contrasted starkly to those of the east. They were largely made up of western and midwestern men, many of whom were rough, rugged characters. "With regard to the general appearance of the Westerners, it is not so different from our own as I had supposed, but certain it is that discipline is most astonishingly lax," wrote Federal staff officer John Chipman Gray that summer.[8] Despite their lack of discipline, the Yankees continued moving south. Johnston next dug in along the Chattahoochie River, where again Sherman turned his line, forcing a withdrawal to Peachtree Creek, two miles farther south and on the outskirts of Atlanta, on July 9. For a week Sherman prepared for a major, coordinated movement across the river. Meanwhile, Jefferson Davis had reached the limits of his tolerance with Joe Johnston, whose repeated movements southward initiated a near panic in the Confederate capital. The replacement for Johnston, assigned on July 17, was Lt. Gen. John Bell Hood, the veteran of many battles that, among other things, left him without his right leg (lost at Chickamauga) and the use of his left arm (at Gettysburg). Now he would attempt to defend the heart of the rail system supporting the Deep South.

In the battle of Peachtree Creek on July 20, Hood attacked and suffered heavy casualties. He then backed into the defenses of Atlanta. The battle of Atlanta, during which McPherson was killed, resulted two days later — as Sherman believed Hood was withdrawing from the city. By July 28 Maj. Gen. Oliver O. Howard, who replaced McPherson, pushed northwestward around the city and toward Ezra Church, two miles west of the city's edge, where he attempted, unsuccessfully, to cut the rail lines and isolate the Confederates. A detachment of cavalry left on a mission to free Union prisoners at Andersonville far to the south but was captured. Sherman finally advanced on August 26, and Hood's groggy response led to the battle of Jonesboro, south of the city, between August 30 and September 1. Hood pulled out of Atlanta in the late afternoon of September 1, when Federal troops marched into the city, escorting civilians out of the area and converting Atlanta into a fortified supply camp. "You cannot qualify war in harsher terms than I will," Sherman wrote Atlanta's mayor, James M. Calhoun, on September 12. "War is cruelty, and you cannot refine it. . . . You might as well appeal against the thunder-storm as against these terrible hardships of war."[9] Hood moved his troops northward into the first phase of what would become a campaign of pure folly.

———

Elsewhere, a variety of land and naval actions were under way. On June 10 at Brice's Crossroads, Mississippi, north of Tupelo, Confederate cavalry great Nathan Bedford Forrest, now a major general, defeated Federal Maj. Gen. Samuel D. Sturgis's force of 7,800 with less than half as many soldiers. The war touched Europe on June 19, when off the coast of Cherbourg, France, the USS *Kearsarge* sank the CSS *Alabama,* the notorious raider that had sunk, burned, or captured sixty-nine ships. In the Shenandoah Valley on June 23, Confederate Maj. Gen. Jubal A. Early began a raid that would bring the terror of war to the outskirts of Washington. Early was checked by Maj. Gen. Lew Wallace along the Monocacy River near Frederick, Maryland, on July 9. Although this battle stopped his advance only briefly, it allowed the Union defenses of Washington to tighten. On July 11 and 12 Early made his closest pass to the capital when he skirmished at Fort Stevens, a battle briefly witnessed by President Lincoln.

The focus, however, remained on the Petersburg defense lines, where the tedium of trench warfare ground on. "I have only one earthly want," Robert E. Lee wrote his son Custis, "that God in His infinite mercy will send our enemies back to their homes."[10] Grant had no such idea, however. The frustrating stalemate led to a novel idea from a regiment of Pennsylvania coal miners — to tunnel underneath the Confederate works, pack the tunnel with black powder, and blow a breach in the line so troops could rush through to victory. Lt. Col. Henry Pleasants of the Forty-eighth Pennsylvania Infantry received permission to proceed with the plan, and by July 23 a shaft measuring 511 feet long extended to a position some 20 feet below the Confederate line. Federal soldiers placed about four tons of black powder — roughly 320 kegs — into the mine adit. Confederates had detected the tunneling operation and constructed a smaller countermine, but they had no indication of the impending explosion. At 4:45 a.m. on July 30, the powder exploded, forming a crater 170 feet long, 80 feet wide, and 30 feet deep. Nine companies of Confederate soldiers were hurled into the air, and some 278 soldiers were killed instantly. In the ensuing melee Union soldiers became mired in the debris rather than pushing forward, and two officers commanding the attack, Brig. Gens. Edward Ferrero and James H. Ledlie, cowered in a bombproof, drinking liquor. It was one of the great disasters of the war. After the smoke, the destruction, and the death, nothing had changed — the Petersburg siege continued.

——

F AR to the southwest, near Mobile, Alabama, a Federal naval force commanded by Rear Adm. David G. Farragut prepared to cut off one of the Confederacy's remaining major ports. In addition to his flagship, USS *Hartford,* Farragut's force consisted of four monitors and thirteen wooden ships. He faced the ironclad ram CSS *Tennessee* and three gunboats, the CSS *Morgan,* CSS *Gaines,* and CSS *Selma,* commanded by Adm. Franklin Buchanan. At 6 a.m. on August 5, Farragut attacked, attempting to run the guns of the nearby forts. The heavy guns of Fort Morgan opened fire on Farragut's fleet slightly more than an hour later. After more than half an hour of intense action, Farragut's lead ship, the USS *Tecumseh,* struck a torpedo (naval mine) and sank. At this point Farragut allegedly stated, "Damn the torpedoes — full speed ahead!"[11] He pressed through, pushed the *Tennessee* into surrender, and captured the imaginations of Northerners as another Union hero.

——

I N Richmond, meanwhile, the Second Congress of the Confederate States of America had convened on May 2. The first session was brief, lasting only until June 14. Despite his sagging relationship with Congress, President Davis attempted to put the best spin on the events that were bearing down on the capital. With Grant's forces on the march toward the city, he wrote, "The recent events of the war are highly creditable to our troops. . . . The armies in northern Georgia and in northern Virginia still oppose with unshaken front a formidable barrier to the progress of the invader, and our generals, armies, and people are animated by cheerful confidence."[12]

Two days later, with Yankees in the neighborhood, the Richmond Tocsin on Capitol Square rang loudly, and members of Congress were thrown into a "patriotic ebullition" that had much in common with near panic. Some wanted to rush to the front to join the fight in the Wilderness. Others wanted to evacuate Richmond and move the entire government to a place of safety. Legislators introduced a flurry of resolutions, amendments, and joint agreements. Members resolved that Congress should form a Congressional Company and take to the field; that Congress should do nothing so as not to alarm the public; that they should formally declare that there was absolutely no danger. Others in Congress pressed for an official explanation that the ringing of the Tocsin did not signal peace, safety, and security; for an exemption of those over fifty from service (which would have included many congressmen); or for an admission that success in the defense of Richmond would depend on everyone — "This is no time for balderdash and jest!" one member snapped. Still others took the floor to suggest that there was no time to refer any response to the Military Affairs Committee, which would only delay any action, or that Congress should rely on the president to tell it what it should do.

In the cacophony some proposed that members should volunteer in various units, affording a great example but not risking the danger of wholesale capture. Others suggested that no member had the right to place his usefulness to his constituency in danger, that Congress should at least defend Richmond as a body and set a good example for the whole country, and that volunteering to fight with the army would mean a virtual dissolution of the government. At last one member declared that since the members of Congress had shown themselves to be sufficiently patriotic, they should table these resolutions and return to other work. This, finally, was what happened — as the Tocsin continued to ring.[13]

The next day Louis Wigfall treated his fellow senators to a tantrum. With Grant bearing down on Richmond, and with "relatively little business" to transact in committee, several senators thought a day for the session's adjournment ought to be set. Robert Johnson of Arkansas pushed the point. "During a campaign like the present," he said, "the whole attention of the President should be free to be devoted to military affairs." Wigfall objected. He had read the papers, but did "not care whether the President thinks there is much for Congress to do or not. The President is not charged with deciding the question what Congress has to do, but Congress itself is." Wigfall ranted that "ours is the only army in the world, civilized or savage, that does not have an inspector general . . . [or] a pay department. . . . The habeas corpus law also demands our attention." He added in a scream, "If Congress has a fault, it is its constant haste to adjourn."[14]

Other politician-generals were much more in control of their emotions, regardless of the dangers. "The feeling is prevalent here that peace is at hand," Lawrence Keitt wrote his wife. "If Lee crushes Grant I know that it is."[15] A week after that letter, however, Keitt was struck down on the battlefield near Gaines's Mill. "I was with [Keitt] all the time not otherwise engaged from the time I heard of his wound until he died," wrote A. S. Talley, a surgeon.

> From the field, he was taken to a house near by, where I found him. . . . I told him he was very dangerously wounded but I hoped not mortally. He asked me if there were as many chances for as against him. I told him I thought then the chances were equal. He was in very great pain was pale and extremely prostrated. I gave him whiskey and morphine. . . . I asked him if he had any message to leave with me. He remained silent for a moment, and then said with a tear from his right eye, which was up, "My two children and my wife." I do not think he spoke after these words. He died quietly.[16]

In the Senate the Braxton Bragg matter would not die. On May 25 James Orr of South Carolina opposed a bill for an additional salary for Bragg while he was charged with military operations in Richmond. Orr despised Bragg, saying the office was "superfluous, and that Bragg is incompetent for the position." Debate followed, with Edward Sparrow defending the assignment as having been made by Davis, while Wigfall said the two least qualified Confederate generals were Bragg and Pemberton, both of whom were now stationed in Richmond. Sparrow declared the bill needed to be acted on, whether the adviser was Bragg or Lee. Orr said he saw Bragg in person for the first time "a week ago, and concluded that he has neither the head nor the heart to lead our armies to victory."[17] Consideration of the bill was postponed.

The next day the matter arose again. Wigfall felt it his duty to say he could not vote for the bill. "The naked question . . . is that there are not two men in the Confederacy more singularly unfit to command armies than Bragg and Pemberton," he snapped, "yet we have them both here."[18] Nonetheless, the bill passed and provided for Bragg to be paid the same amount as a general officer commanding a separate army in the field.

On June 10 the matter came up yet again. Wigfall introduced a bill to repeal the act that would provide a staff and clerical force for Bragg. But with "scarcely more than a dozen members" of the Senate present, Wigfall had no hope of doing anything. Orr agreed with Wigfall but said, "It is too late to do anything with it." Orr ranted on, saying it was strange that the office once filled by Lee was now filled by Bragg — "that was to this Hyperion to a satyr." In the old United States, said Orr, there was a parallel: "The position once filled by George Washington is now filled by Abraham Lincoln."[19]

Beating on Bragg — and by association, Davis — was not Congress's only activity during this stressful time, however. As the armies grappled in the Wilderness, Wigfall also introduced his fellow senators to a resolution of his own to suspend habeas corpus during time of invasion. Now, what Davis had wanted for so long, Wigfall wanted for himself. The proposed bill also asserted that "State courts, being established by State authority, can in no manner be affected by Confederate legislation" and that "State and Confederate governments are separate, distinct, and co-ordinate governments." Trying to have it all ways at once, it also stated the Constitution of the Confederate States is a "compact" of the states between them and is "equally supreme and binding to [citizens] as their State Constitution."[20] On May 11, 1864, Wigfall's resolution was tabled — yet another piece of proposed legislation that sucked up time and went nowhere.

Vampirelike, two days later, the subject came up again. In the Senate Albert Brown of Mississippi shared resolutions of the Mississippi legislature, asking Congress to vote for a bill repealing the act to enable suspending habeas corpus. "The people at home have raised the howl that 'our liberty is in danger,'" said Brown. However, he proclaimed: "I will stand by the president in his heroic efforts to drive back the invaders."[21] On May 16 Henry Chambers of Mississippi declared it inexpedient to repeal the act suspending the writ of habeas corpus. But Burgess Gaither of North Carolina said the whole matter should be delayed because of the immediate danger to the capital. The whole subject was — surprise, surprise — postponed.[22]

Two days later in the House, Henry Foote, "flanked by legal and documentary reports," spoke on habeas corpus for two and a half hours. "The country is engaged in a great war for independence," he said, "the maintenance of State rights and State sovereignty . . . these depend on our failure or triumph in this war. . . . I will do nothing to weaken the Executive arm; nothing to palsy the government vigour; nothing to thwart the common zeal. God forbid!" Foote, quoting from Magna Carta and the Bill of Rights, variously proclaimed, "True, O king!" and "Thank God for James Madison!" He attacked the government for suspending the writ in Richmond and in North Carolina, saying that anyone who called the suspension in those places a necessary act was telling "a garnished lie." He said, "The suspending act clothes the President with extraordinary powers, executive, legislative, judicial — centering in one human being the Congress and the Court. The whole civil fabric and law is under his feet. Great God! What an exhibition for a free people in this boasted nineteenth century!" The disloyalty the act is intended to fight is a "phantom, a myth, a vapour," said Foote, "the mirage arising from a diseased eye. There is no such thing as disloyalty, neither in Richmond nor North Carolina." William Rives of Virginia attempted to reply to the rambling speech, but was cut short and had to promise to speak again on the subject later.[23] Foote's resolution was tabled by a vote of fifty-five to twenty-five.[24]

The next day Davis responded. The president favored suspension, he argued, because it had been beneficial more than once, caused no abridgment of the rights of law-abiding citizens, and no good citizens had suffered wrongfully. "In my opinion the reasons given in the special message transmitted to Congress at its last session, recommending the suspension of the writ of *habeas corpus,* still exist in undiminished force and the present juncture especially requires the continuance of the suspension," he penned. "It would be perilous, if not calamitous, to discontinue the suspension while the armies of the enemy are pressing on our brave defenders."[25] But many members of Congress responded that Davis's claims were vague, general, and mysterious.

As habeas corpus provided fireworks, the old subject of appointments reared its head. In mid-May the Senate Judiciary Committee was asked to rule on whether nominations from the first Senate should still be considered in the second Senate. By a vote of seventeen to zero, the Senate declared all unconfirmed nominations should lapse at the end of the session. This naturally inflamed Davis, who wanted control over such matters. On May 28 the Senate additionally ruled that all nominations not acted upon during a session of the Senate must be renominated (the nomination itself begun again from scratch) and may not be "carried over" to the next session — a step further than the seventeen-to-zero vote.[26]

Matters pertaining to the subject of a general staff bill did not go any more smoothly. Davis insisted on flexibility in staffing to conform to differing requirements in various departments and armies. Specifications for the commissary of subsistence, quartermaster general, adjutant general, inspector general, chief of ordnance, and chief engineer all vary greatly, he argued. Rigid rules for the qualifications of various staff officers would limit those officers for transfer to other assignments. Transfers would be awkward, Davis reasoned, as well as create difficulties for the assignment of aides-de-camp.[27]

Instead of an independent staff corps, with fixed numbers and grades of officers assigned to commanding generals' staffs, Davis favored assignments based on merit made from anywhere within the army. Officers with such staff assignments would retain their line and/or staff commissions. When requirements changed, staff officers would revert to their line and/or staff grades without the loss of relative rank. But Congress disagreed, and the president found himself vetoing the bill they sent forward.[28]

—

AGAIN and again the leaders of the Confederacy chose to spend their energies on questions of bureaucracy and patronage, circling round and round while the Union swept forward. Nothing, however, was gaining more momentum against the administration this long, hot summer than the splintering of loyalty from state governors. The greatest trouble was growing in Georgia, centered around Aleck Stephens. The fire of the vice president's disloyalty had many sources, one of which was his friendship with a cranky, antiadministration newspaper editor, Henry Cleveland, who ran the *Augusta Constitutionalist*. The two struck up a long, detailed correspondence in which they openly discussed the president's incompetence and what ought to be done about it. The two men also raised the idea of a peace conference that could somehow wrest the war from the hands of Davis and restore tranquillity to the South before the Davis administration ruined it forever.

On June 8 Cleveland wrote the vice president, "Since my second letter to you, I have received your last, and confess that I did suppose you had hope of terms from Lincoln. For my self (from reasons I will some day give you) I am satisfied that the States can to day get terms and good terms, but Mr. Davis never can." Continued Cleveland,

> No human power can change Mr. Davis, and consequently, no human power can save the Confederacy from war and speeches. I am satisfied that the immediate secession of Georgia from the Confederate States would be the best thing we could do, and am equally satisfied that nine-tenths of the people of Georgia will follow the lead of the Administration, until our cause is beyond the hand of resurrection. . . . The Stars and Stripes will float over the Government works in Augusta before a year expires, and Mr. Davis be dead or in exile. . . . To win this fight, under this Administration, would be a result without a reason — an effect without a cause. Is this treason? I am afraid you will think so, but it is difficult to look back at all we have suffered, and see blood and life and desperate valor *thrown away,* and still think calmly.[29]

Local politics and business intervened to muzzle Cleveland's public discontent. "A letter from Henry Cleveland informs me that the majority of the stock of the *Constitutionalist* is now owned by Administration men," wrote Joe Brown, a fellow conspirator, "and that he will be obliged to change his course, keep silent, or be ousted. Could not enough of the stock be purchased to control and keep the paper on the rights lines?"[30] But despite the shift more and more people picked up on an increasing and tangled web of conspiracy in Georgia. "Our Vice President is a dangerous man," Brig. Gen. Thomas C. Hindman wrote his friend Louis Wigfall, "the more so because of his stealthy policy and his bogus reputation for fairness and honesty. I consider him the head of a faction that is ready to betray the Confederacy and sell the blood of the Army. 'Crushing him out' is doing God's service."[31]

With Sherman's army bearing down on Atlanta, the conspiracy took a backseat to more practical matters — though these, too, only added to the discontent. "I fully appreciate the importance of Atlanta," Jefferson Davis wrote Governor Brown, "as evinced by my past action. I have sent all available reinforcements, detaching troops even from points that remain exposed to the enemy. The disparity of force between the opposing armies in Northern Georgia is less as reported than at any other point."[32] But Brown wanted more troops, more ammunition, more everything to protect Georgia. "I regret exceedingly that you cannot grant my request as I am satisfied Sherman's escape with his army would be impossible if ten thousand good cavalry under Forrest were thrown in his rear this side of Chattanooga and his supplies cut off," Brown raged. "The whole country expects this, though points of less importance should be for a time overrun. . . . If your mistake should result in the loss of Atlanta and the occupation of other strong points in this State by the enemy, the blow may be fatal to our cause and remote posterity may have reason to mourn over the error."[33]

The president, who was losing patience entirely with Brown, shot back at him sharply. "Your dicta cannot control the disposition of troops in different parts of the Confederate States," the president snapped. "I will be glad also to know the source of your information as to what the whole country expects, and posterity will judge."[34]

Brown and Davis had other problems besides the defense of Atlanta. At Andersonville, Georgia, where thousands of Yankee prisoners were starving and held in the stockade (making the prison temporarily the third largest city in the Confederacy, with more than thirty-three thousand residents), John Winder, the hated former provost marshal of Richmond, had a crisis on his hands. "Matters have arrived at that point *where I must* have reinforcements," he urgently wrote Howell Cobb. "Now General it is morally certain that if the Government or the people of Georgia don't come to my relief and that instantly, I cannot hold these prisoners, and they must submit to see Georgia devastated by the *prisoners.* There is not a moment to spare. . . . Twenty-four hours may be too late."[35] "It is dreadful. My heart aches for the poor wretches, Yankees though they are," wrote Eliza Andrews, a nurse, of the prisoners at Andersonville, "and I am afraid God will suffer some terrible retribution to fall upon us for letting such things happen."[36]

In doubt Davis turned to Lee, as he always seemed to do. "*Genl. Johnston* has *failed* and there are strong indications that he will *abandon Atlanta,*" he wrote. "He urges that *prisoners* should be removed immediately from *Andersonville.* It seems necessary to *relieve him* at once. Who should *succeed* him? What think you of Hood for the position?"[37] Meanwhile, Johnston, seemingly at a loss about what to do, received direction from the president. "You have all the force which can be employed, to *distribute* or *guard prisoners,*" wrote Davis. "Know the condition of the country and the prospects of military operations. I must rely on you to advise *Genl. Winder* as to the proper and practicable action in relation to *U.S. Prisoners.*"[38] How should they be taken care of with the Yankees closing in?

As the situation deteriorated around them, Stephens and Cleveland kept up their correspondence, searching for a newspaper that could be bought and turned into an antagonistic enemy of the administration, perhaps leading to Georgia's secession. "I enclose a letter which speaks for itself," wrote Cleveland of a prospective purchase. "The circulation is exactly that of the *Constitutionalist.* . . . It is the best bargain I have heard of in two years."[39] Soon afterward he wrote again. "I am 'in for the war' against Davis," he declared, "if I can do any good. Mr. Morse to day for the first time, talks about giving up control of the paper [the *Constitutionalist*], but asks a week to decide."[40]

Howell Cobb, meanwhile, still held out hope for Atlanta. "There has been quite a bloody fight at Atlanta resulting favorably to our army," he informed his wife. "As yet we have very few details and the extent of the victory is wholly unknown. . . . The loss of generals is severe on both sides. Genl. McPherson was the next man to Sherman in the Yankee army and some people regard him as the ablest man of the two. The other Yankee generals killed were small potatoes."[41]

Cleveland was not so hopeful. "If the Yankees come to Crawfords-ville [*sic;* Crawfordville, between Atlanta and Augusta, where the vice president lived]," he penned to Stephens, "send your effects to my care and come and stay with me. I would be glad of your society for the next ten years. My little twelve year old would not object to a playmate of her own age, but I would not have room for a family."[42]

Governor Brown, meanwhile, mourned the worsening situation in Georgia and believed it was all Davis's fault. At least now, however, Brown acknowledged the national authorities the ability to control his troops. In the Georgia field Bob Toombs approved of Johnston's removal and felt some confidence in the new commander, whose reputation was as a reckless fighter. "Hood is getting ridd [*sic*] of Bragg's worthless pets as fast as he can," he informed Stephens, "but Davis supports a great number of them, and many other incompts. are sent from other places to take their commands. Hood I think the very best of the generals of his school; but like the rest of them he knows no more of business than a ten year old boy, and [I] don't know who does know anything about it."[43]

Not knowing went straight to the top. Despite the losses, despite mounting evidence of the Georgia conspiracy, despite the sorrowful shape of the Confederate war effort overall, one man still believed fervently that the South would win the war. He was Jefferson Davis, and in his office in Richmond he was fed a regular diet of suspicious information and conclusions that allowed him to believe such a thing regardless of what transpired on the battlefield. "The Northern mind, as a whole, is in an extremely malleable condition," S. J. Anderson, a clerk with Southern sympathies in the mayor's office in New York City, informed the Confederate president. "It fully appreciates the historical fact that Southern Statesmen and Southern policy moulded the character and guided the prosperity of the country prior to the election of Lincoln, and they pant and sigh for the restoration of that statesmanship and policy."[44] With that kind of idea in the Northern mind, how could the Confederacy, in the end, possibly lose?

The answer was: badly, as Davis and his fellow backbiters were soon to learn.

Chapter

17

———

SLAVES AS SOLDIERS?

As Grant and Meade continued in their struggle against Lee at Petersburg, and Sherman pushed more deeply into Georgia, a third operation began in the Union grand strategy of simultaneous movements. In August Maj. Gen. Philip H. Sheridan initiated a campaign to clear the Shenandoah Valley of Confederate troops. He would face Jubal Early, who had threatened Washington so successfully the month before. On September 19 the two forces clashed at Winchester, where Sheridan decisively won and forced Early southward to Fishers Hill. Despite the victory a letter written on this day underscores the uncertainty all parties had about the course of the war and the chances for politics to play a critical role. "The State election of Indiana occurs on the 11th of October," Abraham Lincoln wrote Sherman. "And the loss of it, to the friends of the Government would go far toward losing the whole Union cause. . . . Anything you can safely do to let her soldiers, or any part of them, go home and vote at the State election will be greatly in point."[1]

In the western theater Confederate major general Sterling Price launched a raid across Missouri that had little concrete strategic objective. The idea was to recover the state for the Confederacy, but the realism of such a goal had faded many months before. Nonetheless, Price captured Lexington on September 17–20 and proceeded to attack Fort Davidson, near the distinctive mountain dubbed Pilot Knob, on September 26–27. "Price arrived before Pilot Knob in the afternoon of September 26th," wrote Wiley Britton of the Sixth Kansas Cavalry (U.S.A.), "and skirmished until night with detachments of Federal cavalry. . . . Price opened the attack on [Fort Davidson] at daylight on the 27th, and kept it up all day with great resolution."[2] The campaign was fruitless, however, as Price retreated and then made a circuitous journey through Indian Territory to escape Federal forces. In all this he had done little more than increase the well-being of undertakers.

Meanwhile the situation in the valley between Sheridan and Early accelerated. "To-morrow I will continue the destruction of wheat, forage, etc., down to Fisher's Hill," Sheridan wrote Grant from Woodstock, west of Front Royal, on October 7. "When this is completed the Valley, from Winchester up to Staunton, ninety-two miles, will have little in it for man or beast."[3] He subsequently decisively beat the Confederate force at Tom's Brook, a few miles north of Woodstock, on October 9. Four days later Early made a show of force at Strasburg, forcing Sheridan to recall troops to Middletown, north of Tom's Brook. Having been in Washington for a conference, on October 19 Sheridan returned and approached his army along the Valley Turnpike from Winchester to Cedar Creek. The battle of Cedar Creek, fought in the fields near Middletown, seemed a rout of the Federals. Sheridan's presence, however, sparked his men into regrouping and counterattacking, and the resulting Union victory would spell the end of Confederate resistance in the valley.

Throughout this autumn season the growing legions of prisoners held in both Northern and Southern prisons suffered like never before. "Our quarters were so crowded that none of us had more space to himself than he actually occupied, usually a strip of the bare, hard floor, about six feet by two," wrote Abner Small, a Federal soldier formerly of the Sixteenth Maine Infantry imprisoned in Danville, Virginia. "We lay in long rows, two rows of men with their heads to the side walls and two with their heads together along the center of the room." The scant rations given prisoners led to fantastic rates of death and disease. "A prisoner eating this [spare] diet will crave any kind of fresh meat," wrote Marcus Toney, a Confederate imprisoned at Elmira, New York. "Marching through the camp one day was a prisoner in a barrel shirt, with placard, 'I eat a dog'; another one bearing a barrel, with placard, 'Dog Eater.' . . . It appeared these prisoners had captured a lapdog owned by the baker who came into camp daily to bake bread." The methods to which partisans were resorting to win the war, to free the prisoners, to end the sufferings, and to promote their cause were myriad. On November 25, for example, a band of Confederate agents attempted to burn New York City. The conspirators attacked various hotels and well-known galleries (such as P. T. Barnum's) with incendiary devices, but the fires were controlled, and the whole plan fizzled. "The bottles of Greek fire having been wrapped in paper were put in our coat pockets," wrote John W. Headley, one of the Confederate agents. He continued:

> Each man took ten bottles. . . . I reached the Astor House . . . after lighting the gas jet I hung the bedclothes loosely on the headboard and piled the chairs, drawers of the bureau and washstand on the bed. Then stuffed some newspapers about among the mass and poured a bottle of turpentine over it all. . . . I opened a bottle carefully and quickly and spilled it on the pile of rubbish. It blazed up instantly and the whole bed seemed to be in flames, before I could get out.[4]

That the Confederate managed but to set his own bed ablaze was a symbol few in the Confederate leadership seem to have noticed.

═══

ALTHOUGH progress around the Petersburg trenches was slow, Sherman in mid-November embarked on a march from Atlanta to Savannah, abandoning his base and along the way destroying railroads and much of military value to the Confederacy. He was virtually unopposed. "At three o'clock the watch-fires are burning dimly, and, but for the occasional neighing of horses, all is so silent that it is difficult to imagine that twenty thousand men are within a radius of a few miles," wrote George Ward Nichols, one of Sherman's staff officers. "The ripple of the brook can be distinctly heard as it breaks over the pebbles, or winds petulantly about the gnarled roots. The wind sweeping gently through the tall pines overhead only serves to lull to deeper repose the slumbering soldier, who is in his tent dreaming of his far-off Northern home."[5]

In the South all knew that a major movement was coming. "That Sherman intends to move with this large army upon some point in Georgia I have no doubt," wrote Howell Cobb, "but where it will be is not yet so certain though my opinion is that Macon is the point."[6] Rather than opposing Sherman, Hood believed that by turning northward and threatening lines of supply and communication in Tennessee (as well as endangering Union-held Nashville), he could draw Sherman away from the Deep South. He couldn't have been more wrong. Hood's Tennessee campaign began ingloriously for the Confederates and turned into full-fledged disaster. Hood marched northward from Florence, Alabama, and first encountered Union troops in force near Columbia, Tennessee, with Yankees north of the Duck River on November 27 and Confederates south of it. By midafternoon on November 29, the battle of Spring Hill occurred, with piecemeal and confused attacks mismanaged by Hood.

Hood attacked frontally at Franklin, recklessly exposing his troops to an entrenched position that inflicted murderous casualties to his army. (His ignorance of just how reckless these actions were was summed up in a letter he wrote on the 29th: "I expect to die more proud of my defense of Atlanta & my Tenn. campaign than all my career as a soldier.")[7] The flashpoint of the battle was the Fountain Branch Carter House and a nearby gin mill, around which intense barrages ignited throughout the late afternoon. Hood's frontal attacks cost the army men it could not afford to lose, as he amassed more than six thousand casualties, including six general officers either dead or mortally wounded. Four of these generals were carried to a nearby mansion, where they were laid out on the porch — Maj. Gen. Patrick Cleburne, beloved as one of the greatest Confederate generals in the west, and Brig. Gens. John Adams, Otho F. Strahl, and Hiram B. Granbury. Two other Confederate brigadier generals,

John C. Carter and the unsubtly named States Rights Gist, died fighting at Franklin.

If Hood had bruised his Army of Tennessee into incoherence at Franklin, he ruined it permanently two weeks later at Nashville. As he advanced from Franklin, Federal officers in Nashville prepared to fight a decisive battle with all the resources they had. "Every horse and mare that could be used was taken," wrote Maj. Gen. James H. Wilson. "All street-car and livery stable horses, and private carriage- and saddle-horses, were seized. Even Andrew Johnson, the vice-president-elect, was forced to give up his pair. A circus then at Nashville lost everything except its ponies; even the old white trick horse was taken but it was alleged that the young and handsome equestrienne, who claimed him, succeeded in convincing my adjutant general that the horse was unfit for cavalry service."[8] On December 15 Hood's approach brought on an attack by Maj. Gen. George H. Thomas over a broad front south of the city. The initial battle was a lopsided victory for Union forces, and it continued through part of the next day before the remains of Hood's army fled south.

Anything but obsessed by Hood, Sherman and his sixty-two thousand men were, at this moment, approaching Savannah on his revolutionary March to the Sea. On December 20 he occupied the city and sent Lincoln the message that he could offer Savannah as his Christmas present. A new legend was developing. "General Sherman is the most American looking man I ever saw," wrote John Chipman Gray, a Federal staff officer, on December 14, "tall and lank, not very erect, with hair like a thatch, which he rubs up with his hands, a rusty beard trimmed close, a wrinkled face, sharp, prominent, red nose, small, bright eyes, coarse red hands; black felt hat slouched over the eyes."[9] The final diamonds of the Confederacy were crumbling away, and time was running out rapidly now.

With the Yankees closing in from seemingly every quarter, John H. Winder, still charged with the Union prisoners, let out a cry for help from Columbia, South Carolina. "It is advisable to remove the prisoners from Florence," he pointed out to G. T. Beauregard. "If so, how am I to arrange for Guard. I now have South Carolina reserves.

Cannot carry them into Georgia."[10] Yet again an insistence on state rights, carried to the extreme, left the Confederate military effort little more than an unravelling patchwork.

The military situation was fast becoming untenable.

———

IN Richmond, meanwhile, the second session of the Second Congress of the Confederate States of America began on November 7. On the opening day Jefferson Davis sent a long message to Congress covering many urgent points that needed to be faced. In many ways it was a last attempt for a turnaround and cooperation on a variety of issues that, the president felt, would sink the Confederacy if left unresolved.

"The exemption from military duty now accorded by law to all persons engaged in certain specified pursuits is shown by experience to be unwise, nor is it believed to be defensible in theory," he lectured. "A general militia law is needful in the interest of the public defense," he added. "The employment of slaves for service with the Army as teamsters or cooks, or in the way of work upon the fortifications, or in the Government workshops, or in hospitals or other similar duties, was authorized by the act of the 17th of February last, and provision was made for their impressment to a number not exceeding 20,000, if it should be found impracticable to obtain them by contract with the owners."

Continued the president, "Viewed merely as property, and therefore as the subject of impressment, the service or labor of the slave has been frequently claimed for short periods in the construction of defensive works. The slave, however, bears another relation to the State — that of a person."

This last thought must have struck some of the lawmakers like a clap of thunder. The president then wondered aloud if emancipation should be offered to slaves for faithful military service, and he guessed that, if given, they would not leave their local areas after the war. "A double motive for a zealous discharge of duty would thus be offered to those employed by the Government — their freedom and the gratification of the local attachment which is so marked a characteristic of the negro, and forms so powerful an incentive in his action," the president proposed.[11] This was a conclusion so blind-folded and naive as to be idiotic — morally and politically. Although the president stopped short of suggesting slaves be armed, emancipation for military service — aiding the soldiers in the field and use for manual labor, etc. — was now on the table, confusing many and infuriating others. And yet the whole debate was cloaked in such a supreme air of desperation that many politicians knew something drastic had to be done or the war would be lost.

In the House the topic dominated the day. Members of Congress reported on a conference of governors that had taken place in mid-October in which the chief executives of Virginia, North Carolina, South Carolina, Georgia, Alabama, and Mississippi had concluded "under proper regulation, to appropriate such part of [the slaves] to the public service as may be required," not prohibiting their use as soldiers. They speculated, however, that "no exigency now exists nor is likely to occur in the military affairs of the Confederacy . . . which demands that negroes shall be used as soldiers."[12] The following day Henry S. Foote resolved that arming slaves would be inexpedient, but that they should be used extensively as laborers.

In the House, resolutions were introduced to give the president the opportunity to clarify his opposition to the emancipation of slaves under any conditions. If the public and the European powers got the impression that the government had the power to emancipate slaves, after all, it would be in no better a position than Abraham Lincoln and the United States government.[13]

On November 10 the argument shifted and became murkier. Impressment of up to forty thousand slaves into the army, with prospective emancipation for faithful service, would require consent of the states, Congress concluded. Said a congressman,

> Some have claimed that our army is decreasing by death, disease, and desertion, but our president says it has not suffered half as much as has the Yankee army. President Davis, in his Macon Speech, said that two-thirds of the army is absent, and that this problem should be addressed by Congress, rather than in making plans to recruit negroes as soldiers.

Do the gentlemen of the South propose to fight alongside negroes? Should the slaves be commingled with our brave white troops? The negro race has been ordained to slavery by the Almighty.[14]

Still others opposed the use of slaves as soldiers because it could be seen as a confession of weakness.

On December 12 senators resumed debate on a bill to furnish slaves and free blacks to work on fortifications and provide labor for the armies. "Regarding the limitation of not more than one in five slaves shall be impressed who is working on agriculture, or that the last slave between 18 and 45 shall not be impressed," Virginia congressman Robert M. T. Hunter offered, "as long as any state was not exempted from furnishing its fair quota."[15] The amendment was then adopted, and the bill passed.

Six days later in the House, members proposed a resolution disapproving the government's purchasing slaves as laborers in the army and liberating them after faithful service had been rendered. The topic was referred to committee. Since Davis's opening remarks in November, thousands of Confederate troops had been killed. Amid the blood the politicians argued. "I cannot bring my mind to the conviction that arming our slaves will add to our military strength," wrote William Porcher Miles shortly afterward, "and the prospective and inevitable evils resulting from the measure make me shrink back from the step as only to be taken when on the very brink of the precipice of ruin. At first I was inclined to think we might with some advantage employ negro soldiers — but the more I think of it, the more disinclined I am to resort to what at best can only be regarded as a doubtful experiment."[16] James Leach of North Carolina later offered a House resolution "condemning the use of negroes as soldiers in the Confederate army." Leach said that arming slaves would "be wrong in principle, disastrous in practice, an infringement upon the States rights, an endorsement of the principle contained in President Lincoln's emancipation proclamation, an insult to our brave soldiers and an outrage upon humanity which, if carried into effect, will degrade us in the eyes of the civilized world, endanger our liberties, and jeopardize the lives of our wives and children."[17]

"It would be a fatal stab to the institution of slavery," added Porcher Miles, "and would overturn the whole social fabric of our country. The negro is unfit by nature for a soldier, and he cannot be expected to fight on our side when the Yankees offer him far greater inducements than we can."[18]

——

T H E Davis administration desired nothing but a fight to the end, convinced it could separate successfully and live on as a sovereign nation. But by late 1864 senators and representatives had been calling for peace in more frequent, urgent terms. On November 7 the Senate had resolved that the president should inform the Senate whether he had information that any state in the United States had expressed a willingness to negotiate a peace with the Confederate States. Davis issued no reply, suggesting there had been none.[19]

In mid-December the issue reared its head in the House. Josiah Turner of North Carolina introduced a resolution asking the president to appoint thirteen peace commissioners, one from each state, to seek an end to the war. After discussion, however, debate was postponed.[20]

The next day Representative Lafayette McMullen of Virginia derided the Davis administration for not seeking peace proposals. "Governor Brown and Vice President Stephens have said that we are unwilling to open negotiations with the enemy for securing a peace," screamed McMullen. "Let the Government open negotiations for peace — let Congress despatch its commissioners into the enemy's line — let us show to the world that we are willing to accept an honourable peace — and the mouths of Governor Brown and his friends will be stopped."[21]

Finally, without support of either administration, high officials began to come to terms with opening a negotiation. On December 30 Yankee politician Francis P. Blair Sr. wrote Davis about a meeting to discuss peace terms. "In candor I must say to you, in advance, that I come to you wholly *unaccredited*, except in so far as I may be by having permission to pass our lines and to offer you my own suggestions."[22]

The assistant secretary of war of the Confederacy, John A. Campbell, also took it into his own hands to find a pathway toward peace. He wrote an old colleague, Associate Justice Samuel Nelson of the U.S. Supreme Court, asking for a meeting to discuss possible peace terms. But nothing would come from these political ripples — not for a few weeks, at least.[23]

Meanwhile, the old, tired issue of conscription — who was eligible and who wasn't — again confronted both President Davis and the annoyed Congress. More outraged than either of these two parties was Brig. Gen. John S. Preston, the Virginian who had been appointed chief of the Bureau of Conscription in 1863. Fed up with Congress seemingly meddling in the issue and tying his hands for months, coupled with the fuming anger over the fact that many congressmen disliked him, Preston accelerated an already weeks-long letter-writing campaign to the War Department and to members of Congress. "I am aware that there is a project on foot under high military sanction to abolish the existing system of Conscription and substitute for it a military organization to be regulated by purely rigid military rules," he ranted, "and by the operation of Law to remove me from the control delegated to me by you." As was so often the case for the Confederacy, each state for its own sake could contribute to a distinct individual selfishness. Preston was as much concerned about his own position as he was the war effort; who decided was as important as what was decided. "Nothing will tend more rapidly to disintegrate the Confederacy — than the adoption of these petulant undisguised and revolting schemes of military Conscription." Congress also lashed back. The House

resolved that the report of John S. Preston, Supt. of Conscription, shows laxity, and culpable neglect in the execution of the conscript law. Resolved that neither Congress nor the country looks to Gen. [Gideon] Pillow for a faithful expression of its laws, and any failure, delay, or partiality in their execution must rest on the President and not upon General Pillow. Resolved that General Preston is in error to the number of conscripts furnished by the State of North Carolina, as well as the number of his so-called quasi-volunteers.

On March 6 in the House, a resolution was offered condemning Preston for mismanagement. A week later President Davis returned to Congress, with his approval, an act to regulate the business of conscription. He did ask for one modification: a medical board requested by Congress to examine soldiers for discharge seemed impractical to Davis because it would result in the discharge of too many soldiers.[24] The messy business of conscription would rage on, making everyone unhappy for weeks to come, even as the South's shorthanded military machine gradually fell to pieces.[25]

And with times becoming ever more desperate, the old subject of habeas corpus only inflamed the souls of men in Congress more than ever. "A dangerous conspiracy exists in some of the counties of southwestern Virginia and in the neighboring portions of North Carolina and Tennessee," Davis warned Congress, "which it is found impracticable to suppress by the ordinary course of law. . . . I deem it my duty to recommend the suspension of the writ of *habeas corpus* in order that full efficacy may be given to the military power for the repression of the evil."[26] On December 3 on the floor of the House, Henry Foote demanded his bill on limiting habeas corpus be debated openly. With Foote and William Porcher Miles voting for it, the bill still lost, fifty to forty. By year's end in the House, a resolution that "no exigency exists justifying the [suspension of habeas corpus]" failed to pass, forty-one to thirty-one. The House was betwixt and between, and again, no one would be fully happy with the outcome.

——

In Georgia the little cabal arranged by Vice President Aleck Stephens and comrades Bob Toombs, Howell Cobb, and friends continued to gain momentum. This group now determinedly supported an overthrow of the Davis administration if the South should survive intact. Davis's failure to see the war as it really was frustrated the Georgia cabal to no end. The group clearly believed that some sort of a negotiated end to the struggle was on the horizon. "I see Mr. Davis in his speech at Columbia refers to the traitorous conduct of states that would attempt to negotiate," Georgia governor Joe Brown wrote to his fellow conspirator Aleck Stephens, in wonderment about the sensibility of the chief executive.[27] Aleck Stephens thought that he ought to meet with Gen. William Tecumseh Sherman, seeking an end to the bloodshed. But Bob Toombs steered the frail politician away from the notion. "Do not by any means go to see Sherman," he wrote, "whatever may be the form of his invitation. It will place you in a wrong, *very wrong* position. . . . If Sherman means anything he means to detach Georgia from the Confederacy. Better any fate than that. Davis is impregnable upon the peace issue. In every shape and form and at all times he has professed to seek peace, and in truth up to this time his actions have conformed to his professions."[28]

The rift that existed between Stephens and Davis widened considerably as the year closed. The *Augusta Constitutionalist* printed a letter from Stephens to Senator Thomas Semmes that claimed some in the South, perhaps even Jefferson Davis, would prefer the reelection of Lincoln to the election of George McClellan, the Union general who opposed him. "Perhaps the President belongs to that class," Stephens wrote. "Judging by his acts I should think that he did." Astounded, Davis wrote Stephens: "I am quite at a loss to imagine the basis for your conclusion, and have therefore to ask to what acts of mine you refer."[29]

Setting aside the collapsing military situation, the Confederacy was in a complete shambles. What began as a precarious relationship among Davis, the Congress, and the supporting politicians in key areas had collapsed into total dysfunction. The Confederacy was now — politically and functionally — on the ropes. Its lifeblood was flowing out and running away, and no one on any level seemed to have an idea about how to stop the bleeding.

Chapter

18

=====

PEACE PROPOSALS

As a new year began, the Confederacy was on its last legs. The siege operations around Petersburg ground on, sapping the remaining resources and supplies that could be brought to bear against the Union army. Hood's disastrous campaign in Tennessee had effectively eliminated the Army of Tennessee from further meaningful service in the war. A combined operation by the Federal army and navy was closing in on Wilmington, North Carolina, the last port open to supply the Confederacy. The Lincoln administration had won the autumn election decisively, pushing into the shadows the possibility of a peace movement in the North dominating the Yankees' actions. The Confederacy had lost many a hero in the past couple of years — Stonewall Jackson more important than anyone — and many had lost faith in Jefferson Davis. They had now a single general in the field on whom to place their great hopes: Robert E. Lee.

The growing sense of despair on the Confederate home front and in the ranks led to consideration of some measures that would have been thought insane a year before. An increasing number of officers and politicians toyed with the idea of emancipating slaves as a source of new soldiers. Lee himself supported the idea, which finally gave it the kind of approval to be taken seriously in the Confederate Congress. Still, in January 1865, the measure was debated without a conclusion. Summed up Howell Cobb, "If slaves will make good soldiers, our whole theory of slavery is wrong."[1] And for the moment theory trumped reality.

By contrast the psychology of the Union military was strongly unified. Soldiers and civilians alike began to sense the impending victory, and heroes had multiplied on the Federal side. Grant was locked in the struggle, along with Meade, against Lee in Virginia, and Sherman had emerged in 1864 as a leading figure. "I do think that in the several grand epochs of this war, my name will have a prominent part," Sherman wrote to his wife, Ellen, from Savannah on January 5. "And not least among them will be the determination I took at Atlanta to destroy that place, and march on this city, whilst Thomas, my lieutenant, should dispose of Hood."[2]

Having arrived at Savannah before Christmas, Sherman now trained his armies on the Carolinas. Panic already had struck South Carolina. "Depend upon it," wrote Andrew Magrath, the state's governor, "the order which evacuates Charleston destroys the last hope of our success."[3] Robert E. Lee, meanwhile, wrote to Porcher Miles, who had asked for more troops to be sent to the state. Lee's reply stated that the government would send them, "if any troops could be obtained." It was a very big "if." "It will be impossible for me to send sufficient troops from this army to oppose Sherman's, and at the same time resist Grant," said Lee.[4]

One of the duties of Sherman's invading army would be to liberate Union prisoners wherever they were found. The prisoners at Andersonville had been moved prior to Sherman's approach, but Yankees were released at Millen, Georgia, and other facilities. As Sherman contemplated turning northward, a major attack by the Federal army and navy was planned for Wilmington. Maj. Gen. Benjamin F. Butler had commanded an unsuccessful movement against Fort Fisher, which protected the city's entrance, in December. Now, Maj. Gen. Alfred H. Terry was ordered to take the position. Terry's eight thousand men would be assisted by Rear Adm. David D. Porter's North Atlantic Blockading Squadron, which amounted to sixty ships armed with a total of 627 guns.

The flotilla arrived in the waters off North Carolina's coast on January 12. The Confederate district commander, Maj. Gen. William H. C. Whiting, reinforced the garrison at Fort Fisher so that it consisted of nearly two thousand troops and forty-seven guns. Just after midnight on January 13, the Federal ships opened fire on the fort, and during the following day, troops landed to assault the position. Augustus Buell, a soldier in the Fourth U.S. Artillery, described the heavy bombardment during the thirteenth. "There would be two puffs of blue smoke about the size of a thunder cloud in June," he wrote, "and then I could see the big shell make a black streak through the air with a tail of white smoke behind it — and then would come over the water, not the quick bark of a field gun, but a slow, quivering, overpowering roar like an earthquake, and then, away among the Rebel traverses, there would be another huge ball of mingled smoke and flame as big as a meeting house."[5]

On January 15 a heavy naval bombardment commenced at close range, softening the position where the Federal attack would concentrate. Early in the afternoon a small party rushed forward and dug in close to the fort. Late in the afternoon Federal soldiers stormed the fort in force, breaking into the parapets with axes and firing wildly at the fort's defenders. Before nightfall the Yankees succeeded in capturing the position, nearly two thousand soldiers, all the guns, and the mortally wounded Whiting. The last great Confederate port was closed.

The most progress from Congress during the final weeks of war came from the exact area where Davis wanted it least — peace proposals. As early as January 12, the House passed a resolution to send a peace commission to Washington. The next day Davis reported to the House that his old nemesis, Henry Foote, had been arrested on his way to Washington. Foote had been detained at Occoquan, Virginia, while trying to cross the lines on a private peace mission to the Yankee capital. As Foote was already known as the principal antagonist of Davis's in the House, a special committee was appointed to investigate.[6]

On January 16, members of the House considered all sorts of punishments for Foote. John Clark, leader of the committee of five appointed to investigate, recommended that the whole matter should be referred to the president.[7] Nevertheless, eight days later, Clark and his committee appeared on the House floor and addressed Congress regarding Foote. "Whatever may have been his motive," Clark said, when Foote left the Confederate States, he became "guilty of conduct incompatible with his duty and station as a member of the Congress of the Confederate States, and he is hereby expelled from this House."[8]

On January 30 the House spent much of the day debating peace proposals. It was rumored that a secret peace commission had already met with Lincoln in Washington. (The *Richmond Sentinel* had reported the rumor as fact and claimed those involved were traitors.) The majority of Southerners believed, according to Congress, that there was no intention on the part of the North to acknowledge their independence and that peace and independence could be achieved only by force of arms. Reflecting this position Senator Williamson Oldham offered resolutions from Texas regarding any peace commissioners. Oldham advised against "going back into the old Union," as it could be done only if "we went as a whipped and conquered people."[9] But other leaders, seeing the writing on the wall, remained more flexible.

═══

ALTHOUGH Lee had prevented Grant's forces from taking Petersburg (or destroying the Army of Northern Virginia), time was running out for the Southern hero. "[Grant's] present force is so superior to ours, that if he is reinforced to any extent, I do not see how in our present position he can be prevented from enveloping Richmond," Lee wrote Davis on January 29.[10] At about this time, on January 23, the Confederate Congress reacted to the poor morale and lack of faith in Davis by assigning a general-in-chief of all Confederate armies, naming (after rancorous debate and amendment) Robert E. Lee to the post. Finally, after several years of war, the Confederate government had put the right man in the spot. But in the meantime, the die had been cast. Lee's fears over Grant were about to come true.

On February 2 the emancipation debate spilled over into the Senate. Never one to shy from the spotlight, Wigfall took the floor. "The time has come to settle whether this is to be a free negro free country, or a free white man's free country," he said. "In some of the States the slave population is greater than the white. What is to become of the whites if the negroes should be emancipated?"[11] The following day, however, some senators began to toy with the idea and how it might be established. On February 3 the House resolved to place 100,000 black soldiers into the service. The government should purchase these men from their masters, one by one, and then give one man to each white soldier in the service. The resolution, however, was tabled.

Congress's reluctant proposals to arm black troops rang out like gunshots across the Southern landscape. "The proposition is having a ruinous effect here," Edmund Rhett, an officer, relayed to Porcher Miles from Charleston, South Carolina.

It is breaking down peoples' spirits. Men ask, what are we fighting for? You tell them, "for independence." But what is independence? Independence is the right and the power to make our own laws and to govern our own institutions. But if you take away this power, and destroy those institutions, what independence is left? For God's sake stop it if you can. Our troops are fighting here in the worst way. They do not stand at all before Sherman's men. The demoralization amongst them is very disheartening.[12]

Meanwhile, a peace conference held at Hampton Roads, near Norfolk, Virginia, on February 3 had led nowhere. Initiated by the aged Union politician Francis P. Blair Sr. — a member of Andrew Jackson's "Kitchen Cabinet" — the conference brought Confederate Vice President Alexander H. Stephens, Assistant Secretary of War John A. Campbell, and Senator Robert M. T. Hunter together on board the USS *River Queen*. Meeting them was none other than President Lincoln, who told the agents that the Confederacy had virtually no room for bargaining in terms of surrender.

On February 6 President Davis informed Congress about the failed peace conference held at Hampton Roads. "Having recently received a written notification, which satisfied me that the President of the United States was disposed to confer informally with unofficial agents which might be sent by me with a view to the restoration of peace," Davis explained, "I requested the Hon. Alexander H. Stephens, the Hon. R. M. T. Hunter, and the Hon. John A. Campbell to proceed through our lines, and to hold conference with Mr. Lincoln, or any one he might depute to represent him."[13]

"The Commissioners have returned," the president wrote Senator Benjamin H. Hill. "They met Lincoln and Seward at Fortress Monroe, were informed that neither the Confederate States nor an individual State, could be recognized as having power to enter into any agreement prescribing conditions of peace. Nothing less would be accepted than unconditional submission to the government and laws of the United States, and that Congress had adopted a Constitutional amendment for the emancipation of slaves, which disposed of that question."[14]

On March 1 Representative James Leach of North Carolina proposed that Robert E. Lee ought to be invested with powers to seek peace with the North. But nothing seemed to hold even a glint of promise. "Congress will remember [in the recent Peace Conference] that our commissioners were informed that the government of the United States would not enter into any agreement or treaty whatever with the Confederate States," Davis sternly warned on March 13, "that the only possible mode of obtaining peace was by laying down our arms, disbanding our forces, and yielding unconditional obedience to the laws of the United States, including those passed for the confiscation of our property and the constitutional amendment for the abolition of slavery. . . . There remains, then, for us no choice but to continue the contest to a final issue."[15]

Despite the desperation many Confederates in positions of power failed to see the coming ruin. "Doubtless Lee could protract the war, and, by concentrating farther South, embarrass the enemy by compelling him to maintain a longer line of communication by land and by sea," wrote the war clerk John B. Jones on February 12. "Lee could have an army of 100,000 effective men for years."[16] Such optimism was nothing short of delusional.

If there was to be no peace, war would have to continue, and Lee planned a major attack at Petersburg. His hope was to stun Grant's army, hold Petersburg and Richmond with reduced numbers of men, and head south to unite with Gen. Joe Johnston in the Carolinas, thereby gaining the opportunity to ruin Sherman's army. It was an unlikely plan that would never gain the opportunity for testing except for the initial stage and never assume a form more tangible than rumor. "Something is about to happen," wrote Luther Rice Mills, a North Carolina Confederate, on March 2. "I know not what. Nearly every one who will express an opinion says Gen'l Lee is about to evacuate Petersburg. . . . I would regret very much to give up the old place. The soiled and tattered Colors borne by our skeleton Regiments is sacred and dear to the hearts of every man." On the same day Josiah Gorgas wrote: "People are almost in a state of desperation. Lee is about all we have & what public confidence is left rallies around him, and he it seems to me fights without much heart in the cause."[17]

While the military was crumbling along the Southern lines, politicians were discovering disheartening circumstances in previously ignored corners. On February 7 in the House, information from secret sessions revealed an "enormous blunder" that would require a great increase in taxation. Instead of $114 million, the Confederate government's war debt was recalculated to be in excess of $400 million. Ever greater financial panic struck the Confederacy.[18]

On March 5 Assistant Secretary of War John A. Campbell wrote John Breckinridge, declaring that "a full and exact examination be made of the resources of the Confederate government available for the approaching campaign. It is not a part of statesmanship to close our eyes upon them." Campbell described the current year's debt of the government at a staggering $1.3 billion and said it was "needless to comment" on that. Moreover, he cited "over 100,000 deserters scattered over the Confederacy," and went on to state, "I do not regard the slave population as a source from which" additional troops could be raised. "Their employment since 1862 has been difficult and latterly almost impracticable." Supplies for the army were woefully inadequate, and "the present Commissary General requires the fulfillment of conditions, though, not unreasonable, nearly impossible." The chief of ordnance reported a store of twenty-five thousand arms remaining. "The South may succumb," Campbell wrote, "but it is not necessary that she be destroyed."[19]

As financial woes mounted the Senate also turned toward their lack of confidence in Judah P. Benjamin as secretary of state. Wigfall introduced a resolution of no confidence "because the country and the Congress does not really back him." The measure was voted down fifteen to six, however. On February 15 in the House, it was

> resolved that the views of J. P. Benjamin, Secy. of State, as reported in a speech by him on the tenth instant in the city of Richmond, is derogatory to his position as a high public functionary of the Confederate government, a reflection on his motives of Congress as a deliberative body, and an insult to public opinion. Resolved, our army is *not* composed of mob-materials; that our soldiers are law-abiding men, that in common with their representatives and friends at home they deprecate croakers, official insolence, or mob law, as being repugnant to justice, incompatible with the rights of free men, and revolting to the feelings of patriots and Christians.[20]

Joe Johnston, meanwhile, was busy fighting old battles. Johnston wrote to his friend Wigfall complaining that the secretary of war's report on Johnston's earlier operations in northern Georgia contained lies and inaccuracies. On the receipt of a letter from Aleck Stephens, seventeen senators, including Wigfall and Orr, recommended Johnston be restored to command of the Army of Tennessee. Lee replied: "I entertain a high opinion of Genl. Johnston's capacity, but think a combined change of commanders is very injurious to any troops & tends greatly to thin disorganization."[21] Congress responded by ignoring

Lee's opinion and passed a resolution in favor of Johnston's instatement. Still, no movement would be made by the president toward Johnston. "The Joint Resolution of Congress and other recent manifestations of a desire that General Joseph E. Johnston should be restored to the command of the Army of Tennessee have been anxiously considered by me," Davis wrote, "and it is with sincere regret that I find myself unable to gratify what I must believe to have become quite a general desire of my countrymen."[22]

Finally Lee gave in and assigned Johnston to command the Army of Tennessee on February 25. "I have directed Genl. J. E. Johnston to assume command of [the] Southern Army," Lee penned to Beauregard, "and to assign you to duty with him. Together, I feel assured you will beat back Sherman." Below Lee's telegraphic message Beauregard wrote, "Not without your assistance by concentration."[23]

In Washington on March 4, Abraham Lincoln was inaugurated on the east portico of the Capitol, with Andrew Johnson of Tennessee now becoming his vice president. Lincoln struggled to summarize the horrifying war that had characterized nearly his entire first term and still had not drawn to a conclusion. "With malice toward none, with charity for all, with firmness in the right as God gives us to see the right, let us strive on to finish the work we are in, to bind up the nation's wounds, to care for him who shall have borne the battle and for his widow and his orphan, to do all which may achieve and cherish a just and lasting peace among ourselves and with all nations."[24]

As Lincoln looked forward the politicians in Richmond glared at each other. On the issue of habeas corpus, Davis still demanded action and got nothing. Even some of Davis's enemies tried to assist. "The maxim that it is better one hundred guilty men should escape than that one innocent man should be punished, will not do for a time of war," said Wigfall. "In times like these, it is better that one hundred innocent persons should be arrested than one suspected man would escape."[25]

On March 13 the president scolded Congress: "The Writ of Habeas Corpus must be suspended. Congress has not concurred with me in this opinion. On Congress must rest the responsibility of declining to exercise a power conferred by the Constitution as a means of public safety to be used in periods of national peril from foreign invasion."[26] Two days later the completed habeas corpus bill went to the Senate Judiciary Committee but was rejected by a vote of nine to six. In the House a completed habeas corpus bill was passed thirty-six to thirty-three. The next day in the Senate, the House bill was debated and finally lost by a vote of nine to six. Nothing would come of it in the end.[27]

Lee's attack finally came at Fort Stedman on the Petersburg front on the afternoon of March 25. An attempted breakthrough by Confederate troops worked well at first before a counterattack stalled it. The situation for Lee deteriorated rapidly. Sheridan, who had defeated the scattered remnants of Early's forces in the valley, rejoined Grant, and movements by Maj. Gen. Edward O. C. Ord on March 27–28 allowed Grant to send Sheridan and Warren westward to threaten the Southside Railroad, potentially severing Petersburg from the rest of the country. An explosive engagement along the White Oak Road southwest of Petersburg on March 31 ended in Confederate failure, and the situation for Lee crumbled. At Five Forks, fifteen miles southwest of Petersburg, on April 1, Sheridan and Warren — despite confusion in orders and slowness in executing them — struck the force of forty-five hundred under Maj. Gen. George E. Pickett, capturing them, eliminating the Southside Railroad as a supply route for Lee, and forcing the evacuation of Petersburg.

Struck heavily by Union artillery and a piercing set of attacks on their right flank, Lee's army was in a hopeless situation. Assaults on weak gaps in the Confederate lines continued through April 2, and Grant ordered such thrusts to continue the following day. The main defenses of the Confederacy in the east were collapsing; as soon as Petersburg fell, with its rail lines running north into Richmond, the Confederate capital would be compelled to surrender. Events accelerated. Gen. Robert E. Lee telegraphed Davis, telling him that he could no longer hold his position at Petersburg and could not maintain any protection of Richmond. As the beautiful spring morning infused hope into those who didn't yet know, churchgoers crowded

Richmond's streets. Summoned from the Broad Street Methodist Church, Secretary of War John C. Breckinridge scurried to the War Department to await further telegrams. The telegraph wires went dead, however, spooking the group of officials left at the building. Finally, after a period of silence, the wires reignited, and by 10:40 a.m., word arrived that shocked everyone into silence. Lee sent a message declaring he would have to abandon his positions that evening or perhaps sooner. Now, even those who held out the most hope saw that the Confederacy was coming down around them.

The president, on his way to St. Paul's Episcopal Church, greeted citizens as best he could. "When Davis entered," wrote Adj. Gen. Samuel Cooper, "one who saw him noted his appearance: 'the cold calm eye, the sunken cheeks, the compressed lip, were all as impenetrable as an iron mask.'" In the Davis family pew, sans family, the president listened to the hymn "Jesus, Lover of My Soul" as he waited for the Reverend Charles Minnegerode's sermon.

Davis was kneeling during antecommunion when St. Paul's sexton approached the pew and handed him a telegram from General Lee. Although Davis had heard the news already, he felt he could remain in the pew no longer and, "with his usually quick military tread," walked out. Many in the packed house seemed shocked and noticed the president's "deathly pale, absolutely calm demeanor." "The occurrence probably attracted attention," Davis later recalled, "but the people had been too long beleaguered, had known me too often to receive notice of threatened attacks, and the congregation at St. Paul's was too refined to make a scene at anticipated danger."[28]

A little while after Davis left the church, the sexton returned and pulled Cooper away from his pew; then he returned for Assistant Secretary of War John Campbell. It was clear to all that the great moment of terror was arriving, and whole sections of parishioners rose and walked out of St. Paul's. As befuddled throngs of citizens stood in the church's entryway, the streets were already littered with documents and stacks of military supplies. The Central Hotel on Grace Street, within sight of the church, had served as offices for the Confederate States' auditors. Now, government clerks piled crates of documents carrying the history of the South's war effort outside the hotel, set them ablaze, and transformed them into a tower of black-and-white smoke rising above the Richmond skyline.

Davis walked downhill toward the river, to his office in the former U.S. Customs House. He convened the cabinet, as well as Governor William Smith and Mayor Joseph Mayo, and read Lee's telegram aloud. The suddenness of Lee's evacuation of Petersburg surprised Davis, who knew the rail center would be given up but not necessarily so quickly. Davis felt the collapse was not so "near at hand."[29] The president inquired from Lee by telegraph whether the government could have any further time to prepare for an evacuation. Lee, somewhat irritated by the chief executive, replied that no more time was available. Packing of the government archives had been going on for some time — those documents that would not be burned — but there would still be much that would stay behind.

The Confederate president then walked uphill to his home on Clay Street. He projected a serene air of resignation to Richmond's fate. Ordinary citizens asked him what to do. Should they scatter for the hills? No, they should calmly leave the city. A group of ladies in Capitol Square, frantic, pleaded with the president for guidance. Perhaps General Hardee would come in on time to prevent any catastrophe, he told them. This couldn't have been true, but it reduced the level of panic in their eyes. To a government colleague he was more blunt: "Get out of town."[30]

Davis issued an address to the people of the Confederate States. "The General in Chief of our Army has found it necessary to make such movements of the troops as to uncover the capital and thus involve the withdrawal of the Government from the city of Richmond," he revealed. He went on:

It would be unwise, even were it possible, to conceal the great moral as well as material injury to our cause that must result from the occupation of Richmond by the enemy. It is equally unwise and unworthy of us, as patriots engaged in a most sacred cause, to allow our energies to falter, our spirits to grow faint, or our efforts to become relaxed under reverses, however calamitous. . . . Let us not, then, despond, my countrymen; but, relying on the never-failing mercies and protecting care of our God, let us meet the foe with fresh defiance, with unconquered and unconquerable hearts.[31]

The withdrawal from Richmond began in good order, but quickly collapsed into chaos and frenzy. When he arrived at the Executive Mansion, Davis found a group of friends and ordinary citizens waiting for him. He walked into the house to pack the few personal belongings he would take on the train to Danville. The president bid several people adieu, climbed with a freshly lit cigar into a carriage, and rode toward the station. When the special train was found unprepared, Davis waited in the railway president's office, and then finally, at 11 p.m., he left the beleaguered city accompanied by his cabinet members and Samuel Cooper.

Evacuation fires set to destroy supplies that would otherwise fall into Yankee hands burned out of control, eventually destroying nearly a third of the city. "I was wakened suddenly by four terrific explosions, one after the other, making the windows of my garret shake," wrote Richmond resident Constance Cary on April 4. "It was the blowing up, by Admiral Semmes, by order of the Secretary of the Navy, of our gunboats on the James, the signal for an all-day carnival of thundering noise and flames. Soon the fire spread, shells in the burning arsenals began to explode, and a smoke arose that shrouded the whole town, shutting out every vestige of blue sky and April sunshine. Flakes of fire fell around us, glass shattered, and chimneys fell."[32] As had been the case all war long, much of the damage had been self-inflicted.

Some of the Confederate troops greeted Grant's men with quiet joy. On February 7 the Senate had resolved to take into the army about 200,000 black soldiers and, at the end of the war, emancipate the loyal ones; the matter was referred to committee, where the bill lost nine to eight. By March 13 President Davis had had enough. He sent the Senate a secret message by way of Burton Harrison, his private secretary. The president's alarm read like a final appeal, a search for those who might in the greatest hour of crisis consider themselves old friends and come to his support. The president wrote,

> Recent military operations of the enemy have been successful in the capture of some of our seaports in interrupting some of our lines of communication, and in devastating large districts of our country. These events have had the national effect of encouraging our foes and dispiriting many of our people. The capital of the Confederate States is now threatened, and is in greater danger than it has heretofore been during the war. . . . I desire also to state my deliberate conviction that it is within our power to avert the calamities which menace us.
>
> Long deliberation and protracted debate over important measures are not only natural, but laudable in representative assemblies, under ordinary circumstances, but in moments of danger, when action becomes urgent, the delay thus caused is itself a new source of peril. . . . The bill for employing negroes as soldiers has not yet reached me. Much benefit is anticipated from this measure, though far less than would have resulted from its adoption at an earlier date, so as to afford the time for its organization and instruction during the winter months.[33]

A few days later the Senate had begrudgingly issued a Select Committee report on emancipation. "At what period of the session the president or Secretary of War considered the improbable contingency had arisen," the report began, "which required a resort to slaves as an element of resistance, does not appear by any official document within the knowledge of your committee. . . . The president has never asked, in any authentic manner, for the passage of a law authorizing the employment of slaves as soldiers."[34] (This, of course, was untrue.)

Soon thereafter Congress stopped bickering about communications and passed the bill to enlist black soldiers in the Confederacy. But it was too little too late, and no authenticated African American combat soldiers ever served in the field; the unit that had been issued uniforms was simply drilling in Richmond when the city fell to

Union forces. The mere fact that the official step had been taken was evidence of the Confederacy's desperation.

==

F AR to the south the prospect of the Confederate army meeting up with Joe Johnston was shrinking daily. Sherman had moved out of Savannah and toward Columbia, where on February 17 an evacuation fire also destroyed much of that city. "I began to-day's record early in the evening, and while writing I noticed an unusual glare in the sky," wrote George Ward Nichols, of Sherman's staff, "and heard a sound of running to and fro in the streets, with the loud talk of servants that the horses must be removed to a safer place. Running out, I found, to my surprise and real sorrow, that the central part of the city, including the main business street, was in flames, while the wind, which had been blowing a hurricane all day, was driving the sparks and cinders in heavy masses over the eastern portion of the city."[35] On March 16 a portion of Johnston's command had attempted to block Sherman at Averasboro but was beaten badly. Three days later, at Bentonville, Johnston's force had hit Sherman squarely but again was defeated.

Lee's army had fled westward in what became the Appomattox campaign. The pursuit by Grant's army would be quick and stunning. Lee concentrated at Amelia Court House, thirty-five miles northwest of Petersburg, on April 5, where he expected to find supply trains that never came. The following day, at Sayler's Creek, Federals cut off the Confederate rear guard, capturing more than eight thousand men, including six general officers. On the same day former Virginia governor Henry A. Wise wrote Lee: "[There] has been no country, general, for a year or more. You are the country to these men. They have fought for you."

Varina Davis had been increasingly ill-tempered as the tension had risen in the capital — a family visitor dubbed her "the tigress" — and by the end of March, Davis had sent his wife and their children, Davis's secretary Burton Harrison, Varina's sister Margaret, and Treasury Secretary George Trenholm's daughters fleeing southward to Charlotte, North Carolina, and then on to Abbeville, South

Carolina, home of a family friend. Varina carried a Colt pistol given to her by her husband. If captured, Davis told his wife, "force your assailants to kill you."[36] This would save the family from humiliation in captivity.

"If I live, you can come to me when the struggle is ended," Davis said, "but I do not expect to survive the destruction of constitutional liberty."[37] Now, on the run, he wrote to Varina. "I am unwilling to leave Va and do not know where within her borders the requisite houses for the Depts and the Congress could be found," he told his wife. "May God bless preserve and guide you."[38] His wife could reply only in shell-shocked horror:

> The news of Richmond came upon me like the "abomination of desolation," the loss of Selma like the "blackness thereof." Mrs Joe Johnston is here living with the cashier of the bank and his family and keeps a very pretty fancy carriage and horses. . . . The Wigfalls are staying I believe with Mrs Johnston also. They arrived yesterday. I heard a funny account of Wigfalls interview with Beauregard it seems he went to see him on his way to this place, and then the news of the evacuation of Richmond came, and that the enemy had not yet entered the town. The Genl said Oh they do not understand the situation it is or ought to be a plan of Lees to keep between Richmond and the enemy, if Grant attempts to throw troops between his army and Richmond Lee can whip them in detail with which plan Wigfall was immensely satisfied.[39]

It was fantasy.

On April 7 Lee reached Farmville, west of Petersburg and halfway to Lynchburg, where his starving army received rations and a short rest, but nearby, at High Bridge, the Federal army struck again at his rear guard. On this day Lincoln, who was at City Point, wrote to Grant, "General Sheridan says 'If the thing is pressed I think that Lee will surrender.' Let the thing be pressed."[40]

The thing was pressed. By April 9 Lee was exhausted and surrounded at Appomattox Court House, with Sheridan's cavalry and the infantry of Maj. Gens. Edward O. C. Ord and Charles Griffin blocking his forward movement and the mass of Grant and Meade's army behind him. The jig was up. Lee was forced to meet Grant to discuss surrender terms in the village, and the officers decided on the front parlor of the home of local Wilmer McLean as the best available place. "Shortly comes the order, in due form, to cease firing and to halt," wrote Brig. Gen. Joshua L. Chamberlain, hero of Gettysburg, "but the habit was too strong; they cared not for points of direction, it was forward still, — forward to the end; forward to the new beginning; forward to the Nation's second birth!"

Deep irony attended the location: Grant and Lee would meet in the home of a man who had been driven from his house in Manassas, Virginia, after First Bull Run. Wilmer McLean could state that the war began in his backyard and ended in his front parlor. Lt. Col. Horace Porter, Grant's aide, described encountering Lee before the meeting:

> Lee . . . was fully six feet in height, and quite erect for one of his age, for he was Grant's senior by sixteen years. His hair and full beard were a silver-gray, and quite thick, except that the hair had become a little thin in front. He wore a new uniform of Confederate gray, buttoned up to the throat, and at his side he carried a long sword of exceedingly fine workmanship, the hilt studded with jewels. . . . His top-boots were comparatively new, and seemed to have on them some ornamental stitching of red silk. . . . A felt hat, which in color matched pretty closely that of the uniform, and a pair of long buckskin gauntlets lay beside him on the table.[41]

Years of war, mountains of skulls, an ocean born of tear ducts, and now this, an end.

Grant's generous terms were accepted by Lee, and as the Federal commander returned to the field, he admonished Union soldiers celebrating the Rebels' defeat. "The war is over — the rebels are our countrymen again," said Grant. Lee bade farewell to his beloved army and made plans to return to Richmond, like his soldiers, a paroled prisoner. "With an increasing admiration of your constancy and devotion to your country," he wrote to them, "and a grateful remembrance of your kind and generous consideration of myself, I bid you an affectionate farewell." "How can I write it?" wrote North Carolina diarist Catherine Edmondston. "How find words to tell what has befallen us? *Gen Lee has surrendered!* . . . We stand appalled at our disaster! . . . [That] *Lee,* Lee upon whom hung the hopes of the whole country, should be a prisoner seems almost too dreadful to be realized!"[42] There could be no colder water.

━━

DESPITE the fact that Lee's army was just one of several left in the field, its surrender signaled an obvious end to the conflict. Just five days later a symbolic ending seemed to come with the raising of Old Glory over Fort Sumter, the war's starting place. "The ceremony began with a short prayer by the old army chaplain who had prayed when the flag was hoisted over Fort Sumter on December 27, 1860," wrote Mary Cadwalader Jones, who witnessed the event. "Next a Brooklyn clergyman read parts of several Psalms. . . . Then Sergeant Hart, who had held up the flag when its staff was shot through in the first attack, came forward quietly and drew the selfsame flag out of an ordinary leather mail bag. We all held our breath for a second, and then we gave a queer cry, between a cheer and a yell."[43]

And then, just as the celebrations were gaining steam across the North, the unthinkable happened. On April 14 Abraham Lincoln was assassinated by actor John Wilkes Booth at Ford's Theatre in Washington. Lincoln died across Tenth Street, in the Petersen House, at 7:22 the next morning. "The giant sufferer lay extended diagonally across the bed, which was not long enough for him," wrote Navy Secretary Gideon Welles. "He had been stripped of his clothes. His large arms, which were occasionally exposed, were of a size which one would scarce have expected from his spare appearance. His slow, full respiration lifted the clothes with each breath that he took. His features were calm and striking."[44]

Lincoln's death marked the end of any possibility of a smooth, peaceful reconciliation with the former states in rebellion. Now, radical Republicans would rise to influence and help administer a stern era of Reconstruction. The heartaches of Reconstruction would spread over the coming years: for now the war had to wind down. On

April 17 at Durham Station, North Carolina, Maj. Gen. William T. Sherman forced Gen. Joe Johnston's army into an armistice. Nine days later, after managing the terms and negotiations with the intervention of Grant and the War Department, Sherman received Johnston's formal surrender at Bennett Place, a farm at Durham Station. Johnston's capitulation was the first of the series of smaller surrenders that followed Lee's. On May 4 Lt. Gen. Richard Taylor, son of the twelfth U.S. president, surrendered his force at Citronville, Alabama. Six days later Federal cavalry caught up with the flight of the official party from Richmond, which included Jefferson Davis and his family, at Irwinville, Georgia. An overcoat hastily thrown over Davis's form as he attempted escape incited nasty press in the North about Davis's supposed attempt to impersonate a woman. Also on March 10 Maj. Gen. Samuel Jones surrendered his force at Tallahassee, Florida. The next day Col. M. Jeff Thompson, the famed partisan ranger, gave up his men at Chalk Bluff, Arkansas.

On May 12–13, at Palmito Ranch, Texas (near Brownsville), the last engagement of the Civil War was fought. The action, between a few hundred soldiers on each side, ironically resulted in a decisive Confederate victory. But it was the last gasp of a dead military effort. No more actions of significance took place, and on June 2 in Galveston, Texas, Gen. Edmund Kirby Smith finally surrendered. The Confederacy was gone. "And now, with my latest writing and utterance, and with what will be near to my latest breath, I here repeat, and would willingly proclaim, my unmitigated hatred to Yankee rule," wrote Edmund Ruffin, the fiery South Carolina secessionist, on June 18, "to all political, social, and business connection with the Yankees, and to the perfidious, malignant, and vile Yankee race."[45] He then killed himself.

In Washington, despite the loss of their beloved commander, Northerners celebrated the war's conclusion by marching their two victorious armies through the streets of the capital city. On May 23, as the new President Johnson, Grant, and numerous other officials and military officers watched, Meade's Army of the Potomac, some eighty thousand strong, marched through the city and down Pennsylvania Avenue. The next day Sherman's Army of Georgia and Army of the Tennessee, together some sixty-five thousand strong, marched the same route. The contrast between the well-dressed easterners and the dirty, exhausted westerners (who had just undertaken a two-thousand-mile march) was striking. Bunting and other decor for the fallen president adorned the whole triumphant city. Across the South Jefferson Davis was in captivity, and the Confederate army was out of commission. The wishes of many a Confederate politician, many of those in the House and the Senate, many army officers, many bureau chiefs, and even the vice president had come true. Jefferson Davis had lost his power as Confederate president — but not before the whole cause of the Confederacy was also lost. Dixie was betrayed.

19

EPILOGUE: DESPAIR

A s Sgt. John Worsham would remember it, the morning of April 2, 1865, had witnessed a soft haze settling over Richmond. It had been a Sunday, and the Sabbath was marked by a clear blue sky and the occasional ringing of church bells. A visitor plunked down within the city limits would have had no conception that a great war raged around the city and that its capture by Yankee troops would come at any moment.

Northwest of Capitol Square, in his pew at St. Paul's Episcopal Church, had sat Jefferson Davis. The Confederate president, along with many others in the city's limits, had arrived to celebrate the sacrament of Communion.

At Seventh and Broad streets, just two blocks north of where Davis sat in church, Worsham had lain in his bed. He was not derelict in duty or absent without leave; young Worsham, who had fought so well at the battle of the Wilderness with the Twenty-first Virginia Infantry, had been wounded later in the tumultuous year of 1864. In the Shenandoah Valley, at the second battle of Winchester, on September 19, a bullet had shattered Worsham's left knee, sending him home to Richmond. "I cannot say that I saw or heard much of what went on outside our house," wrote Worsham, "as there was not a man on the place at the time except myself, and the women were too much alarmed to go out."[1]

Nonetheless, Worsham, unable to leave his bed except for brief moments spent on crutches, had heard a flurry of rumors on that Sunday afternoon. About midnight on Monday morning, April 3, the house had awoken when a visitor called, and Worsham's room suddenly was invaded by family members and servants talking to a soldier, a friend of the family who had stopped to bid them all good-bye. Shocked, the Worshams had learned that Jefferson Davis and his family had fled the city. The president's cabinet and other government officials of the Confederacy also had left. The Confederate archives had been carted away. Everything had been loaded onto box-cars on the Richmond & Danville Railroad and sent south. The Confederate government had fled the capital city — lock, stock, and barrel.

Moving in and out of sleep, Worsham had spent a restless night. Shortly before dawn, "a flash of light came into my room, brighter than the brightest lightning," he recalled. "It was accompanied immediately by a loud report that rumbled and shook the house, and by a crash that sounded as if the front had fallen!"[2] The ladies of the house had run into Worsham's room, followed by the servants. Thinking that a great quantity of powder had exploded in the city's warehouse district, the family had explored the house to find shattered windows letting in the sounds of pandemonium from outside.

About sunrise the ladies of the family had discovered that a great fire was raging through Richmond. Fearing the whole city would be up in flames before long, the Worshams had received a friend who stopped by to inform them that the rear guard of General Lee's army had set fire to the tobacco warehouses along Shockoe Slip, down by the river. Stores of military supplies in the arsenals and magazines, along with goods in the Shockoe, Myers, Anderson, and public warehouses, had fueled the fires so voraciously that the flames had spread to adjacent buildings, and the whole district south of Capitol Square was in danger of going up in smoke.

Shouting and screaming on the streets had characterized the chaos that now was spreading throughout Richmond. Glass had been broken, homes and stores looted. Fearful of Union savagery, citizens had taken all the liquor they could find and dumped it in the streets.

Still early in the morning, a small African American child had brought Worsham his breakfast and then had asked, "Marse John, let me run down to the corner and see if I can see any of the Yankees." Returning a little while later, he had said, "Marse John, they is here."[3]

All hell had broken loose. An enormous pall of smoke hung low over the city, illuminated from beneath by the warm glow of orange fire. Worsham recalled that "large chunks of fire were falling on our house and in the yard." The Worsham house had actually caught fire several times, and each time the fire had been extinguished by a watchful house servant. The smoke around the Worsham house had been so dense, he remembered, that the sun had not been visible for most of the day.

And then, as soon as the carnage seemed to be unstoppable, it had ceased. The noise and patter on the streets had died away, the screams and shrieks of tortured souls in the surrounding houses had calmed. Slowly, Richmonders had heard the songs and cheers of Northern boys marching with a clatter along city streets and the clanking of bayonets — just as Worsham had remembered from the battle of the Wilderness, only now, the martial sounds were heard in the place of his boyhood upbringing.

By evening Capitol Square had been transformed into a makeshift refugee camp for those who had lost their homes in the ordeal. Tents were staked all over the area, and campfires burned not for Northern soldiers but for Southern women and children, heating scraps of food, their first meal under Federal occupation. Yankee soldiers patrolled the streets. Quiet spread across the city. Although Union soldiers would soon begin house-to-house searches for Confederate troops in hiding, there were none to be found now. They were scurrying westward with the tattered remnants of Lee's army on a rendezvous with surrender, which would occur a week later in the tiny hamlet of Appomattox Court House.

Three or four days later, as the Worsham household held its collective breath — not knowing what would become of the city — the doorbell had rung. On the step had stood three Yankee officers. At once fearful of what might happen to him and believing he ought to tell the truth, Worsham had confessed he was a wounded Confederate soldier on leave for recovery. The soldiers had hardly reacted, and Worsham had been momentarily relieved. Yet he had worried that the military valuables he kept throughout the house would be stolen or confiscated; two swords were stuck in the lounge near his bed, and the three Yankees had sat right down on the lounge.

The Federals had sat on squeaky springs and moved around in apparent discomfort, but without discovering the booty. Finally, Worsham, unable to stand it, had told them about the hidden swords. All three officers had burst out laughing, and they had advised him to keep the swords hidden and let them know at the headquarters nearby if he needed any further help. The incident had marked a turning point in Worsham's existence. The Yankees were not evil or anxious to persecute him. In fact they were helpful.

A few days later the surviving parolees of the Army of Northern Virginia — many of them young boys and old men — had begun parading back into the city. "As Lee came riding back into Richmond," recalled Worsham, "his old followers immediately recognized him. They formed in line and followed him to his home where, with uncovered heads, they saw him enter his door. Then they silently dispersed."[4] As the white-haired, grandfatherly figure had awaited the noted photographer Mathew Brady, who would come and photograph the war celebrity Lee on the rear porch of his Franklin Street house, the South already was transforming. It was, at this moment, already part of a new United States. And the former soldiers of Lee's army were beginning to discover new lives that they had never known.

Poverty is the great equalizer. With a ruined economy, wrecked buildings, neglected crops, and worthless currency and bonds, the South offered impoverishment to one and all. Worsham recalled seeing a private and a colonel working in the field, side by side, in their old army uniforms. Men who had amassed fortunes in Richmond's financial district now were reduced to cleaning the charred bricks in the burned district of the city.

Although he was just twenty-five at war's end, John Worsham had matured beyond his years, a necessary outcome of the trauma he had lived through. The same could not be said of all the Southern politicians and generals who survived the war. Few wanted to face up to the fact that they had been a cause of the Confederacy's ruin. "You are represented to have manifested surprise that no citizen of the South had appealed to the Government in behalf of Mr. Davis," Howell Cobb wrote the Union secretary of state, William H. Seward, soon after the war ceased. Seward himself was recovering still from hideous injuries suffered on the bloody night of murder in Washington the previous April, when President Lincoln had been killed. "You had evidently inferred from this silence on the part of the people of the South that there existed among them — to say the least — a feeling of indifference on the subject," Cobb continued.

"My object is to disabuse your mind of such erroneous impression," wrote the man who had served as first provisional president of the Confederacy. He continued:

> During the latter portion of the late struggle public opinion in reference to Mr. Davis and his administration was much divided. There were those who fully approved the policy of his administration and as a matter of course gave it their unqualified support. There were others who differed upon many points from his policy who still gave an earnest support to his administration from a conviction that such a course alone promised success to the cause which they had so deeply at heart. There was another class even more opposed to his policy and who believed that success under his lead was impracticable and therefore urged a change of administration. Whilst there existed these differences of opinion there was one point upon which all were agreed, and that was that Mr. Davis was true and faithful to the trust which had been reposed in him.[5]

And so began the remaking of the war, the remolding of the words, the impression of deep unity, which continues in the way many view the war to this day.

And this rewriting of history, this refighting battles on paper, this massaging of the political facts, was just taking hold. Within the year, in force by the end of the century, the Confederacy's politicians would become saints, its generals unsurpassed heroes once again, thanks to the writers of Southern history.

The revisionism began at the top. From the papers of Burton Harrison, Jefferson Davis's secretary, one finds ink notations — corrections — made by the Confederate president. Davis changed the claim he had been "among the keenest and most sagacious of them all in his endeavour to precipitate secession upon the country" to "in his assertion of the rights of the States under the Constitution and of the right of Secession — although the records of Congress show that he cherished the utmost devotion to the Union and consistently opposed extremists of all parties who were endeavouring to precipitate actual secession." A uniter, not a divider. In a passage touching on his address in Montgomery as Confederate president, he reworked "prophesying [*sic*] peace, but threatening that the enemies of the South would be compelled to 'smell Southern powder, and feel Southern steel' " to "expressing his desire for the maintenance of peaceful relations with the States which remained in the Union — asserted that all that the seceding States desired was 'to be let alone' — but announced that, if war should be forced upon them, they would make the enemies of the South 'smell Southern powder and feel Southern steel.' "[6]

Davis always appreciated how his revolution recalled the American Revolution of his generation's grandfathers, how that echo somehow ennobled the cause of Confederate independence. Diehard Confederates churned out such verses as "*Rebels* before / Our fathers of yore / *Rebel's* the righteous name / *Washington* bore / Why, then, be ours the same."[7]

The Confederate president promoted this theme during the war and vigorously stoked it afterward. He also pushed the idea that the Union victory was due to overwhelming odds, that the cleverer and more highly skilled soldiers of the South simply were beaten down in the end by huge numbers of undesirable immigrant troops from the North and by the Union's endless resources. He downplayed or ignored the strategic and tactical victories of Yankee generals. But perhaps most significantly Davis tried to weave a nostalgic view of how the Confederate troops, generals in the field, and politicians all got along. It was a utopia that the Yankees swooped down upon and spoiled, and according to Davis, the world would have been a better place had it continued without ruin from these wicked Northern aggressors.

Davis's harmonic world was a dream — one that ignored the bitter squabbles of those who needed to cooperate the most in order for the Confederacy to succeed. The roll call included Aleck Stephens, Robert Hunter, Henry Foote, Robert Rhett, Louis Wigfall, and Bob Toombs, a gallery of men who held old-school principles — state rights and slavery — higher than the existence of their own creation, the Confederacy.

—

THIS romanticized version of the Confederacy took hold immediately after the war and never let go. Whereas Union military victors had little to prove on paper, Southerners continued to fight the war, invoking numerous "what-ifs" to imagine what could have been, downplaying the role of slavery in going to war, and constructing a new mythology of the Southern soldier. At the war's outset the popular myth had been, "One Southerner can lick ten Yankees." That turned out not to be the case. Now a new mythology arose: "The South lost, even though it fought better and with a superior class of soldiers, because of overwhelming Northern manpower and war matériel."

In the pages of many early Southern histories of the war, the Confederates seem to win practically every battle. The sarcastic question that came later to many observers was, if the South won virtually all the battles, how could it have lost the war?

Americans love myths, and they love imagining what might have been, particularly for underdogs. The popularity of the underdog myth was aided and abetted by the nonresponse from Northern participants, who were much less engaged in recounting the war's actions. The majority of Yankees felt they had won the war, it had been an enormous unwanted distraction, and they wanted to get on with normal life again.

EPILOGUE: DESPAIR

But Southerners great and small continued to fight on paper the war they had lost in reality. Some did it to salvage their reputations; others simply to bolster their damaged sense of pride amid the wreckage of the New South, now experiencing the early days of a painful Reconstruction. Others twisted the truth of what had happened to build a new sense of pride for their children and grandchildren, so the stigma of having lost the war could be lifted as quickly as possible. In this mode of Southern Reconstruction, the revisionists created a powerful Lost Cause mythology that downplayed the actual reasons for secession and put forth the "overwhelming numbers" argument in all its glory.

Many early books published in the South shortly after the war carried the seeds of these themes, including virtually all the general histories of the war published in the South. But the movement really took hold a few years after Appomattox, in Richmond, with the formation of a new organization dedicated to remembering the war and its dead — the Southern Historical Society.

Founded by a group of ex-Confederate officers in 1869, the Southern Historical Society quickly became the preeminent organization aiming to "set the record straight" with regard to the war history. "No Southern man who reads the very personal and partisan chapters of the 'Lost Cause,' or the unjust and unreasonable history of the late war as compiled by Northern writers for the deception of the world and its posterity, can be satisfied," read an announcement for the society's founding. (The book referred to here is Richmond newspaper editor Edward Pollard's *The Lost Cause*, which attacked the foolishness of many Confederate military decisions as well as Jefferson Davis's ability as president.)

Soon after its formation the society began publishing a landmark set of journals collectively termed the *Southern Historical Society Papers*. Containing contributions by ex-officers who included the fiercely unreconstructed Jubal A. Early, Lee's former field general, the *Papers* set about to rewrite history. Their authors attempted to justify secession; promote the theory that overwhelming Union manpower and supplies unjustly defeated a noble Southern band of brothers; suggest within the Confederacy that Virginia and Virginians were the preeminent leaders of the South, the constant battlefield heroes; and — after his death, in 1870 — push Robert E. Lee as a new American cult hero. The conclusions put forth by the Virginians were helped to congeal into popular memory by the fact that few other states or cities had organized societies with the ability to muster a wide-ranging publicity campaign as did the Richmond group.

Moreover, most Northern writers were still racist by today's standards (and would be for a long time to come), and so on all sides of the equation, the moral aspect of the Civil War was downplayed significantly. Few Yankee writers wanted to go on record to support the truth and get into the nitty-gritty details of slavery, and so they abetted the Southern version of events by, in many cases, simply not responding to it.

While the upper class of the Confederate Army, the officers and Virginians, had its *Southern Historical Society Papers,* common soldiers also had a major outlet where they could publish wholesale fabrications of revisionist thought, though it came along a little later. In 1893 the Nashville newspaperman S. A. Cunningham founded *Confederate Veteran,* a monthly journal published "in the interest of Confederate veterans and kindred topics." This title joined *The Land We Love,* published by the former Confederate general D. H. Hill, as a hodgepodge of battle anecdotes, stories about the South, poetry, reports on veterans' activities, and apologia for secession.

Gradually, by attrition, Confederate writers discovered their power of persuasion. If you wrote something often enough, eventually a lot of people would believe it.

And this perception still holds on to the American imagination today. Not just in the Southeast, but everywhere in the United States, the romanticized version of the Confederacy is the one people predominantly believe in and hold out as fact. In the South the perception has been fueled not only by bloodlines and the assumed correctness of anything an ancestor ever did, but also by the adoption of these themes into the "official viewpoint" of such heritage groups as the United Confederate Veterans, the United Daughters of the Confederacy, and the Sons of Confederate Veterans, fraternal organizations that still hold many members. How could any member of the SCV possibly believe that the principle Southern politicians held most sacred, state rights, would be the thing that killed it like a cancer from the inside?

Americans believe in dreams. Dreams caused the Civil War, some have said — different dreams of what the future could be among those in the North and South. The dream of the Confederacy started out with an expectation of nobility and ended cloaked in revisionist elitism. Both dreams contain fantastic, almost unbelievable, stories. But the story of what really happened is far more intriguing — and useful. If we are to learn from the history of men, we must be frank about their humanity. Those who led the Confederacy were not gods. They were men, sometimes bold and sometimes weak, sometimes hateful and sometimes grand, sometimes selfish, not always sober. Together they formed an imperfect union, and together they destroyed it.

POSTLUDE

P. G. T. Beauregard beat the odds. The Little Creole, age forty-seven when the war ended, prospered afterward, returning to New Orleans and employing his engineering talents as superintendent of railroad and street railway companies. Along with former Confederate lieutenant general Jubal Early, he profited greatly as a supervisor of the scandal-plagued Louisiana Lottery. Beauregard fought his last battles on paper, swiping at Jefferson Davis, the adherents to Albert Sidney Johnston, and Joe Johnston and defending his record at First Manassas and his claim to leadership at Shiloh. He served his last years as adjutant general of the Louisiana militia and supervisor of public works in New Orleans, where he died in 1893.

Braxton Bragg was never forgiven by many for helping to orchestrate the removal of Joe Johnston from command of the Army of Tennessee. In the end Bragg had been tragically miscast: he had been assigned a range of responsibilities so unsuited to his personality that failure was almost guaranteed. Bragg caught up with President Davis's party at war's end, just in time to inform the Confederate leader that

286

hope was lost. Afterward Bragg served as superintendent of the New Orleans waterworks before moving to Alabama and then Texas. He died in Galveston in 1876, after suddenly dropping to the ground while walking down a street.

Samuel Cooper is still the forgotten central figure of the Confederacy, as he was after the war. The New Jersey native who married a Southern bride fled Richmond and, on the southward journey from Danville, was allowed to leave the party to surrender. He immediately gave the Yankee authorities his voluminous records, which constituted much of the official paperwork of the Confederacy, as many other caches had been destroyed in the abandonment of the capital. At age sixty-seven, weak from stress and impoverished, Cooper returned from Richmond to Alexandria, Virginia, to quietly live out his remaining days. The much-maligned "glorified clerk" received financial aid from several fellow officers, including Robert E. Lee. He died during the final month of 1876.

Jefferson Davis saw his mental health decline precipitously, draining further his already feeble body. Blamed by Northerners since before Sumter as chief architect of the rebellion, he was not yet accustomed to being held accountable by the majority of Southerners for the Confederacy's collapse. Captured at Irwinville, Georgia, on May 10, 1865, the fifty-six-year-old spent the next two years in prison at Fort Monroe, Virginia, awaiting a trial for treason that never came. Released into a world that had completely changed, Davis nevertheless continued life as a Confederate, albeit one who simply wrote about the past from a study lined with books in Biloxi, Mississippi. Davis's famous tome *The Rise and Fall of the Confederate Government* contained more irrational than useful information, and it attacked Joe Johnston and Beauregard as much as it supported friends such as Bragg and Northrop. Hero status at last came to Davis in his final years, when many rational Southerners decided that he had been in a no-win situation and had done a relatively effective job running the war. Davis died in 1889, survived by his wife and two daughters.

Henry S. Foote spent the first few months of postwar life getting over the embarrassment of his abortive, self-created peace mission to the Yankees. On Andrew Johnson's succession as president, Foote had been ordered by Federal authorities to flee the country or stand trial for treason; he swiftly made tracks for Montreal. Foote finally took the oath of allegiance and was allowed back into the country, settling in Nashville, by 1867. At age sixty-three, the testy politician took up writing, producing two books about the war and his experiences. He then moved to Washington to resume his law practice and write for a newspaper. Ever marked by inconsistency and scathing criticism toward others, Foote attributed the war to a "blundering generation" of sectionalists. He switched parties, becoming a Republican, and subsequently served as superintendent of the U.S. Mint at New Orleans. Returning home in ill health, he died in Nashville, in 1881, "a decrepit old gentleman with a fiery red head."

John Bell Hood continued to fight the war on paper, penning his bitter volume *Advance and Retreat* to defend himself against charges of total incompetency after the Franklin and Nashville campaign. At thirty-four he moved to New Orleans, married — but not the girl he had fallen deeply in love with during the war — and became a cotton merchant. As he searched for a publisher willing to distribute his book, Hood — followed by others in his family — was struck by yellow fever during the epidemic of 1878–79. His wife and daughter succumbed to the disease in August 1879; before the month was out, Hood himself died. *Advance and Retreat* was subsequently published and raised money to help his ten orphaned children.

Robert M. T. Hunter was arrested at war's end and imprisoned in Fort Pulaski, Georgia, until February 1866. On his release Hunter, fifty-seven, learned that his lands in Virginia had been desecrated by soldiers under Maj. Gen. Benjamin F. Butler. He returned to Virginia to resume a law practice and commenced farming. Hunter resumed his role in state politics and served as vice president of the Southern Historical Society, an office that led to more clashes with Jefferson Davis, this time over their recollections of the war. Conscription, emancipation of slaves, and peace proposals continued to be subjects of heated debate between Davis and Hunter. Hunter eventually was named collector of the Port of Tappahannock, northeast of Richmond on the Rappahannock River, by President Cleveland. He died in 1887.

Joseph E. Johnston surrendered what remained of the Army of Tennessee on April 26 at Bennett Place, North Carolina, and resumed a civilian life. At age fifty-eight, he entered the railroad and express transportation businesses, living in Virginia, Alabama, and Washington, DC. Johnston also served a term as U.S. representative from Virginia. Johnston's *Narrative of Military Operations Directed during the Late War between the States,* published in 1874, summarized his arguments with Davis and others and rationalized his actions, hoping to thwart critics. Ironically, Johnston fell ill in the winter of 1891, while standing in the rain acting as an honorary pallbearer at William Tecumseh Sherman's funeral. Beside the coffin of his old nemesis, Johnston caught cold and — just four weeks later — died.

Robert E. Lee towered over the crumbling reputation of Davis as the postwar years dragged on. Lee contemplated writing his memoirs but had too few papers left to get the project going. Instead, he accepted the presidency of Washington College in Lexington, Virginia, and focused on influencing the next generation of Southerners through education. Lee tirelessly raised money for the school, which later would be renamed Washington and Lee University. The general's health eventually deteriorated, however, as it had started to during the final two years of the war. In October 1870, at age sixty-three, he suffered a stroke and died in Lexington.

William Porcher Miles enjoyed a life of relative luxury after marrying into plantation money in 1863. At war's end he began life as a Virginia country gentleman in Nelson County. In 1880 Miles became president of the University of South Carolina. Two years later he took over his father-in-law's Louisiana sugar plantation and grew even richer. His health failed by 1899, when he died at age seventy-six, at his Louisiana estate.

Lucius B. Northrop, stung by the constant criticism of his performance and finally pushed from office as commissary general, was captured by the Yankees in June 1865. A pseudogeneral whose commission had never been confirmed, Northrop's career had crashed and burned. At age fifty-three he spent four months in prison several blocks from his old office, charged with deliberately starving Yankee prisoners. Released in October 1865 he took up farming near Charlottesville, Virginia. Bitter toward a cast of fellow officers, including Robert E. Lee, he stewed over the past and what might have been. In 1890 a stroke limited his physical movement; four years later he died in Maryland, his last home.

Robert Barnwell Rhett never lived down his reputation as the ultimate fire-eater, the self-proclaimed "father of secession." Rhett's angry wartime editorials in the *Charleston Mercury* had scorched the Confederate president. At war's end, at age sixty-four, Rhett fumed over the outcome, writing an unpublished history of his actions against Davis that was finally put into print in 2000 as *A Fire-Eater Remembers.* He eventually moved to Louisiana, where he died in 1876.

Alexander H. Stephens, despite his chronic ill health, lived for nearly twenty years after the war. Disgusted by the mixed motives and complete lack of success of the Hampton Roads Conference, Stephens returned home to await his fate. On May 11, 1865, he was arrested. He spent five months in Fort Warren in Boston Harbor, where he kept a detailed diary before being released. Stephens attempted a return to the U.S. Senate, winning election but eventually barred from taking his seat. Over two years he wrote the ponderous and incredibly dull *A Constitutional View of the War between the States,* a two-volume legal harangue, and in 1873, he reentered politics. Elected from Georgia as a member of the U.S. House of Representatives, Stephens served in that capacity until 1882, when he was elected governor of Georgia. He died in 1883, at age seventy-one, after just three months in office.

Robert A. Toombs fled to Cuba and then Paris immediately after the Confederacy's demise, staying in Europe and then in Canada until 1867. Ultimately returning to the town of Washington, Georgia, he reestablished his law practice at age fifty-seven and reentered Georgia politics. A completely unreconstructed Rebel, Toombs pulled everything he could to thwart Federal authority in the New South. His health deteriorated for a number of years, until he finally died, in 1885.

Louis T. Wigfall blamed Davis for the Confederacy's defeat after the war even more than he had during the contest. After April 1865 he fled to England, where he attempted to incite Great Britain against United States policy. He returned to Maryland in 1872 and moved back to Texas two years later. That same year he died, at age fifty-seven, unheralded in his time but with few equals in his passion for the Southern Nation.

John H. Winder never made it past the war. When he died of a heart attack in Florence, South Carolina, on February 7, 1865, he was wanted by the Union for his authority over the horribly mismanaged Confederate prison camps. Southerners had never learned to like him, either, because of his limiting controls over the citizens of Richmond. It was said that it was "fortunate" for Winder that he died before the Union captured him, or else he might have suffered a fate even worse than death.

John H. Worsham outlived all the elder politicians who controlled his fate in the great war of 1861–65. The young man used his friendship with Richmond's mayor, Joseph Mayo, to become toll keeper at Mayo's Bridge in Richmond soon after he recovered from his wound. He later established a partnership in a tobacco firm, giving him the means to marry Mary Bell Pilcher, in 1871. He then entered the milling business, dabbled in the canal boat business, and subsequently became a bookkeeper, serving his son's printing company for the remainder of his life. Worsham's family included four children and six grandchildren. He remained active in Confederate historical activities, proud both of his part in the war and of what America had become in the Gilded Age. His deep blue eyes often displayed a "twinkle," and he was known around Richmond as a soft-spoken old-timer, a veteran of the war who talked sparingly but was always listened to when he had something to say. In his old age Worsham suffered a fall and contracted pneumonia; he died at age eighty-one, on September 19, 1920, on the fifty-sixth anniversary of his wounding at the battle of Winchester. The South had lost a good man.

APPENDIX

EXECUTIVE OFFICERS OF THE CONFEDERATE STATES, 1861-1865

Presidents
Howell Cobb II, Feb. 4, 1861–Feb. 17, 1862 (Provisional Congress)
Jefferson Davis, Feb. 18, 1861–Feb. 17, 1862 (Provisional)
Jefferson Davis, Feb. 22, 1862–surrendered May 10, 1865

Vice Presidents
Alexander H. Stephens, Feb. 9, 1861–Feb. 17, 1862 (Provisional)
Alexander H. Stephens, Feb. 22, 1862–arrested May 11, 1865

Secretaries of State
Robert A. Toombs, Feb. 21, 1861–resigned Jul. 24, 1861 (Provisional)
Robert M. T. Hunter, July 25, 1861–Feb. 17, 1862 (Provisional)
William M. Browne, Mar. 7, 1862–Mar. 18, 1862 (ad interim)
Judah P. Benjamin, Mar. 18, 1862–May 10, 1865

Secretaries of the Treasury
Christopher G. Memminger, Feb. 21, 1861–Feb. 17, 1862 (Provisional)
Christopher G. Memminger, Mar. 18, 1862–resigned Jul. 18, 1864
George A. Trenholm, Jul. 18, 1864–resigned Apr. 27, 1865
John H. Reagan, Apr. 27, 1865–May 10, 1865 (acting)

Secretaries of War
Leroy P. Walker, Feb. 21, 1861–resigned Sept. 16, 1861 (Provisional)

Judah P. Benjamin, Sept. 17, 1861–Nov. 21, 1861 (Provisional, acting)
Judah P. Benjamin, Nov. 21, 1861–Feb. 17, 1862 (Provisional)
Judah P. Benjamin, Feb. 17, 1862–Mar. 23, 1862 (acting)
George W. Randolph, Mar. 18, 1862–resigned Nov. 17, 1862
Gustavus W. Smith, Nov. 17, 1862–Nov. 21, 1862 (acting)
James A. Seddon, Nov. 21, 1862–resigned Feb. 6, 1865
John C. Breckinridge, Feb. 6, 1865–fled May 10, 1865

Secretaries of the Navy
Stephen R. Mallory, Feb. 28, 1861–Feb. 17, 1862 (Provisional)
Stephen R. Mallory, Mar. 18, 1862–resigned May 2, 1865
John H. Reagan, May 2, 1865–May 10, 1865 (acting)

Postmasters-General
Henry T. Ellett, Feb. 25, 1861–declined Mar. 5, 1861 (Provisional)
John H. Reagan, Mar. 6, 1861–Feb. 17, 1862 (Provisional)
John H. Reagan, Mar. 18, 1862–surrendered May 10, 1865

Attorneys-General
Judah P. Benjamin, Feb. 25, 1861–resigned Nov. 21, 1861 (Provisional)
Thomas Bragg, Nov. 21, 1861–Feb. 17, 1862 (Provisional)

APPENDIX

Thomas H. Watts, Mar. 18, 1862–resigned Oct. 1, 1863
Wade Keyes, Oct. 1, 1863–Jan. 4, 1864 (acting)

George Davis, Jan. 4, 1864–resigned Apr. 26, 1865
John H. Reagan, Apr. 26, 1865–May 10, 1865 (acting)

Derived from John H. Eicher and David J. Eicher, Civil War High Commands *(Stanford, CA: Stanford University Press, 2001).*

CONGRESSES OF THE CONFEDERATE STATES, 1861-1865

Provisional Congress
First session. Assembled at Montgomery, AL, Feb. 4, 1861. Adjourned Mar. 16, 1861, to meet second Monday in May.
Second session (called). Met at Montgomery, AL, Apr. 29, 1861. Adjourned May 21, 1861.
Third session. Met at Richmond, VA, Jul. 20, 1861. Adjourned Aug. 31, 1861.
Fourth session (called). Met at Richmond, VA, Sept. 3, 1861. Adjourned same day.
Fifth session. Met at Richmond, VA, Nov. 8, 1861. Adjourned Feb. 17, 1862.

First Congress
First session. Met at Richmond, VA, Feb. 18, 1862. Adjourned Apr. 21, 1862.
Second session. Met at Richmond, VA, Aug. 18, 1862. Adjourned Oct. 13, 1862.
Third session. Met at Richmond, VA, Jan. 12, 1863. Adjourned May 1, 1863.
Fourth session. Met at Richmond, VA, Dec. 7, 1863. Adjourned Feb. 17, 1864.

Second Congress
First session. Met at Richmond, VA, May 2, 1864. Adjourned Jun. 14, 1864.
Second session. Met at Richmond, VA, Nov. 7, 1864. Adjourned Mar. 18, 1865.

MEMBERS OF THE PROVISIONAL CONGRESS OF THE CONFEDERATE STATES
(FEB. 4, 1861-FEB. 17, 1862)

Alabama
William P. Chilton
Jabez L. M. Curry
Nicholas Davis
Thomas Fearn
Stephen F. Hale
H. C. Jones
David P. Lewis
Colin J. McRae
Cornelius Robinson
John Gill Shorter
Robert H. Smith
Richard W. Walker

Arkansas
Augustus H. Garland
Robert W. Johnson
Albert Rust
Hugh F. Thomason
W. W. Watkins

Florida
J. Patton Anderson
Jackson Morton
James B. Owens
John P. Sanderson
George T. Ward

Georgia
Francis S. Bartow
Nathan Bass
Howell Cobb II
Thomas R. R. Cobb
Martin J. Crawford
Thomas M. Foreman
Benjamin H. Hill
Augustus H. Kenan
Eugenius A. Nisbet
Alexander H. Stephens
Robert A. Toombs
Augustus R. Wright

Kentucky
Henry C. Burnett
Theodore L. Burnett
John M. Elliott
George W. Ewing
L. H. Ford
George B. Hodge
Thomas Johnson
Thomas B. Monroe
John J. Thomas
Daniel P. White

APPENDIX

Louisiana
Charles M. Conrad
Alexander De Clouet
Duncan F. Kenner
Henry Marshall
John Perkins Jr.
Edward Sparrow

Mississippi
William S. Barry
Alexander B. Bradford
Walker Brooke
J. A. P. Campbell
Alexander M. Clayton
Wiley P. Harris
James T. Harrison
John A. Orr
William S. Wilson

Missouri
Caspar W. Bell
John B. Clark
Aaron H. Conrow
Thomas A. Harris
Robert L. Y. Peyton
George G. Vest

North Carolina
W. W. Avery
Burton Craige
A. T. Davidson
George Davis
Thomas D. McDowell
John M. Morehead
R. C. Puryear
Thomas Ruffin
W. N. H. Smith
Abraham W. Venable

South Carolina
Robert W. Barnwell
William W. Boyce
James Chesnut Jr.

Lawrence M. Keitt
Christopher G. Memminger
William Porcher Miles
James L. Orr
Robert Barnwell Rhett
Thomas J. Withers

Tennessee
John D. C. Atkins
Robert L. Caruthers
David M. Currin
W. H. De Witt
John F. House
Thomas M. Jones
J. H. Thomas

Texas
John Gregg
John Hemphill
William B. Ochiltree
Williamson S. Oldham
John H. Reagan
Thomas N. Waul
Louis T. Wigfall

Virginia
Thomas S. Bocock
Alexander R. Boteler
John W. Brockenbrough
Robert M. T. Hunter
Robert Johnston
W. H. Macfarland
James E. Mason
Walter Preston
William B. Preston
Roger A. Pryor
William C. Rives
Charles W. Russell
Robert E. Scott
James A. Seddon
Waller R. Staples
John Tyler

SENATORS OF THE FIRST CONGRESS OF THE CONFEDERATE STATES
(FEB. 18, 1862-FEB. 17, 1864)

Alabama
Clement C. Clay Jr.
Robert Jemison Jr.
William L. Yancey

Arkansas
Robert W. Johnson
Charles B. Mitchell

Florida
James M. Baker
Augustus E. Maxwell

Georgia
Benjamin H. Hill
Herschel V. Johnson
John W. Lewis

APPENDIX

Kentucky
Henry C. Burnett
William E. Simms

Louisiana
Thomas J. Semmes
Edward Sparrow

Mississippi
Albert G. Brown
James Phelan

Missouri
John B. Clark
Waldo P. Johnson
Robert L. Y. Peyton

North Carolina
George Davis

William T. Dortch
Edwin G. Reade

South Carolina
Robert W. Barnwell
James L. Orr

Tennessee
Landon C. Haynes
Gustavus A. Henry

Texas
Williamson S. Oldham
Louis T. Wigfall

Virginia
Allen T. Caperton
Robert M. T. Hunter
William B. Preston

MEMBERS OF THE HOUSE OF REPRESENTATIVES OF THE
FIRST CONGRESS OF THE CONFEDERATE STATES
(FEB. 18, 1862-FEB. 17, 1864)

Alabama
William P. Chilton
David Clopton
Jabez L. M. Curry
E. S. Dargan
Thomas J. Foster
Francis S. Lyon
James L. Pugh
John P. Ralls
William R. Smith

Arkansas
Felix I. Batson
Augustus H. Garland
Thomas B. Hanly
Grandison D. Royston

Florida
James B. Dawkins
Robert H. Hilton
John M. Martin

Georgia
William W. Clark
Lucius J. Gartrell
Julian Hartridge
Hines Holt
Porter Ingram
Augustus H. Kenan
David W. Lewis
Charles J. Munnerlyn
Hardy Strickland

Robert P. Trippe
Augustus R. Wright

Kentucky
Robert J. Breckinridge Jr.
Ely M. Bruce
Horatio W. Bruce
Theodore L. Burnett
James S. Chrisman
John W. Crockett
John M. Elliott
George W. Ewing
George B. Hodge
Willis B. Machem
James W. Moore
Henry E. Read

Louisiana
Charles M. Conrad
Lucius J. Dupré
Duncan F. Kenner
Henry Marshall
John Perkins Jr.
Charles J. Villeré

Mississippi
Ethelbert Barksdale
Henry C. Chambers
J. W. Clapp
Reuben Davis
William D. Holder
John J. McRae

APPENDIX

Otho R. Singleton
Israel Welsh

Missouri
Caspar W. Bell
Aaron H. Conrow
William M. Cooke
Thomas W. Freeman
Thomas A. Harris
George G. Vest

North Carolina
Archibald H. Arrington
Thomas S. Ashe
Robert R. Bridgers
A. T. Davidson
Burgess S. Gaither
Owen R. Kenan
William Lander
Thomas D. McDowell
J. R. McLean
W. N. H. Smith

South Carolina
Lewis M. Ayer
Milledge L. Bonham
William W. Boyce
James Farrow
John McQueen
William Porcher Miles
William D. Simpson

Tennessee
John D. C. Atkins
David M. Currin
Henry S. Foote
E. L. Gardenhire
Meredith P. Gentry
Joseph B. Heiskell
George W. Jones
Thomas Menees
William G. Swan

William H. Tibbs
John V. Wright

Texas
M. D. Graham
Peter W. Gray
Caleb C. Herbert
Frank B. Sexton
John A. Wilcox
William B. Wright

Virginia
John B. Baldwin
Thomas S. Bocock
Alexander R. Boteler
John R. Chambliss
Charles F. Collier
Daniel C. De Jarnette
David Funsten
Muscoe R. H. Garnett
John Goode Jr.
James P. Holcombe
Albert G. Jenkins
Robert Johnston
James Lyons
Samuel A. Miller
Walter Preston
Roger A. Pryor
Charles W. Russell
William Smith
Waller R. Staples

Territories

Arizona
Marcus H. Macwillie

Cherokee Nation
Elias C. Boudinot

Choctaw Nation
Robert M. Jones

SENATORS OF THE SECOND CONGRESS OF THE CONFEDERATE STATES
(MAY 2, 1864-MAR. 18, 1865)

Alabama
Robert Jemison Jr.
Richard W. Walker

Arkansas
Augustus H. Garland
Robert W. Johnson
Charles B. Mitchell

Florida
James M. Baker
Augustus E. Maxwell

Georgia
Benjamin H. Hill
Herschel V. Johnson

Kentucky
Henry C. Burnett
William E. Simms

297

APPENDIX

Louisiana
Thomas J. Semmes
Edward Sparrow

Mississippi
Albert G. Brown
John W. C. Watson

Missouri
Waldo P. Johnson
George G. Vest

North Carolina
William T. Dortch
William A. Graham

South Carolina
Robert W. Barnwell
James L. Orr

Tennessee
Landon C. Haynes
Gustavus A. Henry

Texas
Williamson S. Oldham
Louis T. Wigfall

Virginia
Allen T. Caperton
Robert M. T. Hunter

MEMBERS OF THE HOUSE OF REPRESENTATIVES OF THE SECOND CONGRESS OF THE CONFEDERATE STATES
(MAY 2, 1864-MAR. 18, 1865)

Alabama
William P. Chilton
David Clopton
M. H. Cruikshank
James S. Dickinson
Thomas J. Foster
Francis S. Lyon
James L. Pugh
William R. Smith

Arkansas
Felix I. Batson
David W. Carroll
Augustus H. Garland
Rufus K. Garland
Thomas B. Hanly

Florida
Robert H. Hilton
S. St. George Rogers

Georgia
Clifford Anderson
Warren Atkin
Hiram P. Bell
Mark H. Blandford
Joseph H. Echols
Julian Hartridge
George N. Lester
John T. Shewmake
James M. Smith
William E. Smith

Kentucky
Benjamin F. Bradley
Ely M. Bruce

Horatio W. Bruce
Theodore L. Burnett
James S. Chrisman
John M. Elliott
George W. Ewing
Willis B. Machem
Humphrey Marshall
James W. Moore
Henry E. Read
George W. Triplett

Louisiana
Charles M. Conrad
Lucius J. Dupré
Henry Gray
Benjamin L. Hodge
Duncan F. Kenner
John Perkins Jr.
Charles J. Villeré

Mississippi
Ethelbert Barksdale
Henry C. Chambers
William D. Holder
John T. Lamkin
John A. Orr
Otho R. Singleton
Israel Welsh

Missouri
John B. Clark
Aaron H. Conrow
Robert A. Hatcher
N. L. Norton
Thomas L. Snead
George G. Vest
Peter S. Wilkes

298

APPENDIX

North Carolina
Robert R. Bridgers
Thomas C. Fuller
Burgess S. Gaither
John A. Gilmer
James M. Leach
James T. Leach
George W. Logan
James G. Ramsay
W. N. H. Smith
Josiah Turner Jr.

South Carolina
Lewis M. Ayer
William W. Boyce
James Farrow
William Porcher Miles
William D. Simpson
James H. Witherspoon

Tennessee
John D. C. Atkins
Michael W. Cluskey
Arthur S. Colyar
David M. Currin
Henry S. Foote
Joseph B. Heiskell
Edwin A. Keeble
James McCallum
Thomas Menees
John P. Murray
William G. Swan
John V. Wright

Texas
John R. Baylor
A. M. Branch

Stephen H. Darden
Caleb C. Herbert
Simpson H. Morgan
Frank B. Sexton

Virginia
John B. Baldwin
Thomas S. Bocock
Daniel C. De Jarnette
David Funsten
Thomas S. Gholson
John Goode Jr.
Frederick W. M. Holliday
Robert Johnston
Fayette McMullen
Samuel A. Miller
Robert L. Montague
William C. Rives
Charles W. Russell
Waller R. Staples
Robert H. Whitfield
Williams C. Wickham

Territories

Arizona
Marcus H. Macwillie

Cherokee Nation
Elias C. Boudinot

Choctaw Nation
Robert M. Jones

Creek and Seminole Nations
S. B. Callahan

ACKNOWLEDGMENTS

T HE days I spent with my father tramping around Richmond and among the stacks of many a library in the South were greatly enjoyable. The friendly help I received over the course of this project made it not only possible to write about the Confederacy's glory days, but also a great joy. On the home front I must first thank my wife, Lynda, and son, Christopher, for their never-ending support and encouragement. This work would not have been possible without them. That is true, too, for my father, John Eicher, a superb Civil War historian and fantastic traveling companion who shares stories of the war with an enthusiasm unmatched by anyone I know. My sister, Nancy Eicher, has also shared her support as she has traveled through various battlefields.

I owe a great debt of thanks to Laura Baird for carefully proofreading the manuscript. Many thanks to Terri Field for her exceptional maps created for the book.

For guidance and help with various questions along the way, I thank the following historians: Ed Bearss, John and Ruth Ann Coski, Lance Herdegen, Robert K. Krick, Michael Musick, T. Michael Parrish, and Marion Dawson Phillips. I am indebted to the

ACKNOWLEDGMENTS

staffs of the Library of Congress, the Library of Virginia, Miami University, the Museum of the Confederacy, and the National Archives and Records Administration. Additionally, for fielding queries, I thank Bill Brown, Jennifer Cole, Kevin Gannon, Mark Lause, and Bill Welsch.

For their terrific, on-site help at various institutions, I owe thanks to Betty Allen, Capitol guide, Virginia State Capitol, Richmond, Virginia; Laura C. Brown, head of public services, Manuscripts Department, University of North Carolina, Chapel Hill; Sam Fore, South Caroliniana Library, University of South Carolina, Columbia; Henry G. Fulmer, manuscripts librarian, South Caroliniana Library, University of South Carolina, Columbia; Mark K. Greenough, supervisor and historian, Capitol Guided Tours, Virginia State Capitol, Richmond; Stephanie A. T. Jacobe, visual resources manager, Virginia Historical Society, Richmond; Ginger G. Mauler, Jennifer McDaid, and Tom Crew, the Library of Virginia, Richmond; Patrick McCauley, Department of Archives and History, Columbia, South Carolina; Linda M. McCurdy, director of research services, Rare Book, Manuscript & Special Collections Library, Duke University, Durham, North Carolina; Becky McGee-Lankford, Debbie Blake, Chris Meekins, and Carol Campbell, Department of Archives and History, Raleigh, North Carolina; Jacqueline V. Reid, reference archivist, Duke University Libraries, Durham, North Carolina; Teresa Roane, Valentine Museum/Richmond History Center, Richmond; Gregory H. Stoner, Toni M. Carter, David Ward, Jonathan Bremer, and Sherry Wright, Virginia Historical Society, Richmond; Stacey Tompkins, Eleanor Mills, and Nelda Webb, Perkins Library, Duke University, Durham, North Carolina; Jewel Turpin, Capitol hostess, Virginia State Capitol, Richmond; and Heather A. Whitacre, manager of photographic collections, Museum of the Confederacy, Richmond.

For his patience, skill, and timely suggestions, I owe a great debt to my agent, Michael A. Choate of the Choate Agency. For his patience, editorial guidance, brilliant editorial suggestions, and vision, I have been privileged to work with Geoff Shandler, editor in chief at Little, Brown. His insight and interest in the topic have kept the

ACKNOWLEDGMENTS

project moving along on track. His spectacular editing skill is amazing. Thanks are also due to Elizabeth Nagle, Junie Dahn, and Peggy Freudenthal of Little, Brown, and to Rickie Harvey, who copyedited the book. I also wish to thank Deborah Baker, who brought the book to Little, Brown and showed genuine support for the topic and the writer.

David J. Eicher
Waukesha, Wisconsin
June 2005

NOTES

1. Prologue

1. Worsham, *One of Jackson's Foot Cavalry*, xvi.
2. Putnam, *Richmond during the War*, 314.
3. Adams as quoted in King, *Louis T. Wigfall*, 19.
4. Wigfall as quoted in King, *Louis T. Wigfall*, 40.
5. Russell, *My Diary*, 62.
6. *Congressional Globe*, 36th Cong., 1st sess., 1298–1303.
7. Houston as quoted in King, *Louis T. Wigfall*, 77.
8. *Congressional Globe*, 36th Cong., spec. sess., 1439–41.
9. Wigfall as quoted in King, *Louis T. Wigfall*, 110.
10. Wigfall as quoted in Russell, *My Diary*, 99.
11. King, *Louis T. Wigfall*, 15.

2. Birth of a Nation

1. Rogers, *Confederate Home Front*, 24–25.
2. William C. Davis, *Jefferson Davis*, 171–72.
3. Yancey as quoted in William C. Davis, *Jefferson Davis*, 307.
4. DeLeon, *Four Years in Rebel Capitals*, 23–27.
5. Davis as quoted in William C. Davis, *Jefferson Davis*, 307.
6. Davis, *Papers of Jefferson Davis*, 7: 46–51.
7. Stephens as quoted in Schott, *Alexander H. Stephens*, 334–35.
8. Stephens to R. Schleiden, minister of the Bremen Republic, Richmond, VA, Apr. 26, 1861, in Toombs, Stephens, and Cobb, *Correspondence*, 563–64.
9. Stephens to "a friend" in New York, in Toombs, Stephens and Cobb, *Correspondence*, 504–5.

10. Stephens as quoted in Rable, *Confederate Republic*, 43.
11. Davis, *"Government of Our Own,"* 74–75.
12. As quoted in ibid., 76.
13. As quoted in Rogers, *Confederate Home Front*, 25.
14. Cobb to his wife, New Orleans, LA, Apr. 7, 1861, in Toombs, Stephens, and Cobb, *Correspondence*, 559–60.
15. William Porcher Miles to Howell Cobb, Charleston, SC, Jan. 14, 1861, in Toombs, Stephens, and Cobb, *Correspondence*, 528–29.
16. Cobb to James Buchanan, Macon, GA, Mar. 26, 1861, in Toombs, Stephens, and Cobb, *Correspondence*, 554–55.
17. Cobb to Ambrose R. Wright, Montgomery, AL, Feb. 18, 1861, Stephens Papers, Lib. of Cong.
18. Stephens to Samuel R. Glenn, National Hotel, Washington, DC, Montgomery, AL, Feb. 8, 1861, Stephens Papers, Lib. of Cong.
19. Davis, *Rhett*, 398.
20. Rhett to Robert Branwell Rhett Jr., Montgomery, AL, Feb. 20, 1861, Rhett Papers.
21. Keitt as quoted in Current et al., eds., *Encyclopedia of the Confederacy*, 2:876–79.

3. Portrait of a President

1. Russell as quoted in Cooper, *Jefferson Davis*, 333.
2. Davis to the Congress, Montgomery, AL, Apr. 29, 1861, in Davis, *Jefferson Davis, Constitutionalist*, 5:67–84.
3. Sandburg, *Abraham Lincoln*, 1: 120.
4. Scott, *Memoirs*, 2: 625–28.
5. Donald, *Lincoln*, 282.
6. Lincoln, *Collected Works*, 262–71.

7. Chesnut as quoted in Cooper, *Jefferson Davis*, 334.

8. Klein, *Days of Defiance*, 408.

9. Pease and Pease, *James Louis Petigru*, 156.

10. Pryor as quoted in Klein, *Days of Defiance*, 398.

11. U.S. War Dept., *War of the Rebellion*, I, 1, 13.

12. Ibid., 14.

13. Crawford as quoted in Hewett, *O.R. Supplement*, I, 1, 59.

14. Chester as quoted in Johnson and Buel, eds., *Battles and Leaders*, 1: 65–66.

15. Doubleday, *Reminiscences*, 142.

16. Chester as quoted in in Johnson and Buell, eds., *Battles and Leaders*, 1: 73.

17. U.S. War Dept., *War of the Rebellion*, I, 1, 12.

4. The War Department

1. Rogers, *Confederate Home Front*, 31.

2. Davis as quoted in Dawson, *Be It Known*, 4–5.

3. Jones, *Rebel War Clerk's Diary*, 36–37.

4. Ibid., 38.

5. Moore, *Confederate Commissary General*, 49–50.

6. Jeremy P. Felt, "Lucius B. Northrop and the Confederate Subsistence Department," *Virginia Magazine of History and Biography* 69 (1961): 181–93.

7. Symonds, *Joseph E. Johnston*, 97–98.

8. Mallory diary, Richmond, VA, Sept. 16, 1861, Mallory Papers.

9. Eicher and Eicher, *Civil War High Commands*, 807.

10. Davis to the Congress, Montgomery, AL, May 17, 1861, in Richardson, ed., *Compilation of Messages*, 1: 100–101.

11. Robert H. Smith as quoted in Yearns, *Confederate Congress*, 22–23.

12. Ibid., 24–25.

13. Worsham, *One of Jackson's Foot Cavalry*, 6.

5. A Curious Cabinet

1. Toombs to Alexander H. Stephens, Richmond, VA, Jun. 8, 1861, in Toombs, Stephens, and Cobb, *Correspondence*, 568–70.

2. Toombs to Alexander H. Stephens, Richmond, VA, Jul. 5, 1861, Stephens Papers, Duke University.

3. Kimball, *Capitol of Virginia*, 62.

4. *White House of the Confederacy*, 17–20.

5. Despite the fact that uncountable hours of speeches made from the floor of the Confederate House and Senate were recorded in government documents, evidence of where the sessions took place disappeared in a building collapse after the war. Only hints remain from a few newspaper accounts and a handful of illustrations made for papers such as *Harper's Weekly* and *Frank Leslie's Illustrated News*. In 2002 Mark K. Greenough, supervisor and historian of Capitol Guided Tours in Richmond, analyzed illustrations and accounts of the House and Senate and discovered correlations with some of the window-frame types in two rebuilt rooms. He now believes the Confederate Senate met in a second-floor committee room adjacent to the governor's room, above the House of Delegates Chamber where the 1870 collapse occurred. Ornamental details in a *Frank Leslie's* illustration made after the collapse, but showing the room up through the ceiling above the collapse, seem to confirm this hypothesis. Further, Greenough believes the Confederate House of Representatives met in what is now termed the Old Senate Chamber, on the first floor, based on an 1862 *Richmond Daily Whig* article that described having the windows lengthened in the room used by the House. That room now contains long windows of the same type described that stretch to the floor. After nearly 140 years of uncertainty, Greenough's clever detective work has, seemingly, solved the puzzle of where the Confederacy enacted its laws (Mark K. Greenough, private communication, Richmond, VA, 2002).

6. Hunter to William L. Yancey, P. A. Rose, and A. Dudley Mann, Jul. 29, 1861, in Richardson, ed., *Compilation of Messages*, 2: 49–52.

7. Davis to the Congress, Manassas Junction, VA [Jul. 21, 1861], in Richardson, ed., *Compilation of Messages*, 1: 124–25.

8. Wigfall to her brother, Richmond, VA, Aug. 2, 1861, Wigfall Papers, Museum of the Confederacy.

9. Howell Cobb to his wife, Richmond, VA, Aug. 6, 1861, in Toombs, Stephens, and Cobb, *Correspondence*, 573.

10. Davis to G. T. Beauregard, Richmond, VA, Oct. 30, 1861, in Davis, *Jefferson Davis, Constitutionalist*, 5: 156–57.

11. Davis to Joseph E. Johnston, Richmond, VA, Nov. 3, 1861, in Davis, *Jefferson Davis, Constitutionalist*, 5: 157–58.

12. Woodworth, *No Band of Brothers*, 1–11.

13. Davis to G. T. Beauregard, Richmond, VA, Aug. 4, 1861, in Davis, *Jefferson Davis, Constitutionalist*, 5: 120–21.

6. The Military High Command

1. Putnam, *Richmond during the War*, 67–68.

NOTES

2. Dabney, *Richmond,* 167.

3. Putnam, *Richmond during the War,* 76.

4. Johnston as quoted in Symonds, *Joseph E. Johnston,* 124.

5. Ibid., 128.

6. Lee as quoted in Lee Jr., *Recollections and Letters,* 37.

7. Lee, *Wartime Papers,* 61–62.

8. Andrews, *South Reports the Civil War,* 114–15.

9. Lee as quoted in Worsham, *One of Jackson's Foot Cavalry,* 15–16.

10. Lee as quoted in Lee Jr., *Recollections and Letters,* 39–41.

11. Jackson as quoted in Jackson, *Memoirs of Stonewall Jackson,* 183.

12. Lee as quoted in Lee Jr., *Recollections and Letters,* 43.

13. Ibid., 48–49.

14. As quoted in Andrews, *South Reports the Civil War,* 118.

15. Davis as quoted in Lee Jr., *Recollections and Letters,* 52–53.

16. Pickens as quoted in Davis, *Papers of Jefferson Davis,* 7: 427–28.

17. Davis, *Rise and Fall,* 2: 80.

18. Lee as quoted in Lee, *General Lee,* 129.

19. Lee as quoted in Jones, *Life and Letters,* 156.

20. As quoted in Yearns, *Confederate Congress,* 42.

21. Goode as quoted in Yearns, *Confederate Congress,* 44.

22. Mallory and Keitt as quoted in Yearns, *Confederate Congress,* 218–19.

23. Bonham to William Porcher Miles, near Centreville, VA, Dec. 7, 1861, Miles Papers, University of North Carolina.

24. Toombs to Alexander H. Stephens, Camp near Fairfax Court House, VA, Sept. [30?], 1861, in Toombs, Stephens, and Cobb, *Correspondence,* 577–78.

25. Toombs to Alexander H. Stephens, Camp near Fairfax Court House, VA, Oct. 3, 1861, in Toombs, Stephens, and Cobb, *Correspondence,* 578–79.

26. Thomas to Alexander H. Stephens, Camp Pine Creek, Fairfax Co., VA, Oct. 5, 1861, in Toombs, Stephens, and Cobb, *Correspondence,* 579–80.

27. Thomas to Alexander H. Stephens, Camp Pine Creek, Fairfax Co., VA, Oct. 10, 1861, in Toombs, Stephens, and Cobb, *Correspondence,* 580–81.

28. Davis to G. T. Beauregard, Richmond, VA, Nov. 10, 1861, in Davis, *Jefferson Davis, Constitutionalist,* 5: 163–64.

29. Rhett to Robert Barnwell Rhett Jr., n.p., Dec. 17, 1861, Rhett Papers, University of South Carolina.

7. State Rightisms

1. As quoted in Cooper, *Jefferson Davis,* 372.

2. Richardson, ed., *Compilation of Messages,* 1: 181–83.

3. *Journal of the Congress of the Confederate States of America,* 58th Cong., 2d sess., Doc. 234, 1: 696–97.

4. Davis to the Congress, Richmond, VA, Feb. 25, 1862, in Richardson, ed., *Compilation of Messages,* 1: 189–92; Davis, *Jefferson Davis, Constitutionalist,* 5: 203–6.

5. *Jefferson Davis, Constitutionalist,* 5: 76–77.

6. *Southern Historical Society Papers,* 44:132–35.

7. Davis as quoted in *Journal of the Congress of the Confederate States of America,* 58th Cong., 2d sess., Doc. 234, 2: 22–.

8. Cobb to his wife, Richmond, VA, Feb. 18, 1862, in Toombs, Stephens, and Cobb, *Correspondence,* 587–88.

9. Benjamin to Jefferson Davis, Richmond, VA, Mar. 8, 1862, Davis Papers, Duke University.

10. Davis to Judah P. Benjamin, Richmond, VA, Mar. 11, 1862, in Davis, *Jefferson Davis, Constitutionalist,* 5: 214.

11. Davis to Albert Sidney Johnston, Richmond, VA, Mar. 26, 1862, in Davis, *Jefferson Davis, Constitutionalist,* 5: 225.

12. *Journal of the Congress of the Confederate States of America,* 58th Cong., 2d sess., Doc. 234, 2: 77–.

13. Ibid., 5: 82–84.

14. Ibid., 5: 30–.

15. *Southern Historical Society Papers,* 44: 80.

16. Davis to the Congress, Richmond, VA, Mar. 14, 1862, as quoted in Richardson, ed., *Compilation of Messages,* 1: 215–16.

17. As quoted in Yearns, *Confederate Congress,* 108.

18. *Journal of the Congress of the Confederate States of America,* 58th Cong., 2d sess., Doc. 234, 2: 28–, *Southern Historical Society Papers,* 44: 65–.

19. Davis, proclamation, Richmond, VA, Feb. 27, 1862, as quoted in Richardson, ed., *Compilation of Messages,* 1: 219.

20. Davis, proclamation, Richmond, VA, Mar. 1, 1862, as quoted in Richardson, ed., *Compilation of Messages,* 1: 220–21; Yearns, *Confederate Congress,* 150–51.

21. L. Post, Monroe Co. [N.Y.], [1862], as quoted in Davis Papers, Lib. of Cong.

22. *Southern Historical Society Papers,* 44: 137–38.

23. As quoted in ibid., 45: 26–29.

24. Wigfall and Oldham as quoted in ibid.

25. Davis to Joseph E. Johnston, Richmond, VA, Feb. 28, 1862, in Davis, *Jefferson Davis, Constitutionalist,* 5: 208–10.

26. Brown to Jefferson Davis, Milledgeville, GA, Apr. 22, 1862, Davis Papers, Museum of the Confederacy.

27. Davis to Joseph E. Brown, Richmond, VA, Apr. 28, 1862, in Davis, *Jefferson Davis, Constitutionalist,* 5: 236–37.

8. Richmond, the Capital

1. Dabney, *Richmond,* 171.

2. Jones, *Rebel War Clerk's Diary* 1: 120.

3. Putnam, *Richmond during the War,* 113.

4. Van Brunt, "Report of Captain Van Brunt," to Gideon Welles, Mar. 10, 1862, *Official Records of the Union,* 1: 7: 11.

5. Pugh as quoted in Hedley, *Marching through Georgia,* 46.

6. Stillwell, *Story of a Common Soldier,* 42–52.

7. Stanley, *Autobiography,* 187–200.

8. Garnet Wolseley, "A Month's Visit to Confederate Headquarters," *Blackwood's Edinburgh Magazine* 93 (January–June 1863): 21; Jackson, *Memoirs of Stonewall Jackson,* 249.

9. William Pittenger, "The Locomotive Chase in Georgia," in *Century Magazine* 14 (1886): 141.

10. LeGrand, *Journal,* 39–43; Hawthorne as quoted in Masur, ed., *Real War,* 176.

11. McClellan, *Civil War Papers,* 257.

12. Jones, *Rebel War Clerk's Diary,* 1: 128.

13. Davis to Varina Davis, Richmond, VA, Jun. 2, 1862, in Davis, *Jefferson Davis, Constitutionalist,* 5: 264–65.

14. Evander M. Law, "The Fight for Richmond," *Southern Bivouac* 2 (April 1867): 649.

15. Freeman, *Lee's Lieutenants,* 1: 150–51; Coski, "Abstract of Meetings and Conferences."

16. Davis as quoted in Cooper, *Jefferson Davis,* 379.

17. Johnston to Rosa Johnston, May 10, 1862, and Johnston to Rosa Johnston, May 17, 1862, Johnston Papers, Tulane University.

18. Davis as quoted in *Journal of the Congress of the Confederate States of America,* 58th Cong., 2d sess., Doc. 234, 2: 135.

19. Keitt to Susan Keitt, Charleston, SC, Apr. 10, 1862, Keitt Papers.

20. Davis to Joseph E. Brown, Richmond, VA, May 29, 1862, in Davis, *Jefferson Davis, Constitutionalist,* 5: 254–62.

21. *Journal of the Congress of the Confederate States of America,* 58th Cong., 2d sess., Doc. 234, 5: 251.

22. Gorgas to William Porcher Miles, Ordnance Dept., Richmond, VA, Apr. 4, 1862, Miles Papers, University of North Carolina.

23. Davis to William L. Yancey and Clement C. Clay, senators, Richmond, VA, Apr. 21, 1862, in Davis, *Jefferson Davis, Constitutionalist,* 5: 234.

24. Davis to the Congress, Richmond, VA, Apr. 19, 1862, in Richardson, ed., *Compilations of Messages,* 1: 216–17.

25. Miles to Jefferson Davis, Charleston, SC, May 24, 1862, Davis Papers, National Archives.

26. Pickens to Robert E. Lee, Columbia, SC, Apr. 5, 1862, Pickens Papers.

27. Toombs to Alexander H. Stephens, camp near Richmond, VA, May 17, 1862, in Toombs, Stephens, and Cobb, *Correspondence,* 594–95.

28. Davis to Varina Davis, Richmond, VA, May 28, 1862, in Davis, *Jefferson Davis, Constitutionalist,* 5: 252–54.

29. Davis to Varina Davis, Richmond, VA, May 31, 1862, in Davis, *Jefferson Davis, Constitutionalist,* 5: 264.

9. The Rise of Lee and Bragg

1. Jones to his wife, Richmond, VA, Jun. 13, 1862, Jones Papers.

2. Davis to Varina Davis, Richmond, VA, Jun. 13, 1862, Davis Papers, Museum of the Confederacy; in Davis, *Jefferson Davis, Constitutionalist,* 5: 277–78.

3. Stiles, *Four Years,* 97–99.

4. Livermore, *Days and Events,* 86–90.

5. Dabney, *Life and Campaigns,* 516–18.

6. Sturgis as quoted in Haupt, *Reminiscences,* 78, 80, 82.

7. Edward McCrady Jr., "Gregg's Brigade in the Second Battle of Manassas," *Southern Historical Society Papers* 13 (1885): 32.

8. Charles F. Walcott, "The Battle of Chantilly," *Papers of the Military Historical Society of Massachusetts,* 2:145, 1895.

9. Davis to Francis W. Pickens, Richmond, VA, Jun. 19, 1862, in Davis, *Jefferson Davis, Constitutionalist,* 5: 282–83.

10. Pickens to Jefferson Davis, Columbia, SC, Jun. 12, 1862, Pickens Papers; in Davis, *Jefferson Davis, Constitutionalist,* 5: 275–76.

11. Davis to Francis W. Pickens, Richmond, VA, Aug. 16, 1862, Pickens Papers; Pickens to Jefferson Davis, Columbia, SC, Aug. 20, 1862, Pickens Papers.

12. Bragg as quoted in McWhiney, *Braxton Bragg*, 266.

13. Beauregard to Thomas Jordan, Bladon, AL, Jul. 12, 1862, Beauregard Papers, Duke University.

14. Davis to William Preston Johnston, Richmond, VA, Jun. 14, 1862, in Davis, *Jefferson Davis, Constitutionalist*, 5: 279–80.

15. Davis to Varina Davis, Richmond, VA, Jun. 3, 1862, Davis Papers, Museum of the Confederacy.

16. Davis to James J. Pettus, Richmond, VA, Jun. 19, 1862, in Davis, *Jefferson Davis, Constitutionalist*, 5: 282.

17. Davis to Thomas O. Moore, Richmond, VA, Jun. 25, 1862, in Davis, *Jefferson Davis, Constitutionalist*, 5: 286–87.

18. Rector as quoted in Davis, *Papers of Jefferson Davis*, 8: 193–94.

19. Lubbock to Jefferson Davis, Austin, TX, Jun. 27, 1862, in Davis, *Jefferson Davis, Constitutionalist*, 5: 287–89.

20. Brown to Alexander H. Stephens, Marietta, GA, Jul. 2, 1862, in Toombs, Stephens, and Cobb, *Correspondence*, 597–99.

21. Alexander H. Stephens, draft memorandum, Liberty Hall, Crawfordville, GA, Jun. 24, 1862, Stephens Papers, Duke University.

22. Lubbock, Claiborne F. Jackson, Henry M. Rector, and Thomas O. Moore to Jefferson Davis, Marshall, TX, Jul. 28, 1862, in Davis, *Jefferson Davis, Constitutionalist*, 5: 301–3.

23. Jenkins as quoted in U.S. War Dept., *War of the Rebellion*, 1: 16, 1: 845–47.

24. Horace Greeley, "The Prayer of Twenty Millions," *New York Tribune*, August 20, 1862.

25. Lincoln, *Collected Works*, 5: 388–89.

26. Seward as quoted in Taylor, *William Henry Seward*, 240.

27. Mallory, diary, Richmond, VA, Jun. 24, 1862, Mallory Papers.

10. An Uneasy Brotherhood

1. Davis as quoted in *Journal of the Congress of the Confederate States of America*, 58th Cong., 2d sess., Doc. 234, 2: 226.

2. Ibid.

3. Ibid., 228.

4. *Journal of the Congress of the Confederate States of America*, 58th Cong., 2d sess., Doc. 234, 2: 263; *Southern Historical Society Papers*, 46: 199.

5. Ibid., 278; ibid., 199. Ever since its inception, the U.S. Army had printed an annual register listing its officers and their grades, ranks, and assignments. For the first time the Confederacy now asked for an Army Register of its own when the Senate requested a list of commissioned officers of the Regular and Provisional armies. On September 27 a press run of five hundred copies of this publication was reported. Amazingly, however, not one copy of this register (or any subsequent registers) has been located — not in Richmond, not at the National Archives, not at the Library of Congress.

6. *Southern Historical Society Papers*, 46: 202–5.

7. Phelan as quoted in ibid., 46: 62–65.

8. Semmes, Oldham, and Wigfall as quoted in *Southern Historical Society Papers*, 46: 74–79.

9. *Southern Historical Society Papers*, 45: 176.

10. Miles to Charles Lanman, NY, Oct. 26, 1859, Miles Papers, University of South Carolina.

11. Foote and Singleton as quoted in *Southern Historical Society Papers*, 45: 203–11.

12. Herbert, Miles, and Gaither as quoted in *Southern Historical Society Papers*, 45: 213–16.

13. Foster as quoted in *Southern Historical Society Papers*, 45: 238.

14. Wigfall as quoted in *Southern Historical Society Papers*, 45: 250–54.

15. *Southern Historical Society Papers*, 46: 15–16.

16. Ibid., 46: 17–18.

17. Miller and Crockett as quoted in *Southern Historical Society Papers*, 46: 25–28.

18. *Southern Historical Society Papers*, 46: 176–81.

19. Holt and Jones as quoted in *Southern Historical Society Papers*, 46: 257–59.

20. Davis to Braxton Bragg, Richmond, VA, Aug. 5, 1862, in Davis, *Jefferson Davis, Constitutionalist*, 5: 312–13.

21. Brown to Alexander H. Stephens, Canton, GA, Sept. 1, 1862, in Toombs, Stephens, and Cobb, *Correspondence*, 605–06.

22. Orr as quoted in *Southern Historical Society Papers*, 46: 61.

23. Orr, Phelan, and Wigfall as quoted in *Southern Historical Society Papers*, 46: 113–19.

24. Orr as quoted in *Southern Historical Society Papers*, 46: 127–28.

25. Johnston to his wife, Rosa Johnston, Richmond, VA, Oct. 27, 1862, Johnston Papers.

26. Congress of the Confederate States to Jefferson Davis, Richmond, VA, Sept. 13, 1862, Davis Papers, Duke University.

27. *Southern Historical Society Papers*, 45: 242–47.

28. Foote as quoted in *Southern Historical Society Papers*, 46: 174–75.

29. *Southern Historical Society Papers*, 46: 187–88.

30. Ibid., 49: 87–88.

31. Orr as quoted in *Southern Historical Society Papers*, 46: 215–16.

32. *Southern Historical Society Papers*, 46: 232–34.

33. Davis to the Congress, Richmond, VA, Oct. 13, 1862, in Richardson, ed., *Compilation of Messages*, 1: 262–68.

34. Wigfall as quoted in *Southern Historical Society Papers*, 46: 243–46.

35. Davis to George W. Randolph, Richmond, VA, Nov. 14, 1862, in Davis, *Jefferson Davis, Constitutionalist*, 5: 371–72.

36. Semmes, Clark, and Henry as quoted in *Southern Historical Society Papers*, 49: 7–8.

37. Cobb to his wife, Charlestown, VA, Sept. 17, 1862, as quoted in Toombs, Stephens, and Cobb, *Correspondence*, 606–7.

38. James M. Smythe to Howell Cobb, Augusta, GA, Dec. 17, 1862, in Toombs, Stephens, and Cobb, *Correspondence*, 609.

39. Davis to the Congress, Richmond, VA, Sept. 2, 1862, in Richardson, ed., *Compilation of Messages*, 1: 240–41.

40. Lee to Louis T. Wigfall, Headquarters, Army of Northern Virginia, near Martinsburg, VA, Sept. 21, 1862, Wigfall Papers, Library of Congress.

41. Archer Jones, "Secretary Randolph and Confederate Strategy," *Virginia Magazine of History and Biography* 61 (1953): 45–57.

42. Davis to George W. Randolph, Richmond, VA, Nov. 15, 1862, in Davis, *Jefferson Davis, Constitutionalist*, 5: 374.

43. Mallory, diary, Richmond, VA, Nov. 19, 1862, Mallory Papers.

44. Roy Watson Curry, "James A. Seddon, A Southern Prototype," *Virginia Magazine of History and Biography* 63 (1955): 123–50.

45. Bledsoe to Jefferson Davis, Charlottesville, VA, Nov. 19, 1862, Davis Papers, Duke University.

46. Wigfall to James A. Seddon, Amelia Springs, VA, Dec. 8, 1862, Wigfall Papers, Library of Congress.

47. *Southern Historical Society Papers*, 46: 160–64.

48. Davis to Zebulon B. Vance, Richmond, VA, Oct. 17, 1862, in Davis, *Jefferson Davis, Constitutionalist*, 5: 354–55.

49. Davis to Benjamin H. Hill, Richmond, VA, Oct. 23, 1862, in Davis, *Jefferson Davis, Constitutionalist*, 5: 358–59.

50. Davis to John G. Shorter, Richmond, VA, Oct. 29, 1862, in Davis, *Jefferson Davis, Constitutionalist*, 5: 361.

51. Davis to John Milton, Richmond, VA, Nov. 7, 1862, in Davis, *Jefferson Davis, Constitutionalist*, 5: 366.

52. Lubbock to Jefferson Davis, Austin, TX, Nov. 7, 1862, in Davis, *Jefferson Davis, Constitutionalist*, 5: 369–71.

53. Davis to the state governors, Richmond, VA, Nov. 26, 1862, in Davis, *Jefferson Davis, Constitutionalist*, 5: 377–78.

54. Keitt to Susan Keitt, Sullivan's Island, SC, Dec. 15, 1862, Keitt Papers.

11. Jockeying for Position

1. Davis as quoted in Richardson, ed., *Compilation of Messages*, 1: 276–97.

2. Strother, *Virginia Yankee*, 112.

3. Lincoln, *Collected Works*, 6: 78–79.

4. Davis to the Congress, Richmond, VA, Jan. 12, 1863, in Richardson, ed., *Compilation of Messages*, 1: 276–97; Davis, *Jefferson Davis, Constitutionalist*, 5: 396–415.

5. *Southern Historical Society Papers*, 47: 197–201, 206–11, 223–25.

6. Wigfall and others as quoted in *Southern Historical Society Papers*, 48: 25–27.

7. Phelan as quoted in *Southern Historical Society Papers*, 48: 60–63.

8. Yancey as quoted in *Southern Historical Society Papers*, 48: 318–20, 322–25.

9. As quoted in *Southern Historical Society Papers*, 48: 60, 80.

10. Davis to Edward Sparrow, Richmond, VA, Jan. 20, 1863, in Davis, *Jefferson Davis, Constitutionalist*, 5: 419.

11. Keitt to Louis T. Wigfall, Headquarters, Force on Sullivan's Island, SC, Jan. 16, 1863, Wigfall Papers, Library of Congress.

12. Beauregard to Milledge L. Bonham, Charleston, SC, Jan. 7, 1863, Bonham Papers.

13. *Southern Historical Society Papers*, 47: 211–12.

14. Vest and Foote as quoted in *Southern Historical Society Papers*, 47: 119–23.

15. Foote as quoted in *Southern Historical Society Papers*, 48: 217–18.

16. Johnston to Louis T. Wigfall, Chattanooga, TN, Mar. 8, 1863, Wigfall Papers, Library of Congress.

17. *Southern Historical Society Papers,* 48: 44–.

18. Toombs to the soldiers of Toombs's Brigade, Army of Northern Virginia, Richmond, VA, Mar. 5, 1863, in Toombs, Stephens, and Cobb, *Correspondence,* 612–13.

19. Davis to Abraham C. Myers, Richmond, VA, Feb. 5, 1863, in Davis, *Jefferson Davis, Constitutionalist,* 5: 430.

20. Hood to Louis T. Wigfall, Division Headquarters, Feb. 5, 1863, Wigfall Papers, Library of Congress.

21. Johnston to Louis T. Wigfall, Chattanooga, TN, Mar. 4, 1863, Wigfall Papers, Library of Congress.

22. Davis to Joseph E. Brown, Richmond, VA, Jan. 27, 1863, Davis Papers, Library of Congress.

23. Brown to Alexander H. Stephens, Milledgeville, GA, Jan. 30, 1863, in Toombs, Stephens, and Cobb, *Correspondence,* 610.

24. Toombs to Alexander H. Stephens, Richmond, VA, Mar. 2, 1863, in Toombs, Stephens, and Cobb, *Correspondence,* 611.

25. *Southern Historical Society Papers,* 48: 140–42.

26. Bryan to Jefferson Davis, Waco, TX, Mar. 9, 1863, in Davis, *Jefferson Davis, Constitutionalist,* 5: 442–44.

27. Davis to the senators and representatives of Arkansas, Richmond, VA, Mar. 30, 1863, in Davis, *Jefferson Davis, Constitutionalist,* 5: 460–63.

28. Conrad as quoted in *Southern Historical Society Papers,* 48: 295–96.

12. Politics Spinning Out of Control

1. Putnam as quoted in Jones, *Ladies of Richmond,* 136–39.

2. Jones, *Ladies of Richmond,* 139–42.

3. Wigfall as quoted in ibid., 143–45.

4. John Coski, memorandum by John and Ruth Ann Coski, "Social Life in Wartime Richmond."

5. Ibid.

6. Ibid.

7. Livermore, *Days and Events,* 203.

8. Borcke, *Memoirs,* 2: 241.

9. James Power Smith, "Stonewall Jackson's Last Battle," in *Battles and Leaders,* eds. Johnson and Buel, 3: 211.

10. Darius N. Couch, "The Chancellorsville Campaign," in *Battles and Leaders,* eds. Johnson and Buel, 3: 169.

11. Oliver Otis Howard, "The Eleventh Corps at Chancellorsville," in *Battles and Leaders,* eds. Johnson and Buel, 3: 202.

12. Rowland as quoted in Jones, *Ladies of Richmond,* 165–67.

13. Grierson to John A. Rawlins, Baton Rouge, LA, May 5, 1863, in U.S. War Dept., *War of the Rebellion,* 24: I, 522.

14. Sherman, *Home Letters,* 268–69.

15. Anonymous, Vicksburg, MS, Mar. 20, 1863, as quoted in "A Woman's Diary of the Siege of Vicksburg; Under Fire from the Gunboats," ed., George Washington Cable, *Century* 8 (1885): 767.

16. Andrew Hickenlooper, "The Vicksburg Mine," in *Battles and Leaders,* eds. Johnson and Buel, 3: 542.

17. Wigfall as quoted in Jones, *Ladies of Richmond,* 168–69.

18. Wigfall to "Buddy," her brother, Richmond, VA, May 16, 1863, Wigfall Papers, Museum of the Confederacy.

19. Davis to the people of the Confederacy, Richmond, VA, Apr. 10, 1863, in Davis, *Jefferson Davis, Constitutionalist,* 5: 469–73.

20. Johnston to Jefferson Davis, Tullahoma, TN, Apr. 10, 1863, Davis Papers, Duke University.

21. Vance to Jefferson Davis, Raleigh, NC, May 13, 1863, in Davis, *Jefferson Davis, Constitutionalist,* 5: 485–88.

22. Longstreet to Louis T. Wigfall, Headquarters near Fredericksburg, VA, May 13, 1863, Wigfall Papers, Library of Congress.

23. Beauregard to Louis T. Wigfall, Charleston, SC, May 18, 1863, Wigfall Papers, Library of Congress.

24. Davis to Robert E. Lee, Richmond, VA, May 30, 1863, in Davis, *Jefferson Davis, Constitutionalist,* 5: 500.

25. *Journal of the Congress of the Confederate States of America,* 58th Cong., 2d sess., Doc. 234, 6: 374, 453–54.

26. Foote and Conrad as quoted in *Southern Historical Society Papers,* 49: 87–88.

27. Davis to the Senate, Richmond, VA, Apr. 10, 1863, in Davis, *Jefferson Davis, Constitutionalist,* 5: 478.

28. Brown as quoted in *Southern Historical Society Papers,* 49: 161–62.

29. Davis to William L. Yancey, Richmond, VA, May 26, 1863, in Davis, *Jefferson Davis, Constitutionalist,* 5: 498–99.

30. Cobb to James A. Seddon, Headquarters, Dist. of Middle Florida, Quincy, FL, May 14, 1863, in Toombs, Stephens, and Cobb, *Correspondence,* 616–17.

31. Campbell to "Mrs. Goldthwaite," Richmond, VA, May 23, 1863, Campbell Papers.

NOTES

13. Can't We All Get Along?

1. Joseph G. Rosengarten, "General Reynolds' Last Battle," in *Annals of the War,* ed. McClure, 63.
2. Hood to James Longstreet, Jun. 28, 1875, in *Southern Historical Society Papers,* 4: 150.
3. Gerrish, *Army Life,* 111.
4. Evander M. Law, "The Struggle for Round Top," in *Battles and Leaders,* eds. Johnson and Buel, 3: 327.
5. Longstreet, *Manassas to Appomattox,* 392.
6. Edmund Rice, "Repelling Lee's Last Blow at Gettysburg," in *Battles and Leaders,* eds. Johnson and Buel, 3: 389–90; Haskell, *Haskell of Gettysburg,* 170.
7. Ulysses S. Grant, "The Vicksburg Campaign," in *Battles and Leaders,* eds. Johnson and Buel, 3: 536
8. *New York Tribune* account as quoted in Moore, ed., *Rebellion Record,* 7: 211–14.
9. Davis to Joseph E. Johnston, Richmond, VA, Jul. 8, 1863, in Davis, *Jefferson Davis, Constitutionalist,* 5: 540.
10. Davis to Joseph E. Johnston, Richmond, VA, Jun. 30, 1863, in Davis, *Jefferson Davis, Constitutionalist,* 5: 533–34.
11. Pickens to Louis T. Wigfall, Edgewood, SC, Jul. 28, 1863, Wigfall Papers, Library of Congress.
12. Davis to Joseph E. Johnston, Richmond, VA, Aug. 1, 1863, Davis Papers, Museum of the Confederacy; Davis to Joseph E. Johnston, Richmond, VA, Aug. 1, 1863, in Davis, *Jefferson Davis, Constitutionalist,* 5: 582–83.
13. Johnston to Louis T. Wigfall, Morton, MS, Aug. 12, 1863, Wigfall Papers, Library of Congress.
14. Davis to Joseph E. Johnston, Richmond, VA, Aug. 24, 1863, in Davis, *Jefferson Davis, Constitutionalist,* 6: 1.
15. Davis to William L. Yancey, Richmond, VA, Jun. 20, 1863, in Davis, *Jefferson Davis, Constitutionalist,* 5: 528–30.
16. Davis to Joseph E. Brown, Richmond, VA, Jun. 9, 1863, in Davis, *Jefferson Davis, Constitutionalist,* 5: 510.
17. Lubbock to Jefferson Davis, Austin, TX, Jul. 13, 1863, in Davis, *Jefferson Davis, Constitutionalist,* 5: 544–45.
18. Bonham to the citizens of South Carolina, Columbia, SC, Jul. 13, 1863, Bonham Papers.
19. Bonham to the citizens of South Carolina, Columbia, SC, Aug. 27, 1863, Bonham Papers.
20. Davis to Zebulon B. Vance, Richmond, VA, Jul. 24, 1863, in Davis, *Jefferson Davis, Constitutionalist,* 5: 576–77; Vance Papers.

21. Clay to Louis T. Wigfall, Columbus, GA, Aug. 5, 1863, Wigfall Papers, Library of Congress.
22. Toombs to the editor of the Augusta, GA, *Constitutionalist,* Washington, GA, Aug. 12, 1863, in Toombs, Stephens, and Cobb, *Correspondence,* 622–27.
23. Toombs to Alexander H. Stephens, Washington, GA, Jul. 14, 1863, in Toombs, Stephens, and Cobb, *Correspondence,* 621.
24. Brown to Alexander H. Stephens, Marietta, GA, Aug. 12, 1863, in Toombs, Stephens, and Cobb, *Correspondence,* 621–22.
25. Stephens to Jefferson Davis, Liberty Hall, Crawfordville, GA, Jun. 12, 1863, in Richardson, ed., *Compilation of Messages,* 1: 339–41; Davis, *Jefferson Davis, Constitutionalist,* 5: 513.
26. Davis to Alexander H. Stephens, Richmond, VA, Jul. 2, 1863, in Richardson, ed., *Compilation of Messages,* 1: 341–43; Davis, *Jefferson Davis, Constitutionalist,* 5: 515–16.
27. As quoted in Richardson, ed., *Compilation of Messages,* 1: 343–44.
28. Brown to Alexander H. Stephens, Marietta, GA, Aug. 22, 1863, in Toombs, Stephens, and Cobb, *Correspondence,* 627–28.
29. Hunter to Louis T. Wigfall, near Lynchburg, VA, Jun. 23, 1863, Wigfall Papers, Library of Congress.
30. Davis to R. W. Johnson, Richmond, VA, Jul. 14, 1863, in Davis, *Jefferson Davis, Constitutionalist,* 5: 548–50.
31. Toombs to W. W. Burwell, Washington, GA, Aug. 29, 1863, in Toombs, Stephens, and Cobb, *Correspondence,* 628–29.
32. Toombs to Howell Cobb, Washington, GA, Aug. 29, 1863, Cobb Papers.
33. Davis to Alexander H. Stephens, Richmond, VA, Aug. 31, 1863, in Davis, *Jefferson Davis, Constitutionalist,* 6: 20.

14. Soiled Reputations

1. James R. Carnahan, "Personal Recollections of Chickamauga," in *Sketches of War History, 1861–1865; Papers Read before the Ohio Commandery of the Military Order of the Loyal Legion of the United States, 1883–1886,* vol. 1 (Cincinnati: Robert Clarke, 1888), 410–17; Owen, *In Camp and Battle,* 278–84.
2. Polley, *A Soldier's Letters,* 142–48.
3. Connolly, "Major Connolly's Letters," 35: 298.
4. Bragg to Jefferson Davis, Dec. 1, 1863, in U.S. War Dept., *War of the Rebellion,* 52: II, 745.
5. Edward Porter Alexander, "Longstreet at Knoxville," in *Battles and Leaders,* eds. Johnson

310

NOTES

and Buell, 3: 749; Orlando M. Poe, "The Defense of Knoxville," in *Battles and Leaders,* eds. Johnson and Buell, 3: 743.

6. Lincoln, *Collected Works,* 7: 17–22.

7. Clay to Louis T. Wigfall, Macon, GA, Sept. 11, 1863, Wigfall Papers, Library of Congress.

8. Davis to the soldiers of the Army of Tennessee, Headquarters, Army of Tennessee, Oct. 14, 1863, in Richardson, ed., *Compilation of Messages,* 1: 335–36.

9. Breckinridge to D. H. Hill, Chattanooga, TN, Oct. 15, 1863, Hill Papers, Division of Archives and History. After Hill received the letter relieving him from duty, Archer Anderson, a staff officer, visited Bragg's headquarters with the relieved general. According to Anderson, Bragg said he knew officers were dissatisfied with him and had asked the president to be relieved, but Davis refused! So Bragg suggested to Davis that Hill needed to be removed because he so strongly lacked confidence in Bragg. Hill wanted specifics, rather than a vague condemnation, to repair his reputation (Archer Anderson, memorandum, near Chattanooga, TN, Oct. 16, 1863, Hill Papers, Division of Archives and History).

10. Davis to Leonidas Polk, Atlanta, GA, Oct. 29, 1863, in Davis, *Jefferson Davis, Constitutionalist,* 6: 65–66.

11. Hill to Samuel Cooper, Richmond, VA, Nov. 13, 1863, Hill Papers, Division of Archives and History.

12. Hill to Jefferson Davis, Richmond, VA, Nov. 16, 1863, Hill Papers, Division of Archives and History.

13. Cooper to D. H. Hill, Richmond, VA, Nov. 20, 1863, Hill Papers, Division of Archives and History.

14. Keitt to Susan Keitt, Mt. Pleasant, SC, Oct. 27, 1863, Keitt Papers.

15. Brown to Alexander H. Stephens, Milledgeville, GA, Nov. 27, 1863, in Toombs, Stephens, and Cobb, *Correspondence,* 630–31.

16. Davis to James A. Seddon, Atlanta, GA, Oct. 29, 1863, in Davis, *Jefferson Davis, Constitutionalist,* 6: 72.

17. Vance to Jefferson Davis, Raleigh, NC, Sept. 11, 1863, in Davis, *Jefferson Davis, Constitutionalist,* 6: 30–31.

18. Vance to James A. Seddon, Oct. 1, 1863, Vance Papers, Division of Archives and History; Seddon to Zebulon B. Vance, Richmond, VA, Sept. 17, 1863, Vance Papers.

19. Bonham to P. G. T. Beauregard, Columbia, SC, Oct. 27, 1863, Beauregard Papers, University of South Carolina.

20. Toombs to Alexander H. Stephens, Washington, GA, Nov. 2, 1863, in Toombs, Stephens, and Cobb, *Correspondence,* 630.

21. Davis to the Congress, Richmond, VA, Dec. 7, 1863, in Richardson, ed., *Compilation of Messages,* 1: 345–82; Davis, *Jefferson Davis, Constitutionalist,* 6: 93–128.

22. *Southern Historical Society Papers,* 50: 21–23.

23. Foote as quoted in *Southern Historical Society Papers,* 50: 21–23.

24. Ibid., 140–47.

25. Ibid., 23–24.

26. Wigfall as quoted in *Southern Historical Society Papers,* 50: 109–112.

27. Garland and Foote as quoted in *Southern Historical Society Papers,* 50: 67–69.

28. Vance to Jefferson Davis, Raleigh, NC, Dec. 30, 1863, in Davis, *Jefferson Davis, Constitutionalist,* 6: 141–42; Vance to Jefferson Davis, Raleigh, Dec. 30, 1863, Vance Papers.

15. The President versus the Congress

1. Davis as quoted in Richardson, ed., *Compilation of Messages,* 1: 388–90; Davis as quoted in *Journal of the Congress of the Confederate States of America,* 58th Cong., 2d Sess., Doc. 234, 3: 583–84.

2. *Southern Historical Society Papers,* 50: 273–74.

3. Davis to the Senate, Richmond, VA, Jan. 27, 1864, in Richardson, ed., *Compilation of Messages,* 1: 392–94.

4. Johnston to Louis T. Wigfall, Dalton, GA, Apr. 23, 1864, Wigfall Papers, Library of Congress.

5. Jones, *Artilleryman's Diary,* 166–210; Lee, *Wartime Papers,* 659–60.

6. Porter to Gideon Welles, Flagship *Black Hawk,* mouth of the Red River, May 16, 1864, report quoted in U.S. War Dept., *War of the Rebellion,* 130 [I, 26: 130 (1914)].

7. Cobb to Alexander H. Stephens, Headquarters, Georgia State Guard, Atlanta, GA, Jan. 2, 1864, in Toombs, Stephens, and Cobb, *Correspondence,* 631.

8. Keitt to Susan Keitt, Sullivan's Island, SC, Jan. 31, 1864, Keitt Papers.

9. Wigfall to Robert M. T. Hunter, Albemarle Co., VA, Apr. 12, 1864, Hunter Papers, National Archives, Washington.

10. Davis to Robert M. T. Hunter, Richmond, VA, Apr. 14, 1864, in Davis, *Jefferson Davis, Constitutionalist,* 6: 226–27. Ironically, the Hunter letter was written one year to the day before another act of terror, the assassination of Abraham Lincoln, would take place.

11. Clay to Louis T. Wigfall, Petersburg, VA, Apr. 29, 1864, Wigfall Papers, Library of Congress.

12. Davis as quoted in *Journal of the Congress of the Confederate States of America*, 58th Cong., 2d sess., Doc. 234, 4: 669.

13. Stephens to Jefferson Davis, Crawfordville, GA, Jan. 22, 1864, Stephens Papers, Duke University.

14. Davis to the Congress, Richmond, VA, Feb. 3, 1864, in Richardson, ed., *Compilation of Messages*, 1: 395–400; Davis, *Jefferson Davis, Constitutionalist*, 6: 164–69.

15. Keitt to Alexander H. Stephens, Headquarters, Mt. Pleasant, [SC], Apr. 13, 1864, Stephens Papers, Library of Congress.

16. Johnston to Louis T. Wigfall, Dalton, GA, Jan. 4, 1864, Wigfall Papers, Library of Congress.

17. Gardenhire, Miles, and Foote as quoted in *Southern Historical Society Papers*, 50: 292–94.

18. Barksdale as quoted in *Southern Historical Society Papers*, 50: 356–61.

19. Vance to an unnamed correspondent, Raleigh, NC, Jan. 2, 1864, Vance Papers.

20. Davis to Zebulon B. Vance, Richmond, VA, Jan. 8, 1864, in Davis, *Jefferson Davis, Constitutionalist*, 6: 143–46.

21. Brown to Zebulon B. Vance, Milledgeville, GA, Jan. 16, 1864, Vance Papers.

22. Davis to Zebulon B. Vance, Richmond, VA, Feb. 29, 1864, in Davis, *Jefferson Davis, Constitutionalist*, 6: 193–97.

23. Brown to Alexander H. Stephens, Canton, GA, Jan. 4, 1864, in Toombs, Stephens, and Cobb, *Correspondence*, 631–32.

24. Brown to Alexander H. Stephens, Milledgeville, GA, Jan. 28, 1864, in Toombs, Stephens, and Cobb, *Correspondence*, 632–33.

25. Tucker to Jefferson Davis, Spotswood Hotel, Richmond, VA, Mar. 14, 1864, in Davis, *Jefferson Davis, Constitutionalist*, 6: 204–6.

26. Toombs to Alexander H. Stephens, Washington, GA, Apr. 1, 1864, in Toombs, Stephens, and Cobb, *Correspondence*, 637–39.

27. Rhett to Louis T. Wigfall, n.p., Apr. 15, 1864, Wigfall Papers, Library of Congress.

28. Brown to Alexander H. Stephens, Milledgeville, GA, Apr. 5, 1864, in Toombs, Stephens, and Cobb, *Correspondence*, 639–40.

16. Military Highs and Lows

1. Grant, *Papers*, 10: 273–75.

2. Lee, *Wartime Papers*, 719.

3. J. Harvie Dew, "The Yankee and Rebel Yells," *Century Illustrated Magazine*, 43 (Apr. 1892): 954.

4. Martin T. McMahon, "The Death of General Sedgwick," in *Battles and Leaders*, 4, eds. Johnson and Buel, 175; Augustus C. Brown, *The Diary of a Line Officer*, 43–44.

5. Grant, *Papers*, 10: 422; Ezra J. Warner, *Generals in Gray*, 235.

6. Charles S. Venable, "General Lee in the Wilderness Campaign," in *Battles and Leaders*, 4, eds. Johnson and Buel, 245; Peter S. Michie, *The Life and Letters of Emory Upton, Colonel of the Fourth Regiment of Artillery, and Brevet Major-General, U.S. Army* (New York: D. Appleton, 1885), 108; Richard Corbin, "Letters of a Confederate Officer to His Family in Europe during the Last Year of the War for Secession," *Magazine of History* 24 (1913): 23.

7. Brown, *Diary of a Line Officer*, 77–82.

8. Gray as quoted in John Chipman Gray and John Codman Ropes, *War Letters*, 364–66.

9. William T. Sherman, *Memoirs*, 2: 125–27.

10. Lee as quoted in J. William Jones, *Life and Letters of Robert Edward Lee*, 306.

11. Farragut as quoted in Charles Lee Lewis, *David Glasgow Farragut*, 2: 269.

12. Davis to the Congress, Richmond, VA, May 2, 1864, in Richardson, ed., *Compilation of Messages*, 1: 443–48; Davis, *Jefferson Davis, Constitutionalist*, 6: 239–44.

13. *Southern Historical Society Papers*, 51: 22–26.

14. *Southern Historical Society Papers*, 51: 47–49.

15. Keitt to Susan Keitt, Richmond, VA, May 30, 1864, Keitt Papers.

16. Talley to "Alex," Gaines's Farm, VA, Jun. 8, 1864, Keitt Papers.

17. *Southern Historical Society Papers*, 51: 137–38.

18. Wigfall as quoted in *Southern Historical Society Papers*, 51: 141–42.

19. Orr as quoted in *Southern Historical Society Papers*, 51: 238–39.

20. Wigfall as quoted in *Southern Historical Society Papers*, 51: 36–37.

21. Brown as quoted in *Southern Historical Society Papers*, 51: 66–68.

22. Gaither as quoted in *Southern Historical Society Papers*, 51: 77–80.

23. Foote as quoted in *Southern Historical Society Papers*, 51: 101–5.

24. Rives as quoted in *Southern Historical Society Papers*, 51: 109–114.

25. Davis as quoted in *Southern Historical Society Papers*, 51: 114–15; Richardson, ed., *Compilation of Messages*, 1: 452–53.

26. *Journal of the Congress of the Confederate States of America,* 58th Cong., 2d sess., Doc. 234, 4: 100–101.

27. *Journal of the Congress of the Confederate States of America,* 58th Cong., 2d sess., Doc. 234, 7: 113.

28. *Journal of the Congress of the Confederate States of America,* 58th Cong., 2d sess., Doc. 234, 4: 105–9.

29. Cleveland to Alexander H. Stephens, Office of the *Constitutionalist,* Augusta, GA, Jun. 8, 1864, Stephens Papers, Library of Congress.

30. Brown to Alexander H. Stephens, Milledgeville, GA, Jun. 17, 1864, in Toombs, Stephens, and Cobb, *Correspondence,* 644.

31. Hindman to Louis T. Wigfall, Headquarters, Hindman's Division, in the field, Jun. 26, 1864, Wigfall Papers, Library of Congress.

32. Davis to Joseph E. Brown, Richmond, VA, Jun. 29, 1864, Davis, *Jefferson Davis, Constitutionalist,* 6: 278–79.

33. Brown to Jefferson Davis, Atlanta, GA, July 5, 1864, in Davis, *Jefferson Davis, Constitutionalist,* 6: 280.

34. Davis to Joseph E. Brown, Richmond, VA, Jul. 5, 1864, in Davis, *Jefferson Davis, Constitutionalist,* 6: 280–81.

35. Winder to Howell Cobb, Camp Sumter, Andersonville, GA, Jul. 9, 1864, in Toombs, Stephens, and Cobb, *Correspondence,* 644–45.

36. Andrews, *War-Time Journal,* 76–79.

37. Davis to Robert E. Lee, Richmond, VA, Jul. 12, 1864, in Davis, *Jefferson Davis, Constitutionalist,* 6: 291–92.

38. Davis to Joseph E. Johnston, Richmond, VA, Jul. 12, 1864, in Davis, *Jefferson Davis, Constitutionalist,* 6: 292.

39. Cleveland to Alexander H. Stephens, [SC], Jul. 15, 1864, Stephens Papers, Library of Congress.

40. Cleveland to Alexander H. Stephens, Augusta, GA, Jul. 16, 1864, Stephens Papers, Library of Congress.

41. Cobb to his wife, Macon, GA, Jul. 23, 1864, in Toombs, Stephens, and Cobb, *Correspondence,* 648–49.

42. Cleveland to Alexander H. Stephens, Office of the *Constitutionalist,* Augusta, GA, Jul. 23, 1864, Stephens Papers, Library of Congress.

43. Toombs to Alexander H. Stephens, Atlanta, GA, Aug. 30, 1864, in Toombs, Stephens, and Cobb, *Correspondence,* 651–52.

44. S. J. Anderson, clerk at City Hall, Mayor's Office, Aug. 30, 1864, in Davis, *Jefferson Davis, Constitutionalist,* 6: 324–26.

17. Slaves as Soldiers?

1. Lincoln, *Collected Works,* 8: 11.

2. Wiley Britton, "Resumé of Military Operations in Arkansas and Missouri, 1864–1865," in *Battles and Leaders,* eds. Johnson and Buel, 4: 376.

3. Sheridan to Ulysses S. Grant, Woodstock, VA, Oct. 7, 1864, U.S. War Dept., *War of the Rebellion,* 43: I, 30.

4. Small, *Road to Richmond,* 171–76; Toney, *Privations of a Private,* 93–104; Headley, *Confederate Operations,* 274–77.

5. Nichols, *Story of the Great March,* 48–55.

6. Cobb to his wife, camp near Griffin, GA, Nov. 16, 1864, in Toombs, Stephens, and Cobb, *Correspondence,* 655–56.

7. Hood to Stephen D. Lee, Mount Sterling, KY, Nov. 29, 1864, Hood Papers, University of North Carolina.

8. Wilson, *Under the Old Flag,* 2: 99–121.

9. Gray, in the field near Savannah, Dec. 14, 1864, as quoted in *Proceedings of the Massachusetts Historical Society* 49 (1915–1916): 393–94.

10. Winder to P. G. T. Beauregard, Columbia, SC, Dec. 24, 1864, Winder Papers, University of South Carolina.

11. Davis as quoted in *Journal of the Congress of the Confederate States of America,* 58th Cong., 2d sess., Doc. 234, 7: 258.

12. *Southern Historical Society Papers,* 51: 268.

13. Ibid., 275–76.

14. Ibid., 292–96.

15. Hunter as quoted in ibid., 451–56.

16. Miles to G. T. Beauregard, Richmond, VA, Jan. 14, 1865, Miles Papers, University of North Carolina.

17. Leach as quoted in *Southern Historical Society Papers,* 52: 226–27.

18. Miles as quoted in *Southern Historical Society Papers,* 52: 239–44.

19. *Journal of the Congress of the Confederate States of America,* 58th Cong., 2d sess., Doc. 234, 4: 269–.

20. *Southern Historical Society Papers,* 52: 12–14.

21. McMullen as quoted in ibid., 19–21.

22. Blair to Jefferson Davis, Headquarters, Armies of the United States, Dec. 30, 1864, in Davis, *Jefferson Davis, Constitutionalist,* 6: 432–33.

23. Campbell to Samuel Nelson, Richmond, VA, Dec. 1864, Campbell Papers.

24. Davis to the Congress, Richmond, VA, Mar. 13, 1865, in Richardson, ed., *Compilation of Messages,* 1: 542–43.

25. Preston to James A. Seddon, n.p., Dec. 18, 1864, in Davis, *Jefferson Davis, Constitutionalist,* 6: 422–23.

26. Davis to the Congress, Richmond, VA, Nov. 7, 1864, in Richardson, ed., *Compilation of Messages,* 1: 498; Davis, *Jefferson Davis, Constitutionalist,* 6: 384–98.

27. Brown to Alexander H. Stephens, Milledgeville, GA, Oct. 12, 1864, in Toombs, Stephens, and Cobb, *Correspondence,* 653–54.

28. Toombs to Alexander H. Stephens, Washington, GA, Sept. 23, 1864, in Toombs, Stephens, and Cobb, *Correspondence,* 652–53.

29. Davis to Alexander H. Stephens, Richmond, VA, Nov. 21, 1864, in Davis, *Jefferson Davis, Constitutionalist,* 6: 409.

18. Peace Proposals

1. Cobb to James A. Seddon, Richmond, VA, Jan. 8, 1865, U.S. War Dept., *War of the Rebellion,* 4: III, 1009.

2. Sherman, *Home Letters,* 324–27.

3. Magrath to William J. Hardee, Columbia, SC, Jan. 11, 1865, Magrath Papers.

4. Lee to William Porcher Miles, Headquarters, Army of Northern Virginia, Jan. 19, 1865, Miles Papers, University of North Carolina.

5. Buell, *"The Cannoneer,"* 328–33.

6. *Southern Historical Society Papers,* 52: 144ff.

7. Ibid., 153–54.

8. Clark as quoted in ibid., 215–17.

9. Oldham as quoted in *Southern Historical Society Papers,* 52: 257–59.

10. Lee, *Wartime Papers,* 329–30.

11. Wigfall as quoted in *Southern Historical Society Papers,* 52: 281–83.

12. Rhett to William Porcher Miles, Charleston, SC, Feb. 3, 1865, Miles Papers, University of North Carolina.

13. Davis to the Congress, Richmond, VA, Feb. 6, 1865, in Richardson, ed., *Compilation of Messages,* 1: 519; Davis, *Jefferson Davis, Constitutionalist,* 6: 465–66.

14. Davis to Benjamin H. Hill, Richmond, VA, Feb. 6, 1865, in Davis, *Jefferson Davis, Constitutionalist,* 6: 465.

15. Davis as quoted in *Southern Historical Society Papers,* 52: 415; Davis as quoted in *Journal of the Congress of the Confederate States of America,* 58th Cong., 2d sess., Doc. 234, 4: 705.

16. Jones, *Rebel War Clerk's Diary,* 2: 418.

17. Mills as quoted in George D. Harmon, ed., "Letters of Luther Rice Mills: A Confederate Soldier," *North Carolina Historical Review* 4: (July 1927): 303; Gorgas, *Journals of Josiah Gorgas,* 153–54.

18. *Southern Historical Society Papers,* 52: 311–14.

19. Campbell to John C. Breckinridge, Richmond, VA, Mar. 6, 1865, Campbell Papers.

20. *Journal of the Congress of the Confederate States of America,* 58th Cong., 2d sess., Doc. 234, 4: 550–.

21. Lee to Alexander H. Stephens and 17 senators, Headquarters, Armies of the Confederate States, Feb. 15, 1865, Wigfall Papers, Library of Congress. (Curiously, Lee spelled Stephens's name "Stevens.")

22. Davis to the Congress, Richmond, VA, Feb. 18, 1865, in Davis, *Jefferson Davis, Constitutionalist,* 6: 491–503.

23. Lee to G. T. Beauregard, Headquarters, Feb. 22, 1865, Lee Papers, Museum of the Confederacy.

24. Lincoln, *Collected Works,* 8: 332–33.

25. Wigfall as quoted in *Southern Historical Society Papers,* 52: 235–38.

26. Davis as quoted in *Journal of the Congress of the Confederate States of America,* 58th Cong., 2d sess., Doc. 234, 4: 705–.

27. *Southern Historical Society Papers,* 52: 491–94.

28. Davis as quoted in Hattaway and Beringer, *Jefferson Davis,* 389.

29. Davis as quoted in Cooper, *Jefferson Davis,* 523.

30. Davis as quoted in William C. Davis, *Jefferson Davis,* 605.

31. Davis to the Confederacy, Danville, VA, Apr. 4, 1865, in Richardson, ed., *Compilation of Messages,* 1: 568–70; Davis, *Jefferson Davis, Constitutionalist,* 6: 529–31.

32. Harrison, *Recollections Grave and Gay,* 211.

33. Davis as quoted in *Journal of the Congress of the Confederate States of America,* 58th Cong., 2d sess., Doc. 234, 4: 703–7.

34. *Journal of the Congress of the Confederate States of America,* 58th Cong., 2d sess., Doc. 234, 4: 726–31.

35. Nichols, *Story of the Great March,* 160–66.

36. Davis, *Jefferson Davis,* 601.

37. Ibid., 602.

38. Davis to Varina Davis, Danville, VA, Apr. 6, 1865, in Davis, *Jefferson Davis, Constitutionalist,* 6: 533–34.

39. Davis to Jefferson Davis, n.p., Apr. 7, 1865, in Davis, *Jefferson Davis, Constitutionalist,* 6: 537–39.

40. John Sergeant Wise, *End of an Era,* 434; Lincoln, *Collected Works,* 8: 392.

41. Chamberlain, *Passing of the Armies,* 242; Horace Porter, "The Surrender at Appomattox Court House," in *Battles and Leaders,* eds. Johnson and Buel, 4: 737.

42. Grant as quoted in Johnson and Buel, eds., *Battles and Leaders*, 4: 743; Lee, General Order No. 9, Appomattox Court House, VA, Apr. 9, 1865, *Wartime Papers*, 934–35; Edmondston, *"Journal of a Secesh Lady,"* 694–95.

43. Jones, *Lantern Slides.*

44. Welles, *Diary of Gideon Welles*, 286–87.

45. Ruffin, *Diary of Edmund Ruffin*, 3: 949.

19. Epilogue: Despair

1. Worsham, *One of Jackson's Foot Cavalry*, 183.

2. Ibid.

3. As quoted in ibid., 184.

4. Worsham, *One of Jackson's Foot Cavalry*, 188.

5. Cobb to William H. Seward, Athens, GA, Jul. 18, 1865, in Toombs, Stephens, and Cobb, *Correspondence*, 663–65.

6. Davis corrections on typescript biography, n.p., Nov. 18, 1870, Harrison Family Papers.

7. Hattaway and Beringer, *Jefferson Davis*, 24.

BIBLIOGRAPHY

Akin, Warren. *Letters of Warren Akin, Confederate Congressman.* Edited by Bell Irvin Wiley. Athens: University of Georgia Press, 1959.

Alexander, Edward Porter. *Fighting for the Confederacy: The Personal Recollections of General Edward Porter Alexander.* Edited by Gary W. Gallagher. Chapel Hill: University of North Carolina Press, 1989.

Anderson, Archer. Papers. Eleanor S. Brockenbrough Library, Museum of the Confederacy, Richmond, VA.

Andrews, Eliza. *The War-Time Journal of a Georgia Girl, 1864–1865.* New York: D. Appleton, 1908.

Andrews, J. Cutler. *The South Reports the Civil War.* Pittsburgh: University of Pittsburgh Press, 1985.

Beauregard, P. G. T. Papers. Division of Archives and History, Raleigh, NC.

———. Papers. Duke University, Durham, NC.

———. Papers. Eleanor S. Brockenbrough Library, Museum of the Confederacy, Richmond, VA.

———. Papers. South Caroliniana Library, University of South Carolina, Columbia.

Beringer, Richard E., Herman Hattaway, Archer Jones, and William N. Still Jr. *The Elements of Confederate Defeat: Nationalism, War Aims, and Religion.* Athens: University of Georgia Press, 1988.

———. *Why the South Lost the Civil War.* Athens: University of Georgia Press, 1986.

Bill, Alfred Hoyt. *The Beleaguered City: Richmond, 1861–1865.* New York: Alfred A. Knopf, 1946.

Blair, William. *Virginia's Private War: Feeding Body and Soul in the Confederacy, 1861–1865.* New York: Oxford University Press, 1998.

Boatner, Mark M. III. *The Civil War Dictionary.* 2nd ed. New York: David McKay, 1988.

Boney, F. N. *John Letcher of Virginia: The Story of Virginia's Civil War Governor.* University, AL: University of Alabama Press, 1966.

Bonham, Milledge L., Papers. Department of Archives and History, Columbia, SC.

Borcke, Johann August Heinrich Heros von. *Memoirs of the Confederate War for Independence.* Edinborough: W. Blackwood and Sons, 1866.

Boritt, Gabor S., ed. *Jefferson Davis's Generals.* New York: Oxford University Press, 1999.

———, ed. *Why the Confederacy Lost.* New York: Oxford University Press, 1992.

Bragg, Braxton. Papers. Duke University, Durham, NC.

———. Papers. Eleanor S. Brockenbrough Library, Museum of the Confederacy, Richmond, VA.

———. Papers. Southern Historical Collection, University of North Carolina, Chapel Hill.

Brown, Augustus C. *The Diary of a Line Officer.* New York: Brown, 1906.

Buell, Augustus C. *"The Cannoneer": Recollections of Service in the Army of the Potomac, by "a Detached Volunteer" in the Regular Artillery.* Washington, DC: National Tribune, 1890.

BIBLIOGRAPHY

Campbell, John A. Papers. Southern Historical Collection, University of North Carolina, Chapel Hill.

Carmichael, Peter S. *Lee's Young Artillerist: William R. J. Pegram.* Charlottesville: University Press of Virginia, 1995.

Chamberlain, Joshua L. *The Passing of the Armies: An Account of the Final Campaign of the Army of the Potomac, Based upon Personal Reminiscences of the Fifth Army Corps.* New York: G. P. Putnam's Sons, 1915.

Chesnut, James. Papers. Duke University, Durham, NC.

Chesnut, Mary. *Mary Chesnut's Civil War.* Edited by C. Vann Woodward. New Haven, CT: Yale University Press, 1981.

———. *The Private Mary Chesnut: The Unpublished Civil War Diaries.* Edited by C. Vann Woodward and Elisabeth Muhlenfeld. New York: Oxford University Press, 1984.

Clay, Clement C. Papers. Duke University, Durham, NC.

Clay-Clopton, Virginia. *A Belle of the Fifties: Memoirs of Mrs. Clay, of Alabama, Covering Social and Political Life in Washington and the South, 1853–66.* Edited by Ada Sterling. New York: Doubleday, Page, 1904.

Cobb, Howell. Papers. Duke University, Durham, NC.

Commager, Henry Steele, ed. *The Blue and the Gray: The Story of the Civil War as Told by Participants.* Indianapolis: Bobbs-Merrill, 1950.

Connolly, James A. "Major Connolly's Letters to His Wife, 1862–1865," in *Transactions of the Illinois State Historical Society for the Year 1928.* Springfield, IL: Illinois Historical Society, 1928.

Cooke, John Esten. *Wearing of the Gray: Being Personal Portraits, Scenes, and Adventures of the War.* Baltimore: E. B. Treat, 1867.

Cooper, Samuel. Papers. Eleanor S. Brockenbrough Library, Museum of the Confederacy, Richmond, VA.

———. Papers. Southern Historical Collection, University of North Carolina, Chapel Hill.

Cooper, William J. Jr. *Jefferson Davis, American.* New York: Alfred A. Knopf, 2000.

Coski, John M. Research reports: "Abstract of Specific Documented Business Meetings and Conferences Held in the White House of the Confederacy" and "Social Life in Wartime Richmond and the Confederate White House." Museum of the Confederacy, Richmond, VA, ca. 1990.

Cumming, Kate. *Gleanings from Southland: Sketches of Life and Manners of the People of the South before, during, and after the War of Secession.* Birmingham, AL: Roberts, 1895.

Current, Richard Nelson, Paul D. Escott, Lawrence N. Powell, James I. Robertson Jr., and Emory M. Thomas, eds. *Encyclopedia of the Confederacy.* New York: Simon and Schuster, 1993.

Dabney, Robert L. *Life and Campaigns of Lieut.-Gen. Thomas J. Jackson (Stonewall Jackson).* London: James Nisbet, 1864–66.

Dabney, Virginius. *Richmond: The Story of a City.* Garden City, NY: Doubleday, 1976.

Davis, Jefferson. *Jefferson Davis, Constitutionalist: His Letters, Papers, and Speeches.* Edited by Dunbar Rowland. Jackson: Mississippi Department of Archives and History, 1923.

———. *Jefferson Davis, Private Letters, 1823–1889.* Edited by Hudson Strode. New York: Da Capo Press, 1995.

———. Papers. Division of Archives and History, Raleigh, NC.

———. Papers. Duke University, Durham, NC.

———. Papers. Eleanor S. Brockenbrough Library, Museum of the Confederacy, Richmond, VA.

———. Papers. Library of Congress, Washington, DC.

———. Papers. National Archives and Records Administration, Washington, DC.

———. *The Papers of Jefferson Davis.* Edited by Haskell M. Monroe, James T. McIntosh, Lynda Lasswell Crist, Mary Seaton Dix, and Kenneth H. Williams. Baton Rouge: Louisiana State University Press, 1971–.

———. *The Rise and Fall of the Confederate Government.* New York: Thomas Yoseloff, 1958.

Davis, Varina. *Jefferson Davis: A Memoir by His Wife.* Baltimore: Nautical and Aviation, 1990.

Davis, William C. *"A Government of Our Own": The Making of the Confederacy.* New York: Free Press, 1994.

———. *An Honorable Defeat: The Last Days of the Confederate Government.* New York: Harcourt, 2001.

————. *Jefferson Davis: The Man and His Hour.* New York: HarperCollins, 1991.

————. *Rhett: The Turbulent Life and Times of a Fire-Eater.* Columbia: University of South Carolina Press, 2001.

————. *The Union that Shaped the Confederacy: Robert Toombs and Alexander H. Stephens.* Lawrence: University Press of Kansas, 2001.

Dawson, Marion. *Be It Known to All Men: The Story of General Samuel Cooper, C.S.A., 1798–1876.* Salisbury, MD: Dawson, 2000.

DeLeon, Thomas Cooper. *Four Years in Rebel Capitals: An Inside View of Life in the Southern Confederacy, from Birth to Death, from Original Notes, Collated in the Years 1861 to 1865.* Mobile: Gossip, 1890.

Donald, David Herbert. *Lincoln.* New York: Simon and Schuster, 1995.

Doubleday, Abner. *Reminiscences of Forts Sumter and Moultrie in 1860–'61.* New York: Harper and Bros., 1876.

Dufour, Charles L. *Nine Men in Gray.* Lincoln: University of Nebraska Press, 1993.

Durden, Robert F. *The Gray and the Black: The Confederate Debate on Emancipation.* Baton Rouge: Louisiana State University Press, 1972.

Early, Jubal A., J. William Jones, Robert A. Brock, James P. Smith, Hamilton J. Eckenrode, Douglas Southall Freeman, and Frank E. Vandiver, eds. Southern Historical Society Papers. Richmond: Southern Historical Society and Virginia Historical Society, 1876–1959.

Edmondston, Catherine Ann Devereaux. *"Journal of a Secesh Lady": The Diary of Catherine Ann Devereux Edmondston.* Edited by Beth Gilbert Crabtree and James W. Patton. Raleigh: North Carolina Division of Archives and History, 1979.

Eicher, David J. *The Civil War in Books: An Analytical Bibliography.* Urbana: University of Illinois Press, 1997.

————. *The Longest Night: A Military History of the Civil War.* New York: Simon and Schuster, 2001.

————. *Robert E. Lee: A Life Portrait.* Dallas: Taylor, 1997.

Eicher, John H., and David J. Eicher. *Civil War High Commands.* Stanford, CA: Stanford University Press, 2001.

Escott, Paul D. *After Secession: Jefferson Davis and the Failure of Confederate Nationalism.* Baton Rouge: Louisiana State University Press, 1992.

Esposito, Vincent J., ed. *The West Point Atlas of the Civil War.* Vol. 1, *1689–1900.* New York: Frederick A. Praeger, 1962.

Evans, Clement A., ed. *Confederate Military History: A Library of Confederate States History Written by Distinguished Men of the South, and Edited by General Clement A. Evans.* Ext. ed. Wilmington, NC: Broadfoot, 1987–89.

Faust, Drew Gilpin. *The Creation of Confederate Nationalism: Ideology and Identity in the Civil War South.* Baton Rouge: Louisiana State University Press, 1988.

Faust, Patricia L., ed. *The Historical Times Illustrated Encyclopedia of the Civil War.* New York: Harper and Row, 1986.

Fishel, Edwin C. *The Secret War for the Union: The Untold Story of Military Intelligence in the Civil War.* Boston: Houghton Mifflin, 1996.

Foote, Henry S. *Casket of Reminiscences.* New York: Negro Universities Press, 1968.

Freehling, William W. *The South vs. the South: How Anti-Confederate Southerners Shaped the Course of the Civil War.* New York: Oxford University Press, 2001.

Freeman, Douglas Southall. *Lee's Lieutenants: A Study in Command.* New York: Charles Scribner's Sons, 1942–44.

————. *R. E. Lee: A Biography.* New York: Charles Scribner's Sons, 1934–35.

Fremantle, Arthur J. L. *Three Months in the Southern States, April–June 1863.* Lincoln: University of Nebraska Press, 1991.

Frey, Jerry. *In the Woods before Dawn: The Samuel Richey Collection of the Southern Confederacy.* Gettysburg, PA: Thomas Publications, 1994.

Furgurson, Ernest B. *Ashes of Glory: Richmond at War.* New York: Alfred A. Knopf, 1996.

Gale-Polk Family. Papers. Southern Historical Collection, University of North Carolina, Chapel Hill.

Gallagher, Gary W. *The Confederate War: How Popular Will, Nationalism, and Military Strategy Could Not Stave Off Defeat.* Cambridge, MA: Harvard University Press, 1997.

BIBLIOGRAPHY

Garidel, Henri. *Exile in Richmond: The Confederate Journal of Henri Garidel.* Edited by Michael Benout Chesson and Leslie Jean Roberts. Charlottesville: University Press of Virginia, 2001.

Gay, Mary A. H. *Life in Dixie during the War, 1863–1864–1865.* 3rd ed. Atlanta: Constitution Job Office, 1892.

Gerrish, Theodore. *Army Life: A Private's Reminiscences of the Civil War.* Portland, ME: Hoyt, Fogg, and Donham, 1882.

Goff, Richard D. *Confederate Supply.* Durham: Duke University Press, 1969.

Gorgas, Josiah. *The Civil War Diary of General Josiah Gorgas.* Edited by Frank E. Vandiver. University, AL: University of Alabama Press, 1947.

————. *The Journals of Josiah Gorgas, 1857–1878.* Edited by Sarah Woolfolk Wiggins. Tuscaloosa: University of Alabama Press, 1995.

Grant, Ulysses S. *The Papers of Ulysses S. Grant.* Edited by John Y. Simon, David L. Wilson, J. Thomas Murphy, William M. Ferraro, Brian J. Kenny, and Sue E. Dotson. Carbondale: Southern Illinois University Press, 1967–.

Gray, John Chipman, and John Codman Ropes. *War Letters, 1862–1865, of John Chipman Gray and John Codman Ropes.* Boston: Houghton Mifflin, 1927.

Gunderson, Robert Gray. *Old Gentleman's Convention: The Washington Peace Conference of 1861.* Madison: University of Wisconsin Press, 1961.

Hallock, Judith Lee. *Braxton Bragg and Confederate Defeat.* Vol. 2. Tuscaloosa: University of Alabama Press, 1991.

Hammond, James Henry. *Secret and Sacred: The Diaries of James Henry Hammond, a Southern Slaveholder.* Edited by Carol Bleser. New York: Oxford University Press, 1988.

Hanna, A. J. *Flight into Oblivion.* Baton Rouge: Louisiana State University Press, 1999.

Harrison, Burton N. Family Papers. Library of Congress, Washington, DC.

Harrison, Constance Cary. *Recollections Grave and Gay.* New York: Charles Scribner's Sons, 1911.

Haskell, Frank Aretas. [Frank L. Bryne and Andrew T. Weaver, eds.] *Haskell of Gettysburg: His Life and Civil War Papers.* Madison: State Historical Society of Wisconsin, 1970.

Hattaway, Herman, and Richard E. Beringer. *Jefferson Davis, Confederate President.* Lawrence: University Press of Kansas, 2002.

Hattaway, Herman, and Archer Jones. *How the North Won: A Military History of the Civil War.* Urbana: University of Illinois Press, 1983.

Haupt, Herman. *Reminiscences of General Herman Haupt: Giving Hitherto Unpublished Official Orders, Personal Narratives of Important Military Operations, and Interviews with President Lincoln, Secretary Stanton, General-in-Chief Halleck, and with Generals McDowell, McClellan, Meade, Hancock, Burnside, and Others in Command of the Armies in the Field, and His Impressions of These Men.* Milwaukee, WI: Wright and Joys, 1901.

Headley, John W. *Confederate Operations in Canada and New York.* New York: Neale, 1906.

Hedley, Fenwick Y. *Marching through Georgia: Pen Pictures of Every-Day Life in General Sherman's Army, from the Beginning of the Atlanta Campaign until the Close of the War.* Chicago: R. R. Donnelly, 1885.

Heidler, David S. *Pulling the Temple Down: The Fire-Eaters and the Destruction of the Union.* Mechanicsburg, PA: Stackpole Books, 1994.

Heitman, Francis B. *Historical Register and Dictionary of the United States Army, from Its Organization, September 29, 1789, to March 2, 1903.* Washington, DC: U.S. Government Printing Office, 1903.

Hewett, Janet B., Noah Andre Trudeau, and Bryce A. Suderow, eds. *Supplement to the Official Records of the Union and Confederate Armies.* Wilmington, NC: Broadfoot, 1994–2001.

Hill, Daniel Harvey. Papers. Division of Archives and History, Raleigh, NC.

————. Papers. South Caroliniana Library, University of South Carolina, Columbia.

Hood, John Bell. *Advance and Retreat: Personal Experiences in the United States and Confederate States Armies.* Edited by Richard Current. Bloomington: Indiana University Press, 1959.

————. Papers. Duke University, Durham, NC.

————. Papers. National Archives and Records Administration, Washington, DC.

————. Papers. Southern Historical Collection, University of North Carolina, Chapel Hill.

Hunter, Robert M. T. *Correspondence of Robert M. T. Hunter, 1826–1876.* Edited by Charles Henry Ambler. Washington, DC: U.S. Government Printing Office, 1918.

BIBLIOGRAPHY

———. Papers. The Library of Virginia, Richmond.

———. Papers. National Archives, Washington, DC.

———. Papers. University of Virginia, Charlottesville.

Jackson, Mary Anna. *Memoirs of Stonewall Jackson.* Dayton, OH: Morningside Book Shop, 1993.

Johnson, Robert Underwood, and Clarence Clough Buel, eds. *Battles and Leaders of the Civil War, Being for the Most Part Contributions by Union and Confederate Officers: Based upon "The Century" War Series.* New York: Century, 1887–88.

Johnston, Joseph E. *A Narrative of Military Operations Directed, During the Late War between the States, by Joseph E. Johnston.* Bloomington: Indiana University Press, 1959.

———. Papers. Duke University, Durham, NC.

———. Papers. Eleanor S. Brockenbrough Library, Museum of the Confederacy, Richmond, VA.

Johnston, William Preston. Papers. Tulane University, New Orleans, LA.

Jones, Archer. *Civil War Command and Strategy: The Process of Victory and Defeat.* New York: Free Press, 1992.

Jones, J. William. *Life and Letters of Robert Edward Lee, Soldier and Man.* Harrisburg, VA: Sprinkle, 1986.

Jones, Jenkin Lloyd. *An Artilleryman's Diary.* Madison: Wisconsin History Commission, 1914.

Jones, John B. Papers. Southern Historical Collection, University of North Carolina, Chapel Hill.

———. *A Rebel War Clerk's Diary at the Confederate States Capital.* Philadelphia: J. B. Lippincott, 1866.

Jones, Katherine M. *Ladies of Richmond: Confederate Capital.* Indianapolis: Bobbs-Merrill, 1962.

Jones, Mary Cadwalader. *Lantern Slides.* Boston: Jones, 1937.

Kean, Robert Garlick Hill. *Inside the Confederate Government: The Diary of Robert Garlick Hill Kean.* Edited by Edward Younger. Baton Rouge: Louisiana State University Press, 1993.

Keitt, Lawrence M. Papers. Duke University, Durham, NC.

Kimball, Fiske. *The Capitol of Virginia.* Richmond: Virginia State Library and Archives, 1989.

Kimball, Gregg D. *American City, Southern Place: A Cultural History of Antebellum Richmond.* Athens: University of Georgia Press, 2000.

King, Alvy L. *Louis T. Wigfall: Southern Fire-Eater.* Baton Rouge: Louisiana State University Press, 1970.

Klein, Maury. *Days of Defiance: Sumter, Secession, and the Coming of the Civil War.* New York: Alfred A. Knopf, 1997.

Lee, Fitzhugh. *General Lee.* Wilmington, NC: Broadfoot, 1989.

Lee, Richard M. *General Lee's City: An Illustrated Guide to the Historic Sites of Confederate Richmond.* McLean, VA: EPM, 1987.

Lee, Robert E. *Lee's Dispatches: Unpublished Letters of General Robert E. Lee, C.S.A., to Jefferson Davis and the War Department of the Confederate States of America, 1862–1865, from the Private Collection of Wymberley Jones de Renne, of Wormsloe, Georgia.* Edited by Douglas Southall Freeman. New York: G. P. Putnam's Sons, 1915.

———. Papers. Boston Public Library, Boston.

———. Papers. Division of Archives and History, Raleigh, NC.

———. Papers. Duke University Library, Durham, NC.

———. Papers. Eleanor S. Brockenbrough Library, Museum of the Confederacy, Richmond, VA.

———. Papers. National Archives and Records Administration, Washington, DC.

———. Papers. U.S. Army Military History Institute, Carlisle, PA.

———. Papers. Virginia Historical Society, Richmond, VA.

———. *The Wartime Papers of R. E. Lee.* Edited by Clifford Dowdey and Louis H. Manarin. Boston: Little, Brown, 1961.

Lee, Robert E. Jr. *Recollections and Letters of General Robert E. Lee.* Garden City, NY: Garden City, 1926.

Lee, Stephen Dill. Papers. Southern Historical Collection, University of North Carolina, Chapel Hill.

BIBLIOGRAPHY

LeGrand, Julia. *The Journal of Julia LeGrand: New Orleans, 1862–1863.* Edited by Kate Mason Rowland and Mrs. Morris L. Croxall. Richmond, VA: Everett Waddey, 1911.

Lewis, Charles Lee. *David Glasgow Farragut.* Annapolis, MD: United States Naval Institute, 1941–1943.

Lincoln, Abraham. *The Collected Works of Abraham Lincoln.* Edited by Roy P. Basler. New Brunswick, NJ: Rutgers University Press, 1953–1990.

Livermore, Thomas L. *Days and Events, 1860–1866.* Boston: Houghton Mifflin, 1920.

Long, A. L., and Marcus J. Wright. *Memoirs of Robert E. Lee: His Military and Personal History, Embracing a Large Amount of Information Hitherto Unpublished.* New York: J. M. Stoddart, 1886.

Long, E. B., and Barbara Long. *The Civil War Day by Day: An Almanac, 1861–1865.* Garden City, NY: Doubleday, 1971.

Longstreet, James. *From Manassas to Appomattox: Memoirs of the Civil War in America.* Philadelphia: J. B. Lippincott, 1896.

Loth, Calder, ed. *The Virginia Landmarks Register.* 3rd ed. Charlottesville: University Press of Virginia, 1987.

Lyman, Darryl. *Civil War Quotations.* Conshohocken, PA: Combined Books, 1995.

Magrath, Andrew G. Papers. Department of Archives and History, Columbia, SC.

Mallory, Stephen R. Papers. Library of Congress, Washington, DC.

Manarin, Louis H., ed. *Richmond at War: The Minutes of the City Council, 1861–1865.* Chapel Hill: University of North Carolina Press, 1966.

Marshall, Charles. *An Aide-de-Camp of Lee: Being the Papers of Colonel Charles Marshall, Sometime Aide-de-Camp, Military Secretary, and Assistant Adjutant General on the Staff of Robert E. Lee, 1862–1865.* Edited by Frederick Maurice. Boston: Little, Brown, 1927.

Massey, Mary Elizabeth. *Ersatz in the Confederacy: Shortages and Substitutions on the Southern Homefront.* Columbia: University of South Carolina Press, 1952.

Masur, Louis P., ed. *The Real War Will Never Get in the Books: Selections from Writers during the Civil War.* New York: Oxford University Press, 1993.

McCash, William B. *Thomas R. R. Cobb: The Making of a Southern Nationalist.* Macon, GA: Mercer University Press, 1983.

McClellan, George B. *The Civil War Papers of George B. McClellan: Selected Correspondence, 1860–1865.* Edited by Stephen W. Sears. New York: Ticknor and Fields, 1989.

McClure, Alexander K., ed. *The Annals of the War Written by Leading Participants North and South: Originally Published in the Philadelphia Weekly Times.* Philadelphia: Times, 1879.

McGraw, Marie Tyler. *At the Falls: Richmond, Virginia, and Its People.* Chapel Hill: University of North Carolina Press, 1994.

McMurry, Richard M. *John Bell Hood and the War for Southern Independence.* Lexington: University Press of Kentucky, 1982.

McPherson, James M. *Battle Cry of Freedom: The Civil War Era.* New York: Oxford University Press, 1988.

———. *Drawn with the Sword: Reflections on the American Civil War.* New York: Oxford University Press, 1996.

———. *Is Blood Thicker than Water? Crises of Nationalism in the Modern World.* New York: Vintage Books, 1999.

———. *Ordeal by Fire: The Civil War and Reconstruction.* New York: Alfred A. Knopf, 1982.

McPherson, James M., and William J. Cooper Jr., eds. *Writing the Civil War: The Quest to Understand.* Columbia: University of South Carolina Press, 1998.

McWhiney, Grady. *Braxton Bragg and Confederate Defeat.* Vol. 1: *Field Command.* New York: Columbia University Press, 1969.

Miles, William Porcher. Papers. South Caroliniana Library, University of South Carolina, Columbia.

———. Papers. Southern Historical Collection, University of North Carolina, Chapel Hill.

Military Order of the Loyal Legion of the United States. Papers of the Military Order of the Loyal Legion of the United States, 1887–1915. Wilmington, NC: Broadfoot, 1991–96.

Moore, Frank, ed. *The Rebellion Record: A Diary of American Events, with Documents, Narratives, Illustrative Incidents, Poetry, etc.* New York: G. P. Putnam's Sons, 1861–63, and D. Van Nostrand, 1864–68.

BIBLIOGRAPHY

Moore, Jerrold Northrop. *Confederate Commissary General: Lucius Bellinger Northrop and the Subsistence Bureau of the Southern Army.* Shippensburg, PA: White Mane, 1996.

Moore, Samuel J. T. Jr. *Moore's Complete Civil War Guide to Richmond.* Richmond, VA: Moore, 1978.

Newton, Steven H. *Joseph E. Johnston and the Defense of Richmond.* Lawrence: University Press of Kansas, 1998.

Nichols, George Ward. *The Story of the Great March, from the Diary of a Staff Officer.* New York: Harper and Bros., 1865.

Norton, Oliver W. *Army Letters, 1861–1865, Being Extracts from Private Letters to Relatives and Friends from a Soldier in the Field during the Late Civil War, with an Appendix Containing Copies of Some Official Documents, Papers, and Addresses of a Later Date.* Chicago: O. L. Deming, 1903.

Owen, William M. *In Camp and Battle with the Washington Artillery of New Orleans: A Narrative of Events during the Late Civil War from Bull Run to Appomattox and Spanish Fort.* Boston: Ticknor, 1885.

Patrick, Rembert W. *Jefferson Davis and His Cabinet.* Baton Rouge: Louisiana State University Press, 1944.

Pease, William H., and Jane H. Pease. *James Louis Petigru: Southern Conservative, Southern Dissenter.* Athens: University of Georgia Press, 1995.

Pember, Phoebe Yates. *A Southern Woman's Story: Life in Confederate Richmond.* Edited by Bell Irvin Wiley. Wilmington, NC: Broadfoot, 1991.

Pettigrew, James Johnston. Papers. Division of Archives and History, Raleigh, NC.

Pickens, Francis W. Papers. Department of Archives and History, Columbia, SC.

Pollard, Edward A. *The Lost Cause: A New Southern History of the War of the Confederates.* Baltimore, MD: E. B. Treat, 1866.

Polley, Joseph B. *A Soldier's Letters to Charming Nellie.* New York: Neale, 1908.

Proctor, Ben H. *Not without Honor: The Life of John H. Reagan.* Austin: University of Texas Press, 1962.

Putnam, Sallie. *Richmond during the War: Four Years of Personal Observation.* New York: G. W. Carleton, 1877.

Rable, George C. *Civil Wars: Women and the Crisis of Southern Nationalism.* Urbana: University of Illinois Press, 1991.

———. *The Confederate Republic: A Revolution against Politics.* Chapel Hill: University of North Carolina Press, 1994.

Rhett, Robert Barnwell. *A Fire-Eater Remembers: The Confederate Memoir of Robert Barnwell Rhett.* Edited by William C. Davis. Columbia: University of South Carolina Press, 2000.

———. Papers. South Caroliniana Library, University of South Carolina, Columbia.

Richardson, James D., ed. *A Compilation of Messages and Papers of the Confederacy, Including the Diplomatic Correspondence, 1861–1865.* Nashville: United States Publishing Co., 1905.

Ringold, May Spencer. *The Role of the State Legislatures in the Confederacy.* Athens: University of Georgia Press, 1966.

Rogers, William Warren Jr. *Confederate Home Front: Montgomery during the Civil War.* Tuscaloosa: University of Alabama Press, 1999.

Roman, Alfred. *The Military Operations of General Beauregard in the War between the States, 1861 to 1865.* New York: Harper and Bros., 1884.

Ropes, John Codman, and Theodore F. Dwight, eds. *Papers of the Military Historical Society of Massachusetts.* Wilmington, NC: Broadfoot, 1990.

Rosen, Robert N. *The Jewish Confederates.* Columbia: University of South Carolina Press, 2000.

Ruffin, Edmund. *The Diary of Edmund Ruffin.* Edited by William K. Scarborough. Baton Rouge: Louisiana State University Press, 1972–1989.

Russell, William Howard. *My Diary North and South.* New York: Harper and Bros., 1954.

———. *William Howard Russell's Civil War: Private Diary and Letters, 1861–1862.* Edited by Martin Crawford. Athens: University of Georgia Press, 1992.

Sandburg, Carl. *Abraham Lincoln: The War Years.* New York: Harcourt, Brace, 1939.

Schott, Thomas E. *Alexander H. Stephens of Georgia: A Biography.* Baton Rouge: Louisiana State University Press, 1988.

Scott, Mary Wingfield. *Old Richmond Neighborhoods.* Richmond, VA: Whittet and Shepperson, 1950.

BIBLIOGRAPHY

Scott, Winfield. *Memoirs of Lieut.-General Scott, LL.D.* New York: Sheldon, 1864.

Seddon, James A. Papers. South Caroliniana Library, University of South Carolina, Columbia.

Sherman, William Tecumseh. *Home Letters of General Sherman.* Edited by M. A. DeWolfe Howe. New York: Charles Scribner's Sons, 1909.

———. *Memoirs of General W. T. Sherman: Written by Himself.* New York: D. Appleton and Co., 1875.

Simms, Henry H. *Life of Robert M. T. Hunter.* Richmond, VA: William Byrd Press, 1935.

Small, Abner. *The Road to Richmond: The Civil War Memoirs of Major Abner R. Small of the Sixteenth Maine Volunteers, Together with the Diary Which He Kept When He Was a Prisoner of War.* Edited by Harold A. Small. Berkeley: University of California Press, 1939.

Sparrow, Edward. Papers. Eleanor S. Brockenbrough Library, Museum of the Confederacy, Richmond, VA.

Stanley, Henry M. *The Autobiography of Sir Henry Morton Stanley.* Edited by Dorothy Stanley. New York: Houghton-Mifflin, 1909.

Stephens, Alexander H. *A Constitutional View of the War between the States: Its Causes, Character, Conduct and Results Presented in a Series of Colloquies at Liberty Hall.* Philadelphia: National Publishing Co., 1868.

———. Papers. Duke University, Durham, NC.

———. Papers. Library of Congress, Washington, DC.

———. *Recollections of Alexander H. Stephens: His Diary Kept When a Prisoner at Fort Warren, Boston Harbour, 1865.* Edited by Myrta Lockett Avary. Baton Rouge: Louisiana State University Press, 1998.

Stiles, Robert. *Four Years under Marse Robert.* New York: Neale, 1903.

Stillwell, Leander. *The Story of a Common Soldier of Army Life in the Civil War, 1861–1865.* Kansas City, MO: Franklin Hudson, 1920.

Strother, David Hunter. *A Virginia Yankee in the Civil War: The Diaries of David Hunter Strother.* Edited by Cecil D. Eby. Chapel Hill: University of North Carolina Press, 1961.

Symonds, Craig L. *Joseph E. Johnston: A Civil War Biography.* New York: W. W. Norton, 1992.

Tatum, Georgia Lee. *Disloyalty in the Confederacy.* Lincoln: University of Nebraska Press, 2000.

Taylor, John M. *William Henry Seward: Lincoln's Right Hand.* New York: HarperCollins, 1991.

Taylor, Walter H. *Lee's Adjutant: The Wartime Letters of Colonel Walter Herron Taylor, 1862–1865.* Edited by R. Lockwood Tower. Columbia: University of South Carolina Press, 1995.

Thomas, Emory M. *The Confederate State of Richmond: A Biography of the Capital.* Baton Rouge: Louisiana State University Press, 1998.

———. *Robert E. Lee: A Biography.* New York: W. W. Norton, 1995.

Toney, Marcus B. *The Privations of a Private: The Campaign under Gen. R. E. Lee, the Campaign under Gen. Stonewall Jackson, Bragg's Invasion of Kentucky, the Chickamauga Campaign, Prison Life in the North.* Nashville: Toney, 1905.

Toombs, Robert A. Papers. Duke University, Durham, NC.

Toombs, Robert A., Alexander H. Stephens, and Howell Cobb. *The Correspondence of Robert Toombs, Alexander H. Stephens, and Howell Cobb.* Edited by Ulrich B. Phillips. Washington, DC: U.S. Government Printing Office, 1913.

Upson, Theodore F. *With Sherman to the Sea: The Civil War Letters, Diaries, and Reminiscences of Theodore F. Upson.* Edited by Oscar Osburn Winther. Baton Rouge: Louisiana State University Press, 1943.

U.S. Navy Department. *Civil War Naval Chronology, 1861–1865.* Edited by Ernest M. Eller. Washington, DC: U.S. Government Printing Office, 1971.

———. *Official Records of the Union and Confederate Navies in the War of the Rebellion.* Washington, DC: U.S. Government Printing Office, 1894–1927.

U.S. Senate. *Journal of the Congress of the Confederate States of America.* 58th Cong., 2d sess., Doc. 234. Washington, DC: U.S. Government Printing Office, 1904–1905.

———. *Biographical Directory of the American Congress, 1774–1971.* 92d Cong., 1st sess., Doc. 92–8. Washington, DC: U.S. Government Printing Office, 1971.

U.S. War Department. *The War of the Rebellion: A Compilation of the Official Records of the Union and Confederate Armies.* Washington, DC: U.S. Government Printing Office, 1880–1901.

Vance, Zebulon B. Papers. Division of Archives and History, Raleigh, NC.

BIBLIOGRAPHY

Vandiver, Frank E. *Rebel Brass: The Confederate Command System*. Baton Rouge: Louisiana State University Press, 1993.

Van Felson, Charles A. *The Little Red Book or Department Directory*. Richmond, VA: Tyler, Wise, and Allegre, Printers, Enquirer Job Office, 1861.

Van Lew, Elizabeth. *A Yankee Spy in Richmond: The Civil War Diary of "Crazy Bet" Van Lew*. Edited by David D. Ryan. Mechanicsburg, PA: Stackpole Books, 1996.

Venable, Charles S. Papers. Southern Historical Collection, University of North Carolina, Chapel Hill.

Walther, Eric H. *The Fire-Eaters*. Baton Rouge: Louisiana State University Press, 1992.

Warner, Ezra J. *Generals in Blue: Lives of the Union Commanders*. Baton Rouge: Louisiana State University Press, 1964.

———. *Generals in Gray: Lives of the Confederate Commanders*. Baton Rouge: Louisiana State University Press, 1959.

Warner, Ezra J., and W. Buck Yearns. *Biographical Register of the Confederate Congress*. Baton Rouge: Louisiana State University Press, 1975.

Welles, Gideon. *The Diary of Gideon Welles*. Boston: Houghton Mifflin, 1911.

Welsh, Jack D. *Medical Histories of Confederate Generals*. Kent, OH: Kent State University Press, 1995.

White House of the Confederacy: An Illustrated History. Richmond, VA: Cadmus Marketing, 1994.

Wigfall, Louis T. Papers. Duke University, Durham, NC.

———. Papers. Eleanor S. Brockenbrough Library, Museum of the Confederacy, Richmond, VA.

———. Papers. Library of Congress, Washington, DC.

Wiley, Bell Irvin. *The Road to Appomattox*. Baton Rouge: Louisiana State University Press, 1994.

Williams, T. Harry. *P. G. T. Beauregard: Napoleon in Gray*. Baton Rouge: Louisiana State University Press, 1955.

Wilson, James H. *Under the Old Flag: Recollections of Military Operations in the War for the Union, the Spanish War, the Boxer Rebellion, etc*. New York: D. Appleton, 1912.

Winder, John H. Papers. Duke University, Durham, NC.

———. Papers. South Caroliniana Library, University of South Carolina, Columbia.

———. Papers. Southern Historical Collection, University of North Carolina, Chapel Hill.

Wise, John Sergeant. *The End of an Era*. Boston: Houghton Mifflin, 1902.

Woodworth, Steven E., ed. *The Art of Command in the Civil War*. Lincoln: University of Nebraska Press, 1998.

———, ed. *Civil War Generals in Defeat*. Lawrence: University Press of Kansas, 1999.

———. *Davis and Lee at War*. Lawrence: University Press of Kansas, 1995.

———. *Jefferson Davis and His Generals: The Failure of Confederate Command in the West*. Lawrence: University Press of Kansas, 1990.

———, ed. *Leadership and Command in the American Civil War*. Campbell, CA: Savas Woodbury, 1995.

———. *No Band of Brothers: Problems of the Rebel High Command*. Columbia: University of Missouri Press, 1999.

Worsham, John H. *One of Jackson's Foot Cavalry*. Wilmington, NC: Broadfoot, 1991.

Wright, Louise Wigfall. Papers. Southern Historical Collection, University of North Carolina, Chapel Hill.

———. *A Southern Girl in '61: The War-Time Memories of a Confederate Senator's Daughter*. New York: Doubleday, Page, 1905.

Yearns, Wilfred Buck. *The Confederate Congress*. Athens: University of Georgia Press, 1960.

———. *From Richmond to Texas: The 1865 Journey Home of Confederate Senator Williamson S. Oldham*. Dayton, OH: Morningside Book Shop, 1998.

INDEX

INDEX

INDEX

INDEX

INDEX

INDEX